CA Proficiency
Taxation 2 (RoI)
2021–2022

CHARTERED
ACCOUNTANTS
IRELAND

Published in 2021 by
Chartered Accountants Ireland
Chartered Accountants House
47–49 Pearse Street
Dublin 2
www.charteredaccountants.ie

ISBN: 978-1-913975-08-1

Typeset by Deanta Global Publishing Services
Printed and bound by CPI Group (UK) Ltd, Croydon, CR0 4YY

Contents

Chartered Accountants Ireland *Code of Ethics*   xx

Chapter 1   Appeals, Revenue Audits and Qualifying Disclosures   1

1.1   Appeal Procedures   1

     1.1.1   Introduction   1

     1.1.2   Hearing before the Appeal Commissioners   2

     1.1.3   Hearings before the Courts   2

     1.1.4   Settlement of an Appeal   3

1.2   Revenue Audits, Penalties and Qualifying Disclosures   3

     1.2.1   Introduction to Revenue Audit   3

     1.2.2   Revenue Non-audit Compliance Interventions   3

     1.2.3   Revenue Audit   4

     1.2.4   Revenue Investigation   5

     1.2.5   Tax, Interest and Penalties   6

     1.2.6   Qualifying Disclosures and Mitigation of Penalties   9

     1.2.7   Review Procedures   11

Question   12

Chapter 2   Residence and Domicile   13

2.1   Introduction   13

2.2   Residence   13

2.3   Election to be Resident   14

2.4   Ordinary Residence   15

2.5   Domicile   16

     2.5.1   Domicile of Origin   16

2.5.2	Domicile of Choice	16
2.5.3	Domicile of Dependence	17
2.6	**Location of Assets**	17
Questions		17

PART ONE   CAPITAL GAINS TAX

Chapter 3	**General Principles and Administration – Recap**	21
3.1	**Introduction**	21
3.2	**Computation of Gain or Loss**	22
3.3	**Development Land**	23
3.4	**Losses**	23
3.5	**Exemptions and Reliefs**	23
Questions		24
Chapter 4	**Territoriality Rules**	25
4.1	**Location of Assets**	25
4.2	**Individual is Resident or Ordinarily Resident**	25
4.3	**Individual is not Resident and not Ordinarily Resident**	26
4.3.1	Specified Irish Assets	26
4.3.2	Administration, including Withholding Tax	27
4.4	**Temporary Non-residents**	28
4.4.1	Background	28
4.4.2	Liability to Irish Tax	28
Questions		29
Chapter 5	**Shares**	32
5.1	**Introduction**	32
5.2	**Rights Issues**	33
5.3	**Bonus Issues**	35

5.4 **Acquisition within Four Weeks of Disposal and Disposal within Four Weeks of Acquisition** 36

    5.4.1 Acquisition within Four Weeks of Disposal 36

    5.4.2 Disposal within Four Weeks of Acquisition 36

5.5 **CGT Treatment of Employee Share Options** 37

    5.5.1 General CGT Treatment of Employee Share Options 37

    5.5.2 Key Employee Engagement Programme (KEEP) 38

Questions 41

Chapter 6 **Revised Entrepreneur Relief** 42

6.1 **Introduction** 42

6.2 **Qualifying Conditions** 43

    6.2.1 Relevant Individual 43

    6.2.2 Chargeable Business Asset 43

    6.2.3 Summary of Conditions 44

6.3 **Interaction with Other CGT Reliefs** 45

    6.3.1 Transfer of a Business to a Company 45

    6.3.2 Retirement Relief 45

    6.3.3 Losses and Annual Exemption 46

Questions 46

Chapter 7 **Transfer of a Business to a Company** 47

7.1 **Sole Trader Transfers Trade to Company** 47

7.2 **Relief Available** 47

7.3 **Limitations on the Relief** 53

Questions 54

Chapter 8 **Retirement Relief** 56

8.1 **Introduction** 56

8.2 **Assets Qualifying for Relief** 56

8.3 **Disposal of Sole Trader Business** 59

8.4	**Disposal of Shares**	60
8.5	**Disposal to Person Other than a "Child" (section 598 TCA 1997)**	62
	8.5.1 Individual Aged 55 to 65	62
	8.5.2 Individual Aged 66 or Over	65
8.6	**Disposal to a "Child" (section 599 TCA 1997)**	66
	8.6.1 Individual Aged 55 to 65	66
	8.6.2 Individual Aged 66 or Over	68
8.7	**Summary of Conditions to be Satisfied**	69
	8.7.1 Sole Trader	69
	8.7.2 Shareholder	69
	8.7.3 Land, Buildings, Plant and Machinery Owned by an Individual and Used by the Family Company	69
Questions		70
Chapter 9	**Acquisition by a Company of its Own Shares**	73
9.1	**Overview**	73
9.2	**Quoted Companies**	73
9.3	**Unquoted Companies**	74
	9.3.1 Conditions to be Satisfied	74
	9.3.2 Buyback of Shares to Pay Inheritance Tax	75
	9.3.3 Other Issues	76
Appendix 9.1: Extract from Revenue's *Tax and Duty Manual*, Part 06-09-01: Acquisition by company of its own shares		76
Questions		77

PART TWO   STAMP DUTY

Chapter 10	**General Principles and Conveyance or Transfer on Sale**	81
10.1	**Introduction**	81

10.2	**Charge to Stamp Duty**	81
	10.2.1 Instrument	82
	10.2.2 Schedule 1 SDCA 1999	82
	10.2.3 Executed in the State	82
	10.2.4 Property Situated in the State	82
	10.2.5 "Any matter or thing done, or to be done, in the State"	83
10.3	**Payment and Returns**	83
	10.3.1 When is Stamp Duty Payable?	83
	10.3.2 Who is Liable to Pay Stamp Duty?	83
	10.3.3 e-Stamping via ROS	83
	10.3.4 Self-assessment	84
10.4	**Conveyance or Transfer on Sale**	84
	10.4.1 Stocks and Securities	84
	10.4.2 Property Other than Shares	85
10.5	**Gifts – Deemed Conveyance on Sale**	86
Questions		87
Chapter 11	**Exemptions and Reliefs**	88
11.1	**Exemptions**	88
11.2	**Reliefs**	88
	11.2.1 Young Trained Farmer Relief	88
	11.2.2 Transfers of Farmland between Relations (Consanguinity Relief)	89
	11.2.3 Transfers between Associated Companies	90
Questions		92
Chapter 12	**Transfer of a Business**	94
12.1	**Stamp Duty Consequences on Acquisition of Business Assets**	94
12.2	**Minimising Stamp Duty on Acquisition of Business Assets**	95
Questions		95

PART THREE   CAPITAL ACQUISITIONS TAX

Chapter 13   Capital Acquisitions Tax – Gifts and Inheritances   99

13.1   Introduction to Capital Acquisitions Tax   99

13.2   Gifts and Inheritances   99

13.2.1 Basic Elements of a Gift/Inheritance   100

13.2.2 CAT Differences between Gifts and Inheritances   103

13.2.3 Dates of the Disposition, Gift and Inheritance   103

Questions   105

Chapter 14   Computation of CAT   106

14.1   Introduction   106

14.2   Group Thresholds   106

14.2.1 Group Thresholds 2021   106

14.2.2 Group Thresholds – Special Relationships   107

14.2.3 Group Thresholds – Anti-avoidance: Gift Splitting   110

14.3   Aggregation   111

14.4   Basic Computation   111

Questions   115

Chapter 15   Territorial Scope   117

15.1   Introduction   117

15.2   Taxable Gifts and Inheritances   117

15.2.1 Irish Property – Always Taxable   117

15.2.2 Foreign Property – General Rule   117

15.2.3 Foreign Property – Foreign-domiciled Persons   118

Questions   119

Chapter 16   Taxable Value   121

16.1   General Principles   121

16.2   Market Value   122

16.2.1 Market Value – General Rule 122

16.2.2 Market Value of Shares in Certain Private Companies 122

16.2.3 Valuation of Annuities 122

16.2.4 Market Value of a Limited Interest 122

16.2.5 Valuation of Free Use of Property 123

16.3   Valuation Date 123

16.3.1 Importance of Valuation Date 123

16.3.2 Valuation Date of a Taxable Gift 124

16.3.3 Valuation Date of a Taxable Inheritance 124

16.4   Deduction for Liabilities, Costs, Expenses and Consideration 125

16.4.1 Consideration Paid by Donee/Successor 125

16.4.2 Deductions Specifically Prohibited in Arriving at Taxable Values 126

16.5   Agricultural Relief 126

16.5.1 Calculation of Taxable Value where there is Agricultural Relief 127

16.5.2 Definitions 127

16.5.3 Computation of Relief 128

16.5.4 Computation of Relief: Restriction of Deductions 130

16.5.5 Other Matters 132

16.5.6 Clawback of Relief 132

16.5.7 Ceasing to Farm Land within Six Years 133

16.6   Business Relief 133

16.6.1 Calculation of Taxable Value where there is Business Relief 133

16.6.2 Relevant Business Property 134

16.6.3 Minimum Period of Ownership and Use by Disponer 136

16.6.4 Valuation of Property 136

16.6.5 Other Matters 137

16.6.6 Clawback of Relief 137

Appendix 16.1: Summary Chart 138

Appendix 16.2: Differences between Agricultural Relief and Business Relief 139

Questions 139

Chapter 17   Treatment of Limited Interests 143

17.1   Introduction 143

17.2   Market Value of an Annuity 143

17.2.1 Annuity Charged or Secured on Property 143

17.2.2 Annuity Not Charged or Secured on Property 144

17.3   Taxable Value of Limited Interests 144

17.4   Deduction of Limited Interests as Consideration 145

17.5   Cessation of an Annuity 145

Questions 146

Chapter 18   Exemptions from CAT 150

18.1   Exemption of Small Gifts 150

18.2   Exemption of Gifts and Inheritances taken from a Spouse or Civil Partner and Certain Benefits taken from a Former Spouse or Civil Partner 150

18.2.1 Couples who are Separated 151

18.2.2 Married Couples who are Divorcing or are Divorced, and Civil Partnerships that are being Dissolved or have been Dissolved 151

18.3   Exemption of Certain Government Securities 152

18.4   Exemption of Certain Inheritances taken by Parents 152

18.5   Exemption of Certain Dwelling Houses 152

18.5.1 Definition of "Dwelling House" 154

18.5.2 Clawback of Exemption 154

18.6   Exemption of Certain Receipts 154

18.7   Gifts and Inheritances taken Free of Tax 155

18.8	**Relief in Respect of Certain Insurance Policies**	156
	18.8.1 Policies to Pay Inheritance Tax Only	156
	18.8.2 *Inter Vivos* Dispositions	158
Questions		158
Chapter 19	**Credit for Certain CGT Liabilities**	161
19.1	**Credit for Certain CGT Liabilities**	161
19.2	**Clawback of CGT Credit**	163
19.3	**Identification of CAT Liabilities where more than One Asset**	163
19.4	**Other Matters**	165
Questions		165
Chapter 20	**Administration**	169
20.1	**Accountable Persons**	169
20.2	**Delivery of Returns**	169
	20.2.1 Obligation to File Returns for Capital Acquisitions Tax	169
	20.2.2 Content of a Return	170
20.3	**Payment of CAT and Interest, and Filing Returns**	170
20.4	**Payment of CAT by Instalments**	171
	20.4.1 Agricultural and Business Property	172
20.5	**Overpayment of CAT**	172
20.6	**Surcharge on Undervaluation of Property**	172
Questions		172

PART FOUR   CORPORATE TAXATION

Chapter 21	**Corporation Tax: Residence and Administration**	177
21.1	**Overview**	177
21.2	**Charge to Corporation Tax**	178
	21.2.1 Resident Company	178
	21.2.2 Non-resident Company	178

21.3	**Residence of Companies**	178
	21.3.1 Rules to Establish Residence of a Company	178
21.4	**Rates of Corporation Tax**	180
	21.4.1 Trading Rate of Corporation Tax	180
	21.4.2 Passive Rate of Corporation Tax	180
21.5	**Reporting Requirements**	181
	21.5.1 Country-by-Country (CbC) Reporting	181
21.6	**Transfer Pricing**	181
Questions		183
Chapter 22	**Double Taxation Relief**	184
22.1	**Introduction**	184
22.2	**Foreign Income: Rates of Corporation Tax**	185
	22.2.1 Trading or Professional Services Income	185
	22.2.2 Interest or Rental Income	185
	22.2.3 Dividends	185
22.3	**Methods of Relief**	185
	22.3.1 Deduction Method	186
	22.3.2 Credit Method	186
	22.3.3 Exemption Method	187
22.4	**Ireland as a Holding Company Location**	187
22.5	**Double Taxation Treaties**	188
Questions		189
Chapter 23	**Expenditure on Intangible Assets and Research & Development**	190
23.1	**Intangible Assets: Capital Allowances**	190
23.2	**Research & Development Tax Credit**	192
	23.2.1 Overview	192
	23.2.2 Qualified Company	192

23.2.3 Qualifying R&D Activities   192

23.2.4 Qualifying R&D Expenditure   193

23.2.5 Buildings Used for R&D   193

23.2.6 Groups   194

23.2.7 Reward Key Employees   195

23.2.8 Reduce Corporation Tax   196

23.2.9 Clawback   197

23.2.10 Micro-entities and Small Companies   197

Questions   198

Chapter 24   Group Relief   199

24.1   Introduction   199

24.2   Payments Relief   199

24.2.1 Conditions to be Satisfied   200

24.3   Loss Relief   201

24.3.1 Qualifying Group – 75% Relationship   201

24.3.2 Qualifying Group – Non-resident Company Losses   203

24.3.3 Application of Losses for Group Relief   204

24.3.4 Corresponding Accounting Periods   208

**24.4   Disallowance of Trading Losses following a Change
of Ownership**   210

Questions   211

Chapter 25   Company Capital Gains   214

25.1   Capital Gains Liable to Corporation Tax   214

25.1.1 Irish Resident Companies   214

25.1.2 Non-resident Companies   214

25.2   Capital Gains Liable to Capital Gains Tax   215

25.2.1 Irish Resident Companies   215

25.2.2 Non-resident Companies   215

25.3   **Method of Taxation**   215

25.4   **Exemption from Tax on Disposal of Certain Shareholdings (Participation Exemption)**   216

25.5   **Capital Gains Group**   217

    25.5.1 Definition of a Capital Gains Group   217

    25.5.2 Disposal of Capital Assets within a Group   219

    25.5.3 Disposal of Capital Assets Outside the Group   221

    25.5.4 Company Leaving Group – Anti-avoidance Measure   221

    25.5.5 Pre-entry Losses – Anti-avoidance Measure   223

Questions   223

Chapter 26   **Close Companies**   226

26.1   **Meaning of Close Company**   226

    26.1.1 "Participator"   227

    26.1.2 "Control"   227

    26.1.3 "Associate"   227

    26.1.4 "Director"   227

26.2   **Consequences of Close Company Status**   228

    26.2.1 Certain Expenses for Participators and their Associates   229

    26.2.2 Interest Paid to Directors and their Associates   230

    26.2.3 Loans to Participators and their Associates   233

    26.2.4 Write-off of Loans to Participators   235

26.3   **Close Company Surcharge**   236

    26.3.1 Introduction   236

    26.3.2 7.5% Trading Deduction   236

    26.3.3 Trading Company: Basic Surcharge Calculation   236

    26.3.4 Trading Company Surcharge Calculation: Losses and Charges on Income   238

    26.3.5 Service Company Surcharge   242

26.4	**Other Matters**	245
	26.4.1 Case III Income	245
	26.4.2 Election – Not a Distribution for Surcharge	246
	26.4.3 Payment of Surcharge	247
Questions		247

Chapter 27	**Investment Companies**	252
27.1	**Introduction**	252
	27.1.1 Definition	252
	27.1.2 Relief for Management Expenses	253
27.2	**Management Expenses**	253
	27.2.1 Directors' Remuneration	254
	27.2.2 Carry Forward of Unutilised Management Expenses	254
Questions		255

PART FIVE   INCOME TAX

Chapter 28	**Territoriality Rules**	259
28.1	**Introduction**	259
28.2	**Impact of Residence, Ordinary Residence and Domicile**	259
	28.2.1 Resident and Domiciled	259
	28.2.2 Resident and Domiciled but Not Ordinarily Resident	260
	28.2.3 Resident but Not Domiciled	260
	28.2.4 Not Resident and Not Ordinarily Resident	260
	28.2.5 Not Resident but Ordinarily Resident	261
	28.2.6 Non-resident Individual Entitlement to Tax Credits	261
28.3	**Domicile Levy**	261
28.4	**Split-year Residence**	262
	28.4.1 Year of Arrival	262
	28.4.2 Year of Departure	263

28.5	**Rents Paid to Non-resident Landlords**	263
Questions		264
Chapter 29	**Foreign Investment Income**	265
29.1	**Overview**	265
29.2	**Schedule D, Case III**	265
	29.2.1 Non-EU Deposit Interest	266
	29.2.2 UK Dividends and UK Interest	266
	29.2.3 Foreign Rental Income	267
	29.2.4 Deductions Available	267
	29.2.5 Case III Losses	267
29.3	**Schedule D, Case IV**	267
	29.3.1 EU Deposit Interest	267
	29.3.2 Basis of Assessment	268
	29.3.3 Case IV Losses	268
Questions		268
Chapter 30	**Schedule E – Employment Income**	269
30.1	**Introduction**	269
30.2	**Special Assignee Relief Programme**	269
	30.2.1 Definitions	270
30.3	**Foreign Earnings Deduction**	271
	30.3.1 Qualifying Conditions	272
	30.3.2 Relief Available	272
	30.3.3 Exclusions	273
30.4	**Termination Payments**	273
	30.4.1 Charge to Tax	273
	30.4.2 Tax-exempt Termination Payment	273
30.5	**Retirement Lump Sum Benefits**	276
30.6	**Lump Sum Payments on Account of Death or Disability**	277
Questions		278

Chapter 31   Shares: Employment Incentive Schemes   281

**31.1   Relief for Investment in Corporate Trades: Employment and
Investment Incentive**   281

31.1.1 The Relief   281

31.1.2 Qualifying Criteria for EII Relief   282

31.1.3 Clawback   284

31.2   Share Option Schemes   284

31.2.1 Relevant Tax on Share Options (RTSO)   285

31.2.2 Short Options – Less than Seven Years   285

31.2.3 Long Options – Longer than Seven Years   286

31.2.4 Key Employee Engagement Programme   286

Questions   288

**Chapter 32   Married Couples/Civil Partners: Years of Marriage,
Death and Divorce**   289

32.1   Introduction   289

32.1.1 Joint Assessment   289

32.1.2 Single Assessment   290

32.1.3 Separate Assessment   290

32.2   Tax Treatment in Year of Marriage   290

32.3   Tax Treatment in Year of Death   291

32.3.1 Joint Assessment and Death of Assessable Spouse/
Nominated Civil Partner   292

32.3.2 Joint Assessment and Death of the Non-assessable Spouse or
Non-nominated Civil Partner   293

32.3.3 Single Assessment and Death of a Spouse/Civil Partner   293

32.3.4 Tax Treatment of Surviving Spouse/Civil Partner for
Subsequent Years   294

32.4   Tax Treatment on Separation, Divorce or Dissolution   294

32.4.1 Recap – General Rule   294

32.4.2 Tax Treatment in Year of Separation, Divorce or Dissolution   295

Questions   296

PART SIX   VALUE ADDED TAX

Chapter 33   Cross-border Transactions   301

33.1   Intra-EU Acquisition and Supply of Goods   301

33.1.1 VAT on Purchases from Other EU Member States
and Northern Ireland   301

33.1.2 VAT on Sales to Other EU Member States and
Northern Ireland   302

33.1.3 Intra-EU Distance Sales   303

33.2   Intra-EU Supplies of Services   304

33.2.1 Place of Supply of Services   304

33.2.2 Exceptions to the General Rules   304

33.3   Intra-EU Cross-border Reclaims of VAT   305

33.4   Imports/Exports of Goods from/to Non-EU Countries   305

33.4.1 Imports from Non-EU Countries   306

33.4.2 Exports to Non-EU Countries   306

33.5   Non-EU Supply of Services   306

Questions   307

Chapter 34   VAT and Property   309

34.1   Introduction   309

34.2   Vatable Supplies of Property   309

34.3   Exempt Supplies of Property   310

34.3.1 Option to Tax   310

34.3.2 Letting of Property   311

34.4   Interaction with Stamp Duty   311

Questions   311

Chapter 35   VAT: Advanced Aspects   313

35.1   Partially Exempt VAT-registered Businesses   313

35.2   Group Registration   314

35.2.1 Impact of Group Registration 314

35.2.2 Supply of Property within a VAT Group 315

35.3 VAT and the Transfer of Business 315

Questions 316

Appendix 1: Taxation Reference Material for Tax Year 2021 319

Appendix 2: Taxation and the *Code of Ethics* 335

Appendix 3: Tax Planning, Tax Avoidance and Tax Evasion 337

Suggested Solutions to Review Questions 339

Index 427

Chartered Accountants Ireland *Code of Ethics*

Chartered Accountants Ireland's *Code of Ethics* applies to all aspects of a Chartered Accountant's professional life, including dealing with corporation tax issues, capital gains tax issues, capital acquisitions tax issues and stamp duty issues. The *Code of Ethics* outlines the principles that should guide a Chartered Accountant, namely:

- Integrity
- Objectivity
- Professional Competence and Due Care
- Confidentiality
- Professional Behaviour.

As a Chartered Accountant, you will have to ensure that your dealings with the tax aspects of your professional life are in compliance with these fundamental principles. Set out in **Appendix 2** is further information regarding these principles and their importance in guiding you on how to deal with issues which may arise throughout your professional life, including giving tax advice and preparing tax computations.

Appeals, Revenue Audits and Qualifying Disclosures

Learning Objectives

After studying this chapter you will be able to:

- Advise on the operation of tax appeals.
- Advise on Revenue audits, including qualifying disclosures and mitigation of penalties.

1.1 Appeal Procedures

1.1.1 Introduction

At CA Proficiency 1, students studied income tax, corporation tax, capital gains tax and VAT and the rules pertaining to filing tax returns and paying the relevant tax. Generally, Irish resident persons are assessed to Irish tax on worldwide income and gains; while non-resident persons are subject to Irish tax on some Irish-source income and gains. Individuals and companies subject to self-assessment are obliged to calculate the amount of tax due and to pay and file tax returns with the Revenue Commissioners within the stipulated timeframe. Irish VAT-registered persons are obliged to collect VAT and file returns in accordance with the VAT legislation.

Revenue does not typically issue an assessment in respect of such returns. It will, however, issue a notice of assessment where a return has not been filed, where it is not satisfied with the return or where it believes it is not a full and true return.

If a taxpayer disagrees with Revenue's assessment or with a Revenue decision in relation to their taxes, the taxpayer has the right to appeal the assessment or decision. All appeals (with some exceptions) are submitted directly to the Tax Appeals Commission (TAC).

The taxpayer can **only** appeal if:

1. they have filed a return for the period covered by the assessment; and
2. they have paid the correct tax they believe is due, together with any interest or penalties payable.

An appeal must be submitted to the TAC within 30 days of the issue of the notice of assessment or the decision by Revenue. A taxpayer cannot appeal against a notice of assessment that is in accordance with the information contained in the return of income or that is agreed between Revenue and the taxpayer.

Conditions for a Valid Appeal

For an appeal to be valid it must be made in relation to an appealable matter and it must comply with the following:

1. it must be in writing, sent by post or email or submitted electronically through the TAC's website (www.taxappeals.ie);
2. the precise item in the assessment that the taxpayer disputes must be specified; and
3. the grounds for disputing the item must be detailed.

An appeal should be submitted on a Notice of Appeal form, which may be downloaded from the TAC website. After receipt of the notice of appeal, the TAC will send a copy of the notice of appeal and any documentation attached to it to Revenue. Any objection Revenue may have to the acceptance of the appeal must be sent, in writing, to the TAC within 30 days of receipt of the Notice of Appeal. These objections are copied to the taxpayer, who can respond to Revenue's objection within 14 days from receipt. The decision to accept or reject the appeal application is taken by the TAC only.

1.1.2 Hearing before the Appeal Commissioners

When an appeal has been accepted, the Appeal Commissioner may request that either party provide additional information (a "statement of case") and supporting documentation. Where such a request is made, the party so requested must share their statement plus any associated documents with the other party to the appeal and confirm to the Appeal Commissioner that this has been done. In some instances, the Appeal Commissioner may adjudicate on a matter under appeal without a hearing, provided the Appeal Commissioner notifies both parties of their intention to so do and where, within 21 days of such notification, neither party requests a hearing.

The parties to the appeal must be given at least 14 days' notice of the date for the hearing of the appeal. At the hearing, the Appeal Commissioners will consider the facts of the case and will determine an appeal, either in favour of the taxpayer or of Revenue, as soon as is practicable. The Commissioner will notify the parties, in writing, of their decision within 21 days of the appeal hearing being determined.

All appeal hearings are heard in public but if requested by the taxpayer, the Appeal Commissioners may direct that a hearing or part of a hearing be held *in camera*.

Dismissal or Determination of an Appeal

If an assessment is dismissed, as opposed to determined, there are serious implications for the taxpayer. In the case of a dismissal, the original tax, as assessed by Revenue, is confirmed and becomes immediately payable to Revenue as if no appeal had been lodged against the assessment.

If the assessment is determined, the right of appeal to the High Court, on a point of law only, is available to either party. Tax will neither be collected nor repaid by the Revenue on the basis of the Appeal Commissioner's determination and Revenue will not be obliged to amend the assessment under appeal until the appeal process to the High Court has been fully completed.

1.1.3 Hearings before the Courts

If either party to the appeal is dissatisfied with the determination of the Appeal Commissioner on a point of law, they may request the Appeal Commissioner to sign a 'Case Stated for the Opinion of the High Court' within 21 days from the date of determination of the appeal. This will include details of the Commissioner's findings of fact, an outline of the arguments made and the case law relied on by the parties, the Commissioner's determination and the point of law being appealed.

Either party aggrieved by the decision of the High Court has a right of appeal to the Court of Appeal, unless it is deemed that the matter is of general public importance or in the interests of justice, in which case the appeal will be heard by the Supreme Court.

1.1.4   Settlement of an Appeal

An appeal may be settled where:

- agreement has been reached between the taxpayer and Revenue;
- either party withdraws their appeal;
- the determination of the appeal by the Appeal Commissioner, High Court, Court of Appeal or Supreme Court; or
- by default, i.e. failure to be represented at the appeal hearing before the Appeal Commissioner.

1.2   Revenue Audits, Penalties and Qualifying Disclosures

1.2.1   Introduction to Revenue Audit

For the Revenue Commissioners, it is a fundamental principle of self-assessment tax systems that returns filed by compliant taxpayers are accepted as the basis for computing tax liabilities. Revenue police the self-assessment system by way of:

- non-audit compliance interventions;
- audits; and
- investigations.

Generally, taxpayers are selected for compliance intervention based on the presence of various risk indicators. Cases are selected in a number of ways, including the use of REAP (Revenue's electronic risk analysis system) and through the use of analytics. The REAP system allows for the screening of all tax returns against sectoral and business norms and provides a selection basis for checks or audits. In more recent times, Revenue use e-auditing, which allows the Revenue auditor to use computer-assisted audit techniques on a taxpayer's data as part of its audit process.

In addition to Revenue's risk-based selection approach, it also operates a random audit programme and a re-audit programme.

Revenue's *Code of Practice for Revenue Audit and other Compliance Interventions* (to be found at www.revenue.ie) sets out the guidelines to be followed by Revenue, taxpayers and tax practitioners, in the carrying out of Revenue Compliance Interventions. Under law, Revenue is entitled to make enquiries or investigations and take such actions as it considers necessary to satisfy itself as to the accuracy or otherwise of any statement or other particular contained in any return, list, statement or other particulars.

1.2.2   Revenue Non-audit Compliance Interventions

Revenue's non-audit compliance intervention is usually an enquiry by letter, secure email, telephone or a visit, about a specific issue. An example would be a request for further documentation to support a claim for a particular tax relief. These interventions can be:

- "assurance checks" or "aspect queries" – these are not limited only to self-assessed taxpayers but can also apply to PAYE taxpayers;

- profile interviews;
- sectoral reviews (e.g. a review of a specific trade, profession or economic sector);
- Joint Investigation Unit visits involving other agencies (e.g. Department of Social Protection);
- unannounced visits;
- a request for a person or business to undertake a self-review of a tax liability;
- the pursuit of returns from non-filers.

Where Revenue undertakes any type of non-audit compliance intervention, the taxpayer is still entitled to make an "unprompted qualifying disclosure" (see **Section 1.2.6**) as an audit or investigation is not regarding as having started.

1.2.3 Revenue Audit

The audit programme is mainly concerned with detecting and deterring non-compliance. The *Code of Practice* defines a Revenue audit as an examination of:

- a tax return;
- a declaration of liability or a repayment claim;
- a statement of liability to stamp duty;
- the compliance of a person with tax and duty legislation.

An examination may involve looking at all the risks in a particular case or may focus on a single issue or tax head.

Audit at Company's Place of Business
Where a business is involved, most audits, whether comprehensive or single tax head, include visits to the business premises. The length of such visits depends on the number and complexity of the points at issue. Notice is generally given in such cases to both the company and its agent. In certain exceptional circumstances (e.g. where it is suspected that records are likely to be removed or altered), a visit may take place unannounced.

Desk Audit
Certain audits (mainly verification of specific claims to expenses, allowances or reliefs) are conducted by letter (post, fax or e-mail), or by telephone where straightforward issues are involved. This type of audit, known as a desk audit, may also arise in a review of a director's tax affairs or where a company has unearned income. Similarly, CAT and stamp duty audits are normally desk audits. Taxpayers will be informed of the issues being examined in the course of a desk audit.

It should be noted that a desk audit may subsequently involve fieldwork, if deemed necessary, including visits to the company's premises to examine records.

Audit Notification
Twenty-one days' notice of a Revenue audit is generally given to both the taxpayer and their agent. Where an audit is to be scheduled, the letter issued will include the wording 'Notification of a Revenue Audit' and will show the date the audit will start. All audit notification letters issued to a taxpayer and agent must indicate the nature of the Revenue intervention. The scope of the audit will also be set out and will range from a single tax head or a particular issue for a specific period or year, to a comprehensive audit for a number of years. The Revenue auditor is confined to examining the issues as notified and cannot extend the audit without good reason at the time of the visit. The potential use of e-auditing techniques is noted in all audit notification letters.

As and from the date of the audit notification, the taxpayer can no longer make an unprompted qualifying disclosure. They can, however, make a "prompted qualifying disclosure" before the audit examination begins (see **Section 1.2.6**).

Conduct of a Revenue Audit

At the commencement of any field audit, the Revenue auditor will:

- identify themselves;
- explain the purpose of the audit;
- draw attention to the Customer Service Charter; and
- offer the taxpayer an opportunity to make a prompted qualifying disclosure.

Some of the key points pertaining to the conduct of an audit are:

- Revenue regularly use e-audit techniques to ensure that the business tax returns are based on the information contained in the underlying electronic records.
- The taxpayer (or their information technology supplier) will be required to provide the necessary data downloads.
- A receipt is given for any records removed from the premises. The auditor will try not to retain any records for longer than a month. If more time is required, the taxpayer will be advised of this.
- A written record of all requested, replies and other requirements, whether raised at the initial interview or subsequently, should be kept by the taxpayer to ensure the audit is conducted in an orderly way.
- Issues may arise during the course of the audit that require the auditor to consider opening earlier or later years. If deliberate default/deliberate behaviour is not involved, Revenue may informally draw the taxpayer's attention to these issues and give them the opportunity to make an unprompted qualifying disclosure in relation to these other years.
- If the auditor decides to extend the scope of the audit to other taxes or years not referred to in the audit notice, the taxpayer will be given the opportunity to make a prompted qualifying disclosure in respect of those other taxes or years.

Finalisation of the Audit

At the conclusion of the audit, the Revenue auditor will:

1. Outline the findings of the audit.
2. Quantify the tax, interest and penalties due.
3. Invite the taxpayer to make a written settlement offer.
4. If necessary, require the taxpayer to confirm that any issues identified have been rectified.

When a settlement has been agreed, a final letter will be issued by the Revenue auditor setting out:

- the details of the settlement;
- any inadequacies in the taxpayer's records or tax treatments;
- noting the taxpayer's confirmation that any inadequacies have been rectified.

1.2.4 Revenue Investigation

An investigation is an examination of a taxpayer's affairs where Revenue has evidence or concerns of serious tax evasion. Some investigation cases may lead to criminal prosecution. During the course of a Revenue audit, an auditor may also notify the taxpayer that the audit is ceasing and an investigation commencing.

Where a Revenue investigation is being notified, the letter issued will include the wording: 'Notification of a Revenue Investigation'. Revenue auditors engaged in the investigation of serious tax evasion may visit a taxpayer's place of business without advance notice.

Importantly, once an investigation is initiated, the taxpayer will not have an opportunity to make **any** type of qualifying disclosure and so cannot avail of any mitigation of penalties, avoid publication of final settlement or avoid possible criminal prosecution.

1.2.5 Tax, Interest and Penalties

Tax
Any tax due as a result of the Revenue audit or compliance intervention must be paid.

Interest
Interest is always charged if a failure to pay is identified and **cannot** be mitigated (i.e. reduced). Interest is charged on a daily basis from the date the tax was originally due and payable.

Application of Penalties
Penalties will apply if, in the course of the audit, tax defaults are identified. Penalties are 'tax-geared', which means that the penalty is expressed as a percentage of the tax (but not the interest) in question. Penalties can be mitigated. Penalties will apply in circumstances where there has been:

- careless behaviour; or
- careless behaviour with significant consequences; or
- deliberate behaviour.

Careless Behaviour without Significant Consequences
The penalty for careless behaviour without significant consequences is **20% of the tax due**. Careless behaviour will arise if a person of ordinary skill and knowledge, properly advised, would have foreseen as a reasonable probability or likelihood the prospect that an act (or omission) would cause a tax underpayment, having regard to all the circumstances but, nevertheless, the act or omission occurred. There is also a **materiality test** to determine if the careless behaviour is without significant consequences. The tax shortfall must be **less than 15%** of the tax liability ultimately due in respect of the particular tax.

Careless Behaviour with Significant Consequences
The penalty for this category is **40% of the tax due**. Careless behaviour with significant consequences is the **lack of due care** with the result that tax liabilities or repayment claims are **substantially incorrect** and pass the 15% test described above.

Deliberate Behaviour
The penalty for deliberate default is **100% of the tax due**. Deliberate default has indicators consistent with intent and includes tax evasion and the non-operation of fiduciary taxes, such as PAYE and VAT.

Careless behaviour is distinguished from deliberate behaviour by the **absence** of indicators consistent with intent on the part of the taxpayer.

Example 1.1

George and Rinah were both subject to Revenue audits after filing individual tax returns. After their audits, George and Rinah were deemed to have acted without due care and attention – both had under-declared their tax liabilities for income tax and VAT, respectively. They were not deemed to have deliberately under-declared their respective tax liabilities.

	George	Rinah
Tax amount due	€61,000	€243,000
Tax payable per return submitted	€48,000	€214,000
Tax underpaid	€13,000	€29,000
As a % of tax actually due	21.3%	11.9%
Penalty (before mitigation)	40%	20%

While Rinah underpaid a greater amount of tax, as a percentage of the tax due it was George who was the bigger defaulter.

Innocent Error

A penalty will not be payable in respect of a tax default if the tax default was not deliberate and was not attributable in any way to the failure to take reasonable care to comply with a taxpayer's tax obligations. Factors which will be taken into account in deciding whether a penalty should not be imposed include:

- Whether the auditor concludes that the taxpayer has provided for, and implemented, the keeping of proper books and records so as to fulfil tax obligations.
- The frequency with which the "innocent error" occurs. Repeatedly making such errors could indicate lack of appropriate care which could put the error into the "careless behaviour without significant consequences" category or higher.
- The previous compliance record of the taxpayer.
- Where the error being corrected is immaterial in the context of the overall payments made by the taxpayer.

Interest will, however, be charged even if no penalty is charged.

Technical Adjustments

"Technical adjustments" are adjustments to a tax liability that arise from differences in interpretation or the application of the legislation. A technical adjustment will not give rise to a penalty where:

- due care has been exercised by the taxpayer;
- the treatment concerned was based on an interpretation of law that could reasonably have been considered to be correct.

Interest will, however, be charged even if no penalty is charged.

No Loss of Revenue

The expression "no loss of revenue" is used to describe a situation whereby there is no cost to the State even though tax was not properly charged. For example, if a sale is made between two VAT-registered businesses without the addition of VAT, no VAT is paid on the sale but, correspondingly, no input VAT credit is being claimed by the other party. Basically, there is no loss of revenue to the State.

However, in the event of an audit, Revenue is entitled to seek the VAT, interest and penalties due for the non-operation or incorrect operation of the VAT system.

Taxpayers may make a "no loss of revenue claim" if:

- the tax involved is VAT (no loss of revenue claims may only be made in respect of other taxes in exceptional circumstances);
- the taxpayer can provide conclusive evidence to demonstrate, to the satisfaction of Revenue, that there was no loss of revenue; and
- the taxpayer's compliance record is good and the default in question wasn't as a result of deliberate behaviour.

Where Revenue accepts no loss of revenue claims, statutory interest may be payable but limited to any period where there was a temporary loss of revenue.

Revenue will not accept no loss of revenue claims in the following circumstances:

- where there is a general failure to operate the tax system (and not just a once-off);
- where the default was as a consequence of deliberate behaviour;
- where no loss of revenue has not been proven to the satisfaction of Revenue;
- where the taxpayer has not co-operated;
- where the default is in the careless behaviour category and there is neither a qualifying disclosure nor co-operation;
- where the claim was not submitted in writing; or
- where the no loss of revenue penalty is not agreed and paid.

Self-correction

This category arises outside of the audit or enquiry process. A return may be self-corrected **without** penalty where:

- Revenue is notified in writing of the adjustments to be made, and the circumstances under which the errors arose;
- a computation of the correct tax and statutory interest payable is provided, along with a payment in settlement.

Time Limits for Self-correction

Income Tax	Within 12 months of the due date for filing the return.
Corporation Tax	Within 12 months of the due date for filing the return.
Capital Gains Tax	Within 12 months of the due date for filing the return.
VAT, PAYE and PRSI	Before the due date of the IT or CT return for the period in which the monthly PAYE/PRSI return is due/VAT period ends. E.g. a company with a December year-end must make a self-correction of its Jan. 2021 PAYE/PRSI return or of its Jan/Feb 2021 VAT return before 23 Sept 2022. For bi-monthly/quarterly/half-yearly remitters of VAT, if the net VAT underpayment is less than €6,000, the amount of tax can be included, without interest, as an adjustment in the next VAT return and there is no requirement to notify Revenue.
CAT and Stamp Duty	Within 12 months of the due date for filing the return.
Relevant Contract Tax (RCT)	A return for which a deduction authorisation has been issued may not be amended after the return due date.

The benefit of self-correction does not apply if Revenue had notified a taxpayer of an audit or started to make enquiries in relation to the return in question or if the correction relates to an instance of deliberate behaviour which also featured in a previous period.

1.2.6 Qualifying Disclosures and Mitigation of Penalties

Penalties are mitigated (i.e. reduced) where:

- there is **full co-operation** by the taxpayer;
- a **qualifying disclosure** is made by the taxpayer.

No mitigation of penalties is available where a Revenue investigation has been initiated.

Full Co-operation
Full co-operation includes the following:

- having all books, records, and linking papers available for the auditor at the commencement of the audit;
- having appropriate personnel available at the time of the audit;
- responding promptly to all requests for information and explanations;
- responding promptly to all correspondence;
- prompt payment of the audit settlement liability.

Qualifying Disclosures
The taxpayer may elect to carry out a review of their own tax affairs and identify where mistakes were made **prior** to their discovery by the Revenue auditor. A taxpayer may make a qualifying disclosure, i.e. a disclosure of all information in relation to, and full particulars of, all matters occasioning a liability to tax that gives rise to a penalty. It must be in writing and signed by or on behalf of the taxpayer. It should be accompanied by a declaration that all matters contained in the disclosure are correct and complete, along with full payment of the tax plus any interest incurred on late payment of that tax. There are incentives for taxpayers who wish to make qualifying disclosures.

A qualifying disclosure results in the following:

- non-publication of the tax settlement in the list of tax defaulters published by Revenue;
- no prosecution;
- further mitigation of penalties.

Qualifying disclosures can be either "**unprompted**" or "**prompted**". An unprompted disclosure is one made **before** the taxpayer is notified of an audit or contacted by Revenue regarding an inquiry or investigation relating to their tax affairs.

A prompted disclosure is a disclosure made **after** an audit notice has issued but before an examination of the books and records or other documentation has begun.

Since 1 May 2017, any disclosure made by a taxpayer that relates directly or indirectly to foreign assets, income or gains will **not** be treated as a qualifying disclosure. In addition, where there are liabilities within the State as well as liabilities relating to offshore matters, a qualifying disclosure will be unavailable in respect of **all** of those liabilities except in limited circumstances.

Period to Prepare a Qualifying Disclosure
For a taxpayer to secure an agreed 60-day period of time in which to prepare and make a qualifying disclosure, **notice of the intention** to make a disclosure must be given.

In the case of an **unprompted disclosure**, the notice of the intention to make a disclosure must be given **before**:

■ a notice of audit is issued; or
■ the taxpayer has been contacted by Revenue regarding an enquiry or investigation relating to its tax affairs.

In the case of a **prompted disclosure**, the notice of intention to make a disclosure must be given **within 14 days** of the day of issue of the notification of audit.

A person who has given notice within the time allowed of their intention to make a qualifying disclosure will be given 60 days in which to quantify the shortfall and to make the relevant payment. This period of 60 days will begin from the day on which the notice of intention to make a qualifying disclosure was given and will be communicated to the taxpayer in writing by Revenue. The 60-day period allows the taxpayer or their agent to contact Revenue to discuss any matters arising, including the category of default on which the mitigated penalty is to be based.

Format exact percentages are known of the Qualifying Disclosure

The following conditions must be satisfied for a disclosure to be a **qualifying disclosure** for the purpose of mitigation of penalties:

■ The disclosure must be made in writing and signed by or on behalf of the taxpayer.
■ It must be accompanied by a declaration, to the best of that person's knowledge, information and belief, that all matters contained in the disclosure are correct and complete.
■ The disclosure must, whether prompted or unprompted, state the amounts of all liabilities to tax, interest and penalties, as respects all tax heads and periods, which were liabilities previously undisclosed by reason of *deliberate behaviour* by the taxpayer
■ In the case of a **prompted** disclosure, it must also state the amounts of any liabilities previously undisclosed, for any reason *other than deliberate behaviour*, which are liabilities to tax, interest and penalties within the scope of the proposed audit or audit enquiry.
■ In the case of an **unprompted** disclosure, it must state the amounts of any liabilities previously undisclosed, for any reason other than deliberate behaviour, which are liabilities to tax, interest and penalties in respect of the tax types and periods which are covered by the unprompted qualifying disclosure.
■ The disclosure must be accompanied by a payment of the total liability arising in respect of the tax and interest in respect of that tax. The qualifying disclosure does not need to make reference to the penalty due.

On receipt of the qualifying disclosure the auditor will agree the penalties with the taxpayer and will obtain payment at that stage. Where the taxpayer is unable to pay the full settlement amount at this stage, a real, genuine and acceptable proposal to pay the amount due in accordance with the Revenue instalment arrangement procedures will satisfy the payment requirement. If, however, the taxpayer fails to honour the instalment arrangements, they will be regarded as not having made a qualifying disclosure.

Reduction of Penalties

The amount of the reduction available is determined by whether a qualifying disclosure was made in the previous five years. There are three different tables and the table for the first qualifying disclosure is shown below.

| | **Net Penalty after Reduction where there is:** | | | |
| | | | | |
Category of Tax Default	**Penalty as a % of Tax Underpaid**	**Co-operation Only**	**Co-operation AND a Prompted Qualifying Disclosure**	**Co-operation AND an Unprompted Qualifying Disclosure**
Deliberate behaviour	100%	75%	50%	10%
Careless behaviour **with** significant consequences	40%	30%	20%	5%
Other careless behaviour	20%	15%	10%	3%

It is important to be aware of the different types of default and that the penalty applicable is reduced depending on whether there is co-operation or not and a prompted or unprompted disclosure (although in practice it is not expected that the exact percentages are known).

Where a second or subsequent qualifying disclosure is made within five years of a first qualifying disclosure, there is still a reduction in penalties. However, the reduction in penalties where the category of tax default falls under "deliberate behaviour" or "careless behaviour with significant consequences" is less than the reduction in penalties for the first qualifying disclosure. The same reduction in penalties applies where the tax default is in the category of "careless behaviour without significant consequences". Where a subsequent qualifying disclosure is made more than five years after a first qualifying disclosure was made, the same reduction in penalties applies as if it were a first disclosure.

If a taxpayer deliberately or carelessly files an incorrect return before the due date for filing the return, they are deemed to have filed the return late unless the errors in the return are corrected without unreasonable delay. As the taxpayer is deemed to have filed their return late, a surcharge is payable. If such a taxpayer is also liable to the penalties above, they are not also liable to a surcharge for the late filing of a return. If, however, a taxpayer files their return after the filing deadline and becomes liable to one of the penalties above, the surcharge for the late filing of a return is payable in addition to the tax-geared penalty.

1.2.7 Review Procedures

The taxpayer has the right to request a review of the conduct of an audit, in particular in relation to:

- proposed adjustments to receipts or profits figures, claims for reliefs or allowances or to tax computations;
- penalties to be charged;

The initial review is carried out by the local Revenue office; however, if the taxpayer is not satisfied with the outcome of this review, it may request a review by an external reviewer.

This process cannot be used or requested where:

1. There is disagreement over a point of law; such matters are adjudicated on by Appeal Commissioners or courts.
2. There is a dispute regarding civil penalties as these are determined by the courts.
3. A settlement involves publication in the List of Tax Defaulters as it is a legal requirement.
4. Enforcement proceedings or a court action has been initiated or the debt is the subject of an attachment order.
5. The complaint is being used to delay or obstruct an audit/investigation, or is considered to be frivolous or vexatious.

A taxpayer's statutory right to make an appeal to the TAC or a complaint to the Ombudsman or the Equality Tribunal is not affected by availing of the Revenue's review procedures. Revenue is bound by the outcome of the review unless they are of the view that the decision is not in accordance with the legislation.

Questions

Review Question
(See Suggested Solutions to Review Questions at the end of this textbook.)

Question 1.1

The finance director of Liberworks Ltd recently left the company. Since her departure the shareholders and your clients, Glen and Ursula, have identified a major error in the corporation tax return for the company for the year ended 31 December 2019 (which was submitted to the Revenue Commissioners on time).

The error relates to the deduction claimed for employer's pension contributions. This has resulted in the corporation tax liability for the period being understated. The submitted corporation tax computation included a deduction of €500,000 relating to employer pension contributions. The deduction that should have been claimed was €50,000. Glen has discussed the matter with Ursula; they agree that the finance director probably included an additional zero in the computation by mistake and that the error was not deliberate. They are unsure how to deal with the error.

Requirement
Email Glen and Ursula advising them how they should deal with the error identified in the corporation tax return. In your email include details of how Revenue's penalty regime operates, including the different penalties potentially payable depending upon the behaviour of Glen and Ursula in relation to the error identified. Calculations are not required.

Residence and Domicile

Learning Objectives

After studying this chapter you will understand:

- the importance of the concepts of residence and domicile in assessing an individual's liability to Irish tax;
- the difference between residence, ordinary residence and domicile.

2.1   Introduction

The extent to which an individual is liable to Irish tax on worldwide income and gains depends on the nature and location of the assets (see **Section 2.6**) and on three criteria:

1. the individual's **residence**;
2. the individual's **ordinary residence**; and
3. the individual's **domicile**.

2.2   Residence

An individual's tax residence is determined for each tax year separately. Generally, an individual will be resident in Ireland for a tax year if they are either:

- present in Ireland for a total of 183 days or more during that tax year, or
- present in Ireland for a total of 280 days or more in the current and preceding tax year,

provided that where an individual is present in the State (i.e. Republic of Ireland) for only **30 days or less** in a tax year,

- they will not be Irish resident in that year, and
- no account will be taken of that period in calculating the aggregate of 280 days or more over two tax years.

An individual is present in Ireland for a day if they are in Ireland at **any time during that day**.
   The tests to establish residency are summarised in **Figure 2.1**.

FIGURE 2.1: TEST TO ESTABLISH IRISH RESIDENCY (OTHER THAN ELECTION)

2.3 Election to be Resident

An individual may elect to be Irish resident for a tax year if:

- they are not resident in Ireland in the tax year; and
- they satisfy Revenue that they are in Ireland with the intention and in such circumstances that they will be resident in Ireland for the next tax year.

An individual might elect to be Irish tax resident for the following reasons:

- to qualify for full tax credits;
- to avail of Ireland's network of double taxation agreements; or
- to qualify for joint assessment. The Irish Revenue's view is that both the individual and their spouse must be Irish resident to qualify; however, each case will be examined on an individual basis.

Example 2.1

Anne jets between her home in Barbados and her retreat in West Cork. She spends the following number of days in Ireland over the following tax years:

	No. of Days
2018	Nil
2019	100
2020	125
2021	165

YEAR 2019

Test 1: Does Anne spend more than 30 days in Ireland in 2019?
Answer: Yes, therefore go to Test 2.

Test 2: Does Anne spend 183 days or more in Ireland in 2019?
Answer: No, therefore go to Test 3.

Test 3: Did Anne spend more than 30 days in Ireland in 2018?
Answer: No. Therefore Anne is not resident in 2019.

YEAR 2020

Test 1: Does Anne spend more than 30 days in Ireland in 2020?
Answer: Yes, therefore go to Test 2.

Test 2: Does Anne spend 183 days or more in Ireland in 2020?
Answer: No, therefore go to Test 3.

Test 3: Did Anne spend more than 30 days in Ireland in 2019?
Answer: Yes, therefore go to Test 4.

Test 4: Is Anne's total number of days in Ireland in 2020 and 2019 280 days or more?
Answer: 125 days in 2020 **plus** 100 days in 2019 = 225 days.
No, not 280 days or more. Therefore Anne is not resident in 2020.

YEAR 2021

Test 1: Does Anne spend more than 30 days in Ireland in 2021?
Answer: Yes, therefore go to Test 2.

Test 2: Does Anne spend 183 days or more in Ireland in 2021?
Answer: No, therefore go to Test 3.

Test 3: Did Anne spend more than 30 days in Ireland in 2020?
Answer: Yes, therefore go to Test 4.

Test 4: Is Anne's total number of days in Ireland in 2021 and 2020 280 days or more?
Answer: 165 days in 2021 **plus** 125 days in 2020 = 290 days.
Yes, 280 days or more. Anne is Irish resident for 2021.

2.4 Ordinary Residence

An individual's ordinary residence refers to an individual's pattern of residence over a number of tax years and is determined for each tax year separately. An individual is ordinarily resident in Ireland for a tax year if they have been resident in Ireland for each of the **preceding three consecutive tax years**.

An individual does not stop being ordinarily resident in Ireland unless they have been **non-resident** for the preceding **three consecutive tax years**.

Example 2.2

Tom comes to live in Ireland from the USA on 1 May 2017. He leaves permanently on 28 January 2021.

Tax Year	Resident	Ordinarily Resident
2017	Yes ≥ 183 days	No
2018	Yes ≥ 183 days	No
2019	Yes ≥ 183 days	No
2020	Yes ≥ 183 days	Yes (resident for preceding three consecutive years)
2021	No – fails 30-day test	Yes

Tom will continue to be ordinarily resident in Ireland for 2022 and 2023. He will cease to be ordinarily resident when he has been non-resident for three years, i.e. 2024.

2.5 Domicile

Domicile is a legal term. The main idea underlying the concept is **home**, the permanent home. Generally, a person is domiciled in the country of which they are a national and in which they spend their life. However, the equating of domicile to home must be treated with care as, in certain circumstances, a person may be domiciled in a country that is not and never has been their home. A person can have two homes but can only have **one domicile** at any one time.

Three general points regarding domicile require special attention:

1. a person cannot be without a domicile;
2. a person cannot possess more than one domicile at any time; and
3. an existing domicile is presumed to continue until it is proved that a new domicile of choice has been acquired.

2.5.1 Domicile of Origin

An individual is **born** with a domicile known as the domicile of origin. A child at birth acquires the domicile of the father. If the parents are not married, the domicile of the mother is acquired instead. An individual can reject their domicile of origin and **acquire** a new domicile. In order to abandon the domicile of origin, the individual must prove conclusively that they have **severed all links** with the country in which the domicile of origin lies. A domicile of origin cannot be lost by a mere abandonment, it can only be lost by the acquisition of a domicile of choice.

2.5.2 Domicile of Choice

A domicile of choice is the domicile that any independent person (e.g. an individual who has attained 18 years of age) can acquire by a combination of **residence** and **intention**. To acquire a domicile of choice, an individual must establish a physical presence in the new jurisdiction and have an intention to reside there indefinitely. A domicile of choice can be abandoned. This will involve either the acquisition of a new domicile of choice or the revival of the domicile of origin.

2.5.3 Domicile of Dependence

The domicile of dependent persons (children less than 18 years or incapacitated persons) is **dependent** on the domicile of someone else other than themselves.

2.6 Location of Assets

General law determines where property is located. The main rules are as follows:

1. **Land and buildings** Situated where they are physically located.
2. **Debts**
   (a) A simple contract debt is situated where the debtor resides.
   (b) A speciality debt, i.e. a debt payable under a sealed instrument, is situated where the instrument happens to be.
   (c) A judgment debt is situated where the judgment is recorded.
3. **Securities/Shares** Situated where the share register is kept, if the securities/shares are registered (Irish incorporated companies are required to maintain a register of members in Ireland). Bearer securities/shares are situated where the security/share certificate is physically located.
4. **Tangible property, e.g. cars, furniture, movable goods** Situated where they are physically located.
5. **Cash or currency of any kind** Situated where they are physically located. Bank balances are located in the country where the bank branch in which the account is located
6. **Goodwill of a business** Situated at the place where the trade, business or profession is carried on.

Questions

Review Questions
(See Suggested Solutions to Review Questions at the end of this textbook.)

Question 2.1

Hank is a US citizen seconded to work in Ireland for two years. He arrives on 19 May 2019 and leaves on 1 May 2021. He does not leave the country during that period.

Requirement
Establish Hank's residence status for each year.

Question 2.2

Kenji is a Japanese citizen seconded to work in Ireland for a two-year period. He arrives on 17 December 2018 and leaves on 16 January 2021. He does not leave the country during the period of his secondment.

Requirement
What is Kenji's residence status for each year?

Question 2.3

Aurore is a French woman who has been seconded from France to work in Ireland for three years. She arrives on 1 February 2018 and leaves on 10 January 2021.

Requirement
What is Aurore's residence and ordinary residence status for each year?

Part One

Capital Gains Tax

General Principles and Administration – Recap

Learning Objectives

The purpose of this chapter is to refresh your knowledge of the general principles of capital gains tax (CGT) studied at CA Proficiency 1 where you attained the ability to:

- Advise on and apply the general principles for the computation of CGT liabilities.
- Advise on the payment of CGT and the filing of returns.
- Identify development land for CGT purposes and apply the relevant restrictions to any such disposals.
- Determine and apply the appropriate treatment of capital losses.

Chartered Accountants Ireland's *Code of Ethics* applies to all aspects of a professional accountant's professional life, including dealing with capital gains tax issues. Further information regarding the principles in the *Code of Ethics* is set out in **Appendix 2**.

Students should also be aware of the issues around tax planning, tax avoidance and tax evasion, and these are discussed in **Appendix 3**.

3.1 Introduction

The charge to capital gains tax (CGT) is contained in the Taxes Consolidation Act 1997 (TCA 1997) and arises from a disposal of a chargeable asset by a chargeable person on or after 6 April 1974.

In general, assets are chargeable assets unless specifically exempt. CGT is charged on gains realised by individuals, partnerships and trusts. Companies are only assessed to CGT on disposals of development land. Individuals are entitled to an annual exemption of €1,270. There is no CGT on death.

The general rate of CGT for 2021 is 33% (there is a 10% rate of CGT which applies to disposals of certain business assets qualifying for revised entrepreneur relief (see **Chapter 6**)) and is charged by reference to the year of assessment for individuals (i.e. the calendar year). Where the disposal takes place between 1 January and 30 November, CGT is payable by the following 15 December. For disposals that take place in December, CGT is payable by the following 31 January. A return of chargeable gains must be made on or before 31 October in the year following the year of assessment, i.e. for 2021 the return must be made by 31 October 2022 (usually extended to mid-November if paying and filing using ROS).

The extent to which gains are chargeable, and losses are allowable, depends on the location and nature of the asset (see **Chapter 4**) and the person's tax residence, ordinary residence and domicile (see **Chapter 2**).

3.2   Computation of Gain or Loss

The capital gain is the difference between the deemed consideration for the disposal and the deemed cost of acquisition of the asset, as indexed for inflation if relevant. Enhancement expenditure incurred and reflected in the asset at disposal, as indexed for inflation if relevant, is also deducted in computing the gain. Where the transaction is between connected persons (e.g. relatives) the consideration is deemed to be the open market value. The basic layout of the CGT computation is:

CAPITAL GAINS TAX COMPUTATION FOR 2021

	€	€
Sales proceeds (or market value)	X	
Less: incidental costs of sale	(X)	
		X
Deduct allowable costs:		
Costs of acquisition (or market value) (indexed if applicable)		(X)
Enhancement expenditure (indexed if applicable)		(X)
Gain		X
Deduct: reliefs		(X)
Deduct: losses		(X)
		X
Deduct: annual exemption		(1,270)
Taxable gain		X
CGT payable: taxable gain × CGT rate		X

Where a portion of an asset is sold the portion of the deemed consideration and of the allowable enhancement expenditure allowed as a deduction when computing the chargeable gain/allowable loss is based on the following formula:

$$\text{Original cost or Enhancement expenditure} \times \frac{A}{(A+B)}$$

where: A = deemed proceeds of disposal; and
         B = market value of the asset that is retained.

Example 3.1

Asset cost €10,000 on 10 April 1982. Part of the asset was sold on 10 November 2021 for €27,000. At that time, the market value of the remainder of the asset was €50,000.

The individual is married. Calculate the CGT liability for 2021.

	€
Proceeds	27,000
Indexed cost: (€10,000 × €27,000/(€27,000 + €50,000) × 2.253	(7,900)
	19,100
Annual exemption	(1,270)
Taxable gain	17,830
CGT due @ 33%	5,884

3.3 Development Land

Development land is land which, at the time a disposal is made, the market value exceeds the current use value (CUV) of that land. Indexation relief only applies to the CUV of the land at acquisition and losses from non-development land assets cannot reduce a development land gain. Irish resident companies are only assessed to CGT on disposals of development land; all other disposals by Irish resident companies are assessed to corporation tax.

3.4 Losses

Losses are computed in the same manner as gains. If the asset is sold for less than the allowable cost of acquiring and enhancing the asset, then it is disposed of at a loss and that loss is an allowable loss. However, if the asset disposed of is an exempt asset, then the loss is not allowable. An allowable loss may arise in certain circumstances even where the asset is not disposed of, e.g. a loss arising from the value of an asset becoming negligible.

There are some restrictions in relation to allowable losses where a non-wasting chattel, i.e. a tangible moveable asset with a useful life of in excess of 50 years, such as a painting, is disposed of. Where a non-wasting chattel is disposed of for less than €2,540, any loss on the disposal is computed as if the consideration for the disposal had been €2,540.

Allowable losses arising must be set-off against chargeable gains accruing in the same year of assessment against gains chargeable at the highest rate of tax first and any unused losses must be carried forward and set-off against chargeable gains arising in the earliest **subsequent** year. An exception to this rule is made in the case of losses that accrue to an individual in the year in which they die. These losses may be carried back and set against gains of the three years of assessment preceding the year of assessment in which the individual died.

All available loss relief must be utilised before relief for the €1,270 annual exemption may be taken.

Where a disposal to a "connected person" results in an allowable loss, that loss may only be **set-off against chargeable gains on disposals to the same connected person**.

If a loss is realised on the disposal of an asset that has qualified in full for capital allowances then no relief is available against chargeable gains for that loss.

A loss accruing to a person who is not resident or ordinarily resident in the year of assessment is not an allowable loss for CGT purposes unless, if a gain had accrued instead of a loss on the disposal, the person would have been chargeable on the gain and there is no loss relief available in respect of assets situated outside the State for non-domiciled individuals who are assessed on the remittance basis (see **Chapter 4**).

Indexation cannot increase a loss, nor can it convert a gain into a loss. The substitution of market value at 6 April 1974 for cost can also not increase a loss.

3.5 Exemptions and Reliefs

There are many exemptions from CGT, including winnings from betting and lotteries, government securities and certain life assurance policies. Common exemptions and reliefs from CGT on disposal of assets include:

- transfers between spouses that are living together;
- principal private residence relief;
- disposal of a site to a child;

- non-wasting chattels sold for €2,540 or less;
- wasting chattels not used for business purposes;
- certain land and buildings acquired between 7 December 2011 and 31 December 2014.

These have all been considered at CA Proficiency 1. Further tax reliefs on disposal of business assets will be covered later in this textbook (see **Chapters 6–9**).

Questions

Review Questions
(See Suggested Solutions to Review Questions at the end of this textbook.)

Question 3.1

On 8 March 2021, Mary sold a painting for €40,000. She had purchased the painting in May 1985 for €1,000. On 2 December 2021, she sold an antique table for €12,000, which she had inherited in January 2004 when it was valued at €10,000.

Requirement
Calculate Mary's CGT liabilities for 2021 and state the date(s) payable.

Question 3.2

Dan McLoughlin bought 20 acres of land on 5 March 1973 at €550 per acre, its then current use value. Professional fees and other incidental costs amounted to €450 on the purchase. The value of the land on 6 April 1974 was €600 per acre, also its current use value.

On 7 May 2021, Dan sold four acres of the land as one-acre sites to local families who wished to build residential properties on the sites. Dan received €50,000 for each site while the market value of the remaining 16 acres at the date of sale was €10,000 per acre. The current use value of the four sites sold at the date of sale was €10,000 per acre.

Requirement
Calculate Dan's CGT liability arising on the above disposals. (You can ignore the annual exemption for CGT purposes.)

Territoriality Rules

Learning Objectives

After studying this chapter you will be able to:

- Apply the territoriality rules for CGT as influenced by a person's residence, ordinary residence and domicile, and the location of the asset.
- Identify and apply the rules for temporary non-residence for CGT purposes.

4.1 Location of Assets

The extent to which gains are chargeable, and losses allowable, depends on the location and nature of the asset and the person's tax residence, ordinary residence and domicile (see **Chapter 2**). The general rules for determining the location of assets are set out in **Section 2.6**. However, for CGT, the rule for the location of debts is different to that set down under general law. For CGT purposes, a debt is located in the State only if the creditor is resident in the State.

4.2 Individual is Resident or Ordinarily Resident

An **Irish domiciled** individual who is **resident or ordinarily resident** in the State for 2021 (1 January to 31 December 2021) is chargeable to CGT on **worldwide** chargeable gains made on the disposal of assets.

A **foreign domiciled** individual who is **resident or ordinarily resident** in the State is liable on all **Irish gains** but only on **foreign gains to the extent that they are remitted to the State**, i.e. the remittance basis applies. There is **no loss relief available in respect of assets situated outside Ireland for non-domiciled individuals who are assessed on the remittance basis**.

Where an individual is taxed on a remittance basis, the rate of CGT that applies to remitted gains is the rate of CGT which applied when the disposal was made.

Example 4.1

Hans Vervoort is a Belgian domiciled individual who has been resident in Ireland for many years. On 22 October 2012, when the Irish rate of CGT was 30%, Hans disposed of a property in Belgium. Hans did not remit the proceeds from this disposal to Ireland until 2021. Hans will be liable in 2021 to Irish CGT at 30% on the gain that arose on the disposal of the property.

Anti-avoidance legislation provides that, where a non-domiciled individual transfers outside the State to their spouse or civil partner, any of the proceeds of the disposal of any assets on which chargeable gains accrue and, on or after 24 October 2013, any amounts are received in the State that derive from that transfer, then the amounts will be deemed to have been received in the State by the non-domiciled individual and therefore are liable to Irish CGT.

While an Irish domiciled person who is non-resident, but is still ordinarily resident, is liable to Irish CGT, Irish domiciled individuals had been able to avoid Irish CGT by being resident in certain tax treaty countries. However, there is an anti-avoidance rule that charges to tax certain disposals by temporary non-residents (see **Section 4.4**).

4.3   Individual is not Resident and not Ordinarily Resident

An individual who is neither resident nor ordinarily resident is not liable to Irish CGT on the disposal of an asset unless it is a disposal of a specified Irish asset, i.e. disposals of foreign assets or Irish non-specified assets are outside the charge to CGT for an individual who is neither resident nor ordinarily resident. However, the disposal may be caught under the temporary non-resident anti-avoidance rules dealt with at **Section 4.4**.

4.3.1   Specified Irish Assets

Gains arising on the disposal of certain **specified Irish assets** are chargeable to CGT irrespective of the residence or ordinary residence of the owner. The specified assets are:

1. Land and buildings in the State.
2. Minerals in the State or any rights, interests or other assets in relation to mining or minerals or the searching for minerals, including exploration or exploitation rights within the limits of the Irish Continental Shelf.
3. Unquoted shares deriving their value, or the greater part of their value, from 1. or 2. above.
4. Assets situated in the State that, at or about the time when the gains accrued, were used for the purposes of a trade carried on in the State through a branch or agency, or were used, held or acquired for use by, or for, the purposes of the branch or agency.

You will recall that an individual is ordinarily resident in the State if resident in the State for the preceding three tax years. To become non-ordinarily resident, the individual must not be resident for at least three tax years. Therefore, if an individual wishes to avoid Irish tax on the disposal of a foreign asset or on an Irish asset that is not a specified asset, the individual must become both non-resident and non-ordinarily resident. This would mean that the individual would have to be non-resident for three tax years before the Irish CGT could be avoided under this general rule.

Example 4.2
During 2021, Mary made the following disposals:

1. Gain of €10,000 on sale of shares in Irish Plc, a company quoted on the Irish Stock Exchange.
2. Gain of €100,000 on sale of land in Galway.
3. Gain of €50,000 on sale of shares in UK Plc, a company quoted on the London Stock Exchange.
4. Loss of €5,000 on sale of shares in Completely Irish Plc, a company quoted on the Irish Stock Exchange.
5. Loss of €8,000 on sale of shares in Lyons Plc, a company quoted on the Paris Stock Exchange.

If Mary is Irish domiciled and resident or ordinarily resident, she is liable to Irish CGT on all the gains and is allowed loss relief for all the losses.

continued overleaf

> If Mary is not Irish domiciled, but is resident or ordinarily resident, she is liable to Irish CGT on Irish gains only (i.e. 1. and 2.) and allowed loss relief for Irish losses only (i.e. 4.). Mary will be liable to Irish CGT on the foreign gain (i.e. 3.) if she remits the gain to the State. She will not be entitled to relief for the foreign loss (i.e. 5.).
>
> If Mary is not resident or ordinarily resident, she is liable on specified assets only and therefore is taxable only on 2. and is not entitled to relief for either of the losses.

4.3.2 Administration, including Withholding Tax

Due to the difficulty of collecting CGT due by non-residents, Revenue can issue a notice of assessment at any time, including before the end of the tax year. In this instance the CGT is due either two months after the making of an assessment or three months from the date of disposal, whichever is later.

In respect of certain specified assets, where a tax clearance certificate is not provided by the person making the disposal, the law provides for a withholding tax of **15%** of the purchase price to be withheld by the purchaser and paid directly to Revenue on behalf of the vendor. The purchaser is required to pay the withholding tax and submit information relating to the acquisition of the asset to the Collector-General within 30 days of the payment of the consideration for the asset. The vendor of the asset is entitled to offset the amount deducted against any CGT due on the disposal.

Assets that are potentially liable to the withholding tax are:

- land and buildings in the State;
- minerals in the State or any mineral or mining rights;
- exploration or exploitation rights in a designated area;
- unquoted shares deriving their value from any of the above assets; and
- goodwill of a trade carried on in the State.

While tax law only refers to land, under the Interpretation Act 2005 land is defined, and includes, houses and buildings and any estate, right or interest in or over land. Therefore, any reference to land includes any building(s) on that land.

The requirement to withhold tax of 15% only applies where the **value** of the asset disposed of **exceeds €500,000 or, in the case of a house or apartment, exceeds €1 million**. If an asset exceeding this value is sold in parts to the same person or connected persons, then those disposals are to be treated as one disposal. Where a deduction cannot be made from the purchase price because the consideration is in non-monetary form, the purchaser is still required to pay the 15% withholding tax, but it is recoverable by the purchaser from the vendor. This provision, in relation to consideration in a non-monetary form, does not, however, apply in the case of gifts as Revenue may assess the tax on the donee, i.e. the recipient of the gift.

A vendor may complete a form CG50 and apply for a clearance certificate to receive the proceeds without any withholding tax implications. The Inspector will issue a clearance certificate (CG50A) if satisfied that:

- the vendor is resident in the State;
- no CGT is due on the disposal; or
- the vendor has already paid the CGT due on the disposal of the asset and there is no CGT outstanding from a previous disposal of the asset.

While an Irish resident can obtain the clearance certificate prior to paying any CGT due on the disposal, non-residents must pay any CGT due if they want to receive the clearance certificate and avoid the 15% withholding tax.

4.4 Temporary Non-residents

4.4.1 Background

There is an anti-avoidance rule to tax Irish domiciled individuals who are temporarily non-resident and who would otherwise not pay Irish CGT due to tax treaty protection. This law seeks to prevent individuals who expect to make a gain on the disposal of shares from avoiding Irish CGT by becoming non-resident or becoming tax resident in a treaty country, disposing of the shares so that no Irish CGT is payable, and then returning to Ireland within a few years. If the person is, for more than five consecutive tax years, not tax resident in Ireland, then this anti-avoidance provision does not apply.

4.4.2 Liability to Irish Tax

The law imposes a CGT charge in respect of a *deemed* disposal of "relevant assets" owned by an individual on the last day of the tax year for which the individual is taxable in the State prior to becoming taxable elsewhere.

"Relevant assets" are a holding in a company that, when the person ceases to be chargeable to CGT in the State (i.e. the last day of the tax year in which the person departs),

- is **5% or more by value** of the **issued share capital** of the company; or
- has a **value in excess of €500,000**.

If a person disposes of all or part of such relevant assets during a period of five tax years or less, during which they are outside the charge to CGT under normal rules, the person will be liable to CGT on this disposal as if the person had disposed of those assets, or that part of those assets, on the last day of the tax year in which he/she was resident before departing, i.e. 31 December. For example, if a person leaves in December 2021 and becomes resident again in 2027, there could be a charge under this legislation if the disposal of the relevant assets takes place in the years 2022–2026 inclusive. If the individual waited until 2028 to become resident again, there would be no charge.

While the gain on the deemed disposal arises before the individual ceases to be resident in the State,

- the actual gain is calculated using the actual market value on the date the relevant assets are subsequently disposed of; and
- for self-assessment purposes the gain is required to be included in the individual's tax return, and the CGT in respect of it accounted for, in the year in which the individual again becomes taxable in the State.

Credit will be given in respect of any foreign tax payable on an actual disposal of the assets where such tax is payable in a territory with which Ireland has a double taxation treaty.

Therefore, this CGT charge will only arise if the individual:

- is Irish domiciled and has been Irish tax resident prior to departing temporarily from the State;
- disposes of relevant assets (i.e. certain shares) in the intervening years and only to the extent of the disposal; and
- is not taxable in the State in respect of any gains on the disposal of relevant assets for a period of five years or less before again becoming so taxable.

Example 4.3

Richie Rich owns 40% of the shares in Teleireland Ltd. These shares cost him €200,000 in 1999/2000. On 30 June 2021, he is offered €50 million for his shares. A friend has told him that if he goes to live in Portugal in 2021 and disposes of the shares in 2022, then he will not have any CGT liability on the sale, provided he is regarded as tax resident only in Portugal under the terms of the Ireland/Portugal double taxation treaty, even if he returns to the State in a couple of years' time.

If Richie Rich does as his friend suggests and is non-resident for five years or less between the year of departure and the year of return, and he disposes of the shares in this intervening period, then he would still be liable to CGT in the year in which he returns.

Assuming the shares are worth €51 million on 31 December 2021 and that he sells them for €52 million in June 2022 (and ignoring the annual exemption), the gain will be calculated as follows:

		€
Deemed proceeds:	market value at date of sale (June 2022)	52,000,000
Cost of shares:	€200,000 @ 1.193	(238,600)
Gain		51,761,400

If, however, Richie Rich remained non-resident for more than five years from the year of departure to the year of return, then this anti-avoidance rule would not apply and he would not be liable to CGT.

Questions

Review Questions
(See Suggested Solutions to Review Questions at the end of this textbook.)

Question 4.1

Jacques, a French domiciled individual, has been resident in Ireland since September 2011. During 2021 he made the following disposals.

(a) Disposed of 8,000 shares in a French family trading company for €65,000 on 15 May 2021. Jacques had acquired 16,000 of these shares in August 1994 for €60,000. Jacques used €10,000 of the proceeds received to improve his Dublin home. The remaining €55,000 he put on deposit in a bank in Paris.

(b) Disposed of a UK rental property for €200,000 on 1 October 2021. Jacques acquired this property in November 1997 for €180,000. He carried out extensive renovations on the property in the period January/February 1998, which cost €30,000 in total. He lodged the proceeds in his bank account in Dublin.

(c) Disposed of H Plc shares for €24,000 on 3 December 2021. Jacques had acquired these shares in June 1998 for €8,025. H Plc is an Irish company.

Jacques did not have any chargeable gains in 2020. He did, however, incur a loss of €15,000 on the sale of shares in a German trading company. In 2021, Jacques remitted the proceeds from this sale to an Irish bank account.

Requirement
Calculate Jacques's CGT liability for 2021 (assuming the 33% rate of CGT applies to all disposals).

Question 4.2

Rio Hernandez, a Spanish domiciled individual, moved to Ireland on 15 April 2021 to take up a position as manager of the Irish subsidiary of a Spanish multinational retail clothing company. Rio is resident in Ireland for tax purposes in 2021. He disposed of the following assets during 2021:

1. On 25 January 2021, he disposed of a holiday home he owned in the west of Ireland for €300,000. The holiday home had cost him €150,000 on 5 May 2001. As the holiday home was quite small, Rio no longer felt the need to retain it as he planned on purchasing a larger property to reside in once he had moved to Ireland on a full-time basis.
2. On 30 June 2021, he disposed of a commercial property in Spain for €475,000. The property had cost him €520,000 in 2008 but, as the property had been vacant for a while, Rio decided to dispose of it. Rio lodged the proceeds of the sale to his Irish bank account.
3. On 25 September 2021, he disposed of shares he owned in a UK multinational company for €40,000. He had acquired the shares in 2011 for €22,000. He lodged half of the proceeds to a UK bank account and lodged the other half to his Irish bank account.

Requirement
Outline, giving reasons for your answer, whether each of the above disposals give rise to a chargeable gain or allowable loss for CGT purposes.

Question 4.3

Mark Scanlon is a Scottish domiciled individual who moved to Ireland on 1 June 2008 with his family when Mark was 17 years old. Following a whirlwind romance with a Spanish girl named Maria Sanchez who Mark met while completing a Masters in University College Cork, Mark moved to Spain on 15 May 2015 to reside with Maria. Mark has resided in Spain since 2015 and has only returned to Ireland intermittently since then for short holidays. Maria is a Spanish resident and domiciled individual and only spent a very brief time in Ireland (from 1 September 2013 to 30 April 2015).

Mark enjoyed being in Spain but recently has been missing his family quite a lot (most of whom have remained resident in Ireland) and following a less than amicable break up with Maria, Mark has decided to relocate back to Ireland. Mark returned to Ireland on 1 May 2021 to commence a new job with a company in Dublin. Mark plans to purchase an apartment in Dublin, but in order to do so it was necessary for him to dispose of a number of assets first in order to fund the purchase. Details of those disposals are outlined below:

1. Mark disposed of a cottage in Co. Wicklow on 1 June 2021 for €250,000. Auctioneer's fees and solicitor's fees amounted to €2,000 and €3,000, respectively. Mark had inherited the cottage from his Irish grandmother Lily (who died on 17 September 2011). The market value of the cottage at the date of Lily's death was €200,000.
2. Mark disposed of shares in a UK plc on 20 March 2021 for €35,000. He had acquired the shares in 2014 for €70,000. Stockbroker's fees amounted to €350 on the sale and were €700 on the purchase. Mark lodged the proceeds of the sale to his Irish bank account.
3. On 30 November 2021, Mark gifted his 50% share in an apartment in Madrid, Spain to Maria. Mark and Maria had acquired the apartment on 1 February 2016 for a total of €195,000, inclusive of costs. The total market value of the apartment at the date of transfer was €200,000.
4. Mark and Maria disposed of a site in Spain on 15 December 2021 for €50,000. Legal and professional fees amounted to €3,000 on the sale. Mark and Maria had acquired the site on 5 May 2017 for €42,000 inclusive of costs. They had planned on building a house on the site to reside in. Mark lodged his share of the proceeds to his Irish bank account.

Requirement

(a) Calculate Mark's CGT liability (if any) for the tax year ended 31 December 2021. Give reasons where you believe that a particular transaction does or does not give rise to chargeable gain or allowable loss for Irish tax purposes.

(b) Outline by which date Mark must pay his CGT liability and by which date he must file a CGT return in respect of the above transactions.

Note: You can ignore any potential double taxation relief.

Shares

5.1 Introduction

Shares present special problems when attempting to compute gains or losses on disposal. Consider the scenario in the example below.

Example 5.1

Joe bought the following shares in X Ltd:

	€
1,000 in January 2009 for	2,000
1,000 in January 2014 for	8,000

If Joe sells 1,000 shares today, what determines the cost of acquisition of the shares for CGT purposes?

The general rule is that disposals of shares are to be identified with purchases on a first in/first out (FIFO) basis, i.e. the longest held shares are deemed to be disposed of first. In the example above, the shares purchased first are deemed to be sold first – so Joe's cost of acquisition (base cost) for CGT purposes is €2,000. The FIFO rule offers the taxpayer the maximum advantage as indexation relief is applied to those assets owned for the longest period (see **Example 5.2** below).

Example 5.2

Ordinary shares in Abbott Limited, a trading company

		Number	Cost
			€
May 1981	Bought	100	100
July 1982	Bought	300	300
May 1986	Sold (FIFO)	(100)	
7 April 1989	Bought	400	425
May 1991	Bought	500	600 (i.e. €1.20 each)
May 2014	Sold	(300)	
June 2021	Sold	(525)	Sale proceeds €21,000

The disposals are dealt with on the following basis:

1. **May 1986 disposal:** the FIFO rule applies and the 100 shares sold are deemed to be those purchased in May 1981.
2. **May 2014 disposal:** the sale of 300 shares in May 2014 is deemed to be a disposal of the 300 shares acquired for €300 in July 1982.
3. **June 2021 disposal:** the sale of 525 shares in June 2021 for €21,000 would give rise to the following gains. Two separate disposals are deemed to have taken place:

	€
(a) Disposal of 400 shares acquired on 7 April 1989	
Proceeds: 400 @ €40 (i.e. sale price per share)	16,000
Deduct: €425 indexed @ 1.503	(639)
Chargeable gain	15,361

(b) Disposal of 125 shares out of the 500 originally acquired in May 1991 at a total cost of €600.

	€
Proceeds: 125 @ €40 (i.e. sale price per share)	5,000
Deduct: cost $\frac{125}{500} \times 600 = €150$	
Original cost of 125 shares: €150 indexed @ 1.406	(211)
Chargeable gain	4,789

The CGT liability is therefore:

	€
Total chargeable gains	20,150
Deduct: annual exemption	(1,270)
Taxable gains	18,880
CGT @ 33%	6,230

5.2 Rights Issues

A shareholder may be entitled to purchase additional shares in a company based on their existing shareholding in that company, i.e. by way of a rights issue. The shares acquired will form part of the original block of shares when applying the FIFO rule – they are effectively deemed to be part of the original holding. However, as the cash paid for the additional shares was paid at a later date than the original holding was acquired, the cash paid is treated as enhancement expenditure for indexation relief purposes.

Example 5.3

Jim acquired 1,000 €1 ordinary shares in Axel Plc on 1 May 1989 for €1,000.

On 1 June 1993 he acquired a further 2,000 shares for €5,000.

On 1 January 1997 Axel Plc made a rights issue of 1 for 5 at a price of €3 per share issued.

On 1 May 2021 he sold 1,600 shares at €50 each.

Step 1: Identify the make-up of Jim's holding, prior to the sale on 1 May 2021.

	No. of shares	Cost
Holding acquired 1 May 1989		€
Shares @ €1	1,000	1,000
Rights issue @ €3 (Note)	200	600
	1,200	
Holding acquired 1 June 1993		
Shares @ €1	2,000	5,000
Rights issue @ €3 (Note)	400	1,200
	2,400	

Note: 1996/97 rights issue of one new share for every five shares held (1:5) is deemed to be acquired at same time as the original holding.

Step 2: Apply the FIFO rule to the holdings acquired on 1 May 1989 and on 1 June 1993 to determine which shares are deemed to be disposed of in the sale on 1 May 2021.

The 1,600 shares sold are comprised of:

1,200	Shares from holding at 1 May 1989
400	Shares from holding at 1 June 1993 (i.e. 1/6th of total June 1993 holding)
1,600	

The disposal is treated as the separate disposal of two distinct holdings, those acquired in May 1989 and June 1993.

(a) Disposal of 1,200 shares of May 1989 holding

	€	€
Sale proceeds: 1,200 @ €50		60,000
Deduct:		
Original 1,000 shares cost €1,000		
Indexation: May 1989 @ 1.503	1,503	
Rights issue 200 shares cost €600		
Indexation: January 1997 @ 1.251	751	(2,254)
Chargeable gain		57,746

(b) Disposal of 400 shares of June 1993 holding

	€	€
Sale proceeds: 400 @ €50		20,000
Deduct:		
Original June 1993: 2,000 shares × 1/6 = 333 shares.		
Cost of 333 shares @ €2.50 each = €832 indexed @ 1.331	1,107	
Rights issue 400 shares × 1/6 = 67 shares.		
Cost of 67 shares @ €3 each = €200		
Indexation: January 1997 @ 1.251	250	(1,357)
Chargeable gain		18,643

continued overleaf

Summary	
Gain applicable to May 1989 holding	57,746
Gain applicable to June 1993 holding	18,643
	76,389
Deduct: annual exemption	(1,270)
Taxable gain	75,119
CGT @ 33%	24,789

5.3 Bonus Issues

A shareholder may acquire, at no cost, additional shares in a company based on their existing shareholding in that company, i.e. by way of a bonus issue. The shares acquired will form part of the original block of shares when applying the FIFO rule – they are effectively deemed to be part of the original holding. As no consideration was paid for the additional shares there is no further deductible expenditure for CGT purposes. As no consideration is paid by the shareholders on receipt of the bonus shares, the complex calculations necessary in the case of rights issues are not required.

Example 5.4
Joe originally acquired 1,000 shares on 1 June 1990 for €2,000.

On 1 June 1994, he bought 500 more at a cost of €1,500.
On 1 January 1996, a bonus issue of 2 for 5 was made.
On 1 June 2021, Joe sold 2,000 shares for €20 each.

Prior to the sale on 1 June 2021, Joe's total holding of 2,100 shares was made up as follows:

	No. of shares	Cost €
Holding 1 June 1990		
Original acquisition	1,000	2,000
Bonus issue	400	0
	1,400	2,000
Holding 1 June 1994		
Original acquisition	500	1,500
Bonus issue	200	0
	700	1,500

Computation

The 2,000 shares sold are deemed to have been comprised of:

(a)   the holding of 1,400 acquired 1 June 1990 for €2,000;
(b)   600 of the holding of 700 shares acquired 1 June 1994 for a total of €1,500.

	€
Sale proceeds: 1,400 shares @ €20 each	28,000
Allowable cost: €2,000 @ 1.442	(2,884)
Chargeable gain	25,116
Sale proceeds: 600 shares @ €20 each	12,000
Allowable cost: 600/700 × €1,500 = €1,286 @ 1.309	(1,683)
Chargeable gain	10,317

Note: above gains are subject to the annual exemption.

5.4 Acquisition within Four Weeks of Disposal and Disposal within Four Weeks of Acquisition

These are anti-avoidance provisions designed to prevent taxpayers benefiting by the creation of artificial losses. The transactions involved are commonly referred to as "bed & breakfast" transactions.

5.4.1 Acquisition within Four Weeks of Disposal

In this situation a loss accrues to a person on the disposal of shares and that person then re-acquires shares of the same class within four weeks of the disposal.

In this case, the loss on the shares can only be offset against the gain on the re-acquired shares, i.e. the loss cannot be used against other gains but can only be used when the new shares are disposed of and only against a gain on those shares (if any) and not against any other gains.

Example 5.5

Harry owns 1,000 shares in X Ltd, which he originally purchased at €5 each. On 30 December 2021 the shares are quoted at €1 each. Harry does not wish to sell his 1,000 shares as he believes they will rise in price in the future, but, at the same time, wishes to claim loss relief for the paper loss he has suffered. He cannot do this unless he has a realisation, i.e. a disposal. Accordingly, he arranges to sell his 1,000 shares at €1 each on 30 December 2021 on the understanding that his stockbroker will re-purchase a further 1,000 shares on the market two to three days later. Accordingly, Harry will realise a loss of €4,000 on the disposal which, in the absence of anti-avoidance provisions, would be available to set-off against any gains he has realised in 2021. In addition, he will also still own 1,000 shares in X Ltd.

The legislation prevents the utilisation of the loss by Harry by providing that as the disposal and re-acquisition of the same class of shares took place within four weeks, then the loss arising in 2021 can only be set against the subsequent gain arising on the disposal of the shares which have been re-acquired, i.e. the loss cannot be set against other gains in 2021 or any subsequent year.

Where the number of shares so re-acquired is less than the number of shares disposed of, a proportion of the loss is available for offset in the normal manner. This proportion is the same proportion of the loss on the disposal as the number of shares not re-acquired bears to the number of shares disposed of.

5.4.2 Disposal within Four Weeks of Acquisition

In this situation a person acquires shares and within four weeks after the acquisition disposes of shares of the same class. In this case, the FIFO rule is set aside in relation to the disposal within four weeks, and the shares sold are treated as being those which were acquired within the four-week period. In other words, the 'last in/first out' (LIFO) rule replaces the FIFO rule. It should be noted that LIFO replaces FIFO in all situations where there is an acquisition of shares followed by a disposal of the same class of shares within four weeks of the acquisition, even where the FIFO rule would not result in a loss.

Example 5.6

Joe owns 3,000 shares in a company that have fallen in value by €20,000 since they were purchased. He has other realised gains in the tax year of €30,000 and wishes to offset the losses accrued on his holding of 3,000 shares, but also wishes to retain the investment.

Joe therefore purchases a further 3,000 shares in the company, which he sells within four weeks. If FIFO applied, the disposal of the 3,000 shares would be deemed to come out of the original holding of 3,000 shares purchased at the higher price, thereby realising a loss of €20,000 to set against his other realised gains of €30,000.

continued overleaf

> However, the existence of the anti-avoidance rule means that he is treated as selling the most recently acquired shares (LIFO applies) and his gain or loss on disposal will be calculated on that basis. Therefore the loss of €20,000 is not available.

Where the number of shares disposed of exceeds the number of shares acquired within the four-week period, the excess comes within the normal FIFO rule.

These provisions also apply to married persons and civil partners living together, thus preventing one spouse or civil partner from selling the shares on the open market and having the other spouse or civil partner re-acquire the shares.

5.5   CGT Treatment of Employee Share Options

A share option is the right to subscribe, at a specified price, for a specified number of shares in the employer's company during a specified period of time. The income tax treatment of share options is outlined in **Chapter 31, Section 31.2**.

5.5.1   *General CGT Treatment of Employee Share Options*

An **employee is subject to income tax on the exercise** of a share option and, **possibly, on the grant of the option,** depending on the exercise period.

For CGT purposes, **any gain that is chargeable to income tax is treated as being an additional consideration given by the employee for the shares acquired on the exercise of the option and is an allowable deduction when calculating any gain/loss on a disposal of the shares.**

Example 5.7

Patrick is granted an option by his employer, XYZ Plc, to subscribe for 1,000 €1 ordinary shares at a price of €1 each at any time in the following eight years. He is granted this right by reason of his employment at a time when the shares are valued at €3 each. Some time later Patrick exercises the option, at a time when each €1 ordinary share in XYZ Plc is worth €10, and takes up the 1,000 shares in XYZ Plc.

At the **date of grant** of the option, Patrick is chargeable to income tax on the difference between the option price (€1 per share) and the market value (€3 per share) – total €2,000 taxable at his marginal rate (as the option is longer than seven years).

At the date of exercise of the option he is chargeable to income tax on the full gain, with credit for the tax paid at the date of grant of the option, i.e. **he is charged to income tax on the difference between the amount paid for the shares (€1 per share) and the market value at the date of exercise of the option (€10 per share) – €9,000, with a credit for the tax paid on the gain of €2,000.** He has effectively been charged to income tax on €9,000: €2,000 at the date of grant and €7,000 at the date of exercise.

What is Patrick's base cost for his shares should he now choose to dispose of them?

	€
Actual sum subscribed	1,000
Gain chargeable to income tax to be treated as consideration	9,000
Total	10,000

If Patrick disposed of his shares immediately for €10,000 on exercising his option (which is a frequent occurrence in practice, since employees often cannot finance the holding of the shares they acquire under option schemes), **he would have no gain and no loss for CGT.**

5.5.2 *Key Employee Engagement Programme (KEEP)*

Finance Act 2017 introduced the Key Employee Engagement Programme (KEEP) to facilitate the use of share-based remuneration to attract and retain key employees in unquoted companies. Generally, employees are assessed to income tax, USC and PRSI on the gain arising on exercise of an option to acquire shares in their employer company (see **Chapter 31, Section 31.2**). KEEP provides for an exemption from income tax, USC and PRSI on the gain arising on exercise of a qualifying share option by a qualifying individual to acquire shares in a qualifying company in the SME sector, provided certain conditions are met by both the company and the individual throughout the period from the date of the grant to the date of exercise. Tax on such shares will be deferred until the shares are disposed of and CGT will be payable on the gain arising on the difference between the sales proceeds received and the price paid on exercise for the shares. The relief applies to qualifying share options **granted** in the period from 1 January 2018 to 31 December 2023.

Qualifying Share Options

A qualifying share option is a right granted to an employee or director of a qualifying company to purchase a predetermined number of shares in that company at a predetermined price where the following conditions are met:

- the shares must be ordinary fully paid-up shares in a qualifying company or qualifying holding company of a qualifying group;
- the option price at date of grant cannot be less than the market value of the same class of shares at that date;
- there must be a written contract in place setting out the number and type of shares, the option price, and the period during which the options can be exercised;
- options cannot be exercised within 12 months of grant other than in limited circumstances;
- options cannot be exercised more than 10 years from the date of grant; and
- the share option must have been granted for bona fide commercial purposes, the main purpose of which is to recruit or retain employees in the qualifying company, and not part of a tax avoidance scheme or arrangement.

Qualifying Company

The company must:

- be incorporated in the State, an EEA state or the UK and be resident in the State or carry on business in the State through a branch/agency;
- exist wholly or mainly for the purpose of carrying on a qualifying trade;
- at the date of the grant:
  - be an SME (i.e. less than 250 employees, annual turnover less than €50 million, and/or balance sheet not exceeding €43 million), and
  - total market value of issued but unexercised qualifying shares options cannot exceed €3 million;
- from date of grant to date of exercise:
  - be an unquoted company, other than a ESM or its equivalent in a EEA/DTA country, and
  - not be a company in difficulty under EU state aid rules.

A qualifying company is required to make an annual return to Revenue giving details of all options granted and exercised in the year.

Qualifying share options can be issued by a **qualifying holding company** to a qualifying individual who is an employee or director of a qualifying company (i.e. a qualifying subsidiary of the qualifying holding company). The qualifying holding company and qualifying subsidiary must be members of a **qualifying group**.

Qualifying Group

A qualifying group must consist of the following companies **and no other company**:

- a qualifying holding company;
- qualifying subsidiary or subsidiaries (i.e. one whose share capital is owned directly by more than 50% by the qualifying holding company);
- a relevant subsidiary or subsidiaries (i.e. one that is owned more than 50% indirectly by the qualifying holding company). A relevant subsidiary is not regarded as a qualifying company in relation to a qualifying holding company.

For at least 12 months from the date of the grant of the option to the date of exercise, the following conditions apply:

- the qualifying group must include at least one qualifying company in the group that is also a qualifying subsidiary (i.e. more than 50% of shares held directly);
- the activities of the group, excluding the qualifying holding company, consist wholly or mainly of carrying on a qualifying trade;
- each company in the qualifying group is unquoted;
- each company in the qualifying group is not in financial difficulty under EU Commission's guidelines on state aid.

At the date of the grant of the share option, the group is an SME and the total market value of the issued, but unexercised, qualifying shares options does not exceed €3,000,000.

Qualifying Holding Company

A qualifying holding company is a company:

- that is not under the control, directly or indirectly, of another company;
- that does not carry on a trade or trades; and
- whose business consists wholly or mainly (i.e. more than 50%) of holding shares **only** in its qualifying subsidiaries and its relevant subsidiaries.

Qualifying Trade

A qualifying trade is defined as trading activities other than excluded activities, such as:

- adventure or concerns in the nature of trade;
- financial activities;
- specified professional service companies;
- dealing in shares and other financial assets;
- dealing in or developing land, building and construction;
- forestry;
- coal, steel and shipbuilding.

Specified professional services include medical, dental, architectural, accountancy, geological and legal services. The qualifying trade must be undertaken on a commercial basis with a view to the realisation of profit, the profits or gains of which are charged to tax under Case I of Schedule D.

Qualifying Individual

A qualifying individual is an employee or director of the qualifying company (including a qualifying company that is a member of a qualifying group) who is required to work a minimum of 20 hours per week for the company or devote not less than 75% of their working time to the qualifying company. This applies for the duration from date of grant to date of exercise. The employment must be capable of lasting at least 12 months from the date of grant of the share option. These working time conditions are deemed to be satisfied if the share options are exercised within 90 days of leaving the employment.

An individual will cease to qualify if they, together with connected parties, directly or indirectly become the beneficial owner of more than 15% of the ordinary share capital of the qualifying company or of the qualifying holding company of a qualifying group during the option period. If an individual ceases to qualify during the option period they will be assessed to income tax, PRSI and USC on any gain arising on the exercise of the option granted.

Limits on the Relief

The market value of all shares in respect of which qualifying share options have been granted to an employee or director cannot exceed:

■ €100,000 in any one tax year;
■ €300,000 in any three consecutive tax years; or
■ the amount of annual emoluments of the qualifying individual in the year of assessment in which the option is granted.

Example 5.8

Hannah works full-time as a food scientist for Veganberries Ltd, a small, Irish-incorporated and tax-resident company. She earns €75,000 per annum. At 1 January 2021, the company grants her the option to acquire shares in the company. The shares are valued at €1 at 1 January 2021 and the option price is €1 per share. She can exercise her option anytime between 1 April 2022 and 31 March 2026. The maximum share options are the lower of:

■ €100,000 in 2021;
■ €300,000 in 2021, 2022 and 2023; or
■ €75,000, being her annual emoluments in the year of the grant.

Hannah is granted options on 30,000 shares at €1 each.

Example 5.9

Following on from **Example 5.8**, Hannah decides to exercise the option at 1 March 2026 when the market value is €6 per share.

In the absence of any relief, Hannah would be assessed to income tax, PRSI and USC at her marginal rate (52%) on the difference between the amount paid for the shares and their market value at the date of exercise:

30,000 × (€6 – €1) @ 52% = €78,000

As Hannah, the company and the share options fulfil all of the KEEP conditions, this gain is exempt from income tax, USC and PRSI.

Hannah sells the shares immediately. Ignoring the annual exemption and assuming she does not qualify for revised entrepreneur relief, Hannah is liable to CGT of:

30,000 × (€6 – €1) @ 33% = €49,500

In essence, Hannah has saved €28,500 in tax.

Questions

Review Questions
(See Suggested Solutions to Review Questions at the end of this textbook.)

Question 5.1

Louise, a single person, disposed of 5,000 shares in Tedu Ltd, a trading company, for €15,000 in June 2021. She acquired 4,000 shares in July 2006 for €1.50 per share. In October 2007 the company declared a 1: 2 bonus issue.

Requirement
Calculate Louise's CGT liability for 2021.

Question 5.2

On 2 May 2021, Lorraine McCarthy, a single person, gifted 10,000 shares in Arco Ltd, a trading company, to her sister, Mary. Lorraine had acquired her shares in Arco Ltd as follows:

1 July 1972	6,000 shares @ 19c each
1 November 1983	Rights issue 2 for 1 @ 34c each

She took up her rights issue fully.
At 6 April 1974 the shares were worth 22c each, and at 2 May 2021 they were worth €1.68 each.

Requirement
Compute Lorraine's CGT liability for 2021 (assume that the 33% rate of CGT applies).

Question 5.3

Martin Doyle, a married man, acquired 4,000 ordinary shares in Dublin Ltd, a trading company, in May 1973 for €1,000. The market value of each share at 6 April 1974 was 75c. On 6 January 1988, Dublin Ltd made a rights issue to existing shareholders. The offer was 1 share for every 2 held at a rights price of €3 per share. Martin took his full entitlement under the rights issue. The market value per share after the rights issue was €4.

On 6 July 2021, Martin sold 1,500 shares in Dublin Ltd to his wife, Orla, and 900 shares to his only son, Gerry, for €1,500 and €900, respectively. The market value of each share on that date was €10.

On 6 October 2021, Martin sold the balance of his shares on the market for €12 each.

Requirement
Compute CGT payable by Martin Doyle (assume that the 33% rate of CGT applies).

Revised Entrepreneur Relief

6.1 Introduction

Section 597AA TCA 1997 (introduced by Finance Act 2015) provides for a revised entrepreneur relief under which a reduced **rate of CGT of 10%** applies in respect of chargeable gains on the disposal of **chargeable business assets** made by a **relevant individual** on or after 1 January 2016, up to **a lifetime limit of €1 million of gains**. The 10% rate applies from 1 January 2017, with disposals in 2016 subject to the previous rate of 20%.

Note: the original entrepreneur relief (section 597A TCA 1997) still exists and is available if it is more favourable to the taxpayer, but is beyond the scope of this textbook.

Example 6.1

On 6 February 2021, Helen disposes of shares that are chargeable business assets, and she satisfies all of the other conditions for revised entrepreneur relief. Helen has not previously disposed of any chargeable business assets. The shares are sold for €1.5 million. Ignoring the annual exemption, what would Helen's CGT liability be if she realised a gain of:

(a) €800,000?
(b) €1.3 million?

(a) **Gain of €800,000** As Helen qualifies for revised entrepreneur relief and her gain is less than €1 million, she is taxed at 10% on the gain. Capital gains tax is €800,000 @ 10% = €80,000.

(b) **Gain of €1.3 million** As Helen qualifies for revised entrepreneur relief she is taxed at 10% on the first €1 million of the gain. The balance is taxed at the standard CGT rate of 33%. Therefore, CGT is:

€1,000,000 @ 10%	€100,000
€300,000 @ 33%	€99,000
Total	€199,000

To qualify for revised entrepreneur relief a number of conditions must be satisfied in relation to the asset being disposed of and the individual disposing of the asset.

6.2 Qualifying Conditions

6.2.1 Relevant Individual

An individual can qualify for the relief if they have held the asset for a continuous period of three years out of the five years prior to the disposal. In the case of ordinary shares, with effect from 1 January 2021 the individual must have owned not less than 5% of the ordinary share capital of the company for a continuous period of three years at any time prior to the disposal.

6.2.2 Chargeable Business Asset

To qualify for revised entrepreneur relief, there must be a disposal of a **"chargeable business asset"** by an individual. "Chargeable business asset" means:

1. An asset used for the purpose of a "qualifying business" carried on by the individual. (A "qualifying business" is any business that is not in the business of holding investments, holding development land or the developing or letting of land.)
   This would include, for example, goodwill, buildings, plant and machinery.
2. Ordinary shares in a company where the following conditions are satisfied:
   (a) the individual has owned not less than 5% of the ordinary share capital of the company for a continuous period of three years at any time prior to the disposal;
   (b) the individual has been a director or employee of the company, or a group member, in a managerial or technical capacity for a continuous period of at least three of the five years before the disposal;
   (c) during the three-year period working for the company, or group company, the individual was required to spend not less than 50% of their working time working for the company, or group company.

   Shares in a holding company can qualify for relief. A holding company is a company whose business consists wholly or mainly of holding shares in 51% subsidiary companies.
   Revised entrepreneur relief applies to disposals of shares in public and quoted companies, provided the conditions are satisfied.
   If a company reorganisation qualifies for tax relief, any period of ownership of, and working for, the original company will be taken into account in determining whether or not the three-year test is satisfied.

The legislation specifically states that chargeable business assets do not include:

(i) shares held as investments;
(ii) development land;
(iii) any asset that would not give rise to a chargeable gain if sold (e.g. inventory);
(iv) goodwill disposed of to a company if, immediately after the transfer, the individual is connected with the company (e.g. incorporation of sole trade); or
(v) shares disposed of to a company if, immediately after the transfer, the individual is connected with the company sold.

Goodwill and shares referred to in (iv) and (v) above, will however qualify as chargeable business assets if it would be reasonable to consider that the disposal was made for bona fide commercial reasons and did not form part of a scheme or arrangement the main purpose, or one of the main purposes, of which was tax avoidance. If arrangements are made to circumvent the connected parties test, the reduced rate of CGT will not apply.

Where a shareholder owns an asset that is leased to and used by the company, the disposal of that asset by the shareholder does not qualify for revised entrepreneur relief.

6.2.3 Summary of Conditions

For the disposal of a **sole trader business**, the 10% rate applies if the following conditions are satisfied:

1. The business is a qualifying business (i.e. the business does not consist of holding investments, holding development land or developing or letting land).
2. The sole trader has disposed of chargeable business assets (for example, goodwill, buildings and plant and machinery used for the business).
3. The disposal was for bona fide commercial reasons and did not form part of a scheme or arrangement the main purpose of which was to avoid tax in circumstances where the sole trader disposed of goodwill to a company and is connected with the company immediately after the transfer.
4. These assets have been held for a continuous period of three years out of the five years prior to the disposal.
5. The lifetime limit on gains arising on the disposal of chargeable business assets since 1 January 2016 of €1 million has not been exceeded.

For the disposal of **shares** in a company, the 10% rate applies if the following conditions are satisfied:

1. The business of the company is a qualifying business (i.e. the business does not consist of holding investments, holding development land or developing or letting land).
2. The individual is disposing of chargeable business assets – they are ordinary shares and they owned at least 5% of the ordinary shares for a continuous three years at any time prior to disposal.
3. The disposal was for bona fide commercial reasons and did not form part of a scheme or arrangement the main purpose of which was to avoid tax in circumstances where the disposal is of shares to another company and the individual is connected with the transferred company immediately after the transfer.
4. The shareholder has owned at least 5% of the ordinary shares in the company for a continuous period of three years at any time prior to disposal.
5. The shareholder has been a director or employee of the company in a managerial or technical capacity for a continuous period of at least three of the last five years before the disposal.
6. During the three-year period working for the company, the shareholder was required to spend not less than 50% of their working time working for the company.
7. The lifetime limit on gains arising on the disposal of chargeable business assets since 1 January 2016 of €1 million has not been exceeded.

> **Example 6.2**
>
> Emily and her spouse, Hugh, set up a distribution company, Together Ltd, in 2012. Each owns 50% of the shares in the company. Emily works full-time as managing director for the company; Hugh is a non-executive director of the company. They have been offered €2.1 million for the company by Takeover Ltd, an unconnected company, which would generate a gain of €1 million each.
>
> Ignoring the annual exemption, what would be the CGT payable by Emily and Hugh?
>
> | Condition | Company | Emily | Hugh |
> |---|---|---|---|
> | Qualifying business? | Yes – distribution | | |
> | Ordinary shares? | | Yes | Yes |
> | Owned at least 5% for 3 continuous years at any time | | Yes | Yes |
> | Connected to Together Ltd after disposal? | | No | No |
> | Held for 3 continuous years? | | Yes | Yes |
> | During 3 of last 5 years, have: | | | |
> | – managerial/technical role, | | Yes | No |
> | – for not less than 50% of working time? | | Yes | N/a |
>
> Emily satisfies all of the conditions, therefore she will pay CGT of €1 million @ 10% = €100,000.
>
> Hugh's situation is different. Although most of the conditions are satisfied, he has not worked for the company in a managerial or technical capacity so he is not entitled to the 10% rate. Therefore Hugh will pay CGT of €1 million @ 33% = €330,000.

6.3   Interaction with Other CGT Reliefs

6.3.1   Transfer of a Business to a Company

Where there is a transfer of a business to a company, and relief under section 600 TCA 1997 is claimed (see **Chapter 7**), the reduced rate of 10% will not apply to any portion of a gain relating to non-share consideration, unless it is reasonable to consider the transfer is done for bona fide commercial reasons and not as part of a tax avoidance arrangement or scheme.

As the company must be trading, etc. for three years before the 10% rate can apply to a disposal of its shares, any period of being a sole trader before incorporation is ignored when assessing the three-year period of ownership of, and working for, the company tests.

6.3.2   Retirement Relief

Retirement relief (see **Chapter 8**) also contains a definition of chargeable business assets, which is specific for the purposes of that relief and should not be confused with its meaning for revised entrepreneur relief.

Where an individual satisfies the conditions for retirement relief and revised entrepreneur relief, the individual will qualify for retirement relief but the relieved gain will use up part (or all) of the €1 million gain that may be taxed at 10% under this relief. For example, say Joe disposes of chargeable business assets giving rise to a gain of €1 million and Joe qualifies for both retirement relief and revised entrepreneur relief. The taxable gain of €1 million is fully relieved under retirement relief and he pays no tax. Even though he has not paid CGT at the 10% rate, he has realised gains of €1 million, since 1 January 2016, on the disposal of chargeable business assets and therefore he cannot benefit from the 10% rate of tax on any subsequent disposals of chargeable business assets.

6.3.3 Losses and Annual Exemption

If an individual has gains taxed at 10% and 33% during the tax year and has losses (forward or current year), the losses are offset first against gains taxed at 33% and then against gains taxed at 10%. The annual exemption is also offset first against gains taxed at 33%.

Questions

Review Questions
(See Suggested Solutions to Review Questions at the end of this textbook.)

Question 6.1

Carmel, a sole trader aged 39, has run her own upholstery business for a number of years. She has one workshop in Dublin (acquired in March 2008 for €280,000) and another in Cork (acquired in June 2011 for €85,000). There has been a downturn in sales in Cork and so, on 28 September 2021, she sold the Cork workshop for €120,000. Carmel did not make any other capital disposals since 2015.

Requirement
Calculate the CGT due on the sale of the workshop in Cork, on the basis that all reliefs and/or exemptions are claimed.

Question 6.2

Simon, aged 48, owns a 30% shareholding in Direct Computers Ltd (DCL), an Irish incorporated and Irish tax resident company that designs and sells hi-tech computer equipment. He acquired his shareholding at its market value of €60,000 on 10 May 2011. Simon is the finance director of DCL and has worked full-time for the company since 2010.

On 24 December 2021, Simon gifted his entire shareholding in DCL to his brother, Dan. The value of Simon's shareholding at that date was €1,220,000. The value of DCL's assets as at 24 December 2021 was as follows:

	€000
Premises	2,160
Investment property	1,320
Inventory	690
Receivables	450
Total	4,620

More than 50% of DCL's turnover and profits are derived from its trading activities.

Requirement
Calculate the CGT arising, if any, on the gift of shares by Simon to Dan in December 2021. Simon had no disposals prior to the transfer to Dan. Your answer should identify and explain any CGT relief(s) available **and** include a full analysis of how the conditions to qualify for any relief(s) are met.

Transfer of a Business to a Company

Learning Objectives

After studying this chapter you will be able to:

- Advise on the CGT exposure for a sole trader transferring the business to a company upon incorporation.
- Advise on the potential deferral of CGT arising on the transfer of a business to a company and the future base cost of shares in the company.

7.1 Sole Trader Transfers Trade to Company

Where a sole trader carries on a trade, the individual owns all the assets of the trade, including the capital assets. If any capital assets are disposed of, the individual sole trader must calculate a gain or loss on the disposal and pay any CGT due. If the individual sole trader decides to incorporate the business, i.e. transfer the trade, including some or all of its assets and liabilities, to a company, then the individual will typically have a disposal of capital assets (e.g. goodwill, building, machinery, etc.) to the company and therefore will have to consider the CGT implications and any reliefs – see **Section 7.2** below. When transferring the assets, it is critical to remember that this is a disposal between connected parties and therefore all assets must transfer at market value, including goodwill. This chapter deals with the taxation of these gains and the relief that is available, provided the conditions are satisfied.

When the assets are transferred to the company, they now belong to the company. If the capital assets are subsequently sold by the company, it will be liable to corporation tax (CGT in the case of development land) on any gain in excess of the market value of the assets at the date of transfer. **Chapter 25** deals with companies and capital gains.

7.2 Relief Available

As an individual and a limited company are separate legal entities, the transfer of business assets to a company by an individual will be a chargeable event for CGT purposes. That is, the disposal of capital assets, such as goodwill, buildings and machinery, by the individual to the company may trigger a CGT liability for the individual. However, under section 600 TCA 1997, CGT on the disposal of business assets to a company may be deferred, provided the business and all its assets (or all its assets other than cash) **are transferred in consideration for the issue of shares in the company** (see **Example 7.1** below). To avail of this relief, the business must be transferred as a going concern to the company. The deferral continues until the shares are disposed of by the individual who transferred the assets to the company (see **Example 7.3** below).

As with many CGT reliefs, the relief will not apply unless it is shown that the transfer has been effected for bona fide commercial reasons and does not form part of any arrangement or scheme of which the main purpose, or one of the main purposes, is avoidance of liability to tax.

The net gain on the transfer of the chargeable assets to the company is calculated in the usual way, and the proportion appropriate to any cash or deemed cash consideration is assessed immediately. The balance of the total net gain, i.e. the deferred gain, is apportioned rateably over the shares received, thereby reducing the base cost of the shares for the purposes of any subsequent disposal. The allowable cost of future disposals of the shares for the purposes of indexation is the original cost of the shares (at the time they are first issued) less the amount of the deferred gain.

If any liabilities of the trade, such as trade payables, are taken over by the company, then this is treated as a cash payment to the former proprietor and the deferred gain is reduced accordingly. Similar treatment applies if part of the consideration is satisfied by the creation in the company of a loan account in favour of the individual.

When the normal gain arising on the transfer of the chargeable assets to the company has been calculated, the amount to be deferred is calculated by applying the formula:

$$\frac{\text{Value of shares}}{\text{Total consideration}} \times \text{Chargeable gain (after indexation relief)}$$

If more than one class of shares is issued, the deferred gain is deducted from the cost of the shares on the basis of the relative market values of each class of shares at the time of acquisition.

Note: the greatest problem many students have with this topic is an accounting/shares issue and not a tax issue, i.e. how to value the shares. Once you remember that the value of the shares is the difference between the market value of the assets and the amount received in cash and deemed cash (e.g. liabilities taken over), then the computation is significantly easier.

Example 7.1
Mr X transferred his business, with all its assets other than cash, to a company on 30 November 2021. He had acquired the business on 5 December 1999. In consideration for the transfer, the company, X Ltd, issued 10,000 ordinary shares at par fully paid and paid Mr X €600,000 in cash. Mr X has not previously disposed of any chargeable business assets.

At the date of transfer the balance sheet of the business was as follows:

		€
Assets:	Goodwill at cost	29,000
	Inventories	250,000
	Buildings	250,000
	Cash	50,000
		579,000
Liabilities:	Trade payables	100,000
	Capital account	479,000
		579,000

continued overleaf

At the date of transfer the market value of the assets was as follows:

	€
Goodwill	250,000
Inventories	300,000
Buildings	<u>1,300,000</u>
	1,850,000
Trade payables	<u>(100,000)</u>
Net value of assets transferred	<u>1,750,000</u>

The market value of the assets was €1,850,000. The cash (€600,000) and deemed cash (payables €100,000) totalled €700,000. Therefore, the shares are worth €1,150,000 (€1,850,000 – €600,000 – €100,000).

The cost of the chargeable assets at acquisition on 5 December 1999 was as follows:

	€
Goodwill	29,000
Buildings	250,000

The chargeable gains are computed as follows:

	Dec 1999	Index	Adjusted Base Cost	Current Market Value	Chargeable Gain
	€		€	€	€
Inventories (not chargeable – gain liable to income tax)					
Goodwill	29,000	1.193	34,597	250,000	215,403
Buildings	250,000	1.193	298,250	1,300,000	<u>1,001,750</u>
					<u>1,217,153</u>

Deferred gain:

$$\frac{\text{Value of shares issued}}{\text{Total consideration}} \times €1,217,153$$

$$\frac{€1,150,000}{€1,850,000} \times €1,217,153 = €756,609 \text{ deferred gain}$$

Chargeable gain:	€
€1,217,153 – €756,609	460,544
Less: annual exemption	<u>(1,270)</u>
	<u>459,274</u>

This gain will be taxed at 33% unless Mr X satisfies the conditions required for revised entrepreneur relief, which would reduce the CGT rate to 10%.

Allowable cost of shares for future disposal:	€
Cost of shares	1,150,000
Less: deferred gains	<u>(756,609)</u>
Base cost for subsequent disposals of the shares issued to Mr X	<u>393,391</u>

There is a Revenue concession that, where an individual transfers a business to a company in exchange for shares only and assets exceed liabilities, bona fide trade payables taken over will not be treated as consideration.

Example 7.2

Ms Y set up her business in June 2005, buying a business premises at the same time. On 30 June 2021, Ms Y transferred her business, with all its assets (other than cash) and liabilities, to a company. In consideration for the transfer, the company, Y Ltd, issued 10,000 ordinary shares at par fully paid.

At the date of transfer the balance sheet of the business was as follows:

		€
Assets:	Inventories	250,000
	Buildings (at cost)	300,000
	Cash	50,000
		600,000
Liabilities:	Trade payables	100,000
	Capital account	500,000
		600,000

At the date of transfer the market value of the assets was as follows:

	€
Goodwill (Note)	250,000
Inventories	300,000
Buildings	1,300,000
	1,850,000
Trade payables	(100,000)
Net value of assets transferred	1,750,000

Note: the goodwill has no base cost as it was not acquired.

The chargeable gains are computed as follows:

	Cost June 2005	Market Value	Gain
	€	€	€
Inventories (not chargeable – gain liable to income tax)			
Goodwill	Nil	250,000	250,000
Buildings (no indexation as acquired post 01/01/03)	300,000	1,300,000	1,000,000
			1,250,000

Under the Revenue concession, where an individual transfers a business to a company in exchange for **shares only,** and assets exceed liabilities, **bona fide trade payables taken over will not be treated as consideration**. As this transfer satisfies these conditions, all of the gain may be deferred.

Allowable cost of shares for future disposal:	€
Cost of shares	1,750,000
Less: deferred gains	(1,250,000)
Base cost for subsequent disposals of the shares issued to Ms Y	500,000

Example 7.3

On 31 July 2021, Bill sold his 15,000 ordinary shares in FCS Ltd to Buy Ltd for €300,000. Bill had acquired these shares on 31 March 1999 when he transferred all his business assets, other than cash, and liabilities to FCS Ltd in exchange for 15,000 ordinary shares of €1 each in FCS Ltd and €25,000 cash.

Bill's balance sheet at 31 March 1999 read as follows:

		Cost	Market Value at 6 April 1974	Market Value at 31 March 1999
	€	€	€	€
Premises (at cost – 19 August 1970)		10,000	18,000	200,000
Goodwill		15,000	8,000	100,000
Receivables		13,000	N/A	13,000
Inventories		12,000	N/A	18,000
Cash		4,000		
		54,000		331,000
Less: payables	5,000			
Tax due	1,000	(6,000)		
		48,000		

At 31 March 1999 FCS Ltd had agreed to pay payables €5,000 and taxation €1,000 on behalf of Bill.

What is the chargeable gain arising from this transaction in 2021?

To calculate the CGT on Bill's disposal in 2021 it is necessary to calculate the base cost of the shares when he acquired them at 31 March 1999. Bill received the shares in 1999 in consideration for transferring his business to the company, FCS Ltd. Therefore, we must first calculate the deferred gain that arose on the transfer of his business to the company in return for the shares in FCS Ltd at 31 March 1999.

Disposal 31 March 1999 (disposal of business)

	€	€
Value of assets transferred at 31 March 1999		331,000
Taken in cash	25,000	
Debts paid by FCS Ltd	6,000	31,000
Value of shares (balance)		300,000
Proportion of consideration taken in shares	300	
	331	
Premises: 06/04/74 value: €18,000 @ 6.215	111,870	
Proceeds	200,000	
Gain		88,130
Goodwill: 06/04/74 value: €8,000 @ 6.215	49,720	
Proceeds	100,000	
Gain		50,280
{Receivables}		
{Inventories} No chargeable gain		
{Cash}		
Total chargeable gains		138,410

continued overleaf

Bill would have claimed relief to the extent that the sale proceeds were taken by way of shares in the company. In effect, this relief consisted of a deferral of the CGT payable on the amount of the consideration taken in the form of shares in the company.

Deferred gain: $\dfrac{300}{331} \times €138,410 = €125,447$

The deemed share value for future disposals following the application of the relief is calculated as follows:

	€
Value of shares	300,000
Less: deferred gain	(125,447)
Base cost of shares for CGT	174,553

Disposal 31 July 2021 (shares)

	€
Sale proceeds	300,000
Cost €174,553 @ 1.212	(211,558)
Chargeable gain	88,442

Bill will be assessed to CGT on this chargeable gain in 2021.

This relief merely defers some or all of the CGT arising on the disposal of a business by an individual. It is important to remember that such a disposal may also entitle the individual to other CGT reliefs, such as revised entrepreneur relief (see **Chapter 6**) as demonstrated in the following example, and retirement relief (see **Chapter 8**).

Example 7.4

Mr Harris, aged 48, carried on a wholesale distribution business from 8 May 1999 to 5 May 2021.

With effect from 6 May 2021, Mr Harris agreed to merge his business with a similar one carried on by Mr Hoyle. The merger is for bona fide commercial reasons and not as part of an arrangement the main purpose of which would be to avoid tax. A new company, H&H Ltd, will take over their businesses as going concerns.

Proceeds for disposal of Mr Harris's assets will be as follows:

(1) Goodwill valued at €60,000 is to be satisfied by issue of 50,000 €1 ordinary shares in H&H Ltd, valued at €50,000 and €10,000 cash. The market value of goodwill at 8 May 1999 acquired on purchase of business was €5,000.

(2) Receivables and inventories as per the balance sheet at 5 May 2021 are €8,000 and €10,000, respectively. Inventories per balance sheet was valued at historical cost. Having regard to current cost prices, it was agreed that inventories would be taken over at a value of €12,000. Mr Harris agreed to take 10,000 ordinary shares and €10,000 cash for these two items. There were no other business assets.

What is Mr Harris's CGT liability for 2021 on the basis that this was his only disposal for that year, and that he has not previously disposed of any chargeable business assets? Indicate the cost of shares in H&H Ltd for CGT purposes.

continued overleaf

	€	€
Consideration – goodwill		60,000
Market value at 8 May 1999: €5,000 × 1.193		(5,965)
Gain		54,035
Value of assets transferred (€60,000 + €8,000 + €12,000)	80,000	
Amount taken other than in shares (i.e. cash)	(20,000)	
Amount taken in shares	60,000	
Gain chargeable in 2021: $\frac{20}{80}$ × €54,035		13,509
Less: annual exemption		(1,270)
		12,239
CGT @ 10%		1,224
Cost of shares	60,000	
Less: deferred gains (€54,035 – €13,509)	(40,526)	
Base cost for CGT purposes	19,474	

7.3 Limitations on the Relief

1. The fact that liabilities of the trade taken over by the company are treated as cash consideration for the purposes of calculating the deferral relief seriously reduces the benefit to be gained from claiming the relief.
2. Capital gains that arise in a company in effect suffer CGT twice: once on the company on disposal of the asset by the company; and again on the shareholder on disposal (by sale or liquidation) of the shares. Thus, appreciating assets, such as land and buildings, are open to an effective double charge to CGT if owned by a company.
3. The relief is not available unless all the assets of the trade, including land and buildings, are transferred to the company. An exception for cash was noted above.
4. The deferred gain reduces the base cost of the shares in the event of a subsequent disposal. However, if it is the individual's intention to benefit from retirement relief (see **Chapter 8**) or to never sell the shares, then this is not a concern.
5. Neither revised entrepreneur relief (**Chapter 6**) nor retirement relief (**Chapter 8**) will apply to reduce the CGT on the non-share based proportion of the gain unless the transfer is done for bona fide commercial reasons and not part of a tax avoidance scheme. However, as relief under section 600 itself will only apply if the transfer is done for bona fide commercial reasons and not as part of a tax avoidance scheme, this condition will generally be satisfied.

Questions

Review Questions
(See Suggested Solutions to Review Questions at the end of this textbook.)

Question 7.1

Jack O'Dowd has run a successful retail business for a number of years. To facilitate expansion of the business he decided to form a limited company, O'Dowd Ltd. The business (i.e. all assets and liabilities) was transferred to O'Dowd Ltd on 30 June 2021 in exchange for 200,000 €1 ordinary shares and cash of €50,000. The cash was left outstanding on a loan account. Jack has not previously disposed of any chargeable business assets.

The balance sheet of the business immediately prior to the transfer was as follows:

	€	€
Warehouse at cost (purchased May 2001)	120,000	
Depreciation to date	(12,000)	108,000
Plant and machinery at cost	46,000	
Depreciation to date	(14,000)	32,000
Receivables	117,000	
Inventories	48,000	
Payables	(55,000)	
Net current assets		110,000
		250,000
Jack O'Dowd's capital account		250,000

Market values as at 30 June 2021 were as follows:

	€
Warehouse	400,000
Plant and machinery (Note 1)	40,000
Goodwill (Note 2)	130,000
Net current assets	110,000

Notes:

1. The market value of no individual item exceeded its original cost.
2. The value of goodwill was ascertained by professional valuers. It relates entirely to the business as it was built up over the years by Jack.

He sold shares in ABC Plc for €5,000 on 7 December 2021, which cost him €10,000 on 9 July 2009. Jack, who is single, has no other disposals in the year ended 31 December 2021. He had a capital loss forward of €10,000.

Requirement
(a) Calculate the CGT liability of Jack O'Dowd for the tax year 2021.
(b) State when this CGT liability is payable.
(c) Calculate the base cost of the shares in O'Dowd Ltd for CGT purposes.

Retirement Relief

Learning Objectives

After studying this chapter you will be able to:

■ Explain the principles of, and conditions for, CGT retirement relief.
■ Determine the availability of CGT retirement relief on disposal of shares and other business assets to a person other than a child and calculate the relief due.
■ Determine the availability of CGT retirement relief on disposal of shares and other business assets to a child and calculate the relief due.

8.1   Introduction

Certain gains arising on the disposal of "qualifying assets" by an individual who is at least 55 years of age may be relieved from CGT if certain conditions are satisfied. There is no requirement that the individual in question actually retires. The amount of relief available depends upon whether the assets are disposed of to third parties or, alternatively, to the taxpayer's children as defined (see **Sections 8.5** and **8.6** respectively).

If retirement relief is applied, the annual exemption of €1,270 is not due for other disposals in the year of assessment, i.e. there is no annual exemption in the year retirement relief applies, including any marginal relief.

The relief will not apply to disposals to third parties where the sole or main purpose of the disposal of qualifying assets is the avoidance of tax and not for genuine commercial reasons.

8.2   Assets Qualifying for Relief

Relief is available in respect of disposals of **qualifying assets**. The main qualifying assets, excluding farmland which has been rented to a tenant, are:

1. **Chargeable business assets** of the individual owned by them for at least 10 years ending with the date of disposal, and which have been their chargeable business assets throughout this 10-year period. The requirement for **10-year ownership does not apply to assets that are tangible, movable property**, e.g. movable plant and equipment.

In the context of retirement relief, chargeable business assets are **assets used for the purposes of a trade, profession, farming or employment carried on by the individual, or by the individual's family company**. Note that the definition of chargeable business assets for retirement relief differs from its definition under revised entrepreneur relief.

While stocks (inventories) and debtors (receivables) are assets used for the purposes of the trade, any gain on disposal of these assets is not subject to CGT. They are therefore not considered to be chargeable assets for this purpose.

Goodwill is a chargeable business asset for retirement relief purposes. However, as with revised entrepreneur relief (**Chapter 6**), the legislation provides that goodwill will not be a chargeable business asset if the goodwill is disposed of to a company and the individual is connected with the company immediately after the disposal unless it is reasonable to consider that the transfer was done for bona fide commercial reasons and not as part of a tax avoidance arrangement or scheme. This bona fide test for goodwill is in addition to the general bona fide test detailed in **Section 8.1**.

Assets not employed for the purposes of a trade, such as assets held as investments (shareholdings or rented property), are not chargeable business assets.

2. **Shares owned by the individual in a trading or farming company that is the individual's family company**. To qualify, the following conditions must be satisfied:

   (a) the shares must have been owned by the individual for at least 10 years ending on the date of the disposal;
   (b) the shares must be in a company that has been a trading or farming company, and the individual's "family company" for at least 10 years ending on the date of the disposal; and
   (c) the individual has been a working director of the company for at least 10 years, during which time the individual has been a full-time working director for at least five years;
   (d) if the shares are transferred to a company and the shareholder remains connected with the transferred company, retirement relief will not apply unless it is reasonable to consider that the transfer was for bona fide commercial purposes and not a part of a scheme or arrangement to avoid tax. This bona fide test for shares is in addition to the general bona fide test detailed in **Section 8.1**.

Note: the 10-year period for which the individual must have been a working director of the company does not have to be the 10-year period ending with the date of the disposal.

The legislation provides the following definitions:

▨ **Family company** A company in which the individual claiming relief controls:
  ● at least 25% of the voting rights; or
  ● at least 10% of the voting rights and at least 75% of the total voting rights (including the individual's own 10%) are controlled by members of the individual's family or a member of the family of their spouse or civil partner.

  "Family", for this purpose, means the individual's spouse or civil partner, or a brother, sister, ancestor or lineal descendant of the individual or their spouse or civil partner.

▨ **Full-time working director** A director who is required to devote substantially the whole of their time to the service of the company in a managerial or technical capacity.
▨ **Trading company** A company whose business consists wholly or mainly in the carrying on of a trade or trades. It also applies to professions.

3. Shares owned by the individual in a company that is a **member of a trading group, the holding company** of which has been the individual's **family company**. Conditions 2(a)–(d) above and the definitions of family company and full-time working director also apply to these shares. The specific terms are defined as:

   - **Holding company**   A company whose business (disregarding any trade carried on by it) consists wholly or mainly of the holding of shares or securities in one or more companies that are 75% subsidiaries.
   - **75% subsidiary**   A company is a 75% subsidiary of another company if not less than 75% of its ordinary share capital is owned directly or indirectly by that other company.
   - **Trading or farming group**   A group of companies consisting of the holding company and its 75% subsidiaries, the business of whose members consists wholly or mainly of carrying on a trade(s).

   As the relief applies to the disposal of shares by an individual, it generally covers the sale of shares in a holding company.

4. **Land and buildings, machinery or plant** that the individual has owned for a period of not less than **10 years** ending with the disposal and which:
   (a) was **used throughout that period** for the purposes of the relevant company (i.e. the family company referred to in **2. and 3.** above); and
   (b) is **disposed of at the same time and to the same person as the shares** in the family company.

   Personally owned assets can qualify for retirement relief provided that they were used for the business of the company and are disposed of at the same time and to the same person as the shares in the company. This is similar to the rule that applies in capital acquisitions tax (CAT) business relief (see **Chapter 16, Section 16.6.2**). Unlike CAT business relief however, there is no requirement that the vendor should have control of the company whose shares are being sold in order for assets let to the company to qualify for retirement relief.

   The definition of qualifying assets also includes certain farming and fishing payments and assets.

In applying the 10-year tests, the following periods can be taken into account.

1. The period of ownership by the individual's spouse or civil partner is treated as a period of ownership by the vendor.
2. The period of use by the spouse or civil partner of the individual where the spouse or civil partner is deceased is treated as a period of use by the vendor.
3. The period immediately before the death of a deceased spouse/civil partner, throughout which the deceased was a full-time working director is counted as a period when the vendor was a full-time director.
4. The period of ownership of the business prior to incorporation by the individual will qualify as a period of ownership and throughout which they were a full-time working director if the individual was entitled to "transfer of a business to a company" relief.
5. The period that an individual was a director of a company will be deemed to include the period during which the individual was a director of another company where, under a scheme of reconstruction or amalgamation, shares in that other company were exchanged for shares in the first-mentioned company.

6. As indicated above, it is not necessary to satisfy the 10-year test in the case of tangible movable property.

8.3 Disposal of Sole Trader Business

If the sole trader, who is aged 55 or more, only owns chargeable assets which are used for the purposes of the trade and the assets (other than tangible movable property) have been owned for at least 10 years, then full relief may be available. However, if the proceeds on the disposal of these chargeable business assets exceed €750,000 (or €500,000 if the individual is at least 66 years old) and the disposal is to someone other than a child, then either marginal relief applies or no relief is available (see **Section 8.5**).

Example 8.1

Anna, aged 56, disposes of her sole trader business for €800,000 to an unconnected third party, Gregoria Ltd. The value is derived from the following assets and liabilities:

	€
Premises	600,000
Goodwill	90,000
Equipment	50,000
Receivables	100,000
Inventories	70,000
Liabilities	(110,000)
	800,000

Anna set up the business in 2002, when she bought the premises.

Does Anna qualify for retirement relief?

▪ She is at least 55 years of age.

▪ She has owned the chargeable business assets (other than the equipment, which is tangible movable property) for at least 10 years.

▪ The chargeable business assets have been used in the business for at least 10 years.

Anna does therefore qualify for retirement relief. Is full or marginal relief available to her?

▪ The value of the chargeable business assets is €740,000 (€600,000 + €90,000 + €50,000), i.e. it does not exceed the €750,000 limit. (Remember, receivables and inventory are not subject to CGT and so are not considered chargeable business assets for retirement relief.)

▪ She is less than 66 years of age.

▪ As Anna is not connected with the company after the transfer of goodwill to the company, the goodwill qualifies as a chargeable business asset for retirement relief purposes.

Therefore, Anna qualifies for full relief and the disposal of the business is relieved from CGT.

Example 8.2

Tom, aged 58, disposes of his sole trader business for €900,000 to an unconnected third party. The value is derived from the following assets and liabilities:

	€
Premises	600,000
Goodwill	90,000
Equipment	50,000
Investment (cost €50,000 in 2006)	80,000
Receivables	100,000
Inventories	90,000
Liabilities	(110,000)
	900,000

Tom set up the business in 2001, when he bought the premises.

As Tom is at least 55 but not 66 years old, has owned the chargeable business assets (other than equipment) for at least 10 years and the value of the chargeable business assets is not greater than €750,000 (it is €740,000, i.e. €600,000 + €90,000 + €50,000), he qualifies for relief from CGT on disposal of the trade assets. However, the disposal of the investment is liable to CGT because it is not a chargeable business asset, i.e. used for the purpose of the trade. On the basis that this is his only chargeable disposal in 2021 his CGT is:

	€
Proceeds	80,000
Cost	(50,000)
Gain	30,000
CGT @ 33%	9,900

No annual exemption available in 2021 as retirement relief applies in 2021.

8.4   Disposal of Shares

If the assets subject to disposal are shares in a family company or a holding company that is a family company, then the following points are relevant.

Where shares are sold and the company owns assets comprised of chargeable business assets (within the definition specific to retirement relief) and other chargeable assets, only a portion of the gain qualifies for retirement relief. The amount of the gain that qualifies for relief is the proportion of the gain which the value of the company's **chargeable business assets** bears to the value of the company's **total chargeable assets**, i.e.:

$$\text{Gain on disposal of shares} \times \frac{\text{Value of chargeable business assets}}{\text{Value of total chargeable assets}}$$

where total chargeable assets is chargeable business assets plus other chargeable assets (e.g. assets held as investments).

Where the shares are disposed of to someone other than a "child" (see **Section 8.5**), in determining whether the consideration limit has been exceeded, sale proceeds are apportioned between the value of the company's **chargeable business assets and other chargeable assets that are not chargeable business assets**, i.e.:

$$\text{Sale proceeds of shares} \times \frac{\text{Value of chargeable business assets}}{\text{Value of total chargeable assets}}$$

Example 8.3 – Family trading company

John owns 100% of the shares in Durun Ltd, which he acquired in 2009 for €350,000. He has been a full-time working director since then. The company's assets have the following market values:

	€
Land and buildings	700,000
Equipment	10,000
Goodwill	30,000
Inventories	30,000
Trade receivables	40,000
Quoted investments	50,000
	860,000
Deduct: liabilities	(60,000)
	800,000

Assume that all the conditions for retirement relief are met and that John, aged 58, is disposing of the shares to an individual who is not a child. Therefore, the limit on proceeds from qualifying assets is €750,000.

The sale proceeds to be taken into account for the purposes of determining whether or not retirement relief applies is calculated as follows:

$$\text{Sale proceeds of shares} \times \frac{\text{Chargeable business assets}}{\text{Total chargeable assets}}$$

$$€800,000 \times \frac{(€700,000 + €10,000 + €30,000)}{(€700,000 + €10,000 + €30,000 + €50,000)} = €749,367$$

As the portion of sales proceeds representing chargeable business assets is less than the €750,000 lifetime limit for retirement relief on disposals to persons other than a child, retirement relief may be claimed on the portion of the gain relating to chargeable business assets.

The chargeable gain not relieved from CGT is calculated as follows:

	€
Sales proceeds	800,000
Deduct: cost of acquisition (no indexation, post-31/12/2002)	(350,000)
Gain	450,000
Deduct: retirement relief (€450,000 × €740,000/€790,000)	(421,519)
Chargeable gain	28,481

In the case of a holding company, the formula would take into account the asset position of the whole trading group, i.e.:

Sales price of shares in holding company $\times$ $\dfrac{\text{Value of chargeable business assets of trading group}}{\substack{\text{Value of total chargeable assets of trading group} \\ \text{(excluding shares in other group members)}}}$

8.5 Disposal to Person Other than a "Child" (section 598 TCA 1997)

8.5.1 Individual Aged 55 to 65

Section 598 TCA 1997 provides for retirement relief on disposals of qualifying assets to a person other than a child, where the individual is aged between 55 and 65 years old and the sales proceeds do not exceed €750,000. This is a lifetime limit. The assets may be sold piecemeal over a number of years, but if the aggregate consideration for all the qualifying assets sold since 6 April 1974 exceeds €750,000, then the relief will be withdrawn from all disposals that qualified for relief under this section.

  Note: **qualifying assets** only include assets in respect of the disposal of which retirement relief could have been claimed. Accordingly, disposals of business assets by an individual before they are aged 55 are ignored in determining whether the lifetime limit has been breached.

Example 8.4: Disposal of sole trader business
Sam, a sole trader aged 65, sold his business to Barry, an unconnected person, for €250,000 in October 2021. Sam had acquired the business on 6 April 1984.

	€	Cost 6 April 1984 €
Freehold	150,000	2,000
Goodwill	19,000	3,000
Investments (also acquired 6 April 1984)	20,000	1,000
Receivables	71,000	
Payables	(10,000)	
	250,000	

Freehold and goodwill are relieved from CGT as total proceeds on chargeable business assets does not exceed €750,000.

Investments		20,000
€1,000 @ 1.819		(1,819)
		18,181
CGT @ 33%		6,000

No annual exemption is available as retirement relief applies in 2021.

Example 8.5
David and Joe Sheahan (brothers), both aged at least 55 but less than 66, own a successful Irish trading group. The trade has grown from humble beginnings when Joe and David set it up for almost nothing – assume Joe's indexed cost of acquisition is €1,000. The group is now valued at an estimated €7 million (on the basis of the trade/goodwill and asset portfolio within the group). The group structure is as follows:

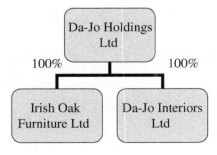

continued overleaf

Da-Jo Holdings Ltd is a 100% parent of both companies in the group. **David owns 90% of Da-Jo Holdings Ltd and Joe owns 10%.** They have owned the company shares for over 20 years. Both men devote all their working time to the group's business and have been directors of Da-Jo Holdings Ltd since the 1990s. Joe wishes to sell his 10% holding to an unconnected third party for €0.7 million. Joe has not previously disposed of any chargeable business assets.

Requirement Compute the retirement relief available if the chargeable business assets of the group are €5.5 million, and the chargeable assets of the group that are not chargeable business assets are €0.5 million.

Assets available in the group

	€
Chargeable business assets of the group	5.5m
Chargeable assets that are not chargeable business assets	0.5m
Non-chargeable assets (net)	1.0m
Market value of the group	7.0m

Retirement relief is available to Joe on his 10% holding as he satisfies all the conditions. The proceeds re qualifying assets are:

$$\frac{€700,000 \times €5,500,000}{€6,000,000} = €641,667$$

€641,667 is within the €750,000 limit; however, part of the gain does not qualify for relief as some of the chargeable assets are not chargeable business assets. Therefore the taxable gain is as follows:

	€
Proceeds	700,000
Indexed cost of shares assumed	1,000
Gain on sale of shares	699,000
Retirement relief: €699,000 × €5.5m/€6m	(640,750)
Gain liable to CGT	58,250
CGT @ 10% (Note)	5,825

Note: the 10% rate of CGT would apply as the conditions for revised entrepreneur relief (see **Chapter 6**) are also satisfied.

Marginal relief applies where the proceeds of disposal are in **excess of €750,000**. In such cases, the CGT payable cannot exceed half the excess of the aggregate proceeds over €750,000 (or €500,000, if appropriate) (see **Section 8.5.2**).

Example 8.6: Disposal of shares
Joe is married and aged 65. He bought shares in a family trading company in 1980/81 for €1,000. He has been a full-time working director since then. He sold the shares in October 2021 for €780,000 to an unconnected third party. Joe has not previously disposed of any chargeable business assets.
The net assets of the company at the date of sale were as follows:

	€
Factory	645,000
Goodwill	125,000
Receivables	60,000
Liabilities	(50,000)
	780,000

continued overleaf

Proceeds	780,000
Cost: €1,000 @ 3.240	(3,240)
	776,760
Less: annual exemption	(1,270)
	775,490
CGT @ 10%	77,549

The 10% rate of CGT applies as the conditions for revised entrepreneur relief (see **Chapter 6**) are also satisfied.

The maximum CGT payable if marginal relief were to apply would be:

€780,000 − €750,000 = €30,000 × 50% = €15,000

Therefore marginal relief should apply.

When considering whether or not the lifetime limit of €750,000 has been exceeded, the following should be noted:

1. Qualifying assets transferred to a spouse/civil partner are included at market value. Thus, while the transfer of a qualifying asset to a spouse/civil partner will not be a chargeable disposal for CGT purposes, it may restrict the relief available.
2. Disposals of qualifying assets to "children" are not included.
3. If the disposal arises due to the receipt by an individual of a payment made by a company on the acquisition of its own shares, which is not treated as a distribution but as a capital disposal (see **Chapter 9, Section 9.3** for the conditions to be satisfied), this capital receipt will be treated as coming within the scope of retirement relief and will therefore be taken into account for the purpose of the €750,000 threshold.

Example 8.7: Disposal of sole trader business
A newsagent, aged 58, who meets the conditions for retirement relief, gives one of his two shops to his wife (market value €700,000) and sells the other shop to an unconnected third party for €90,000 (allowable indexed cost, say, €30,000). Both shops were owned for 11 years and disposed of on 1 May 2021.

	€
Market value of transfer to wife	700,000
Sale to third party	90,000
Total proceeds	790,000
Excess proceeds over €750,000	40,000
Max. CGT liability (€790,000 − €750,000) × 1/2	20,000
CGT if no retirement relief:	
CGT on transfer to wife	Exempt

CGT on disposal to third party:	€
Sale proceeds	90,000
Less: indexed cost	(30,000)
Gain	60,000
Less: annual exemption	(1,270)
Taxable	58,730
CGT @ 10% (Note)	5,873

continued overleaf

Notes:

Revised entrepreneur relief applies (see **Chapter 6**) as the asset is a business asset that has been owned for at least three of the last five years and, assuming the newsagent has not sold any other business assets since 31 December 2015, cumulative gains on the sale of business assets do not exceed €1 million. The 10% rate of CGT applies.

As the CGT liability computed in the normal way is below €20,000, marginal relief does not apply.

8.5.2 Individual Aged 66 or Over

With effect from 1 January 2014, where the individual disposing of chargeable business assets is aged at least 66, the lifetime proceeds limit is €500,000 instead of €750,000.

Example 8.8

Carol Edwards has a very successful trading company, Edwards Limited, the shares in which she has owned for more than 10 years. She has been a full-time working director of the company during that time. The only chargeable assets of the company are chargeable business assets for retirement relief. The company is worth €740,000. The shares cost €1,000 in 2007. Carol has not previously disposed of any chargeable business assets. She advises you that she is going to retire during 2021 and sell her shares to Purchase Limited. Advise her as to the capital gains tax implications of disposing of the shares in 2021, (a) if she sells in February when she is 65 years of age; or (b) in May when she is 66.

Sell in February 2021 (aged 65)

If Carol disposes of the shares to someone other than her "child" in February 2021, when she is 65, she will have no taxable gain as all the conditions for retirement relief have been satisfied and the proceeds do not exceed the limit of €750,000.

Sell in May 2021 (aged 66)

If she disposes of the shares in May 2021 when she is 66 years of age, again all the conditions will be satisfied, but the proceeds limit will be only €500,000. As the proceeds limit is exceeded, she may qualify for marginal relief. Her maximum tax will be limited to

$$(€740,000 - €500,000) \times \tfrac{1}{2} = €120,000$$

This is compared to the CGT she would pay if retirement relief did not apply.
CGT payable if retirement relief does not apply:

	€
Proceeds	740,000
Cost (no indexation (2007))	(1,000)
Gain	739,000
Annual exemption	(1,270)
Liable to CGT	737,730
CGT @ 10% (Note)	73,773

Note: the 10% rate of CGT applies as the conditions for revised entrepreneur relief (see **Chapter 6**) are also satisfied.

As the CGT payable is less than it would be using the marginal relief formula, marginal relief does not apply. Therefore, she will pay €73,773 of CGT. However, by disposing of the shares in February 2021, instead of May 2021, Carol would avoid paying **any** CGT and would thereby save €73,773.

Example 8.9

Sean O'Brien is 67 years of age. He has a very successful trading company, O'Brien Limited, the shares in which he has owned for over 30 years. He has been a full-time working director of the company during that time. At all times, the only chargeable assets of the company are chargeable business assets for retirement relief. In 2018, when Sean was 64, he disposed of 75% of the shares in O'Brien Limited to Jones Limited for €450,000. He qualified for retirement relief and so did not have to pay CGT of €44,423. Now in 2021, when he is 67, he is disposing of the remaining 25% of his shares in O'Brien Limited to Jones Limited for €160,000. Advise him as to the CGT implications of disposing of the shares to Jones Limited in 2021, on the basis that the indexed cost of 25% of the shares in the company is €1,500. Other than the disposal of shares in 2018, Sean did not dispose of any other chargeable business assets since 1 January 2016.

All the conditions for retirement relief have been satisfied by Sean. However, as the proceeds limit is €500,000 and he has received proceeds of €610,000 (€450,000 + €160,000) since he was 55 years of age, he will have to pay the CGT on the disposal in 2021, and there will be a clawback of all the relief granted in 2018; or alternatively, marginal relief may apply if this results in a lesser amount of CGT being payable.

CGT before marginal relief
CGT would be calculated as follows:

		€
Disposal in 2021		
	Proceeds	160,000
	Indexed cost	(1,500)
	Gain	158,500
	Annual exemption	(1,270)
	Liable to CGT	157,230
	CGT @ 10% (Note)	15,723
2018 CGT as retirement relief no longer available		44,423
Total CGT payable		60,146

Note: the 10% rate of CGT applies as the conditions for revised entrepreneur relief (see **Chapter 6**) are also satisfied.

Marginal relief
The maximum tax is: (€610,000 − €500,000) × ½ = €55,000
Therefore marginal relief will apply and Sean will pay CGT of €55,000 (rather than €60,146).

8.6 Disposal to a "Child" (section 599 TCA 1997)

8.6.1 Individual Aged 55 to 65

Section 599 TCA 1997 permits unlimited retirement relief on disposals of qualifying assets to a child of the individual, where the individual is aged between 55 and 65 years old.

In addition to natural children, stepchildren and adopted children, the definition of "child" includes:

- A child of the civil partner of the individual.
- **Nieces** or **nephews** who have **worked substantially on a full-time basis for five years ending with the date of the disposal** in the business or company also qualify. The reference to nephew/niece does *not* include nephews/nieces of the spouse or civil partner of the individual disposing of the asset.
- A foster child who resided with and was under the care of and maintained at the expense of the individual making the disposal for a period of five years, or periods that together amounted to five years, up to the time that such foster child reached 18 years of age. A claim cannot be based on the uncorroborated testimony of one witness.

■ A **child of a deceased child** of the individual or the civil partner of the individual, a child of the civil partner of a deceased child of the individual and a child of the civil partner of a deceased child of the civil partner of the individual.

For the purposes of any subsequent sale by the child, the child is deemed to have acquired the assets at **market value** at the **date of disposal**.

If the child **disposes of the assets within six years** of the date they acquired the assets, the "child" will have to pay the CGT that would have been payable by the individual had the individual not qualified for section 599 relief (retirement relief on a disposal to a child). In such circumstances you should check if the individual would have qualified for section 598 retirement relief or marginal relief (see **Section 8.5**) or revised entrepreneur relief (see **Chapter 6**) when computing the CGT now payable by the child in respect of the original disposal by the individual who qualified for retirement relief. This CGT is payable in addition to any CGT arising on any gain that the child realises on the disposal of the assets by the child.

Example 8.10

Andrew, who is aged 60, transferred his 100% shareholding in his wholesale company to his daughter, Louise, in 2021. The market value of the shares at the date of transfer was €800,000. He had acquired the shares in January 1994 for €1,000. He was a full-time director of the company and the company held no investment assets.

The conditions for retirement relief are met and, as the disposal is to his child and Andrew is aged between 55 and 66 years, there is no limit on the amount of the proceeds. Therefore, no CGT is due. If Louise were to dispose of the shares within six years, not only would she have a liability to CGT on her disposal, but would also be liable for the CGT that would have been payable on the original disposal by her father to her if he had not qualified for relief under section 599.

Example 8.11

Paddy, who is aged 57, is in a civil partnership with Joe. He transferred his 100% shareholding in Paddy Ltd, a trading company, to Joe's daughter, Carol, in August 2021. The market value of the shares at the date of transfer was €1 million. Paddy had not previously disposed of any chargeable business assets.

The shares were acquired 15 years ago for €40,000. Assume an indexation factor of 2.5. Paddy was a full-time working director of the company throughout the period of ownership.

The market value of the assets of the company at the date of transfer were:

	€
Premises	450,000
Goodwill	350,000
Inventories and receivables	300,000
Investments	150,000
	1,250,000
Payables	(250,000)
Net value	1,000,000

As Paddy is less than 66 years of age and because Carol is the daughter of Paddy's civil partner, Joe, this is a disposal to a "child" and there is no limit on the proceeds.

continued overleaf

	€
Deemed proceeds	1,000,000
Cost €40,000 @ 2.5	(100,000)
Gain	900,000

Less: retirement relief:

$$€900,000 \times \frac{€450,000 + €350,000}{€450,000 + €350,000 + €150,000} \qquad (757,895)$$

Gain liable to CGT	142,105

CGT @ 10% = €14,210.

Paddy also satisfies the conditions for revised entrepreneur relief (see **Chapter 6**), therefore the 10% rate of CGT applies

8.6.2 Individual Aged 66 or Over

With effect from 1 January 2014, if the individual is aged 66 or over, retirement relief is only available on qualifying assets with a value up to €3,000,000. Any excess is subject to CGT. The limit of €3,000,000 is in respect of all disposals to children, as defined, by a parent while the parent is aged 66 or over. Once the limit has been used, there is no further relief.

Example 8.12

Joanne Phelan is 65 years of age. She has a very successful trading company, Prime Limited, the shares in which she has owned for over 30 years. She has been a full-time working director of the company during that time. The only chargeable assets of the company are chargeable business assets for retirement relief. The company is worth €10 million. Joanne has not previously disposed of any chargeable business assets. The shares cost €5,000 and the indexation factor is, say, 4. She advises you that she is going to retire when she is 66, in 2022, and give her shares to her son, Jack. Advise her as to the CGT implications of disposing of the shares to Jack in 2021 (when she is 65) versus 2022 (when she is 66), assuming no change in value of the company or in tax law.

If Joanne disposes of the shares in 2021, she will have no taxable gain as all the conditions for retirement relief have been satisfied. If Jack sells the shares within six years, he will have to pay the CGT Joanne did not pay in addition to any CGT due by him.

If she disposes of the shares in 2022 when she is 66, there will be relief but it will only be given as if the consideration for the disposal had been €3 million. Therefore, assuming no change in the value of the company, the rate of tax, etc., her CGT would be calculated as follows:

	€
Deemed consideration	10,000,000
Indexed cost: €5,000 × 4	(20,000)
Gain	9,980,000
Relief: €3,000,000 – €20,000	(2,980,000)
Taxable gain	7,000,000
CGT @ 10% of €1,000,000 (Note)	100,000
@ 33% of €6,000,000	1,980,000
Total CGT payable	2,080,000

Therefore, by disposing of the shares in 2021, Joanne has avoided CGT of €2.08 million. If Jack sells the shares within six years, he will have to pay the CGT that Joanne did not pay in addition to any CGT due by him.

Note: the 10% rate of CGT would apply to €1 million of the gain as the conditions for revised entrepreneur relief (see **Chapter 6**) will also be satisfied.

8.7   Summary of Conditions to be Satisfied

The summary below sets out the key issues only and does not deal with all issues which may arise. Therefore, it is important to read all of the chapter.

8.7.1   Sole Trader

- At least 55 years of age.
- Owned chargeable business assets for at least 10 years (plant and machinery – no minimum period), or owned by spouse or civil partner and individual for 10 years.
- Proceeds limit of €750,000 (or €500,000 if aged 66 or over) on qualifying assets if disposed of to someone other than a child. If the disposal is to a child and the individual disposing of the assets is aged 66 or over, there is a limit of €3,000,000 on the proceeds that can qualify for retirement relief.
- Must be for genuine commercial reasons and not the avoidance of tax.

If there are any chargeable assets which are not chargeable business assets, any gain on these assets will be taxable.

8.7.2   Shareholder

- At least 55 years of age.
- Shares owned for at least 10 years ending on the date of the disposal (or owned by spouse or civil partner and individual for 10 years; if qualified for transfer of business to a company, can include period as sole trader).
- Shareholder cannot be connected with the transferred company if the disposal is to another company, unless it is reasonable to consider the transfer was for bona fide commercial purposes and not part of a scheme to avoid tax.
- Shares in trading company or trading group.
- Shares in family company (at least 25% or, alternatively, 10% with 75% owned by family).
- Working director for at least 10 years, of which at least five years were full-time (or working by spouse or civil partner if spouse or civil partner is deceased; if qualified for transfer of business to a company, can include period as sole trader).
- Proceeds limit of €750,000 (or €500,000 if aged 66 or over) on qualifying assets if disposed of to other than a child (remember to count the value of a building if it is transferred separately – see **Section 8.7.3**). If the disposal is to a child and the individual disposing of the assets is aged 66 or over, then there is a limit of €3,000,000 on the proceeds that can qualify for retirement relief.
- Must be for genuine commercial reasons and not the avoidance of tax.

Even if the relief is due, if there are any chargeable assets in the balance sheet of the company and these are not chargeable business assets, then there is only part relief, i.e. chargeable business assets/total chargeable assets.

8.7.3   Land, Buildings, Plant and Machinery Owned by an Individual and Used by the Family Company

- At least 55 years of age.
- Owned land, buildings, plant or machinery for at least 10 years ending with the date of the disposal.

- Land/buildings/plant used by family/trading company for at least 10 years ending with the date of disposal.
- Disposed of land, etc. at same time and to same person as shares in family trading company.
- Shares in family/trading company must also qualify for retirement relief.
- Proceeds limit of €750,000 (or €500,000 if aged 66 or over) on qualifying assets if disposed of to other than a child (remember to count the value of the shares – see **Section 8.7.2**). If the disposal is to a child and the individual disposing of the assets is aged 66 or over, then there is a limit of €3,000,000 on the proceeds that can qualify for retirement relief.
- Must be for genuine commercial reasons and not the avoidance of tax.

Questions

Review Questions
(See Suggested Solutions to Review Questions at the end of this textbook.)

Question 8.1

On 1 August 2021, Jim Hughes, who is 60 years old, transferred 20% of his 100% shareholding in his family trading company to his son, Paul. The market value of the 20% is €800,000 and all chargeable assets are chargeable business assets. Jim had acquired these shares in the family company on 1 December 1994 when their market value was €40,000. He has been a full-time working director since 1994 and has not previously disposed of any chargeable business assets.

Requirement
(a) Compute the CGT payable in respect of this transaction, indicating the year for which it will be assessed and by whom it will be payable.
(b) If Paul Hughes, who is single, were to sell his 20% of the private company for €900,000 on 1 December 2021, what would be the CGT liability and by whom would it be payable?

Question 8.2

Since 1987, Sean Humbert, aged 63, has operated Tara Foods Ltd as a very successful company in the catering sector. Sean is now considering, in December 2021, the transfer of his business by way of gift to his only son, Michael. Sean has been a full-time working director of the company since it was incorporated in 1987, with himself as the 100% beneficial owner. Sean has not previously disposed of any chargeable business assets.

The share capital of the company comprises 100 ordinary shares of €1 each. Sean subscribed for his shares at par value in July 1987. Of the 100 shares, 99 are registered in Sean's name and the remaining share is registered in the name of Sean's wife, and is held in trust for Sean.

The shares in Tara Foods Ltd carry a current value of €800,000, derived from the following assets and liabilities:

	Market Value
	€
Goodwill	600,000
Equipment	50,000
Inventories	40,000
Trade receivables	25,000
Quoted investments	120,000
Trade payables	(35,000)
	800,000

The property from which the company operates is owned personally by Sean and it is his intention to transfer the property to Michael by way of gift, in addition to the shares in Tara Foods Ltd. The property was purchased by Sean for €28,000 in July 1987. The current market value of the property is €300,000.

Requirement

(a) Set out your views on Sean's eligibility for retirement relief on the proposed transfer of his shares and business premises to Michael. The basis for your views should be outlined together with an indication of the amount of relief available in the circumstances as set out.

(b) Compute the CGT liability that will arise if Sean makes the proposed transfers to Michael.

(c) Under what circumstances would the retirement relief claimed at (b) be withdrawn?

(d) How would Revenue recover the CGT due should the retirement relief fail to be clawed back?

Question 8.3

On 1 November 2021, on the occasion of his 60th birthday, Colin, a widower, made the following gifts:

	Notes	Market Value at 1 November 2021
(a) To his son Sean:		
100% of the shares in an unquoted trading company, Crawford Sportswear Ltd	1.	€500,000
Premises occupied by Crawford Sportswear Ltd	1.	€250,000
(b) To his daughter Esther:		
A holiday cottage in France	2.	€120,000
Cash		€50,000

Notes:

1. Crawford Sportswear Ltd is engaged in the sale of sportswear. Colin had carried on this trade as a sole trader since 1990 until he incorporated Crawford Sportswear Ltd on 1 January 2013. On 1 January 2013 Colin transferred the entire assets and liabilities of the trade, other than the cash and the shop premises, to Crawford Sportswear Ltd in exchange for shares in the company. On 31 December 2012, the market value of the trade's assets and liabilities were as follows:

	Market Value €
Premises*	125,000
Fixtures and fittings*	50,000
Goodwill	80,000
Inventories	120,000
Receivables	25,000
Cash	10,000
Payables	110,000

* Colin acquired the premises on 1 June 1990 for €20,000. Following the transfer of the business to Crawford Sportswear Ltd, the premises were let at full market rent by Colin to the company.

The market value of no single item of fixtures and fittings exceeded its original cost at 1 January 2013.

Colin has always been a full-time working director of the company.

At 1 November 2021, all of the company's assets consisted of assets in use, and which have always been in use, for the purpose of the company's trade.

Apart from the disposals set out above, Colin has not previously disposed of chargeable business assets.

2. Colin inherited the holiday cottage in France from a French cousin. Colin's cousin died on 10 October 2003, when the cottage was valued at €25,000. A number of complexities arose in the administration of his cousin's estate and the legal ownership of the cottage was not transferred to Colin until 11 January 2005, when the cottage was valued at €30,000.

Requirement

Calculate Colin's CGT liability for 2021 on the assumption that no other assets were disposed of during the year.

Acquisition by a Company of its Own Shares

Learning Objectives

After studying this chapter you will be able to:
- Apply the CGT (and income tax) rules appropriate to the purchase by a company of its own shares.

9.1 Overview

A company is legally entitled to acquire/buy back its own shares or shares of its parent company. A company, particularly a quoted company, might do this if its management were of the view that the shares were good value at present; an unquoted company might do this **if a shareholder wished to dispose of shares and another shareholder did not want to buy the shares**.

As we saw at CA Proficiency 1, if the shareholder is an individual, any distribution out of assets of the company in respect of shares, except any part of it which represents a repayment of capital, is a distribution for tax purposes, i.e. the difference between what the shareholder subscribed for the shares and what he/she is now receiving is taxable under Schedule F. The income tax liability is typically at 40%, plus Universal Social Charge of up to 11% and PRSI at 4%.

Chapter 9 of Part 6 TCA 1997 sets out the tax treatment of an acquisition by a company of its own, or its holding company's, shares. Where the relevant conditions are satisfied, the sale of the shareholder's shares is subject to CGT treatment rather than income tax treatment. The law deals separately with quoted and unquoted companies.

9.2 Quoted Companies

A buyback (including the redemption, repayment and purchase) of its own shares by a quoted company (or of its own shares by a subsidiary of a quoted company) is not treated as a distribution. Consequently, the disposal of the shares by the shareholders(s) concerned is within the charge to CGT.

There is a condition that must be satisfied by quoted companies, i.e. a share buyback must not be part of a scheme or arrangement, the main purpose (or one of the main purposes) of which is to enable the owner of the shares to participate in the profits of the company, or of any of its 51% subsidiaries, without receiving a dividend. If this condition is not satisfied, the share buyback is treated as a distribution. Quoted companies must include in their annual corporation tax return details of any share buybacks undertaken in an accounting period, indicating whether or not the buyback is to be treated as a distribution.

9.3 Unquoted Companies

Where an unquoted trading or holding company buys back its own shares (or its holding company's shares) from a shareholder who is not a dealer in those shares, the payment made to the shareholder is, subject to certain conditions being satisfied, not to be treated as a distribution. As the payment is not to be treated as a distribution, **CGT treatment** applies to the shareholder's disposal of the shares.

9.3.1 Conditions to be Satisfied

The conditions that **must** be satisfied if such a purchase is not to be treated as a distribution are:

- The company must be a trading company or a holding company of a trading company.
- The motive test, i.e. the acquisition of the shares by the company must be wholly or mainly for the **benefit of the trade** of the company or any of its 51% subsidiaries. See **Appendix 9.1** for an extract from Revenue's *Tax and Duty Manual*, Part 06-09-01: Acquisition by a company of its own shares, dealing with its interpretation of "the benefit of the trade" test.
- The buyback must not be part of a scheme or arrangement the purpose of which is to enable the shareholder to participate in the profits of the company or any of its 51% subsidiaries without receiving a dividend.
- The vendor of the shares, if an **individual**, must be **resident and ordinarily resident** for the year of assessment in which the shares are bought back; if the vendor is a **company**, it must be **resident** in the accounting period in which the shares are bought back. This ensures that the vendor is within the charge to Irish CGT.
- The vendor must have **owned the shares throughout a five-year period** ending with the date of the buyback. The period of ownership of a spouse or civil partner living with a vendor at the date of the buyback is aggregated with that of the vendor. However, where an Approved Profit Sharing Scheme has appropriated the shares to a participant, the period is reduced to three years. If the vendor inherited the shares from the previous owner, the vendor's period of ownership is deemed to include the period of ownership of the previous owner. In addition, where the shares are inherited, the required period of ownership is reduced to three years.
- Where the vendor's shareholding in a company is not fully purchased, redeemed or repaid, then generally their **shareholding** and entitlement to **share of profits** must be **substantially reduced**. Both the nominal value of shareholding and the profit entitlement must, after the sale of the shares, be reduced **by at least 25%**.

Example 9.1
D Ltd has an issued share capital of 100,000 €1 ordinary shares, of which E holds 20,000 (that is, 20/100ths or 20%). If E sells 5,000 shares to D Ltd, D Ltd's issued share capital is reduced for tax purposes to 95,000 shares, of which E holds 15,000, a fraction of 15/95ths or 15.79%.

Thus, although E has sold 25% of the original holding, E's percentage holding has been reduced by only 21%, and the buyback will not qualify for CGT treatment (i.e. it will be treated as a distribution). To achieve a reduction of 25%, E would need to sell 5,890 shares.

▨ The **vendor is not connected with the company**, or group company, after the buyback, i.e. the vendor and the vendor's associates must not, after the buyback of the shares, be entitled to more than 30% of the capital, voting rights or assets on a winding up of the company.

There is a very long definition of an associate in the law. The **main** people are:

- a husband and wife or civil partners living together are associated with one another and a person under the age of 18 is an associate of his or her parents and their spouses or civil partners (no other relatives are treated as associated);
- a person who has control of a company is associated with that company;
- two companies which are controlled by the same person are associated.

The legislation states that in order for CGT treatment to apply, the vendor is only required to reduce their shareholding by 25% and also provides that the vendor must not be entitled to more than 30% of the share capital of the company after the buyback. Thus the legislation envisages situations where a vendor continues to have a shareholding in the company. However, as set out in **Appendix 9.1**, Revenue's interpretation of how it sees the "benefit of the trade" test being satisfied does not envisage the vendor continuing to have a shareholding in the company of in excess of 5%. In practice, therefore, in order to satisfy the "benefit of the trade test" so that CGT treatment will apply, the vendor will generally have to reduce their shareholding to 5% or less. Furthermore, Revenue's view is that the shareholder should also cease to be a director of the company in order for the "benefit of the trade" test to be satisfied. In this context, Revenue state that it would be acceptable for a shareholder to stay on as a director for no longer than six months after the sale of their shares.

9.3.2 Buyback of Shares to Pay Inheritance Tax

The various conditions necessary for a buyback not to be treated as a distribution are waived where it can be shown that shares had to be disposed of in order to discharge inheritance tax in respect of an inheritance by that shareholder of the company's shares or to repay borrowings used to pay the inheritance tax. For this rule to apply, the shareholder must not otherwise have been able to discharge the inheritance tax owed without undue hardship.

Example 9.2

Harry and Peter, two Irish resident and ordinarily resident individuals, set up Super Friends Ltd in 1995 to sell electronic equipment. Harry owns 80% of the shares, while Peter owns 20%. The company has been very profitable and now has revenue reserves of €2 million. Harry believes that the success of the company is due totally to his efforts. He believes that Peter does not really contribute to the success of the company and is more interested in his golf handicap. There have been a number of acrimonious board meetings and as a result Harry has decided to "buy out" Peter. Peter is happy to dispose of his shares provided that he receives €1 million and pays CGT at 33%, or 10% if revised entrepreneur relief applies (see **Chapter 6**), and not the higher tax on income.

If Harry were to buy the shares, he would need €1 million. As Harry does not have that amount of cash, he would have to either borrow the money (which would have to be repaid) or get money from the company (on which he would be liable to income tax).

If Super Friends Ltd bought back the shares from Peter, then Harry would own all the shares without having to find the cash to actually buy the shares. Peter will be liable to income tax on the cash received from Super Friends Ltd in excess of the amount he contributed for the shares. However, if he satisfies the following conditions, he will be liable to CGT on the gain, and not income tax:

continued overleaf

1	Trading or holding company?	Yes
2	Will the acquisition benefit the trade?	Yes, there is disagreement between shareholders
3	Is Peter resident and ordinarily resident in Ireland in 2021?	Yes, resident and ordinarily resident
4	Has Peter owned the shares for five years?	Yes
5	Is Peter selling all his shares, or at least substantially reducing his shareholding?	Yes, he is selling all his shares
6	Is Peter not connected with Super Friends Ltd after the disposal?	Yes

As all the conditions have been satisfied, Peter will be liable to CGT on the disposal of the shares to Super Friends Ltd.

9.3.3 Other Issues

Even though the buyback is not treated as a distribution for the shareholder, it is a distribution for the purposes of the close company surcharge (see **Chapter 26**), i.e. it would reduce the amount liable to the surcharge. It does not matter whether the buyback is treated as a distribution or a capital gain – there is no tax deduction for the company.

In respect of treasury shares:

- treasury shares that are not cancelled by a company are treated as cancelled immediately when they are acquired by the company;
- no allowable loss arises on cancellation of treasury or other shares by a company, regardless of whether the shares are actually cancelled or are treated as cancelled for tax purposes; and
- reissues of treasury shares are treated as new issues of shares.

A return is required to be made to the Inspector by companies that buy back their own shares or acquire their holding company's shares, where such companies consider exemption from the distribution treatment applies to those acquisitions. The time limit for making such a return is nine months from the end of the accounting period in which the acquisition takes place. There is provision for penalties for failure to make returns.

Appendix 9.1: Extract from Revenue's *Tax and Duty Manual*, Part 06-09-01: Acquisition by company of its own shares

The following is taken from Appendix II of the *Tax and Duty Manual*, Part 06-09-01: Acquisition by a company of its own shares. It outlines Revenue's guidance on the application of the trade benefit test.

"Revenue will normally regard a buy-back as benefiting the trade where for example:

- There is a disagreement between the shareholders over the management of the company and that disagreement is having or is expected to have an adverse effect on the company's trade and where the effect of the transaction is to remove the dissenting shareholder
- The purpose is to ensure that an unwilling shareholder who wishes to end his/her association with the company does not sell the shares to someone who might not be acceptable to the other shareholders.

Examples of this would include:

- An outside shareholder who has provided equity finance and wishes to withdraw that finance.
- A controlling shareholder who is retiring as a director and wishes to make way for new management.
- Personal representatives of a deceased shareholder where they wish to realise the value of the shares.
- A legatee of a deceased shareholder, where she/he does not wish to hold shares in the company.

The above examples envisage the shareholder selling his/her entire shareholding in the company and making a complete break from the company. If the company is not buying **all** the shares owned by the vendor or if the vendor is selling all the shares but retaining some connection with the company (e.g. directorship) it would seem unlikely that the transaction would benefit the company's trade.

However, there may be situations where:

- For sentimental reasons a retiring director of a company wishes to retain a small shareholding in the company. In this context, **Revenue would consider that a small shareholding would not exceed 5% of the share capital of the company**.
- A controlling shareholder in a family company is selling his/her shares to allow control to pass to his/her children but remains on as a director for a specified period purely because his/her immediate departure from the company at that time would otherwise have a negative impact on the company's business. **Revenue would consider that the specified period that the director remains with the company should not exceed 6 months**.

In such circumstances it may still be possible for the company to show that the main purpose is to benefit its trade.

Given that the underlying concept is that the buy-back will benefit the company's trade, consideration will be given as to whether the proposed manner of funding the buy-back will place the company in a weak financial position. Where the manner of paying for the shares leaves the company in a position where, for example, it would be undercapitalised or its cash flow situation jeopardised this would unlikely to be considered to be of benefit to the trade.

In some circumstances it may be necessary for the company to borrow in order to pay for the share buy-back. It is accepted that, in principle, where the buy-back is to be funded or part funded by a loan that this will not in itself mean that the trade benefit test isn't satisfied. However, where any such borrowing would seem to materially weaken the company's financial situation it is very unlikely that a positive advance opinion will be given."

Questions

Review Questions
(See Suggested Solutions to Review Questions at the end of this textbook.)

Question 9.1

Alan Doyle has been a director of Annally Ltd since the company was incorporated in August 1990. The company is a large importer of toys from the Far East, which it distributes in Ireland and the UK.

Alan is 60 years old and intends retiring from the business shortly. His original investment in company shares was €10,000 in €1 ordinary shares. There was no share premium account. His brothers, Mark and Colm, also own 10,000 €1 shares between them, and they will continue to run the company as directors after Alan's retirement.

Alan has recently had his shares valued and was pleasantly surprised to discover that they are worth €600,000. He has asked Mark and Colm to purchase these shares, but they have told him that they do not have sufficient funds.

You have been approached for advice on the possibility of the company acquiring its own shares from Alan.

Requirement
(a) State the conditions that must be in place in order that the proceeds from a company acquiring its own shares can be treated as a share disposal for CGT purposes.
(b) Compute Alan's liability to CGT if all the conditions are met.
(c) State the tax consequences for Alan and the company if the conditions are not met.

Part Two

Stamp Duty

General Principles and Conveyance or Transfer on Sale

Learning Objectives

After studying this chapter you will be able to:

■ Advise on and calculate the stamp duty implications of certain transactions involving certain written documents either executed in the State or relating to property situated in the State.

■ Advise on the stamp duty administrative requirements and the implications of non-compliance.

Chartered Accountants Ireland's *Code of Ethics* applies to all aspects of a Chartered Accountant's professional life, including dealing with stamp duty issues. As outlined at the beginning of this textbook, further information regarding the principles in the *Code of Ethics* is set out in **Appendix 2**.

Students should also be aware of the issues around tax planning, tax avoidance and tax evasion, and these are discussed in **Appendix 3**.

10.1 Introduction

Prior to 15 December 1999, the law governing stamp duties was contained in the Stamp Act 1891 and the Stamp Duties Management Act 1891, with subsequent Finance Acts amending and adding to these provisions. The Stamp Duties Consolidation Act 1999 (SDCA 1999) was brought into law with effect from 15 December 1999, consolidating the legislation into a single Act and subsequent Finance Acts.

10.2 Charge to Stamp Duty

Section 2 SDCA 1999 provides that any "instrument" specified in Schedule 1 to the SDCA that is:

1. **executed in the State**; or
2. relates to any **property situated in the State**; or
3. relates to any matter or thing done, or to be done, in the State

is chargeable with stamp duty, subject to exemptions provided for in the Act.

An explanation of the meaning of these terms and the wording used is required, and is given below.

10.2.1 Instrument

While an instrument is defined as "including every legal document", the important thing to note is that it is a written document of some sort that acts as a mechanism for doing something. Accordingly, **where no written document is produced, no stamp duty can arise**.

For example, oral agreements that are not then put into writing or transactions executed by conduct (such as delivery) do not attract stamp duty. Nor do agreements recorded on film, tape, etc.

Example 10.1
Pat and Catherine agree that Pat will buy Catherine's collection of antique books for €10,000.
No written agreement was drawn up and, accordingly, no stamp duty arises.

10.2.2 Schedule 1 SDCA 1999

Schedule 1 SDCA 1999 lists instruments of various types and describes the stamp duties attaching to them. Any instrument not falling within Schedule 1 is not subject to stamp duty. Certain instruments which do not themselves fall within Schedule 1 are deemed to be instruments within it for stamp duty purposes (e.g. conveyance of a gift).

Stamp duty can be one of two types:

1. *Ad valorem* – where the amount of stamp duty depends on the value of the consideration or property affected by the instrument concerned (e.g. land).
2. Fixed – where the instrument attracts a set amount of stamp duty regardless of the value of the property affected by the transaction (e.g. cheque).

10.2.3 Executed in the State

Executing an instrument means doing whatever is necessary to make the instrument operable or effective. For most written agreements, this means signing the agreement. In some cases instruments are not executed until signed and sealed (e.g. deed of convenant).

Example 10.2
An agreement is signed in Killarney to transfer ownership of a painting kept in Bermuda from one party to another. The agreement is subject to Irish stamp duty as it is executed in the State, i.e. in the Republic of Ireland.

10.2.4 Property Situated in the State

The rules relating to where property is situated are, generally, the same as those for CGT (see **Chapter 4**). In summary, the legal status of various types of property is as follows:

Property	Location
Shares in registered form	Where share register is kept
Simple contract debts	Where debtor resides*
Land and buildings	Where located
Goodwill	Where business is carried on
Patents/trademarks	Where registered

* The rule for the location of debts is different from the rule for CGT purposes. For CGT purposes, a debt is located in Ireland only if the creditor is resident in Ireland. The stamp duty legislation does

not state the location of different types of property, so general legal principles apply. Under general legal principles a debt is located where the debtor is resident.

> **Example 10.3**
> An agreement is signed in Chicago to transfer the ownership of a building in Dundalk. The document is stampable as it relates to property situated in the State.

10.2.5 "Any matter or thing done, or to be done, in the State"

This a very wide provision that rarely arises in practice. The view of the Revenue Commissioners in relation to this criterion is that the instrument and/or the underlying transaction should relate to, or involve, a substantive action or obligation to be carried out or undertaken in the State. For example, where an instrument is executed abroad and the only connection with the State is that one of the parties is an Irish resident, the Revenue Commissioners' view is that in such a case the instrument would not be liable to duty.

10.3 Payment and Returns

10.3.1 When is Stamp Duty Payable?

Stamp duty is payable within 30 days of execution of the instrument concerned. However, as a matter of practice, Revenue extends this date so that the duty on the instrument must be paid **within 44 days** of the date of first execution of the instrument.

10.3.2 Who is Liable to Pay Stamp Duty?

In theory, it is a matter for agreement between the parties to the transaction as to who is responsible for the stamp duty, the "accountable person". The legislation does contain provisions to decide who the "accountable person" is, in the event that the Revenue Commissioners has to sue for the stamp duty, as follows:

- the purchaser or transferee in the case of a transfer on sale;
- the lessee in the case of a lease;
- either party in the case of a gift or sale at undervalue (voluntary disposition *inter vivos*).

Where a person buys shares in a public company through a stockbroker, the stamp duty is collected by the stockbroker and paid to Revenue. Where a person buys shares in a private company, the person dealing with the share transfer document, for example the accountant, will deal with collecting the stamp duty and paying it to Revenue. Where a person buys land and buildings, the solicitor will convey the property and will collect the stamp duty and pay it to Revenue.

10.3.3 e-Stamping via ROS

Under e-stamping, a person uses ROS (Revenue Online Service) to file the stamp duty return and pay stamp duty online and receive a stamp certificate as part of that online transaction. This stamp certificate is printed and attached to the instrument, to denote the instrument as stamped.

Alternatively, the statutory return may be filed in paper format. However, this is only allowed where Revenue has excluded a person from the requirement to file electronically, i.e. where the accountable person:

■ does not have sufficient access to the internet to comply with the requirements; or

■ in the case of an individual, is prevented by age or mental or physical infirmity from being able to comply with the requirements.

10.3.4 Self-assessment

Similar to other taxes, under self-assessment for stamp duty the accountable person (usually the purchaser) files the return, calculates and pays the stamp duty and may be subject to audit at a later stage. As with other taxes, if the accountable person has a doubt about the application of stamp duty law to a particular transaction, the person can lodge an "expression of doubt". If Revenue does not agree with the position adopted by the accountable person, they have a right of appeal against Revenue's decision.

Under self-assessment, a return must be filed within 30 days of the date of the execution of the document in question, although in practice Revenue will accept that a return is filed on time if it is filed up to 44 days after the date of execution. If a return is not filed on time, there is a fine of €3,000 plus a surcharge of:

■ 5% of the stamp duty liability or €12,695, whichever is lower, if the return is filed within two months of the due date, i.e. within 92 days from the date of execution; and

■ 10% of the stamp duty liability or €63,485, whichever is lower, if the return is filed more than two months after the due date, i.e. after 92 days from the date of execution.

As with other taxes, if stamp duty is paid late, interest is payable at 0.0219% per day or part of a day.

10.4 Conveyance or Transfer on Sale

A conveyance is an instrument whereby ownership of any property, immovable or movable, tangible or intangible, is transferred from one person to another.

The term "conveyance" is usually thought of as being the document that transfers ownership in land following the signing of contracts for sale. However, it has a much wider meaning. For instance, it includes court orders. The term "on sale" implies that two considerations have been satisfied:

1. there has been an agreement to sell the property with all the necessary conditions of contract law satisfied (offer, acceptance, consideration); and
2. the consideration is in the form of money.

In Schedule 1 SDCA 1999, there are three heads of charge for conveyances or transfers on sale. The two of importance here are:

1. "Conveyance or transfer on sale of any stocks or marketable securities".
2. "Conveyance or transfer on sale of any property other than stocks or marketable securities".

10.4.1 Stocks and Securities

For stamp duty to arise under this head, there must be a sale (including a gift) of stocks or securities.

Stamp duty is chargeable at 1% of the consideration, rounded down to the nearest euro, subject to a minimum payment of €1. There is an exemption on share transfers where the duty involved is €10 or less.

Example 10.4
Paul sells shares in Damascus Ltd, an Irish incorporated private company, to Peter for €1,250.

	€
Stamp duty liability: 1% × €1,250	12.50
Stamp duty	<u>12.00</u> (rounded down)

The stamp duty due would be payable by Peter (the purchaser).

The instrument (document) that is the conveyance for these purposes is the share transfer form. Generally the transfer or conveyance on sale of shares and marketable securities of **a company not registered in the State** is **not subject to Irish stamp duty**. This is provided that the conveyance is not executed in the State, nor does it relate to:

1. any Irish immovable property;
2. any Irish-registered stocks and marketable securities.

Stocks must be in a company registered in the State or relate to Irish immovable property.

Finance Act 2017 introduced a stamp duty anti-avoidance section that applies the 7.5% stamp duty rate on the disposal of certain shares deriving their value from non-residential property (which is beyond the scope of this textbook).

Issue of Shares by a Company
Where an Irish company issues shares in return for cash, this is not liable to stamp duty.

Purchase by a Company of its Own Shares
Technically, when a company purchases its own shares, a liability to stamp duty arises. In practice, however, shares in unquoted companies can be converted into redeemable shares and redeemed. No stamp duty arises on redemption of these shares.

Alternatively, the shares can be bought back on foot of a contract or share purchase agreement. If the shareholder and the company enter into an agreement and the shareholder simply hands over the share certificates to the company, there is no need for a stock transfer form and no duty is charged.

10.4.2 Property Other than Shares

The most common example of stamp duty arising under this head is on sales of land and buildings. Sales of freehold land, transfers of business property (e.g. goodwill) and assignments of leasehold interests in land are also covered under this head of charge. The creation of a leasehold interest is charged under the "lease" heading.

The rates of stamp duty applicable depend on whether the property is residential property or non-residential property. In either case, it is the purchaser who pays the stamp duty, not the vendor.

Residential Property
With effect from 8 December 2010 the rates of stamp duty, as set out in **Appendix 1**, are **1% on the first €1,000,000 of the consideration and 2% on the balance**, rounded down to the nearest euro.

Example 10.5
Mary buys a residential property with a value of €1,250,000. The stamp duty payable by Mary is as follows:

	€
First €1,000,000 @ 1%	10,000
Balance €250,000 @ 2%	5,000
Total	15,000

With effect from 20 May 2021, there is an increased rate of stamp duty of 10% on purchases of 10 or more residential houses/duplexes at one time or cumulatively in a 12-month period. Houses and duplexes bought before 20 May 2021 can be counted towards the threshold of 10 units, but the higher rate only applies to those units bought after this date. For example, if a person buys six houses in April 2021 and five houses in June 2021, the threshold is exceeded in June 2021 and the stamp duty will be charged at 10% on the June purchases. The increased rate does not apply to apartments.

Non-residential Property

In the case of non-residential property, such as commercial buildings, farms, land and goodwill, the rate is 7.5% of the consideration, rounded down to the nearest euro, for instruments executed on or after 9 October 2019 (previously the rate was 6% from 11 October 2017). Transitional provisions apply to instruments executed after 9 October 2019 and before 1 January 2020 where a binding contract was entered into before 9 October 2019 (instrument must contain a certificate to this effect in such form as Revenue specifies).

Mixed-use Property

In the case of a mixed-use property, the consideration must be apportioned on a just and reasonable basis between the residential and non-residential parts of the property.

Example 10.6
Susan buys a shop and an apartment over the shop for €900,000. The estate agent advises that the value of the shop is €750,000 and the apartment is €150,000. The stamp duty payable by Susan is:

Shop (€750,000 @ 7.5%)	€56,250
Apartment (€150,000 @ 1%)	€1,500
Total stamp duty	€57,750

Where VAT is charged on the acquisition of a property, it is the amount of the consideration exclusive of VAT that is liable to stamp duty (see **Chapter 34**).

10.5 Gifts – Deemed Conveyance on Sale

Certain transfers are deemed to be "conveyances on sale" for stamp duty purposes, even though the consideration is not in the form of money. A conveyance of property by way of gift is not a conveyance on sale as there is no sale; however, it is a deemed conveyance on sale for stamp duty purposes. The consideration is the market value of the property conveyed.

This is a point of particular importance in estate planning when assessing whether assets should be gifted now or transferred as part of a person's estate by inheritance. Stamp duty is payable in relation to a gift. No stamp duty arises on inheritance.

Example 10.7: No stamp duty arises on foot of an inheritance

Mr X approaches you for advice in relation to whether or not he should gift Irish shares worth €200,000 to his brother now, or provide that his brother will receive the shares on his death by way of an inheritance.

Stamp duty implications if he gifts now: €200,000 @ 1% = €2,000.

This will be a liability of Mr X's brother.

Stamp duty implications if it is an inheritance: no stamp duty payable by Mr X's brother on receipt of the shares by inheritance.

Questions

Review Questions

(See Suggested Solutions to Review Questions at the end of this textbook.)

Question 10.1

Frank is considering acquiring the following assets:

(a) Shares in an Irish Plc at a cost of €30,000.
(b) Shares in a US Plc at a cost of €20,000.
(c) Land in Galway for €80,000.
(d) An apartment in Kilkenny for €120,000.

Requirement

Frank would like advice regarding whether any stamp duty is payable and, if so, the amount payable.

Question 10.2

The following transactions have taken place in September 2021:

(a) Ann Murphy bought an apartment for €200,000 on 1 September.
(b) Frank Gibbons received a gift of shares in an Irish private company from his brother on 5 September. The market value of the shares is €300,000.

Requirement

Advise each of these individuals as to the amount of stamp duty payable and the date by which it must be paid.

Exemptions and Reliefs

Learning Objectives

After studying this chapter you will be able to:

■ Identify and advise on the main exemptions from stamp duty.
■ Advise on the availability of certain reliefs from stamp duty, including young trained farmer relief, transfers of farmland between relatives relief, and transfers between associated companies relief.

11.1 Exemptions

The **main** exemptions from stamp duty are as follows:

1. Transfers of government stocks.
2. Wills.
3. **Conveyance or transfer of property between spouses or civil partners.** This exemption applies provided the spouses or civil partners are legally married or in a civil partnership (even if they are separated); it is only after divorce or dissolution of the civil partnership that a conveyance or transfer becomes liable to stamp duty. Furthermore, upon divorce or dissolution of a civil partnership, any transfer of property made under an Irish court order (or a foreign court order recognised as valid in the State) is also exempt from stamp duty.
4. Conveyance, transfer or lease of land made for **charitable purposes** in the State or Northern Ireland.
5. Any instrument for the sale, transfer or other disposition of **intellectual property**, as defined. Intellectual property includes patents, trademarks, copyright, registered designs, inventions, domain names, etc. (The definition of intellectual property is the same as the definition of intangible assets for corporation tax purposes in **Chapter 23, Section 23.1**).
6. Conveyances of **immovable property situated outside the State** (subject to some conditions).

11.2 Reliefs

11.2.1 Young Trained Farmer Relief

Under section 81AA SDCA 1999, there is a full relief from stamp duty on a transfer of an interest in land to a "young trained farmer" up to 31 December 2021. The purpose of this relief is to encourage the transfer of farmland (including the farmhouse and other buildings on the farmland) to a new generation of farmers with relevant qualifications. The transfer may be by way of gift or sale.

With effect from 1 January 2019 there is an aggregate limit of €70,000 on the amount of state aid that may be granted to a young trained farmer under this relief and other income tax reliefs, including section 667B TCA 1997 (stock relief). The limit applies to the aggregate of relevant reliefs claimed since 1 July 2014. For example, any such relief claimed in 2017 would reduce the amount of relief available in 2021, subject to the total reliefs claimed from 1 July 2014 not exceeding €70,000.

To qualify for the relief the farmer must:

1. be less than 35 years of age on the date of execution of the deed of transfer;
2. have attained a recognised agricultural qualification; and
3. furnish a declaration to the effect that:
    (a) for a period of **five years** from the date of execution of the deed of transfer they will:
        (i) spend not less than 50% of their normal working time farming the land, and
        (ii) retain ownership of the land;
    (b) they will submit a business plan to Teagasc before the execution of the instrument concerned; and
    (c) they come within the EU Commission definition of a micro or small enterprise.

If the young farmer does not have a relevant qualification at the date of execution of the deed of transfer but acquires one within four years of that date, they will be entitled to a refund of stamp duty paid. To qualify for a refund the farmer must: submit a business plan to Teagasc; come within the EU Commission definition of a micro or small enterprise; and intend to, for five years from the date of the repayment claim, spend not less than 50% of their normal working time farming the land and to retain ownership of the land.

If the land is disposed of within five years from the date of execution of the deed of transfer and is not replaced by other land within one year of the disposal, then the exemption will be **clawed back** by way of a penalty. If only part of the land is disposed of, then any clawback will relate only to the portion disposed.

11.2.2 Transfers of Farmland between Relations (Consanguinity Relief)

Consanguinity relief applies to transfers between close relatives of **farmland only**, subject to certain conditions being satisfied. Farmland includes buildings on farmland used for farming purposes, but not a farmhouse as this is considered a residential property. The relief applies to transfers by way of sale or gift.

The relief operates by applying a 1% rate of stamp duty to qualifying transfers of farmland between close relatives before 1 January 2024.

Conditions

The following conditions must be satisfied:

1. The individual to whom the land is transferred/conveyed must either:
    (a) farm the land for a period of not less than six years, or else
    (b) lease it for a period of not less than six years to someone who farms the land.

2. The person farming the land must do so on a commercial basis and with a view to the realisation of profits. The person must also spend not less than 50% of their normal working time farming land, including the land transferred, **or** be the holder of one of the agricultural qualifications set out in legislation.
3. The transfer/conveyance must be to a relative.
4. The transfer must take place on or before 31 December 2023.

The Revenue Commissioners considers that "normal working time", including on-farm and off-farm working time, is about 40 hours per week. Therefore a farmer with off-farm employment would qualify provided he/she spends a minimum average of 20 hours working on the farm per week. Farmland includes any farm buildings on that land.

(Note: there is a relief in capital acquisitions tax called agricultural relief. The conditions for this stamp duty relief also apply to CAT agricultural relief (see **Section 16.5.2**), namely: farming the land or leasing it to someone who farms it for six years; and the person having a farming qualification or farming the land for at least 50% of their time and doing so on a commercial basis. However, the tests at 3. and 4. above apply for stamp duty relief only.)

This relief applies to transfers of the **entire** beneficial interest to most relatives, i.e. where the person to whom the property is being transferred (or each of them if there is more than one transferee) is related to the transferor in one of the following ways:

- Lineal descendant (child, grandchild, etc.)
- Parent
- Grandparent
- Step-parent
- Husband, wife or civil partner
- Brother/sister of parent (i.e. aunt, uncle)
- Brother or sister
- Lineal descendant of a parent (e.g. step-brother/sister)
- Lineal descendant of a husband/wife (e.g. stepchild)
- Lineal descendant of a brother/sister (e.g. nephew/niece)
- Civil partner of a parent
- Lineal descendant of a civil partner.

Example 11.1
Ben gives his granddaughter, Jane, Irish land worth €100,000 on 4 March 2021.
The stamp duty payable on this voluntary disposition *inter vivos* would be €100,000 @ 7.5% = €7,500.
As there is no mention of farming, relief cannot be claimed.

Example 11.2
Peter wishes to transfer 100 acres of land valued at €1.2m to his nephew, Eoin, on 23 May 2021. What is the stamp duty payable if Eoin is a farmer?

The stamp duty will be €1.2m × 1% = €12,000.

11.2.3 Transfers between Associated Companies

Stamp duty chargeable under the "conveyances on sale" headings in Schedule 1 SDCA 1999 (deemed transfers included) can be reduced to 0% where a transaction is between "associated companies" as defined in section 79 SDCA 1999. In order for the relief to apply, the transfer must be for bona fide commercial reasons and not to avoid tax.

One company is associated with another if there is a 90% direct or indirect relationship between them in terms of:

1. ordinary share capital (ordinary shares excluding fixed rate preference shares);
2. profits available for distribution; and
3. assets available for distribution on a winding up.

Example 11.3

Conveyances on sale between A Ltd and B Ltd will qualify for the reduced rate of 0%.

Example 11.4

Transfers between A Ltd and B Ltd, and between B Ltd and C Ltd will qualify for the relief.

Example 11.5

Transfers between A Ltd and C Ltd will not qualify as there is only an 81% relationship, i.e. A Ltd owns 90% of B Ltd's ownership in C Ltd, 90% of 90% = 81%.

If the companies cease to be associated within two years of the date of the conveyance or transfer, then full stamp duty will be payable. However, the relief is not clawed back where the companies cease to be associated because the transferor company is liquidated, provided the transferee continues to own the property that was transferred for at least two years.

Example 11.6

Arklow Ltd transfers freehold land worth €1 million to its 100% subsidiary, Gorey Ltd.

The transfer will qualify for the associated companies relief, therefore no stamp duty will be payable. However, if the 90% relationship is broken within two years, Gorey Ltd will have to pay €75,000 in stamp duty.

Example 11.7

Arklow Ltd grants Gorey Ltd, its 100% subsidiary, a leasehold interest in land. The premium payable is €900,000 with no annual rent.

The transaction is chargeable under the "Lease" heading and therefore associated companies relief is not available.

Stamp duty liability is 7.5%, i.e. €67,500.

Questions

Review Questions

(See Suggested Solutions to Review Questions at the end of this textbook.)

Question 11.1

Joseph is married to Anne and they have two sons, Alex and Shane. Joseph has decided to make the following gifts:

(a) land worth €100,000 to Alex for him to build a house;
(b) a cottage in Galway worth €500,000 to Anne;
(c) land in Mayo to an Irish charity to build a hostel for homeless people;
(d) shares in his company, XYZ Limited, worth €200,000 to Shane; and
(e) land in the UK worth €90,000 to Alex.

Requirement

Joseph would like advice regarding whether or not stamp duty is payable and, if so, the amount payable. He would also like to know the stamp duty consequences if, instead of making the gifts now, he leaves them to the same people in his will.

Question 11.2

Holdings Limited owns shares in three companies as follows:

(a) 100% of the shares in Private Limited;
(b) 85% of the shares in Free Limited; and
(c) 95% of the shares in Major Limited.

In each case, Holdings Limited is entitled to the same percentage of profits available for distribution and assets available for distribution on a winding up.

Holdings Limited is proposing to transfer the following assets:

(a) a commercial building worth €1 million to Private Limited;
(b) a residential property worth €1.5 million to Free Limited;
(c) a holding of shares in an Irish plc worth €1 million to Major Limited; and
(d) a patent worth €3 million to Free Limited.

Requirement

Advise Holdings Limited as to the stamp duty payable if these transfers are made.

Transfer of a Business

Learning Objectives

After studying this chapter you will be able to:

■ Advise on the stamp duty arising on sale or incorporation of a business and how to minimise the liability.

12.1 Stamp Duty Consequences on Acquisition of Business Assets

Contracts for the sale of property can be deemed to be a conveyance on sale and therefore liable to stamp duty. Where a business is sold, the contract for the sale is liable to stamp duty as a deemed conveyance on sale. However, if assets are already chargeable to stamp duty (e.g. a building) or the asset is goods and merchandise of the business (e.g. inventories and machinery), then there is no deemed conveyance of those assets. In practice, this means that contracts for the sale of intangible assets such as goodwill, debtors and cash on deposit are deemed conveyances on sale.

Where a contract for the sale of property (e.g. the sale of a sole trader's business) comprises both chargeable and non-chargeable property, the consideration must be apportioned as only the chargeable property is liable to stamp duty under this rule. This will also apply where a sole trader/partnership decides to incorporate the business.

Example 12.1

X Ltd agrees to sell its business to Y Ltd for a cash sum of €300,000. It is agreed that the following assets and liabilities will be transferred to Y Ltd.

	€
Machinery	150,000
Goodwill	30,000
Receivables	250,000
Patents and designs	100,000
	530,000
Payables	(230,000)
Net worth of business	300,000

A written agreement is drawn up to evidence the sale of the business.

continued overleaf

Therefore, Y Ltd will have the following stamp duty liability (before claims for exemptions, etc.):

1. The contract for sale is stampable as a deemed conveyance on sale due to the fact that the sale of certain intangibles has been dealt with by it, i.e. goodwill, debts, patents and designs.
2. As the entire transaction has been dealt with in one agreement, the total consideration for stamp duty purposes is split between that which is liable to stamp duty and that which is not. As the machinery is not liable, stamp duty is charged on:

	€
Goodwill	30,000
Receivables	250,000
Patents and designs	100,000
Stampable consideration	380,000
Stamp duty @ 7.5%	28,500

12.2 Minimising Stamp Duty on Acquisition of Business Assets

From **Example 12.1** above, Y Ltd can minimise its stamp duty liability as follows:

1. Do not transfer receivables and payables to Y Ltd. Instead, let X Ltd (or Y Ltd as its agent) collect the debts and use them to pay off the payables.
2. The patents and designs – avail of exemption for intellectual property.

Therefore, only the goodwill is liable, i.e. €30,000 @ 7.5% = €2,250.

Example 12.2

Clive is selling the Irish goodwill of his business to Denis for €80,000. As it will be sold under contract, Denis will be liable to pay 7.5% stamp duty.

Clive is a client of the firm where you are employed. Before the contract is drawn up he contacts your office to speak with your manager, who is on lunch, and is put through to you instead. Clive explains that Denis has suggested that the contract be drafted to reflect consideration of €50,000 and he will give Clive the balance of €30,000 in cash. In this way, Denis can reduce his stamp duty liability. Clive is unsure how to proceed. What should you do?

What Denis is suggesting is not legal nor ethical. As Clive is a client of your manager, it is more appropriate that your manager explain this to him. You tell Clive that your manager will discuss the matter with him after lunch. You inform your manager of the details of the conversation.

Questions

Review Questions
(See Suggested Solutions to Review Questions at the end of this textbook.)

Question 12.1

Jack Feeley carried on his sole trader business for many years. He has decided to incorporate the business for commercial reasons. He will transfer all of his trading assets and his trade payables to the company in return for shares in the company. The assets and liabilities of the business are as follows:

	€
Land and buildings	500,000
Machinery	30,000
Goodwill	180,000
Receivables	40,000
Inventories	120,000
Trade payables	(70,000)

Requirement

(a) Advise Jack as to whether any CGT will be payable. You are not required to calculate the CGT or base cost of the shares.

(b) What would be the stamp duty if the transaction is evidenced by a contract?

Part Three

Capital Acquisitions Tax

Capital Acquisitions Tax – Gifts and Inheritances

Learning Objectives

After studying this chapter you will be able to:

- Identify and discuss how and when gifts and inheritances arise, and distinguish between them.

Chartered Accountants Ireland's *Code of Ethics* applies to all aspects of a Chartered Accountant's professional life, including dealing with capital acquisitions tax issues. As outlined at the beginning of this textbook, further information regarding the principles in the *Code of Ethics* is set out in **Appendix 2**.

Students should also be aware of the issues around tax planning, tax avoidance and tax evasion, and these are discussed in **Appendix 3**.

13.1 Introduction to Capital Acquisitions Tax

Capital acquisitions tax (CAT) is a tax on the acquisition of a benefit by a person for less than full consideration. The benefit can be either a gift or an inheritance. It is an aggregable tax, i.e. when assessing an individual's exposure to CAT all benefits taken by them on or after 5 December 1991 must be included. However, gifts and inheritances up to certain values may be taken tax-free in a person's lifetime, depending on their relationship with the person providing the benefit.

The Capital Acquisitions Tax Consolidation Act 2003 determines:

- If the benefit is a gift/inheritance.
- If the benefit is within the charge to CAT (**Chapter 15**).
- How the taxable value of the benefit is computed (**Chapters 16** and **17**).
- If there are any reliefs or exemptions available (**Chapters 16** and **18**).
- How the tax is calculated (**Chapter 14**).
- The administration of the CAT system (**Chapter 20**).

13.2 Gifts and Inheritances

All benefits, be they gifts or inheritances, are taxed together. When the legislation was originally introduced there were significant differences assessing CAT on gifts and on inheritances, and the legislation was structured accordingly. However, over the years these differences have been reduced and you will find that the rules for dealing with gifts and inheritances are almost completely the same.

Broadly speaking, if an individual becomes entitled to any property or benefit, for less than full consideration, and there is no death involved, then that individual is deemed to have received a **gift**. The amount of the gift is represented by the full market value of the property or benefit taken as reduced by any consideration given, and any debts or encumbrances taken over. Where a private company makes or receives a gift, the liability to CAT is determined by looking through the company, or series of companies, to the ultimate individual shareholders and by treating the shareholders as having made or received the gift.

If the benefit or property is received as a result of a death, the beneficiary is deemed to have taken an **inheritance**. The amount of the inheritance is calculated in the same manner as for gifts.

13.2.1 Basic Elements of a Gift/Inheritance

Section 5 CATCA 2003 provides that a **gift is deemed to be taken** when:

- a **disposition** is made,
- by a **disponer**,
- whereby a **donee**,
- becomes **beneficially entitled in possession**,
- otherwise than **on a death**,
- to **any benefit**,
- otherwise than for **full consideration in money or money's worth paid by the donee**.

Section 10 CATCA 2003 provides that **an inheritance** is taken when:

- a **disposition is made**,
- by a **disponer**,
- whereby a **successor**,
- becomes **beneficially entitled in possession**,
- **on a death**,
- to any **benefit**,
- otherwise than for a full consideration in money or money's worth **paid by the successor**.

We see, therefore, that most of the basic elements constituting an inheritance correspond to those constituting a gift. These definitions contain many elements that need to be examined carefully.

Disposition

The disposition represents the **method by which the ownership of the property or benefit involved is transferred**. For every gift, there must be a disposition; but every disposition is not necessarily a gift. For example, if one sells a car at market value, this is a disposition but it is not a gift. The term is specifically defined in section 2 CATCA 2003 for the purposes of CAT. This definition is intentionally very wide and includes:

1. Any act or omission by a person as a result of which the value of that person's estate is reduced, e.g. the transfer of property otherwise than for full consideration.
2. The release of any debt or failure to exercise a right by an individual, as a result of which the value of that person's estate is reduced.

> **Example 13.1**
> The passing of a resolution by a company that results, directly or indirectly, in one shareholder's property being increased in value at the expense of the property of any other shareholder, if that other shareholder could have prevented the passing of the resolution by voting against it.

3. Payment of money.
4. The grant or creation of any benefit.
5. The transfer of any property or benefit by will or on intestacy (intestacy means that a person dies without making a will).

The "disposition" may, therefore, be said to be the legal method of alienating the property in favour of a beneficiary, e.g. the deed of conveyance in respect of the transfer of a farm, the trust deeds in relation to the transfer of property to a trust fund, or the act of delivery in the case of the transfer of movable property.

Disponer

The **disponer** is the person who, directly or indirectly, is the **source of the financial benefit** comprised in the disposition. This is usually very straightforward, e.g. a parent who gifts shares to a child is the disponer. It is important to establish who the disponer is as the amount of benefit that can be taken tax-free depends on the recipient's relationship with the disponer.

Other examples of the disponer include:

- the deceased, in the case of a will or an intestacy;
- the settlor, in the case of property transferred to express or discretionary trusts;
- a person who has made a reciprocal arrangement with a third party to provide property comprised in a disposition to a second person.

> **Example 13.2**
> Brian owes Alan €10,000. Alan agrees to waive the debt if Brian transfers shares valued at €10,000 to Alan's brother, James. The financial source of James's benefit (and therefore the disponer) is Alan, and not Brian who actually provided the property.

Donee/Successor

The **donee** is simply the person who receives the **gift**, whereas the recipient of an inheritance is known as the **successor**. In the example of a parent gifting shares to a child, the child is the donee. Alternatively, if an aunt dies leaving money to a niece, the aunt is the disponer, the niece is the successor.

Entitled in Possession

"Entitled in possession" is defined in CATCA 2003 as "**having a present right to the enjoyment of property** as opposed to having a future such right".

A gift/inheritance is not deemed to be taken until the happening of the event upon which the donee/successor (i.e. the beneficiary) becomes beneficially entitled in possession to the benefit. For example, if a father gives his solicitor €20,000 to give to his son when the son marries, the gift will only arise when the son actually gets married, as it is only at that time that the son will have a present right (as opposed to a future right) to enjoy the funds.

On a Death

Section 3 CATCA 2003 defines this term as meaning a benefit taken under any of the following circumstances:

1. Under the terms of a will (whether the benefit is taken immediately or after an interval).
2. Under an intestacy, i.e. individual dies without leaving a will.
3. Under a disposition where the disponer dies within two years of the date of the disposition. In such cases, the gift is effectively deemed to be an inheritance. Previously, the distinction was relevant as the rates of gift tax and inheritance tax differed. As both rates are now the same, the distinction is no longer significant.
4. An appointment of property from a discretionary trust where the trust was created by the will of a deceased person.
5. On the termination of a life interest by the death (or the deemed death) of the life tenant or at a definite interval after such a death. Advance termination of a limited interest is beyond the scope of this textbook.
6. On the death of a person who is a joint tenant.
7. On the happening of any event following the termination of an intervening life interest which gives rise to the benefit in question.

If a person becomes beneficially entitled in possession to any benefit on a death otherwise than for full consideration, then he is deemed to take an inheritance. A "gift", therefore, arises *otherwise* than on a death.

Benefit

For CAT purposes, a benefit refers to a gift or inheritance. Section 2 CATCA 2003 defines it to include "any estate, interest, income or right". Such a wide definition would clearly include:

- an absolute interest/ownership in property;
- a life interest in property; and
- an annuity or other periodic payment.

Example 13.3

1. Jim transfers ownership of his farm to Joe – Joe takes an absolute interest in the farm. As full ownership passed, the gift taken was equal to the full value of the farm.
2. Jim gives Joe a right to the use of his farm for Joe's lifetime – Joe takes a limited interest in the farm (i.e. a life interest). Obviously, the benefit taken is less than the full value of the farm as it is not full ownership of the property.

It is only the value of the actual benefit taken that is taxable and not necessarily the full value of property comprised in the gift or inheritance. Where the benefit involved does not comprise an absolute interest it is a "limited interest" and CATCA 2003 provides a statutory method of valuing the benefit. The calculation of the taxable value of a limited interest, be it an annuity or a life interest, is dealt with in **Chapter 17**.

Consideration in Money or Money's Worth Paid by the Beneficiary

There can be no gift or inheritance if full consideration in money or money's worth is paid by the recipient of the benefit. As such, it would not be subject to CAT. Payment can be non-monetary, hence the "money's worth".

Any consideration, monetary or otherwise, given by the recipient therefore reduces the value of any benefit taken for the purposes of CAT.

Example 13.4

1. Tony transfers his hotel, valued at €2,000,000, to Mary for €2,000,000 – clearly there is no gift here as full consideration has been paid.
2. Tony transfers the hotel to Mary for €1,200,000 – here the gift comprises the full value of the hotel reduced by the consideration paid by Mary, i.e. €2,000,000 – €1,200,000, i.e. €800,000.
3. Tony transfers the hotel to Mary, subject to Mary giving Colin €500,000 – this involves two gifts as follows:
   (a) the hotel less €500,000 from Tony to Mary, i.e. Mary receives a gift of €1,500,000; and
   (b) €500,000 from Tony to Colin.

13.2.2 CAT Differences between Gifts and Inheritances

In essence, an inheritance is distinguished from a gift in that an inheritance is taken *on a death* while a gift is taken otherwise than on a death. The recipient of a gift is known specifically as the *donee* whereas the recipient of an inheritance specifically is the *successor*. (The general term for the recipient of a benefit, be it a gift or inheritance, is "the beneficiary".)

There are some differences in the treatment of gifts and inheritances for CAT purposes. Where relevant, these will be addressed in the following chapters. However, it should be noted at this stage that the main difference between gift tax and inheritance tax is that **the first €3,000** of the total taxable value of the total **gifts taken from a single disponer in the same year is exempt from CAT** (known as the small gift exemption, see **Section 18.1**). There is no equivalent exemption for inheritances.

13.2.3 Dates of the Disposition, Gift and Inheritance

We have seen that in order to have a gift or an inheritance there must be a disposition by a disponer. It should be noted that the date of the disposition may differ from the date of the gift/inheritance. These dates are defined in the legislation.

Date of the Disposition
Section 2 CATCA 2003 defines the date of the disposition to mean:

1. the date of death of the deceased in the case of a benefit taken by will or an intestacy;
2. the date of death of the deceased in the case of benefits derived under the Succession Act 1965 (i.e. basically a widow's legal right or claims of children to a share in the estate);
3. the latest date when the disponer could have exercised the right or power which has been waived, where the disposition consisted of a failure or omission to exercise a right or power;
4. in any other case, the date of the disposition is the date on which the act or, where more than one act is involved, the last act of the disponer was done by which he provided or bound himself to provide, the property comprised in the disposition.

Example 13.5

1. If Pat leaves €200,000 to his son in his will, the date of disposition is Pat's date of death.
2. If Pat gives his solicitor €200,000 to give to his son when the son marries, the date of the disposition is the date of payment of the money to the solicitor.

The date of the disposition is important as it determines the tax rules that apply. This is covered in greater detail in **Chapter 15**. It is also important in determining if certain CAT exemptions apply (**Chapter 18**).

Date of the Gift

Section 2 CATCA 2003 defines the date of the gift as "the date of the happening of the event on which the donee becomes beneficially entitled in possession to the benefit". In other words, something has to happen for the donee to be in possession of the benefit, and it is only when this has happened that the donee becomes liable to CAT.

Example 13.6
Following from **Example 13.5** above, while the date of the disposition was the date Pat gave his solicitor the money, the date of the gift will be the date the son marries as it is only at that time that the son will have a present right (as opposed to a future right) to enjoy the funds.

If Pat had merely given his son €200,000 on a certain day, the date of the disposition is the actual date of payment of the money and the date of the gift is the same date because the son immediately becomes entitled in possession to the benefit.

Example 13.7
A father gives (by deed of conveyance) his son the right to use a property for a period of 10 years with absolute ownership of the property passing to his grandson after the 10-year period has expired. The deed of conveyance is the disposition.

In the son's case, he receives an immediate benefit, i.e. the use of the property (though for a limited period only). In that instance, the date of the gift corresponds to the date of the disposition.

The grandson is not treated as having received a gift until he becomes entitled in possession, i.e. until the 10-year period has elapsed. In his case, the date of the disposition (i.e. the date of execution of the deed) and the date of the gift are completely different. When the 10-year period has elapsed, the grandson is treated as having received the gift direct from his grandfather, and only then does he becomes entitled in possession.

The date of the gift is important as it determines the tax rates and tax-free thresholds that apply to the calculation of CAT arising on that gift. In subsequent chapters we will see that the date of the gift is also important for determining whether or not a gift is liable to CAT (**Chapter 15**) or whether the gift qualifies for certain reliefs (**Chapter 16**) or exemptions (**Chapter 18**).

Date of the Inheritance

The term "date of the inheritance" normally means the date of the death which has to occur in order for a successor to become entitled to an inheritance. An exception is where a gift becomes an inheritance because the disponer dies within two years of the date of the disposition, in which case the date of the inheritance is the date of the gift.

Example 13.8
Jack dies on 1 February 2021. Under the terms of Jack's will, he leaves a life interest in a property to his son, Joe, and provides that the property is to pass absolutely to Joe's son, George, on Joe's death. The date of Joe's inheritance from his father is 1 February 2021. The date of George's inheritance from his grandfather will be the date of Joe's death.

The date of the inheritance is important as it determines the tax rates and tax-free thresholds that apply to that inheritance. So, if the date of inheritance is 2021, the 2021 CAT rate and tax-free group thresholds will apply – even if the successor does not receive the inheritance until a later date (when different rates or thresholds may well be in place), as is common with inheritances. As with gifts, we will see in subsequent chapters that the date of the inheritance is also important for determining whether or not an inheritance is liable to CAT (**Chapter 15**) or whether it qualifies for certain reliefs (**Chapter 16**) or exemptions (**Chapter 18**).

Questions

Review Questions
(See Suggested Solutions to Review Questions at the end of this textbook.)

Question 13.1

Mary owes John €8,000. John tells her to give €8,000 to Peter, in settlement of the debt.

Requirement
Who is the disponer for the €8,000?

Question 13.2

A mother agrees to give a farm to her daughter when the daughter has her first child.

Requirement
When is the gift taken by the daughter?

Question 13.3

Joyce gives Paddy the family company worth €1 million, subject to Paddy giving €100,000 to Nora.

Requirement
What gifts are taken?

Question 13.4

You are a tax specialist in a firm of Chartered Accountants. The managing partner has asked you to write a memo dealing with the following CAT queries.

Requirement
(a) What is regarded as a "disposition" for CAT purposes?
(b) What is the "date of the disposition"?
(c) What does "beneficially entitled in possession" mean?
(d) Explain what is meant by "date of the gift".

Computation of CAT

14.1 Introduction

The computation of CAT depends upon a number of factors, including:

■ The **relationship** between the recipient of the gift/inheritance (beneficiary) and the person from whom the gift/inheritance is taken (disponer). This relationship governs the **group threshold** to be applied.
■ The **taxable value** of the gift/inheritance received.
■ The **aggregate** of the taxable value of all previous benefits taken by the beneficiary from persons within the **same group threshold** on or after **5 December 1991**.
■ The date on which the gift/inheritance is taken (because group threshold can change).

14.2 Group Thresholds

14.2.1 Group Thresholds 2021

The amount of the **group threshold** applicable in computing the CAT arising on receipt of a benefit depends on the relationship between the recipient of the benefit (beneficiary) and the provider of the benefit (disponer) and the year in which the benefit is taken. The group thresholds to be used when taxing a gift or inheritance taken in 2021 are:

Group A   **€335,000** where the beneficiary is, on the day the gift or inheritance is taken:

■ the child of the disponer; or
■ the child of the civil partner of the disponer; or
■ the minor child of a deceased child (see **Section 14.2.2**); or

  ▒ a parent of the disponer taking an inheritance that is not a limited interest on the death of the disponer (see **Section 14.2.2**); or
  ▒ a "favorite niece/nephew" of the disponer taking a gift/inheritance of business property (see **Section 14.2.2**).

A child includes an adopted child and a stepchild. For the purposes of the Group A threshold, it is also deemed to include a natural child who has been adopted by someone else and also a foster child, subject to certain conditions.

Group B **€32,500** where the beneficiary is, on the day the gift or inheritance is taken:

  ▒ a lineal ancestor of the disponer (some exceptions for a parent (see **Section 14.2.2**)); or
  ▒ a lineal descendant of the disponer (other than relationships as set out in Group A); or
  ▒ a brother or sister of the disponer; or
  ▒ a child of a brother or sister, or a child of a civil partner of a brother or sister of the disponer (other than relationships as set out in Group A).

Group C **€16,250** in all other cases.

Example 14.1
David gives (by deed of conveyance) his son, Nigel, the right to use a property for a period of 10 years with absolute ownership of the property passing to his grandson, Dylan, after the 10-year period has expired. David also gifts his own mother, Kate, and her sister, Mary, €20,000 each. The group thresholds that apply when assessing each beneficiary's CAT exposure are:

  ▒ Nigel is a child of the disponer, David – Group A
  ▒ Dylan is a grandchild (i.e. lineal descendant) of the disponer, David – Group B
  ▒ Kate is a parent (i.e. lineal ancestor) of the disponer, David – Group B
  ▒ Mary is David's aunt (his mother's sister). She is not a lineal ancestor, nor a lineal descendant, nor a sister, nor a child of a brother/sister of the disponer – Group C

We will see that, when computing CAT, the fact that *prior* gifts/inheritances were taken in a different year is irrelevant. **When taxing a benefit taken in 2021, use only the group threshold figures and CAT rates for 2021.** The group thresholds for earlier periods are set out in **Appendix 1** at the end of this textbook. Earlier thresholds are only relevant when computing CAT for a year earlier than 2021. Such calculations are beyond the scope of this book.

14.2.2 Group Thresholds – Special Relationships

Minor Child of Deceased Child
The Group A €335,000 threshold applies where the beneficiary is, on the day the gift or inheritance is taken:

  ▒ the minor child of a deceased child of the disponer; or
  ▒ the minor child of a deceased child of the civil partner of the disponer; or
  ▒ the minor child of the civil partner of a deceased child of the disponer; or
  ▒ the minor child of the civil partner of a deceased child of the civil partner of the disponer.

A minor child is defined in CATCA 2003 as a child who is under 18 years of age and has never been married.

Example 14.2

Anthony and Harriet are Jim's parents. Jim is married to Nora, and they have a daughter, Emma, who is five years old. Jim died on 1 January 2021. On 2 February 2021, Anthony gave Emma €200,000. On 1 March 2021, Alan, Nora's father, gave Emma €100,000.

The gift of €200,000 by Anthony to Emma will be subject to the Group A €335,000 tax-free threshold, as Emma is a minor child of a deceased child (i.e. Jim) of Anthony's.

The gift by Alan to Emma is in the Group B €32,500 tax-free threshold as Alan is Emma's grandparent. Emma is not a minor child of a deceased child of Alan's and therefore the Group A threshold is not applicable.

Benefit taken by a Parent

A parent is a lineal ancestor of their child so, generally, Group B threshold applies to gifts and inheritances taken by a parent from their child unless:

1. the parent takes an inheritance from their child, on the death of that child, and the inheritance is not a limited interest, the applicable threshold is Group A for that inheritance (see **Section 14.2.1**); or
2. the parent takes an inheritance from their child, on the death of that child, and that child had taken a non-exempt gift or inheritance from either parent within five years immediately prior to the death of that child, in which case the inheritance by the parent is **exempt** from CAT (see **Chapter 18, Section 18.4**).

Example 14.3

Tara, a wedding planner, died intestate (i.e. without a will), leaving an estate valued at €500,000. She is survived only by her mother, Colette. As Colette is inheriting absolute ownership of Tara's estate on Tara's death, the Group A threshold applies when assessing Colette's CAT liability.

However, if Colette had made a non-exempt gift to Tara in the five years preceding Tara's death, Colette's inheritance from Tara would be exempt from CAT.

Benefit taken by a Spouse/Civil Partner

Gifts and inheritances taken by a spouse/civil partner from their spouse/civil partner while married are exempt from CAT – so no group threshold is necessary (see **Chapter 18, Section 18.2**).

Favourite Niece/Nephew

Schedule 2 CATCA 2003 provides that, in certain circumstances, a nephew or niece may be deemed to be the child of a disponer and, therefore, qualify for the Group A threshold of €335,000 rather than the Group B threshold of €32,500. The beneficiary must be a child of the disponer's brother or sister or a child of the civil partner of the disponer's brother or sister.

In order to qualify for the Group A threshold in respect of the benefit, the niece/nephew must have:

- **worked substantially on a full-time basis for the disponer for the relevant period** in carrying on, or assisting in carrying on, the trade, business or profession of the disponer and the benefit consists of property which was used in connection with that trade, business or profession, or
- **worked substantially on a full-time basis for a company controlled by the disponer** for the **relevant period** in carrying on, or in assisting in carrying on, the trade, business or profession of the company and the benefit consists of **shares** in that company.

The term "worked substantially on a full-time basis" requires that the beneficiary:

- works **more than 24 hours a week** for the disponer/company at a place where the business, trade or profession is carried on; or
- works **more than 15 hours a week** for the disponer/company at the place where the business, trade or profession is carried and such business, trade or profession is carried on exclusively by the disponer, the disponer's spouse/civil partner and the beneficiary.

The **"relevant period"** means:

- the period of **five years** ending on the date of the disposition; or
- in the case where, at the date of the disposition, an interest in possession is limited to the disponer under the disposition, the period of five years ending on the coming to an end of that interest.

Reasonable periods of annual or sick leave are allowed.

A **"company controlled by the disponer"** means a company that:

- is a **private trading company** (as defined in **Chapter 16, Section 16.2.2**);
- has the **disponer as one of its directors**; and
- is under the **control** of the disponer, or nominees of the disponer.

"Control" generally means holding 50% or more of the nominal value of the shares in a company or more than 50% of the voting share capital.

Example 14.4
June leaves her farm, worth €800,000, to her niece Catherine, who had worked full-time on the farm with her for the last eight years. She also left her shares in Abbey plc worth €50,000. The group threshold in respect of the farm is Group A €335,000, as she has worked on the farm for at least five years and it is an inheritance of a trade asset. The group threshold in respect of the shares is the normal Group B threshold of €32,500.

Surviving Spouse/Civil Partner of a Deceased Person

CATCA 2003 provides a specialised relief that effectively permits the surviving spouse or civil partner of a deceased person to "stand in the shoes of the deceased person" in certain circumstances. The relief applies where:

- at the date of the gift or inheritance,
- the beneficiary is the surviving spouse or civil partner of a deceased person who at the time of their death was of a closer blood relationship to the disponer than the beneficiary.

In these circumstances, for the purposes of calculating the liability, the beneficiary is deemed to take up the same relationship to the disponer as the deceased spouse or civil partner had at the time of death. This can result in the use of a more favourable tax-free threshold for the computation of any liability due.

Example 14.5
Jim died on 28 February 2021 and left €200,000 to his son-in-law, James. James' wife, Ann, (i.e. Jim's daughter), had died some years previously. In these circumstances, James is deemed to stand in Ann's shoes, *vis-à-vis* her blood relationship with her father and, accordingly, the €335,000 group threshold applies. If this rule did not apply, James would be treated as a stranger and a threshold of only €16,250 would apply. If James also received a gift from Ann's aunt, the group threshold would be €32,500 instead of the usual €16,250.

14.2.3 Group Thresholds – Anti-avoidance: Gift Splitting

In the absence of anti-avoidance legislation, the practice of 'connected dispositions' (i.e. gift splitting) could save substantial CAT through the utilisation of more advantageous tax-free thresholds than might otherwise be available if the gift were made directly from the original disponer to the final recipient, as shown in the following example.

Example 14.6

Peter wishes to give his grandson, Mark, €200,000 in January 2021. If the gift is made directly to Mark, the tax-free threshold applicable is only €32,500. However, if Peter were to first gift the €200,000 to his son, John (Mark's father), the tax-free threshold applicable between father and son is €335,000. John could then subsequently gift the €200,000 to Mark without attracting CAT liability.

Section 8 CATCA 2003 is an **anti-avoidance** provision designed to prevent the avoidance of CAT by passing property through one or more intermediaries before vesting ownership in the final recipient, as suggested in **Example 14.6**. Section 8 provides that where a gift is made within three years before or three years after the original gift, then *two gifts* are deemed to have been made by the original disponer as follows:

1. a gift by the original disponer to the first recipient; and
2. a gift by the original disponer to the final recipient.

Both gifts are taxable in the normal way (including if the original disponer dies within two years of the original gift the beneficiaries will be deemed to have taken an inheritance).

Example 14.7

(a) In 2021, Peter gives a gift to his son, John, and John subsequently gives a gift to his son, Mark, in 2022. John and Mark will be assessed to CAT as follows:

- John takes a gift from Peter, his father – Group A threshold.
- Mark is deemed to take a gift from Peter, his grandfather – Group B threshold.

(b) In 2021, John borrows €100,000 from the bank and gifts it to his son, Mark. Subsequently, in 2022, Peter gives a gift of €100,000 to his son, John. John uses the gift to repay his bank loan. John and Mark will be assessed to CAT as follows:

- John takes a gift from Peter, his father – Group A threshold.
- Mark is deemed to take a gift from Peter, his grandfather – Group B threshold.

Section 8 does not apply in the following circumstances:

- Where it can be shown that the original disposition was not made with a view to enabling or facilitating the making of the subsequent disposition or with a view to facilitating the recoupment in any manner of the cost of the disposition to the final recipient.
- Section 8 only applies to gifts, and therefore will not have effect unless the original and subsequent benefits are gifts rather than inheritances, i.e. if the gift splitting occurs as a result of an **intervening death, then the provisions are not invoked**.
- Revenue will not invoke this legislation where a gift is taken by a **married child** of the disponer of a house or site for a house, and the married child has to **transfer the property into the names of that child and their spouse in order to get a mortgage** from a lending institution.

14.3 Aggregation

The aggregate taxable values of all taxable gifts and taxable inheritances taken **on or after 5 December 1991** by the recipient from **all disponers** *within the same group threshold*, are taken into account to determine the amount of CAT payable on the current benefit. This means that in a lifetime, from 5 December 1991 an individual can currently receive taxable gifts and inheritances totaling up to €335,000 from Group A disponers, plus €32,500 from Group B disponers, plus €16,250 from Group C disponers without crystallising a CAT liability.

While all benefits from persons within the one group threshold are aggregated, there is only one group threshold (i.e. tax-free) amount. For example, if benefits are received from a brother, a sister and an aunt, all three benefits are aggregated, but the maximum tax-free group threshold that can be availed of is €32,500, i.e. one cannot get €32,500 tax-free from each person within the same group threshold.

14.4 Basic Computation

CAT payable on a gift or inheritance is calculated as follows:

Step 1: Calculate "**Aggregate A**", which is the aggregate of:

    (i)   the taxable value of the current gift or inheritance; PLUS

    (ii) the taxable value of all previous taxable gifts and inheritances taken from persons within the **same group threshold** on or after **5 December 1991**.

Step 2: Calculate the CAT chargeable on "**Aggregate A**":

    CAT on Aggregate A = (Aggregate A − Group threshold) × 33%

Step 3: Calculate "**Aggregate B**", which is:

    (i)   Aggregate A, i.e. the aggregate taxable value in Step 1; MINUS

    (ii) the taxable value of the current gift or inheritance (i.e. (i) in Step 1. above).

Step 4: Calculate the CAT chargeable on "**Aggregate B**" (i.e. the notional amount of CAT that would arise on the prior benefits if they were received using the current tax rate and group threshold):

    CAT on Aggregate B = (Aggregate B − Group Threshold) × 33%

Step 5: Calculate the **CAT on the current benefit**:

    CAT on current benefit = CAT on Aggregate A − CAT on Aggregate B

It should be noted that where current group threshold exceeds Aggregate B (total prior taxable benefits), the notional tax on prior benefits (i.e. CAT on Aggregate B) will be nil, resulting in the full amount of CAT on Aggregate A being payable. Also, where total prior taxable benefits (Aggregate B) exceed the current group threshold, the CAT on the current taxable benefit will be 33% of the current benefit.

Example 14.8

On 1 February 2021, Mary O'Hagan received an inheritance with a taxable value of €350,000 from her father. Mary had previously received the following benefits:

- gift of €10,000 on 1 December 1989 from her aunt;
- inheritance of €5,000 on 20 December 2005 from her sister;
- gift of €255,000 on 1 June 2006 from her mother;
- gift of €15,000 on 1 November 2007 from her uncle.

What is Mary's CAT liability, if any, on the February 2021 inheritance from her father? (Ignore small gift exemption.)

As Mary is inheriting from a parent, Group A is the relevant threshold. Assess prior benefits for other Group A gifts and inheritances:

- gift of €10,000 on 1 December 1989 from her aunt – pre-5 Dec 1991, not applicable.
- inheritance of €5,000 on 20 December 2005 from her sister – Group B, not applicable.
- gift of €255,000 on 1 June 2006 from her mother – Group A, aggregable.
- gift of €15,000 on 1 November 2007 from her uncle – Group B, not applicable.

Computation

1. Calculate Aggregate A, i.e. total taxable gifts and inheritances taken since 5 December 1991 from persons in the Group A threshold:

Current inheritance from father	€350,000
Gift from mother 2006	€255,000
Total benefits Group A	€605,000

2. Calculate CAT on Aggregate A:

Deduct: Group A threshold	(€335,000)
Taxable	€270,000
CAT @ 33% on Aggregate A	€89,100

3. Calculate Aggregate B, i.e. total taxable gifts and inheritances taken since 5 December 1991 from persons in the Group A threshold excluding the current benefit:

Gift from mother 2006	€255,000

4. Calculate CAT on Aggregate B:

Deduct: Group A threshold	(€335,000)
Taxable	NIL
CAT @ 33% on Aggregate B	NIL

5. Calculate CAT on current benefit:

CAT on Aggregate A	€89,100
Less: CAT on Aggregate B	Nil
CAT on current benefit	€89,100

Example 14.9

On 4 April 2021, Mary Ryan received an inheritance with a taxable value of €60,000 from her uncle. She had received no other gifts or inheritances from any source since 5 December 1991. What is Mary's CAT liability on the inheritance from her uncle?

As she has no previous benefits, there is nothing to aggregate. Therefore, simply calculate CAT on the current benefit.

	€
Taxable value	60,000
Deduct: Group B threshold	(32,500)
	27,500
CAT @ 33%	9,075

Example 14.10

Louise and Ellen are civil partners. On 5 October 2021, Louise's sister Catherine gifts €30,000 to Ellen's daughter, Olivia. Olivia has received no other benefit since 5 December 1991. (Ignore small gift exemption.) What is the CAT liability, if any, on the gift taken by Olivia?

As Olivia is the daughter of Ellen, who is the civil partner of Catherine's sister, Louise, the Group B threshold applies.

As she has no previous benefits, there is nothing to aggregate. Therefore, simply calculate CAT on the current benefit.

	€
Taxable value	30,000
Deduct: Group B threshold	(32,500)
	NIL

As the taxable value is less than the Group B threshold, no liability arises.

Example 14.11

During October 2021 Michael Moran received the following gifts:

1. a gift of a rental property worth €220,000 from his father;
2. a gift of shares worth €30,000 from an aunt; and
3. a gift of €5,000 cash from a cousin.

He had previously received the following benefits:

- an inheritance of investments valued at €200,000 from his mother on 1 June 1991;
- an inheritance of shares valued at €30,000 from an uncle on 6 May 2004;
- an inheritance of a holiday cottage valued at €50,000 from a friend on 11 December 2010.

What is the CAT liability, if any, on the gifts received in 2021 (ignoring the small gift exemption)?

Computation

1. Gift of rental property from father – the only other Group A benefit is the inheritance from his mother, but as this was received before 5 December 1991 it is ignored. Therefore, no aggregation is necessary and the total taxable value of the current gift is €220,000. This is below the Group A threshold of €335,000; therefore, no CAT is payable on this gift.

continued overleaf

2. Gift of shares from aunt:

		€
	Current gift	30,000
	Prior gift from uncle	30,000
	Aggregate A	60,000
	Group threshold B	(32,500)
		27,500
	CAT on Aggregate A @ 33%	9,075
	Prior gift from uncle	30,000
	Group B threshold	(32,500)
		NIL
	CAT on Aggregate B @ 33%	NIL
	CAT on Aggregate A	9,075
	CAT on Aggregate B	NIL
	CAT on shares from aunt*	9,075

* As the threshold exceeds previous taxable benefits CAT due equals CAT on Aggregate A.

3. Gift of cash:

		€
	Current gift	5,000
	Previous gift from friend	50,000
	Aggregate A	55,000
	Group C threshold	(16,250)
		38,750
	CAT on Aggregate A @ 33%	12,787
	Aggregate B, i.e. previous gift from friend	50,000
	Group C threshold	(16,250)
		33,750
	CAT on Aggregate B @ 33%	11,137
	CAT on Aggregate A	12,787
	CAT on Aggregate B	(11,137)
	CAT on cash from cousin**	1,650

** As the threshold is already fully used, €5,000 is taxable at 33%.

4. Total CAT payable on gifts taken during 2021:

		€
	Rental property from father	NIL
	Shares from aunt	9,075
	Cash from cousin	1,650

We will see later that these liabilities are payable by 31 October 2022 as the valuation date, in this case the date of the gift, is in October 2021.

Example 14.12
Frank and Jonathon are civil partners. On 15 April 2021, Frank died. Under the terms of his will he left property worth €500,000 to Jonathon, cash of €100,000 to his daughter, Alexa, and cash of €70,000 to Jonathon's son, Ryan. None of the beneficiaries has received a gift or inheritance since 5 December 1991, except for Ryan, who received a gift of €270,000 from his mother in May 2019.

What is the CAT liability, if any, of each beneficiary on the inheritances taken in 2021? (Ignore small gift exemption.)

Computation
As Jonathon is Frank's civil partner, he is exempt from CAT on the benefit of €500,000 which he receives from Frank.

As Alexa is Frank's daughter, the Group A threshold of €335,000 applies. As this is the first benefit she has received in Group A and the taxable value is less than the threshold, there is no tax payable on the €100,000 she receives.

As Ryan is the son of Frank's civil partner Jonathon, the Group A threshold applies. The prior gift of €270,000 from his mother must be aggregated:

	€
Current inheritance	70,000
Previous gift from mother	270,000
Aggregate A	340,000
Group A threshold	(335,000)
	5,000
CAT on Aggregate A @ 33%	1,650
CAT on Aggregate B*	NIL
CAT on cash from Frank	1,650

* Previous benefit below group threshold of €335,000.

Questions

Review Questions
(See Suggested Solutions to Review Questions at the end of this textbook.)

Question 14.1

Identify the **group threshold amounts** applicable to the following gifts/inheritances in 2021:

1. Gift of investment property by father to daughter.
2. Gift of shares by son to father.
3. Gift of 25% of shares in a private trading company by uncle to nephew. Remaining 75% of shares owned by unrelated parties. Nephew has worked for company on a full-time basis for last 10 years.
4. Gift of farmland by uncle to nephew. Nephew has worked on a full-time basis for uncle farming this land for previous 10 years.
5. Gift of shares by father-in-law to daughter-in-law, son still alive.
6. Gift of shares by grandfather to 19-year-old grandson, grandson's father is deceased.
7. Gift of cash from cousin.
8. Gift of cash from uncle to niece.
9. Gift of cash from nephew to uncle.

10. Gift of 75% of shares in trading company by aunt to niece. Remaining 25% of shares owned by two unrelated parties. Niece has worked for company on a full-time basis for last 10 years. Aunt is a director in the company.
11. Gift of farmland to sister's civil partner's son who had worked on a part-time basis farming the land for the previous 10 years.
12. Gift of cash by stepfather to stepchild.
13. Gift of investment property by grandfather to grandson's wife. Grandson is deceased.
14. Gift of 100% of shares in trading company by uncle to nephew. Nephew has worked for company on a full-time basis for previous four years.
15. An inheritance of cash from mother's civil partner.
16. Gift of shares to brother's wife. Brother is deceased.
17. Gift of antique vase by granddaughter to grandmother.
18. Gift of cash to adopted child of brother.
19. Gift of farmland to wife's nephew. Nephew has been working on a full-time basis farming the land for the previous 10 years.
20. Gift of cash by Tom to Alannah. Alannah, aged 17, is Tom's civil partner's son's civil partner's child. Tom's civil partner's son died tragically six months before the gift from Tom to Alannah.

Question 14.2

During his lifetime, Peter made the following gifts, net of small gift exemption, to his son, Edward:

(a) on 17 June 1990 he gifted €300,000 to Edward; and
(b) on 8 June 2003 he gifted €100,000 to Edward.

On 11 April 2021, Peter died and left his estate, valued at €350,000, to Edward.

The only other gifts or inheritances that Edward had received were an inheritance of €30,000 on the death of his mother on 15 May 2018 and of €40,000 on the death of his uncle Harry on 13 January 2019. All gifts are net of small gift exemption.

Requirement
Compute the CAT payable by Edward on the inheritance of €350,000 on the death of his father.

Territorial Scope

15.1 Introduction

The territorial scope of CAT must clearly be limited, as is the case for other taxes, such as income tax and CGT. CATCA 2003 therefore sets out a number of rules which determine whether or not a particular gift or inheritance is within the scope of CATCA 2003, i.e. whether a particular gift is a **"taxable gift"** or whether a particular inheritance is a **"taxable inheritance"**. A liability may not necessarily result even where these territorial rules are satisfied. For example, the particular gift or inheritance may be covered by a tax-free threshold or may be exempt altogether.

15.2 Taxable Gifts and Inheritances

15.2.1 Irish Property – Always Taxable

A benefit, i.e. a gift or inheritance, is a taxable benefit to the extent that it, or a portion of it, consists of property that is situated in the State (i.e. Republic of Ireland) at the date of the gift/inheritance. The law determining the location of assets is outlined in **Chapter 2, Section 2.6**.

15.2.2 Foreign Property – General Rule

The current rules apply to benefits where the date of the disposition is on or after 1 December 1999. Before this date, one looked at the domicile of the disponer.

Foreign property is taxable if:

- the disponer is resident or ordinarily resident in the State in the year of assessment in which the disposition is made; or
- the beneficiary is resident or ordinarily resident in the State in the year of assessment in which the benefit falls.

The income tax rules for determining residence, ordinary residence and domicile apply (see **Chapter 2**). However, this general rule would mean that foreign-domiciled persons who were only in Ireland for a short time could trigger an Irish CAT liability. To ensure that this does not happen, there is a special five-year rule for foreign-domiciled persons.

15.2.3 Foreign Property – Foreign-domiciled Persons

For CAT purposes, foreign-domiciled persons are not treated as resident or ordinarily resident on a date unless:

- the date occurs on or after 1 December 2004;
- the person has been resident in the State for **five consecutive years of assessment immediately preceding the year of assessment in which that date falls**; *and*
- the person is either **resident or ordinarily resident** in the State on that date.

The date is:

- the date of the disposition in the case of the disponer;
- the date of the gift or the inheritance in the case of the beneficiary.

Example 15.1
On 1 April 2021, Joe gives Ray one acre of land in Dublin. As this is Irish property it is liable to CAT. It does not matter where either of them is domiciled, resident and ordinarily resident.

Example 15.2
On 31 August 2021, Mary, who is domiciled, resident and ordinarily resident in Ireland, gifts her villa in Spain to her friend Manuel, who is Spanish and lives in Spain. As Mary is Irish resident (or ordinarily resident) and domiciled, the gift is subject to Irish CAT, i.e. Manuel must pay CAT.

Example 15.3
On 31 August 2021, Martin, who is domiciled, resident and ordinarily resident in Germany, gifts his shares in a German company to his cousin Joe, who is domiciled, resident and ordinarily resident in Ireland. As Joe is Irish resident (or ordinarily resident) and domiciled, the gift is subject to Irish CAT, i.e. Joe must pay CAT.

Example 15.4
On 31 August 2021, Peter, who is domiciled, resident and ordinarily resident in France, gifts his shares in a US company to his brother Ivan, who moved to Ireland in early 2017. Ivan is French domiciled, but resident and ordinarily resident in Ireland under the income tax rules for 2021. However, as Ivan is foreign domiciled, he is only liable on foreign property if he has been resident in Ireland for the five tax years preceding the year in which he receives the gift, i.e. 2021. As he has not been so resident, he is not liable to Irish CAT.

Example 15.5

On 31 October 2021, Joey, who is domiciled, resident and ordinarily resident in Italy, gifts his house in Rome to his brother Bart, who moved to Ireland in 2012. Bart is Italian domiciled, but resident and ordinarily resident in Ireland under the income tax rules. As Bart is foreign domiciled, he is only liable on foreign property if he has been resident in Ireland for the five tax years preceding the year in which he receives the gift, i.e. 2021. As he has been so resident, he is liable to Irish CAT on the gift of the house in Rome.

(The rules regarding benefits where the date of the disposition is before 1 December 1999 are beyond the scope of this textbook. The above definitions, and those that follow in later chapters, exclude rules regarding discretionary trusts, which are also beyond the scope of this textbook.)

Questions

Review Questions

(See Suggested Solutions to Review Questions at the end of this textbook.)

Question 15.1

A gift or inheritance of property situated in the State is within the charge to Irish CAT regardless of the domicile/residence position of the disponer or the donee/successor.

Requirement

Outline the general rules which determine where property is situated.

Question 15.2

The following gifts/inheritances were taken during the year ended 31 December 2021:

1. Donal, an Irish domiciled and resident individual, died on 19 April 2021. He left all his assets, consisting of Irish and UK property, to his son Brendan, also Irish domiciled and resident.
2. Gordon, an Irish domiciled and UK resident person, died on 11 July 2021. He left shares in a UK trading company to his Irish resident and domiciled nephew, Dermot.
3. Jonathan, a UK domiciled and resident person, died on 15 August 2021 and left land in Cork to his son John, also UK domiciled and resident.
4. Noel, a UK domiciled and resident person, died on 16 September 2021 and left a house in the UK and €20,000 in a Sterling bank account in London to his son, Nevin, also UK domiciled but resident in Ireland since 2013.
5. Michael, an Irish domiciled and resident individual, died on 1 February 2021. He left all his assets equally to his two children, David and Jane. His assets consisted of a house in Clare and €30,000 in an Irish bank account. David and Jane are both Irish domiciled; however, while David is also Irish resident, Jane has been resident in the UK for many years.
6. On 23 August 2021, Maurice, an Irish domiciled and UK resident person, gave shares valued at €10,000 in various UK companies to his nephew Darren, also Irish domiciled and UK resident. Maurice has been living in the UK since 2002. Darren only moved to the UK in June 2020. Prior to moving to the UK, Darren had always lived in Cork.

7. Jim, an Irish domiciled and resident individual, gave his daughter Brid, also Irish domiciled and resident, a rental property in the UK by deed dated 12 December 2021.

8. Jean, an individual domiciled in France but resident in Ireland since 2012, gifted her daughter Amelie, also domiciled in France and resident in Ireland since 2012 except for the year 2019 when she was non-resident, shares in an Irish trading company and shares in a French trading company on 31 December 2021.

Requirement

(a) Outline the rules for determining whether a gift or inheritance taken during the year ended 31 December 2021 is a taxable gift or inheritance.

(b) For each gift or inheritance outlined above, state whether the gift/inheritance is a taxable gift/inheritance, giving reasons for your answer.

Question 15.3

Calculate the CAT payable in respect of the gift/inheritance taken in 2021 in each of the following cases:

(a) Michael, who is Irish domiciled and resident, gave his daughter, also Irish resident and domiciled, a cash gift of €40,000 on 1 January 2021. His daughter had previously received the following benefits:

    (i) a house in Sligo valued at €80,000 inherited from her grandmother, also Irish domiciled and resident, in June 2009; and

    (ii) jewellery valued at €20,000 inherited on the death of her mother, also Irish domiciled and resident, in August 2011.

(b) Bridget, who is domiciled in the State but resident in the USA, inherited a property in the UK valued at €120,000 from an uncle, who is Irish domiciled and resident, on his death in October 2021. Bridget had previously received the following benefits:

    (i) shares in an Irish quoted company valued at €50,000 inherited on the death of an aunt, US domiciled and resident, in March 2008;

    (ii) a gift of a car valued at €15,000 from a cousin, Irish domiciled and resident, in January 2009; and

    (iii) €25,000 in an Irish bank account inherited on the death of Bridget's grandmother, Irish domiciled and resident, in September 1990.

Taxable Value

16.1 General Principles

We have seen that CAT is levied on the **taxable value** of the gift or inheritance concerned. The basic steps involved may be illustrated as follows:

	€
Market value	X
Less: liabilities, costs and expenses payable out of the taxable benefit	(X)
Incumbrance-free value	X
Less: market value of consideration paid by the beneficiary	(X)
Taxable Value	X

We will now examine in detail the meaning of the above terms.

16.2 Market Value

CATCA 2003 contains specific provisions setting out the method by which the market value of different types of property is to be computed.

16.2.1 Market Value – General Rule

The general rule is that the market value of any property is to be the price that, in the opinion of the Revenue Commissioners, the property would fetch if sold on the open market, **on the valuation date**, in such manner and subject to such conditions as might reasonably be expected to obtain for the vendor the best price for the property.

CATCA 2003 sets out the general market value rule and specifically states that the Revenue Commissioners will not make any reduction in the estimate of market value on the grounds that the whole property is to be placed on the market at the same time.

Revenue has the power to authorise the inspection of property by any person it considers fit at all reasonable times. If Revenue requires a professional valuation, then the cost of such valuation is to be paid for by Revenue.

For the purposes of estimating the market value of unquoted shares or securities if sold on the open market, it is to be assumed that there is available to any prospective purchaser of the shares or securities all the information a prudent prospective purchaser might reasonably require if they were proposing to buy them from a willing vendor at arm's length.

The meaning of the term **valuation date** is dealt with at **Section 16.3**.

16.2.2 Market Value of Shares in Certain Private Companies

A **private company** is defined to mean a body corporate (wherever incorporated) that:

1. is under the control of not more than five persons; and
2. is not a quoted company which is excluded from the corporation tax close company rules (as adjusted for CAT purposes to counter tax avoidance).

Therefore most companies in Ireland, particularly family-owned companies, are covered by the definition.

CATCA 2003 provides that the market value of each share in a private company that is (after the taking of the gift or inheritance), on the date of the gift or inheritance, a **company controlled by the beneficiary** (see **Section 16.6.2** for definition) is to be computed on a market value basis, i.e. each share is valued as if it formed an apportioned part of the market value of the shares in that company. Such apportionment, as between shares of a particular class, is by reference to nominal amount and, as between different classes of shares, is with due regard to the rights attaching to each of the different classes.

16.2.3 Valuation of Annuities

CATCA 2003 contains special provisions for calculating the value of a gift or inheritance of an annuity. The method of valuation depends on whether or not the annuity is charged/secured on any property. These are dealt with separately in detail in **Chapter 17**.

16.2.4 Market Value of a Limited Interest

CATCA 2003 contains specific provision for the valuation of limited interests (e.g. a house for life). These are dealt with separately in detail in **Chapter 17**.

16.2.5 *Valuation of Free Use of Property*

A charge to CAT arises where a person has the use and enjoyment of property either for no consideration or for less than full consideration. If the "free" use is ongoing, the benefit is deemed to be taken on 31 December each year. The benefit taken is deemed to be the difference between the consideration given by the person for the use, occupation or enjoyment of the property and the best price obtainable in the open market for such use, occupation or enjoyment. If the free use is of land or a house, the best price obtainable would be the market rent payable for such a property. If the free use is of cash, for example an interest-free loan, the best price obtainable would be the income from the investment of such cash, i.e. the bank deposit rate applicable to such sum and not the rate which a bank might apply to a loan. The following examples explain how the benefit is calculated.

Example 16.1 Market value of benefit in "free" use case involving a loan
Joe gives an interest-free loan of €100,000 to his nephew, John, on 1 January. The **bank deposit rate of interest is, say, 2%**. John is deemed to take a gift of €2,000 on 31 December. He is also deemed to take a gift each year, on 31 December, until the loan is repaid and each such deemed gift is taken into account for aggregation purposes. If the loan is repaid during the year, the date of the deemed gift for that year is the date of repayment. If the loan was repaid after six months, the value of the gift for that year would be €1,000.

Example 16.2 Market value of benefit in "free" use case involving accommodation
Anne gives the use of her house, worth €200,000, to her cousin, Colette. The annual market rent is €15,000. Colette pays Anne €5,000 per annum. Colette is deemed to take a gift of €10,000 on 31 December each year that she has the use of the house and each deemed gift is taken into account for aggregation purposes.

16.3 Valuation Date

16.3.1 *Importance of Valuation Date*

The valuation date is very important for a number of reasons:

- It is the market value of the gift/inheritance at the valuation date that is assessed to CAT.
- It is the date used to determine when the CAT is paid and the return filed. If the valuation date is from 1 January to 31 August 2021, CAT is payable and the return must be filed on or before 31 October 2021. If the valuation date is from 1 September to 31 December 2021, CAT is payable and the return must be filed on or before 31 October 2022. Where a return is filed on ROS (the Revenue Online Service) for the period ending 31 August 2021, the filing date is extended to 17 November 2021.
- It is the date used to determine whether certain conditions are fulfilled for agricultural relief (**Section 16.5**) and business relief (**Section 16.6**).

For example, if a parent is considering gifting shares to a child on 1 April 2021 but delays actually making the gift for six months until 1 October 2021, then the valuation date is 1 October 2021. If the shares increase in value by, say, 20% during that period, then the child will bear a 20% higher market value and taxable value and probably an increased CAT liability. The due date for the payment of the CAT would be 31 October 2022, rather than 31 October 2021.

16.3.2 *Valuation Date of a Taxable Gift*

CATCA 2003 sets out the rules for determining the valuation date. The valuation date is normally the **date of the gift**. The valuation date in relation to a **gift which subsequently becomes an inheritance** as a result of the death of the disponer within two years of the disposition is specifically deemed to remain the **date of the gift**.

16.3.3 *Valuation Date of a Taxable Inheritance*

The determination of the valuation date for inheritances is complex. The following are the main rules:

1. For cases not covered by 2. below, the valuation date of a taxable inheritance will be the **earliest** of the following dates:

    (a) the earliest date on which any person is **entitled** to retain the subject matter of the inheritance for the benefit of the successor; or
    (b) the date on which the subject matter of the inheritance **is** actually retained; or
    (c) the date of **actual delivery/payment** of the inheritance to the successor.

2. The valuation date for a gift which has become an inheritance as a result of the disponer dying within two years of the date of the disposition is deemed to be the date of the gift.

Generally speaking, the residue of an estate cannot be regarded as retained for the benefit of the beneficiary until the estate is finally administered. This is, of course, subject to the possibility of interim payments having been made to the legatee in question.

The basic principle to be applied therefore is **that the valuation date will be the date of delivery or payment** of the subject matter of the inheritance to the beneficiary, or the date of retainer on their behalf, whichever is the earliest.

The valuation date for assets passing under a will or intestacy is usually the date on which the Grant of Representation issues from the Probate Office or District Probate Registry. (The Grant of Representation is the document which allows the people distributing the assets to the beneficiaries to do so.) If assets are passing outside of the will or intestacy, the valuation date will normally be the deceased's date of death.

There can be several valuation dates where multiple benefits are taken from the same estate.

Examples of when date of death is the valuation date include where the beneficiary is in occupation of the property and where there is joint ownership of the property.

Litigation and family disputes may cause the valuation date to be put back to a later time.

Example 16.3

Jim dies in 2021. He bequeaths his farm to his wife, who lives on the farm with him, a cash legacy to his nephew and the residue of his estate to his son for life with the remainder to his grandson. The valuation dates would be as follows:

(i)   the date of death in the case of the inheritance taken by the wife, as this is probably the earliest date on which the personal representatives are entitled to retain the farm for the benefit of his wife;
(ii) the valuation date in the case of a cash legacy would be the date the personal representative actually paid the legacy to the nephew;
(iii) his son has a life interest in the residue of the estate and the valuation date in this case would be the date of retention of the residue for him by the personal representative. This will be sometime after the issue of the grant of probate when the personal representatives have collected the assets and the liabilities of the estate have been established, but not necessarily paid;
(iv) the grandson's valuation date would probably be the date of the son's death, as the grandson would become beneficially entitled in possession to the benefit at that time.

> **Example 16.4**
>
> On 1 November 2021, Ian, by deed, transfers property to trustees on trust for Brian for life with remainder to Conor absolutely. On creation of the trust, Brian would immediately become beneficially entitled to his benefit and the date of the gift would therefore be 1 November 2021. The valuation date in respect of this gift would be the same date.
>
> The date of Conor's inheritance is the date of Brian's death, as that is the date when Conor becomes beneficially entitled in possession to the benefit. Again, the valuation date is probably the same date.

It is clear from CATCA 2003 that different parts of the same inheritance may have different valuation dates, e.g. if interim payments are made out of a deceased's estate prior to the date of final retainer, the valuation date of each interim payment will be the date on which the advances are actually paid.

The Revenue Commissioners are entitled to determine the valuation date for a particular inheritance, but this determination is subject to an appeal by the taxpayer if they wish.

Appendix 16.1 contains a summary of the definitions of the date of the disposition, date of the gift/inheritance and the valuation date.

16.4 Deduction for Liabilities, Costs, Expenses and Consideration

We have seen that the market value of the taxable benefit is reduced by any liabilities, costs and expenses that are properly payable out of the taxable gift or taxable inheritance in order to arrive at what is known as the incumbrance-free value.

Any legal or other cost associated with the transfer of property will normally fall under this heading, e.g. solicitors' fees or stamp duty.

The most common examples of expenses that are deductible in calculating CAT are debts owed by the deceased at the date of death, funeral expenses and costs of administering the estate.

Where the property transferred is charged with the payment of a liability, then that liability is properly deductible under this heading also in arriving at the incumbrance-free value.

> **Example 16.5**
>
> Ann transfers a house worth €500,000 to Barbara, subject to a mortgage charged on the house on which there is an outstanding amount due of €150,000. In this case the incumbrance-free value is €500,000 less €150,000, i.e. €350,000. This assumes, of course, that Barbara takes over the property subject to the mortgage. If Barbara also paid stamp duty and solicitor's costs in connection with the transfer, such expenses would also be deducted.

> **Example 16.6**
>
> Joe dies and leaves a business worth €5,000,000 to his son, Ray. The executor of Joe's will paid legal expenses of €50,000. These legal expenses are a deductible expense in calculating the taxable value of the benefit taken by Ray, i.e. €5,000,000 – €50,000 = €4,950,000.

16.4.1 Consideration Paid by Donee/Successor

CATCA 2003 permits the incumbrance-free value of the property transferred to be reduced by any "bona fide consideration in money or monies worth paid by the donee or successor" in computing the taxable value of the gift or inheritance.

Consideration is the last deduction to be made in arriving at the taxable value and is deductible in effect from the value of the interest taken by the donee, whether absolute or limited. The treatment of limited interest will be dealt with separately (**Chapter 17**).

CATCA 2003 particularly mentions that consideration will *include*:

1. Any liability of the disponer which the beneficiary undertakes to discharge as their own **personal** liability.
2. Any other liability to which the gift or inheritance is subject under the terms of the disposition under which it is paid. For example, Claire transfers property to Damien on condition that Damien pays €1,000 to Emer. The €1,000 paid by Damien to Emer would represent consideration to be deducted from the incumbrance-free value of the property taken from Claire in calculating the final taxable value.

Consideration paid by a beneficiary may take many forms:

- a part payment;
- an annuity payable to the disponer (**Chapter 17**);
- a CGT liability of the disponer arising out of the disposal, which the donee agrees to pay.

16.4.2 Deductions Specifically Prohibited in Arriving at Taxable Values

Set out below are the main deductions not allowable in arriving at taxable values.

1. Contingent liabilities: where the payment of a liability is contingent upon the happening of some future event, no deduction is permitted. If the contingent liability eventually becomes payable by the donee/successor, then an adjustment is allowed.
2. Liabilities, costs, etc. for which reimbursement can be obtained.
3. The tax, penalties or interest payable under CATCA 2003 and any costs of raising money to pay those liabilities.
4. Liabilities connected with exempt assets cannot be used to reduce the taxable value of non-exempt property.

16.5 Agricultural Relief

Provided certain conditions are fulfilled, section 89 CATCA 2003 permits the market value of specified "**agricultural property**" to be **reduced by 90%** in computing the taxable value of the gift/inheritance taken by a "**farmer**".

Example 16.7
Joe received a gift of a farm, livestock and machinery worth €1 million. The value for CAT purposes is calculated as follows:

	€
Market value of agricultural property	1,000,000
Agricultural relief (90%)	(900,000)
Agricultural value	100,000

The relief was lower in the past. Previous rules are not covered in this textbook.

16.5.1 Calculation of Taxable Value where there is Agricultural Relief

The calculation of taxable value where there is agricultural relief is as follows:

Market value	X
less: agricultural relief (90%)	(X)
Agricultural value	X
less	
Proportion of liabilities, costs and expenses	(X)
equals	
Incumbrance-free value	X
less	
Proportion of consideration	(X)
equals	
Taxable value	X

16.5.2 Definitions

"**Agricultural property**" is defined as:

- agricultural land, pasture and woodlands situated in the EU or the UK;
- crops, trees and underwood growing on such land;
- such farm buildings, farm houses, and mansion houses (together with the lands occupied therewith) as are of a character appropriate to the agricultural property;
- farm machinery, livestock and bloodstock thereon;
- a payment entitlement under the EU Basic Payment Scheme to a farmer.

To qualify for the relief, the gift/inheritance must be agricultural property at the date of the gift/inheritance *and* at the valuation date.

The term "**agricultural value**" refers to the **market value of the agricultural property as reduced by 90%**.

"**Farmer**"

To qualify for the relief, the beneficiary must qualify as a "farmer" on the valuation date. For gifts or inheritances taken on or after 1 January 2015, there are two tests to be satisfied: an "asset test" and an "activity test".

Asset Test

A "**farmer**" is defined as a beneficiary who is, **on the valuation date and after taking the gift or inheritance**, an individual in respect of whom **not less than 80% of the market value** of the property to which they are beneficially entitled in possession is represented by the market value of property in the EU or the UK which consists of **agricultural property** (as defined above). The gross value of all property is used for the purposes of the 80% test, i.e. no deduction is made for mortgages, etc. except **borrowings on an off-farm principal private residence are deductible for the purpose of the 80% test** provided that the borrowings have been used to purchase, repair or improve that residence.

Activity Test

In this situation, the beneficiary must:

(a) farm the agricultural property for a period of not less than six years commencing on the valuation date; or

(b) lease the agricultural property to a tenant who farms the land for a period of not less than six years commencing on the valuation date.

In addition, the beneficiary (or the lessee, where relevant) must:

(c) have one of the agricultural qualifications set out in the legislation; or

(d) farm agricultural property, including the agricultural property, for not less than 50% of their normal working time.

Revenue will accept working 20 hours per week on average as satisfying the condition of farming for not less than 50% of their normal working time. The agricultural property must also be farmed on a commercial basis and with a view to the realisation of profits.

(Note: there is a stamp duty relief called consanguinity relief. The same conditions for this CAT agricultural relief also apply to stamp duty consanguinity relief (see **Chapter 11, Section 11.2.2**), namely: farming the land or leasing it to someone who farms it for six years, the person having a farming qualification or farming the land for at least 50% of their time and doing so on a commercial basis. However, the asset test applies for CAT relief only. Also, for the stamp duty relief to apply, the transferor must be related to the transferee).

16.5.3 Computation of Relief

In the computation of taxable value, the market value of the agricultural property comprised in the gift or inheritance is reduced to its agricultural value.

Example 16.8: Gift of agricultural property

John gives the following to his daughter, Mary, who has no other assets and who intends to farm the land on a full-time basis for at least six years:

	€
Farmland	300,000
Woodland	100,000
Farm buildings	50,000
Farm machinery	20,000
Bloodstock	30,000
Total	500,000

If there were no agricultural relief, the full gift would be taxable, i.e. taxable value of €500,000. The relief would not be due, for example, if she had other assets and could not satisfy the 80% test or if the land is not farmed.

She is a "farmer" as at least 80% of her assets (in this case, 100%) are agricultural assets and she intends to farm the land. Therefore, agricultural relief is due and the taxable value is reduced. The agricultural value is calculated as follows:

	€
Market value of agricultural property	500,000
Relief @ 90%	(450,000)
Agricultural value	50,000

Example 16.9

Assume the same facts as in **Example 16.8** except that Mary has other assets, as follows:

	€
Bank deposit account	10,000
Shares	20,000
Principal private residence (PPR)	300,000
Mortgage to buy PPR	250,000

Gross market value of all Mary's assets (less mortgage re off-farm PPR) is €580,000, i.e. €500,000 + €10,000 + €20,000 + €300,000 − €250,000.

Gross value of agricultural assets is €500,000.

Is Mary a farmer? $\dfrac{€500,000}{€580,000} = 86\%$

Yes, Mary is a farmer as she satisfies the asset and activity tests. So, agricultural relief is due and the taxable value is reduced as follows:

	€
Market value of agricultural property	500,000
Relief @ 90%	(450,000)
Agricultural value	50,000

Example 16.10: **Inheritance of agricultural property**

Jack, who has no other assets, inherits the following from his aunt:

	€
Farmland and buildings	200,000
Crops growing on the land	30,000
Livestock and machinery	20,000
Total	250,000

He intends to farm the land for not less than six years from the valuation date.

If there were no agricultural relief, the full inheritance would be taxable, i.e. taxable value of €250,000.

Due to agricultural relief, the taxable value is reduced. The agricultural value is calculated as follows:

	€
Market value of agricultural property	250,000
Relief @ 90%	(225,000)
Agricultural value	25,000

Example 16.11: **Client may have given incorrect information**

If, in **Example 16.10**, you deal with Jack's tax affairs, you know that when you filed his last return on his behalf he owned property. However, he has stated that he does not have any property in his recent correspondence to your manager.

You should advise your manager of the fact that his last tax return showed that Jack had property. Your manager can raise this with Jack to establish whether there was some other explanation, such as having sold the property to pay off debt or whether there was an error made by Jack.

16.5.4 Computation of Relief: Restriction of Deductions

CATCA 2003 also provides that the **allowance for debts, incumbrances and consideration connected with the agricultural property** that has been artificially reduced in value must be **proportionately reduced** to ensure that the final deduction is proportionate to the agricultural value of the property *vis-à-vis* its market value.

Example 16.12

Jim gives agricultural land worth €600,000 to John (who qualifies as a "farmer"). The lands are charged with a mortgage of €100,000. John is required by Jim, in consideration for the transfer, to give Stewart €50,000.

Computation of Taxable Value

	€
Market value of agricultural property, i.e. lands	600,000
Less: agricultural relief @ 90%	(540,000)
"Agricultural value"	60,000
Less: mortgage charged on land (as restricted):	
€100,000 × agricultural value/market value (i.e. 10%)	
€100,000 × $\dfrac{60,000}{600,000}$	(10,000)
Incumbrance-free value	50,000
Less: consideration (as restricted):	
€50,000 × $\dfrac{60,000}{600,000}$ (i.e. 10%)	(5,000)
Taxable value	45,000

Example 16.13

Colin died leaving agricultural land worth €100,000 to Desmond (who qualifies as a farmer). The executors of Colin's will incur legal expenses of €1,400.

Computation of Taxable Value

	€
Market value of agricultural property	100,000
Less: agricultural relief @ 90%	(90,000)
Agricultural value	10,000
Less: legal expenses €1,400 × $\dfrac{10,000}{100,000}$	(140)
Taxable value	9,860

Computation where Agricultural Property and Other Property are Involved

Where the gift/inheritance comprises both agricultural and non-agricultural property, then the taxable value of each must be computed separately. This is because:

- any expenses, etc. related to agricultural property will only be 10% allowable;
- any expenses, etc. related to non-agricultural property will be fully allowable; and
- any expenses, etc. related to both agricultural and non-agricultural properties will have to be apportioned between the two, and then allowed to the extent of 10% for the agricultural one and fully for the non-agricultural.

Example 16.14

Michael transfers the following assets to his brother, Sean:

	Market Value
	€
Agricultural land	1,200,000
Shares	100,000
Total value	1,300,000

Sean, in consideration of the gift, has paid €39,000 to Michael's nephew, Jim.

Sean, who has been a salesman, intends to become a farmer. His only asset is his private residence, which is worth €160,000 (mortgage outstanding of €100,000 for the purchase of the residence).

Legal fees and other costs of the transfer amount to €13,000 and are payable out of the gift.

Computation

Is Sean a "farmer"?

Yes, as he satisfies the activity test. After accepting Michael's gift he also satisfies the asset test, i.e. more than 80% of his **gross assets** comprise agricultural property, bloodstock and farm machinery, i.e.

$$\frac{€1,200,000}{€1,360,000^*} \times 100 = 88\%$$

* €1,300,000 + €160,000 − €100,000

(a) Computation of Taxable Value of Agricultural Property

	€
Market value	1,200,000
Less: Relief: €1,200,000 @ 90%	(1,080,000)
Agricultural value	120,000

Less: Liabilities, costs, etc.
    Legal (relating to total property transferred)
    Portion applicable to agricultural property only:

$$€13,000 \times \frac{€1,200,000}{€1,300,000} \qquad €12,000$$

    Restricted for agricultural value, i.e. allow
      €12,000 @ 10% (1,200)

Incumbrance-free value	118,800

Less: consideration (relates to total property)
    Portion applicable to agricultural property:

$$€39,000 \times \frac{€1,200,000}{€1,300,000} \qquad €36,000$$

Allowable 10%	(3,600)
Taxable value of agricultural property	115,200

(b) Computation of Taxable Value of Non-agricultural Property

	€
Market value	100,000
Less: Liabilities, costs, etc.	
Legal (balance €13,000 − €12,000)	(1,000)
Incumbrance-free value	99,000

continued overleaf

Less: Consideration:		
Balance €39,000 − €36,000		(3,000)
Taxable value of non-agricultural property		96,000
(c) Computation of Total Taxable Value of Property		
Taxable value of agricultural property		115,200
Taxable value of non-agricultural property		96,000
Total		211,200

Note: Sean must farm the land for not less than six years from the valuation date.

16.5.5 Other Matters

1. If a taxable gift/inheritance is taken by a beneficiary subject to the **condition that it is to be invested in agricultural property** and this condition is complied with **within two years** of the date of the benefit, then the benefit is deemed to be agricultural property. Therefore, the individual will initially pay the CAT but get a refund of any overpaid CAT, based on availing of agricultural relief. The six-year period from which the property must be farmed runs from the date the beneficiary invests in the agricultural property.
2. In the case of agricultural property which consists of **trees or underwood**, it is **not necessary for the beneficiary to satisfy the "farmer test"**.
3. Agricultural relief of 90% can be claimed in respect of **all** qualifying gifts and inheritances, i.e. there is no limit on the relief.
4. If an individual does not qualify for agricultural relief (e.g. does not satisfy the test that 80% of assets are agricultural property), the individual **may qualify for business relief** (see **Section 16.6**). The differences between agricultural relief and business relief are set out in **Appendix 16.2**.
5. The farmhouse or farm buildings qualify for agricultural relief when disposed of with the farmland. If the farmhouse or farm buildings are not received at the same time as the farmland, they will not qualify as agricultural property and therefore agricultural relief will not be due. For example, farmland, excluding the farmhouse, is given to a son. One year later the farmhouse is given to the same son. While the gift of the farmland may qualify, the gift of the farmhouse cannot qualify for agricultural relief. If the farmhouse had transferred at the same time, it would have qualified as agricultural property and agricultural relief would have been available, assuming the son is a "farmer" for CAT purposes.

Ranking of Agricultural and Business Relief
An individual does not have the option of claiming either agricultural or business relief – agricultural relief applies if the conditions are satisfied.

16.5.6 Clawback of Relief

Agricultural relief which was previously applied will be recaptured if the agricultural property (other than crops, trees or underwood), or part of it, **is disposed** of or compulsorily acquired within six years from the date of the gift or inheritance, *and* **not replaced by other agricultural property**:

- within a year in the case of a sale; or
- within six years in the case of a compulsory acquisition.

The reinvestment does not have to be in the same type of agricultural property.

This clawback **does not apply where the beneficiary dies** before the property is sold or compulsorily acquired.

If there is **full reinvestment** of proceeds, there is **no clawback**. If there is **no reinvestment** of proceeds, there is **full clawback**. If a proportion of the proceeds are reinvested, only a proportion of the relief is clawed back.

Example 16.15

Joe inherited a farm, with a market value of €1,000,000 on the valuation date. He qualified for agricultural relief and therefore the taxable value of the inheritance was €100,000. Joe paid CAT at the then rate of 33% on the inheritance as his tax-free threshold was fully utilised. Two years later, Joe sold the farm for €1,400,000. He reinvested none of the proceeds. What is the CAT due as a result?

The CAT payable on clawback is calculated as follows:

	€
Original relief claimed is clawed back	900,000
Additional CAT payable (at the rate that prevailed when the inheritance was received) (€900,000 @ 33%)	297,000

16.5.7 Ceasing to Farm Land within Six Years

If within six years of qualifying for agricultural relief, the beneficiary or lessee ceases to satisfy the activity test due to ceasing to farm the land or ceasing to lease it to a person who farms the land (otherwise than on the death of the beneficiary or lessee), then the benefit is treated as not being agricultural land. For example, the individual takes up full-time 'off the farm' employment and no longer spends at least 20 hours a week farming the land. Agricultural relief is clawed back and CAT is payable accordingly.

16.6 Business Relief

Provided certain conditions are fulfilled, sections 90–101 CATCA 2003 permit the taxable value of any "relevant business property" to be **reduced by 90%** in computing the taxable value of the gift/ inheritance taken.

In the case of sole traders and partnerships, the relief applies to the value of the net assets of the business that are used in the course of its qualifying business activities. In the case of companies, the relief applies to that proportion of the value of the shares of the company derived from qualifying business activities. Assets that are not used for the purposes of a qualifying business activity are excluded.

16.6.1 Calculation of Taxable Value where there is Business Relief

The calculation of taxable value where there is business relief is as follows:

Market value	X
less	
Liabilities, costs and expenses	(X)
equals	

Incumbrance-free value	X
less	
Consideration	(X)
equals	
Taxable value before relief	X
less	
Business relief @ 90%	(X)
equals	
Taxable value	X

16.6.2 Relevant Business Property

The property that can qualify for relief is "relevant business property", which is:

1. A business or an **interest in a business**.
2. **Unquoted shares** in a company subject to the condition that on the valuation date:

   (a) the **beneficiary** holds **more than 25%** of the voting rights; or
   (b) the company is **controlled by the beneficiary**; or
   (c) the **beneficiary** holds at least **10%** of the issued share capital of the company **and has worked full-time** in the company (or a group company) for the **five years** prior to the date of the gift or inheritance.

   In (a)–(c) the per cent ownership test is carried out **after taking the benefit**.

   A company is controlled by a beneficiary if it is controlled by any one or more of the following:

   - the beneficiary;
   - relatives, civil partner or children of the civil partner of the beneficiary; and
   - certain nominees and trusts.

   "Controlled" generally means holding 50% or more of the nominal value of the shares in a company, or more than 50% of the voting share capital. There is no minimum ownership requirement for the beneficiary. The following are relatives of a beneficiary: their spouse, parent, child, aunt/uncle, the children of those persons and the children of those children, the spouse of any of these relatives; their grandparents. For this purpose, a company controlled by a beneficiary under the definition above is deemed to be a relative of a beneficiary.

3. **Land, buildings, machinery and plant** owned by the disponer but **used by a company controlled** by the **disponer**, or by the disponer and his or her spouse or civil partner, or used by a partnership of which the disponer was a partner. The land, etc. must, however, be **transferred to the beneficiary at the same time as the partnership interest or the shares** or securities of the company are transferred, and the partnership interest or shares must be relevant business property. The definition of "control" for this purpose is different from the definition in 2. above. In order for a company to be controlled by the disponer, and his or her spouse or civil partner, they must hold a majority of the voting rights in the company.

4. **Quoted shares** or securities of a company only where:

   (a) they were **owned by the disponer prior** to their becoming **quoted**; and
   (b) **one of the ownership tests** set out at 2. above is satisfied.

Example 16.16

If a sole trader gifts his or her **business** to a child, this is a gift of relevant business property.

If a partner in a partnership leaves the share in the partnership to a child, this is relevant business property.

If a sole trader gifts **just the premises** in which the trade is carried on (and not the trade itself) to a niece, this is **not relevant business property,** i.e. it is a gift of a premises only and not of a business.

Example 16.17

In order to qualify for business relief, the shares generally must be unquoted and **minimum ownership conditions** must be satisfied.

If a parent gifts shares in AIB plc to a child, this is not relevant business property and business relief will not apply.

If a parent owns a company and leaves it equally to their five children, then the shares are relevant business property. This is due to the fact that the company is controlled by the beneficiary and relatives.

A parent owns 30% of an unquoted company. The other 70% is owned by people who are not related to the parent. If the parent gifts these shares to a child, the child receives relevant business property – holds more than 25% of voting power.

If, alternatively, the parent wants to gift shares equally to two children, then the 15% shareholding received by each child will only be relevant property if the child has worked full-time in the company for the preceding five years.

This means that minority (non-controlling) shareholders in a company (which is not their family company), who want a beneficiary to benefit from business relief, must ensure that they give/leave shares to one person who will have:

- **more than 25% of voting rights** after receiving the shares; or
- **worked in the business** for five years and will hold **at least 10% of the shares** after receiving the shares.

Non-qualifying Property

A business or interest in a business, or shares or securities in a company, are **not qualifying property** where the business, or the business of the company, consists wholly or **mainly of dealing in currencies, securities, stocks or shares, land or buildings, or making or holding investments**. A business of "dealing in land" would not include genuine building and construction businesses or businesses which acquire land with a view to its development and disposal where most of the profit is derived from the increase in value of the land as a result of its development.

A holding company can qualify provided that its value is primarily attributable, directly or indirectly, to trading activities.

16.6.3 Minimum Period of Ownership and Use by Disponer

The minimum period of ownership by the disponer depends on the type of benefit taken and is as follows:

- in the case of an **inheritance taken on the date of death of the disponer**, the property must have been owned by the **disponer or their spouse or civil partner** for at least **two** years prior to the date of the inheritance; and
- in any other case (i.e. a gift, or an inheritance taken on the death of a person other than the disponer) the property must have been owned by the **disponer or their spouse or civil partner** for at least **five** years prior to transfer.

The two-/five-year minimum period of ownership is modified in two situations, namely replacement assets and successive benefits. These are beyond the scope of this book.

If it is to qualify for relief, an asset must have been **used** wholly or mainly for the purpose of the business concerned for the two-year period prior to the gift or inheritance. However, in the case of land, buildings, machinery or plant that qualifies for business relief because it has been used by a company controlled by the disponer (see **Section 16.6.2**), the period for which such assets must have been used by the company is at least two years in the case of an inheritance received on the death of the disponer or five years in any other case.

16.6.4 Valuation of Property

Value of a Business
The value of the business or an interest in a business (e.g. share in a partnership) is computed on **a net value basis**, i.e. the market value of the *assets used in the business* (including goodwill), reduced by the aggregate market value of any *liabilities incurred for the purposes of the business*.

Valuing Groups
There are specific rules for valuing groups, but these are beyond the scope of this book.

Assets Excluded in Determining the Value Attributable to Relevant Business Property
Having determined that the property is relevant business property, one must then value the property. As noted above, normal market value rules are used. However, CATCA 2003 provides that the value of **certain assets must be excluded** when determining how much of the total value of the business will actually qualify for business relief. The most important are assets used wholly or mainly for **personal use and any non-business assets**. In determining the amount of the value of a company which can qualify for relief, the value of business assets which were used wholly or mainly for the purposes of the business concerned throughout the last two years before the gift or inheritance may qualify for relief. Where an asset has been owned for less than two years, its value can qualify for relief if it has been used for the business of the company for the entire period of ownership.

Example 16.18

Harry Porter owned Hogmount Ltd since its formation in 2011 and transferred his 100% shareholding to his son, Trevor, in October 2021. The company is valued as follows:

	€
Rental property	310,000
Goodwill	300,000
Equipment	70,000
Inventories	30,000
Trade receivables	50,000
Trade payables	(60,000)
	700,000

The company operated a number of fast-food outlets and used surplus funds to invest in a rented residential property.

Trevor's CAT liability is as follows:

	Qualifying Property	Non-qualifying Property
	€	€
Market value	450,000	310,000
Less: liabilities		
Trade payables	(60,000)	
Taxable value before relief	390,000	310,000
Business relief 90%	(351,000)	0
Taxable value	39,000	310,000

Total taxable value is €349,000.

16.6.5 Other Matters

■ The relief is deducted from taxable value, i.e. **after deduction of expenses and consideration**. (*Agricultural relief is deducted from market value with a proportionate reduction in expenses and consideration.*)

■ Where agricultural relief applies, business relief does not also apply. Agricultural relief will apply, if available. Where the beneficiary does not satisfy the 80% asset test, then business relief should be considered.

16.6.6 Clawback of Relief

Disposal within Six Years

There is a clawback of the relief if at any time within six years after the gift or inheritance:

■ the business concerned ceases to be a qualifying business, other than by reason of bankruptcy or a bona fide winding up on grounds of insolvency; or

■ to the extent that the relevant business property is sold, leased, redeemed or compulsorily acquired within that six-year period and not replaced within one year by another qualifying business property.

Reinvestment

If there is **full reinvestment** of proceeds, there is **no clawback**. If there is **no reinvestment** of proceeds, there is **full clawback**.

If a proportion of the proceeds are reinvested, a similar proportion of the relief is clawed back.

Example 16.19

Albert inherited a business, with a market value of €1 million on the valuation date. He qualified for business relief at 90% of €900,000 and therefore the taxable value of the inheritance was €100,000. Albert paid CAT at 33% on the inheritance as his tax-free threshold was fully utilised. Two years later, Albert sold the business for €1,400,000. He did not reinvest any of the proceeds in buying another business. What is the CAT due as a result?

	€
Original relief claimed is clawed back	900,000
Additional CAT payable (€900,000 @ 33%)	297,000

Appendix 16.1: Summary Chart

Gift

Date of the disposition	▪ The date the person (disponer) does something which binds them to provide the property.
	▪ In the case of failure to act, the latest date when the disponer could have acted.
Date of gift	▪ The date the person (donee) becomes beneficially entitled in possession.
Valuation date	▪ The date of the gift.

Inheritance

Date of the disposition	▪ Normally the date of death.
	▪ Date when the person (disponer) is bound to provide the property (including situation where a gift becomes an inheritance).
	▪ In the case of failure to act, the latest date when the disponer could have acted.
Date of the inheritance	▪ Date of latest death.
	▪ Date of death of life tenant.
	▪ Date of gift where it becomes an inheritance.
Valuation date	▪ Normally it is the earliest of the following dates:
	● when entitled to retain property;
	● retain property;
	● property is delivered.
	▪ Gift becomes an inheritance, date of the gift.

Appendix 16.2: Differences between Agricultural Relief and Business Relief

- There is no minimum ownership period for the disponer for agricultural relief, while there is a two-year (inheritance) or five-year (gift) minimum ownership period for business relief.
- Agricultural relief applies to the market value of property, while business relief applies to taxable value.
- Agricultural relief applies to the farmhouse, but business relief does not apply to a residential property.
- Non-agricultural assets can be used to purchase agricultural assets, in certain circumstances, and can qualify for relief. There is no such provision for business relief.
- Unsecured liabilities are apportioned pro rata between agricultural and non-agricultural assets, while in business relief only liabilities applicable to the business are deductible from the business assets and all other liabilities (as far as possible) are deductible from the non-business assets.
- There must be a farming business for business relief to apply. It is not sufficient that there is an asset that could be used for a business, e.g. property.
- There is no 80% asset test for business relief. While there is no activity test that has to be satisfied for agricultural relief **before** the transfer, if the activity test is not satisfied after the transfer, then the relief is effectively not available as it is clawed back immediately.
- A beneficiary does not have the option of claiming either agricultural or business relief. If the property is agricultural and the beneficiary qualifies as a farmer, then agricultural relief applies. It is only in the event of failure to qualify for agricultural relief that business relief will apply to agricultural property.
- If land is disposed of because it has been compulsorily acquired and agricultural relief applied, replacement land must be acquired within six years; whereas if business relief applied, replacement business property must be acquired within one year.

Questions

Review Questions
(See Suggested Solutions to Review Questions at the end of this textbook.)

Question 16.1

You are a tax specialist in a firm of Chartered Accountants. The managing partner is meeting with a client who is considering gifting a substantial amount of land and farm assets to his son. The managing partner has asked you to write a memo to him outlining the conditions which would need to be satisfied if his client's son is to qualify for agricultural relief on the transfer.

Requirement
Write a memo to the partner outlining the conditions which must be satisfied if agricultural relief is to be claimed. Your memo should cover the following items:

(a) What relief is given.
(b) The definition of "agricultural property".
(c) The definition of "farmer".
(d) Withdrawal of the relief.

Question 16.2

Amy Smyth died on 1 February 2021 and her estate was administered in accordance with the terms of her will as follows:

1. To her niece, Margaret:

	Market value at 1 February 2021 and at the valuation date
	€
Holiday home in France	180,000
Quoted stocks and shares	230,000
€120,000 6% Irish Government Loan Stock	101,500

2. To her nephew, Liam:

	€
Farmland	850,000
Farm buildings	90,000
Bloodstock	100,000
Farm machinery	50,000

The farmland was charged with a mortgage of €120,000 and with the payment of farm creditors. Farm creditors amounted to €15,000 at 1 February 2021 and at the valuation date. Liam intends to farm the land on a full-time basis for at least six years from the valuation date.

3. To her daughter, Eva:
    100% of the shares in Fine Arts Ltd, which were valued at €950,000. Amy owned the shares for many years. The company's net assets at the valuation date were as follows:

	€
Factory premises	130,000
Goodwill	215,000
Investment property	360,000
Plant and machinery	70,000
Inventories	180,000
Receivables	80,000
Net liabilities	(75,000)
Net assets	960,000

4. The residue of her estate, charged with the payment of funeral expenses, was also left to her nephew, Liam. The residue consisted of cash on deposit of €50,000. Amy's funeral expenses amounted to €20,000.

    Prior to his inheritance from Amy, Liam's only asset was his residence, which had a market value of €200,000 on 1 February 2021 and at the valuation date was subject to a mortgage used to buy the residence of €130,000.

    Margaret, Liam and Eva had previously received no gifts or inheritances other than the inheritance received from Amy.

    Amy, Margaret, Liam and Eva are all Irish domiciled and resident.

Requirement

Calculate the CAT payable, if any, by Margaret, Liam and Eva.

Question 16.3

Sandra and John are married with one son, James, and all are Irish domiciled, resident and ordinarily resident. On 1 June 2021, Sandra died, leaving the following estate:

	Market value at 1 June 2021 and date of retainer
	€
Investment property	520,000
Proceeds of non-exempt life policy	104,000
Bank accounts	60,000

In addition to the above assets, Sandra owned 20% of the issued share capital of the family trading company, Tyrex Ltd, which owns and operates a number of retail outlets. The total issued share capital comprised of 1,000 €1 ordinary shares which, prior to Sandra's death, were held as follows:

John	350	€1 shares
James	50	€1 shares
Sandra	200	€1 shares
Sandra's brother	400	€1 shares
	1,000	

The company has been valued at €1 million on a net assets basis. Included in the company's net assets is a house occupied by Sandra's brother as his main residence that has been valued at €300,000. There is a mortgage charged on the house of €50,000 included in the company's liabilities. This is the only non-trade asset and liability included in the company's net assets. Sandra had owned these shares since 2006.

Sandra's estate had the following liabilities:

	€
Funeral expenses	10,600
Income tax	3,800
Rates on investment property	1,600
	16,000

All these liabilities are to be met from the residue.

Sandra's will contained the following provisions:

- The investment property was left jointly to her husband, John, and son, James.
- Her 20% shareholding in the family company was left to her son, James.
- The residue was left equally to her husband, John, and her son, James.

James has received the following gifts:

- A gift of €15,000 from his aunt on 1 July 2002.
- A gift of €16,000 from his uncle, Sean, on 1 July 2009.

- A gift of 50 shares in Tyrex Ltd from his mother on 1 November 2008. For CAT purposes, the taxable value of these shares was €167,000 on that date. This figure was net of the small gift exemption.

None of the other beneficiaries has previously received gifts or inheritance from any source.

Requirement
Compute the CAT liabilities, if any, in respect of:

(a) The benefits taken by James under Sandra's will.
(b) The benefits taken by John under Sandra's will.

Treatment of Limited Interests

Learning Objectives

After studying this chapter you will be able to:

■ Determine and calculate the taxable value of gifts/inheritances received for a limited period or where the interest is not an absolute interest, including annuities.

■ Determine the appropriate deduction available where a limited interest forms part of the consideration given for a gift/inheritance.

17.1 Introduction

Section 2 CATCA 2003 defines "limited interest" as meaning:

"(a) an interest (other than a leasehold interest) for the duration of a life or lives or for a period certain, or
(b) any other interest which is not an absolute interest".

This includes an annuity (i.e. an annual fixed payment for a limited period).

Obviously a limited interest, whether a life interest or for a period certain, is less than an absolute interest and therefore the taxable value will be lower. The taxable value of a limited interest is achieved by reducing the incumbrance-free value of the benefit (i.e. the market value less expenses, costs and liabilities but before deducting consideration). The rules for ascertaining the market value of a benefit, other than an annuity, have been outlined in **Chapter 16, Section 16.2**.

17.2 Market Value of an Annuity

Section 5 CATCA 2003 contains special provisions for calculating the value of a gift or inheritance of an annuity. The method of valuation depends on whether or not the annuity is charged or secured on property.

17.2.1 Annuity Charged or Secured on Property

Where an annuity or limited interest is charged on any property, the value of the gift or inheritance is deemed to consist of the **appropriate part** of the property on which the annuity or limited interest is charged. The **appropriate part** is ascertained using the following formula:

$$\text{Entire property} \times \frac{\text{Gross annual value of benefit}}{\text{Gross annual value of entire property}}$$

Example 17.1

Gary gives an annuity of €5,000 to his son, Stephen, and charges a specific block of investments owned by him with payment of the annuity. The investments have a capital value of €150,000 and produce an annual income of €10,000. The gift given by Gary to Stephen is deemed to consist of the appropriate part of the entire block of investments, i.e.

$$€150,000 \times \frac{€5,000}{€10,000} = €75,000$$

This €75,000 is used as the market value of the gift received by Stephen from his father.

17.2.2 Annuity Not Charged or Secured on Property

Where a gift or inheritance of an annuity is given that is not charged on any particular property, the value of the benefit is calculated by deeming it to be equal to the market value of a capital sum required to be invested in the latest Government security issued prior to the date of the gift/inheritance, which is not redeemable within 10 years, to yield an income equal to the annuity.

Example 17.2

Eoin covenants to pay his mother Bernadette, aged 62, €10,000 per annum. The value of the benefit taken by Bernadette is calculated as follows.

Say the latest Government stock issued which was not redeemable within 10 years was a 4% Government Bond and this was quoted at €0.90 for €1 of stock.

In order to produce an annual income of €10,000 by investing in this Government stock, it would be necessary to buy €250,000 of the stocks, i.e. €10,000/4%. At the current price of €0.90 per €1 of stock, it would cost €225,000 to buy €250,000 of this stock, i.e. €250,000 × 0.9. Accordingly, the market value of the benefit received by Bernadette is deemed to be €225,000.

Having ascertained the market value, deduct any liabilities, costs and expenses to give the **incumbrance-free value**.

17.3 Taxable Value of Limited Interests

The taxable value of a limited interest is achieved by reducing the incumbrance-free value of the benefit (i.e. the market value less expenses, costs and liabilities). The incumbrance-free value of the benefit is reduced by applying a factor (i.e. a figure of less than 1) as prescribed in Tables A and B of Schedule 1 Part 2 CATCA 2003 (which are reproduced in **Appendix 1**). Table A applies to the valuation of life interests (i.e. the interest is for the duration of a person's life), while Table B applies to the valuation of interests for "periods certain" (i.e. a fixed amount of time).

Example 17.3: Use for remainder of life (life interest)

John receives a life interest in his deceased uncle's farm. If John was aged 45 at the date of his uncle's death, and the incumbrance-free value of the farm was valued at €100,000, the taxable value of his benefit would be computed as follows:

€100,000 × 0.7897 = €78,970 (Table A, Column 3)

> **Example 17.4: Use for a fixed period of time (period certain)**
> If John had instead been granted the use of the farm for a period of eight years, his taxable value would have been computed as:
>
> €100,000 × 0.4177 = €41,770 (Table B, Column 2)

> **Example 17.5**
> Following on from **Example 17.2**, as Bernadette has received the annuity for life, she has received a life interest in €225,000. The €225,000, assuming no deductible costs are incurred, must be multiplied by the factor in *Table A for a female aged 62, i.e. 0.6162,* to arrive at the taxable value of the benefit received. The taxable value of the gift received by Bernadette is, therefore, €138,645 (€225,000 × 0.6162).

There are special rules for valuing interests involving one or more lives and for periods not equal to a year, which are beyond the scope of this textbook.

17.4   Deduction of Limited Interests as Consideration

It is quite common for a beneficiary to be required to pay an annuity to another person, for a limited period, as a consequence of receiving a benefit. For example, a son inherits his father's estate subject to the son paying his aunt an annuity for the rest of her life. The market value of the annuity is "consideration" paid by the beneficiary for the benefit.

> **Example 17.6**
> Ann inherited an investment property valued at €1,750,000 from her father. The property yields an annual income of €125,000. The property was to be charged from the time of his death with the payment of an annuity of €25,000 to his sister, Mary, aged 60, for Mary's lifetime.
>
> Taxable value of Mary's inheritance:
>
> €1,750,000 × $\frac{25,000}{125,000}$ = **€350,000** × 0.6475 = €226,625
>
> Taxable value of Ann's inheritance:
>
> €1,750,000 − **€350,000** = €1,400,000

17.5   Cessation of an Annuity

A taxable gift or inheritance arises on the cessation of the payment of an annuity charged or secured on a property. The "slice" of the property subsequently received is taxable. The value of the "slice" is calculated by reference to the relative values at the date the annuity payments cease.

> **Example 17.7**
> Following on from **Example 17.6**, Mary dies when the property is valued at €2,000,000 and yields an annual income of €160,000. Therefore Ann takes a further inheritance, being Mary's "slice" of the property at Mary's date of death, the valuation date. The value of the annuity is calculated based on current values as follows:
>
> €2,000,000 × 25,000/160,000 = €312,500
>
> Ann will be assessed to CAT on an additional inheritance of €312,500 from her father.

Questions

Review Questions

(See Suggested Solutions to Review Questions at the end of this textbook.)

Question 17.1

Calculate the CAT payable in respect of the gift/inheritance taken in 2021 in each of the following cases:

(a) Tom, who is Irish domiciled but UK resident and ordinarily resident, executed a deed of covenant on 8 April 2021 for €10,000 per annum for life in favour of his mother, who is Irish domiciled and resident. Tom's mother is a widow aged 59. Assuming the latest Government stock issued before 8 April, which is not redeemable within 10 years, was 5% Government bond quoted at €0.92 for €1 of stock.

Tom's mother had previously received the following benefits:

   (i) assets valued at €250,000 on the death of her husband, also Irish domiciled and resident, in 2014;

   (ii) €25,000 in cash on the death of her own mother, Tom's grandmother, also Irish domiciled and resident, in 1998; and

   (iii) jewellery and other assets valued at €30,000 on the death of her sister, also Irish domiciled and resident, in March 2008.

(b) Martha, an Irish domiciled and resident person, died in January 2011. Under the terms of her will she left a life interest in a UK property to her brother, Jason, who is Irish domiciled and resident, and on his death absolutely to his son, Mark, also Irish resident and domiciled. Jason died on 5 September 2021, at which date the absolute ownership of the UK property reverted to Mark, then aged 56. The market value of the UK property at the date of Jason's death was €300,000.

Under the terms of Jason's will, Mark also inherited cash in a Dublin bank account of €260,000.

Apart from the above, the only previous benefit received by Mark was €190,000 worth of savings certificates inherited from his mother, also Irish domiciled and resident, on her death in June 2004, and €10,000 inherited from a nephew in May 2010.

Question 17.2

Calculate the taxable value of the following gifts/inheritances arising in the year 2021.

(a) Martin, a grocer for many years, died on 1 March 2021. He left his entire estate to his brother Dermot, aged 42, for life. His estate consisted of the following at the valuation date:

	€
Grocery business and premises	600,000
House and contents	150,000
Bank accounts	15,000

Funeral and other expenses of €8,000 were outstanding.

(b) Jack, a publican for many years, died on 2 June 2021. He left his pub premises and business, valued at €600,000, to his son, John, absolutely. The pub produces an annual income of €150,000. Jack charged the premises and business with the payment of an annuity to his sister Margaret, aged 54, of €15,000 for 10 years.

Jack also left the residue of his estate to his son John. Any liabilities are to be paid out of the residue. These were as follows at the valuation date:

	€
Residue	50,000
Income tax liabilities outstanding	20,000
Funeral expenses and expenses of administering the estate	9,000

(c) In 2015 David inherited an investment property from his father valued at €250,000. The property was charged with the payment of an annuity to David's brother, Larry, for six years of €10,000. In 2015 the property produced an annual rental income of €20,000.

The last payment was made to Larry in April 2021. In April 2021 the property was valued at €375,000 and produces an annual rental income of €30,000.

(d) On 7 August 2021, Alan executed a deed of covenant of €10,000 per annum for life in favour of his widowed mother, aged 65.

It may be assumed that the latest Government stock issued before 7 August, which is not redeemable within 10 years, was 4% Government bond quoted at €0.89 for €1 of stock.

(e) Tom died on 11 October 2021. He left his entire estate absolutely to his son, Fintan. His estate consisted of the following:

	€
Farmland	950,000
Farm buildings	120,000
Stocks and shares	50,000
Cash	25,000

Funeral expenses of €9,500 were also outstanding.

Under the terms of Tom's will, he charged the farmland and farm assets with the payment of an annuity of €15,000 per annum to his daughter Emer, aged 40, for life. Annual income produced by letting the farmland and farm buildings to a lessee who farms the land full-time amounts to €50,000. Fintan has no other assets. Emer's only asset is a house valued at €120,000 that she rents to a tenant.

Question 17.3

Andrew McNeill has owned and farmed land for 16 years. On 6 August 2021 he took his son, David, into partnership on a 75/25 (25% to David) basis, and at that time transferred to David 25% of the farm and farm assets. Andrew had made no previous lifetime transfers.

Andrew and David McNeill continued farming in partnership on a full-time basis until Andrew's death on 25 November 2021 when all of Andrew's remaining assets, which consisted of the remainder of the farm, other farm assets and a number of investments, passed to David. The values of the assets were as follows:

	Value at 6 August 2021	Value at 25 November 2021 and at valuation date
Assets (Farming)	€	€
300 acres of farmland	2,200 per acre	3,600 per acre
Farm buildings	28,200	33,600
Machinery	15,600	19,300
Livestock	24,400	31,700
Other investments		95,000

The transfer of the investments to David under Andrew's will was subject to and charged with the payment of an annuity of €5,000 to Andrew's sister, Rachel. The investments produce an annual income of €8,000.

During 2020, David had inherited assets valued at €120,000 from an uncle. By 6 August 2021, David had sold all these assets and had cash in the bank of €126,000. On 10 October 2021, David spent €120,000 on farmland adjoining his father's land. This land was valued at €150,000 on 25 November 2021 and at the valuation date.

Legal fees associated with Andrew's estate amounted to €25,000.

Apart from the gifts and inheritances outlined above, David had not previously received any taxable gifts or inheritances.

All persons outlined above are Irish domiciled and resident persons.

Requirement

Compute the CAT payable by David on:

(a) the gift from Andrew on 6 August 2021, assuming all available reliefs and exemptions were utilised; and
(b) Andrew's death, assuming that no lifetime transfers had been made after 6 August 2021.

You may ignore stamp duty.

Question 17.4

Peter O'Connor, a farmer aged 57, gifted farmland and farm assets located in Co. Monaghan to his son, Stephen, valued at €5 million on 18 August 2021, on condition that Stephen would pay him €30,000 per annum for the rest of his life. (It may be assumed that the latest Government stock issued before 18 August 2021, which is not redeemable within 10 years, was 5% Government bond quoted at 90c for €1 of stock.)

Peter had inherited this farmland and assets from his own father in January 2003, at which time the lands were valued at €200,000. Peter had farmed this land since he'd inherited it; and Stephen will continue to farm the land on a full-time basis.

Stephen paid stamp duty and legal fees of €165,000 on the transfer of the land to him.

Stephen had previously inherited a site valued at €10,000 on the death of his mother in May 2013. At the time of his mother's death, the land had planning permission for residential development. Stephen subsequently built apartments on the site, which are now fully let.

Stephen had also previously inherited land in Co. Antrim (Northern Ireland) from an uncle, Peter's brother, in March 2010, valued at €300,000.

On 18 August 2021, Stephen's assets consisted of the following:

	€
His house (Note)	350,000
A car	20,000
Farmlands in Co. Antrim (Northern Ireland)	500,000
Site, now fully developed, inherited from mother	450,000

All the O'Connor family are Irish domiciled. Peter and his wife have always been Irish resident. Stephen's uncle was Irish domiciled and UK resident at the date of his death.

Note: in respect of the purchase of the house there was a mortgage outstanding of €100,000 on 18 August 2021.

Requirement
(a) Calculate the CGT liability, if any, arising on the transfer to Stephen on 18 August 2021.
(b) Calculate the CAT liabilities, if any, arising on the same transfer.

18

Exemptions from CAT

Learning Objectives

After studying this chapter you will be able to:

- Identify and advise on certain gifts and inheritances that are exempt from CAT, including:
  - €3,000 gift per disponer per annum;
  - between spouses/civil partners;
  - Government securities;
  - certain inheritances taken by parents;
  - certain dwelling houses;
  - gifts/inheritances taken free of tax;
  - certain receipts and insurance policies.

18.1 Exemption of Small Gifts

Under section 69 CATCA 2003, the first **€3,000** per annum in **gifts** made by any one disponer to any one donee is exempt, i.e. in computing the amount of a gift to be aggregated, the first €3,000 of total value taken from the *same disponer* in each year is disregarded. The amount of the exemption was lower for gifts taken before 1 January 2003.

The annual exemption does not apply to inheritances. However, where a gift subsequently becomes an inheritance, due to the death of the disponer within two years of the date of the gift, then the annual exemption is not recaptured.

The annual exemption applies to gifts taken during **calendar years**.

> **Example 18.1**
> John receives a gift of €10,000 from his uncle. In consideration of the gift he has to give €1,000 to his sister. John's taxable value is €10,000 − €1,000 = €9,000. The small gift exemption of €3,000 is deducted so that the final taxable value is €6,000. John's sister will have received a gift of €1,000 from her uncle. As the amount is less than the small gift exemption no CAT arises and it will not be aggregated in future.

18.2 Exemption of Gifts and Inheritances taken from a Spouse or Civil Partner and Certain Benefits taken from a Former Spouse or Civil Partner

Inheritances taken by the surviving spouse or civil partner of a deceased spouse or civil partner and gifts taken from a spouse or civil partner are exempt from CAT, and also are not aggregated for the purposes of calculating CAT payable on any other gifts or inheritances taken by that person in the future.

18.2.1 Couples who are Separated

In order for the exemption to apply, the couple must be legally married or be a party to a civil partnership registration. If they are separated but are not divorced or their civil partnership has not been dissolved, then they are still legally married or in a civil partnership and the exemption applies.

Example 18.2
Darren and Tracey signed a deed of separation on 1 July 2021. Under the terms of the deed, Darren agreed to sign over to Tracey his interest in a house he owns. As they are still married, the gift from Darren to Tracey is a gift to a spouse and is, therefore, exempt from CAT. (Note: the transfer is exempt from stamp duty as they are married. For CGT purposes, the disposal is exempt as it is a transfer on foot of a deed of separation. If, however, in a subsequent year Darren voluntarily gives Tracey shares, while the CAT and stamp duty exemptions would be available, for CGT purposes there would be no relieving provision.)

18.2.2 Married Couples who are Divorcing or are Divorced, and Civil Partnerships that are being Dissolved or have been Dissolved

Where a couple obtains an Irish divorce or a dissolution of a civil partnership, transfers between former spouses or civil partners made on foot of an Irish court order governing the divorce or dissolution of a civil partnership are exempt from CAT. This exemption also applies to a foreign divorce or dissolution of a civil partnership that is recognised as valid under Irish law.

Once divorced or the civil partnership has been dissolved, any transfers made voluntarily between the former spouses or civil partners are not exempt and Group C would be the relevant threshold.

Example 18.3
Grace and Ivan divorced on 1 August 2021. Under the terms of their divorce, Grace agreed to sign over her interest in the family home to Ivan. The transfer of the house from Grace to Ivan is exempt from CAT as it arises under the terms of the divorce. (Note: the transfer is exempt from stamp duty and CGT also.)

If, three years later, Ivan had financial problems and Grace decided to give him €20,000, he would be liable to CAT on this receipt of a gift and the relevant group threshold would be Group C.

Example 18.4
Leopold and Peter registered their civil partnership on 8 April 2014. Having lived apart for two of the last three years, they decided that they would separate and get the civil partnership dissolved. When they are granted the decree of dissolution, any provision made under the decree regarding transfer of property, etc. is exempt from CAT, stamp duty and CGT. If, two years after the dissolution, Leopold decided to make a gift of shares to Peter, that gift would be taxable and the Group C threshold would apply.

18.3 Exemption of Certain Government Securities

Irish assets are always liable to Irish CAT. However, to get non-Irish persons to hold Irish Government securities, **certain Government securities are exempt from CAT**, provided the following conditions are satisfied:

1. the **beneficiary** must **neither be domiciled nor ordinarily resident** in the State at the date of the gift or inheritance; and
2. the **disponer was the beneficial owner** of the securities for **15 years** prior to the date of the gift or inheritance. This **condition does not apply** where the **disponer is neither domiciled nor ordinarily resident** in the State at the date of the disposition.

18.4 Exemption of Certain Inheritances taken by Parents

Inheritances (not gifts) taken by a **parent on the death of a child** are exempt **if the deceased child had taken a non-exempt gift or inheritance from either parent** in the **five-year period prior to the death of the child** (see **Chapter 14, Section 14.2.2**).

Example 18.5
On 1 June 2018 Frank gave a gift of €100,000 to his daughter, Joanne, which she used as part-payment to acquire an apartment. Joanne died in 2021 and Frank inherited her entire estate, which was valued at €500,000. The €500,000 inherited by Frank is exempt from CAT as Frank had given Joanne a non-exempt gift within five years before her death.

18.5 Exemption of Certain Dwelling Houses

There has been a dwelling house exemption for many years. However, the exemption was significantly changed in respect of gifts of dwelling houses taken on or after 25 December 2016. Provided conditions are satisfied, any inheritance of a dwelling house may be exempt, but gifts are only exempt if taken by a relative who is aged 65 or over or who is permanently and totally incapacitated (i.e. a dependent relative).

For an **inheritance** of a dwelling house to be exempt from CAT, the conditions that must be satisfied are as follows:

1. The donor must have occupied the dwelling house as their only or main residence at their date of death. This requirement is relaxed in situations where the deceased person had to leave because of ill health, e.g. to live in a nursing home. This condition does not apply to an inheritance by a dependent relative on or after 25 December 2017.
2. The beneficiary must have occupied the dwelling house continuously as their only, or main, residence for a period of **three years** prior to the date of the inheritance. Where the dwelling house has directly or indirectly replaced other property, this condition may be satisfied where the recipient has continuously occupied both properties as their only or main residence for a total period of three out of the four years immediately prior to the date of the inheritance.

3. The beneficiary must **not**, at the date of the inheritance or on the valuation date if it is later, be beneficially entitled to any **other dwelling house** or to any interest in any other dwelling house (including a dwelling house that is subject to a discretionary trust under, or in consequence of, a disposition made by the successor where that successor is an object of the trust). For example, if Cathal owns an apartment in Limerick and inherits the family home in Waterford he will not qualify for the dwelling home exemption. Beneficial entitlement to any other dwelling house also includes a situation where the beneficiary acquires an interest in another dwelling house as part of the same inheritance.

4. The beneficiary must continue, except where the recipient was aged 65 years or more at the date of the inheritance, to **occupy** that dwelling house as their only or main residence for a period of **six years** commencing on the date of the inheritance (the **relevant period**). A period of absence while working elsewhere, due to a condition of their employment, counts as a period of occupation for this purpose, as does absence from the dwelling due to ill health.

For **gifts of dwelling houses** to be exempt from CAT, conditions 2 to 4 above must be satisfied (with the relevant date being the date of the gift instead of the date of the inheritance). Condition 1 above does not have to be satisfied, however, there is an extra condition – that the **donee must be a dependent relative**. A **dependent relative** is a direct relative of the donor or of the donor's spouse or civil partner, who is permanently and totally incapacitated because of physical or mental infirmity from maintaining himself or herself, or who is aged 65 or over. (Where a gift becomes an inheritance, due to the donor dying within two years of the disposition, it continues to be a gift for the purposes of this exemption and it is therefore these conditions that must be satisfied.)

Example 18.6

Pat and Joe are two brothers, aged 45 and 47, who have lived together in the house they inherited from their parents in December 2010. The house was valued at €100,000 in December 2010. In January 2021, Pat moved out and gave his half share in the house to Joe, together with contents valued at €20,000 (in total). The house was valued at €500,000 at the date of Pat's gift. Apart from the inheritance from his parents, Joe has not previously received any other taxable gifts or inheritances.

What is Joe's CAT liability arising from his gift from Pat (ignoring small gift exemption)?

Computation

The half share in the house is valued at €250,000. This is **not exempt**, as Joe is not a dependent relative, i.e. he is neither incapacitated nor aged 65 or over.

Taxable gift	€	
House	250,000	
50% share in contents	10,000	
Taxable inheritance	260,000	€
Group threshold	32,500 @ Nil	Nil
Balance	227,500 @ 33%	75,075
CAT payable		75,075

Note: as no previous gifts or inheritances were taken from persons within the same group threshold, therefore tax on Aggregate B is nil.

If, instead, Pat had died and left his share of the house to Joe, then the inheritance of the house would be exempt as (1) the donor, Pat, occupied it as his main residence at the date of his death; and (2) the beneficiary, Joe, has lived in the house for the previous three years; and (3) owns no other dwelling house. Joe must continue to own and occupy the house (or a replacement) for six years after the inheritance to avoid a clawback. The share of the contents (€10,000) will be taxable, although no actual CAT will be payable as this is less than the threshold of €32,500.

18.5.1   Definition of "Dwelling House"

A "dwelling house" means:

1. a building or part of a building which was used or suitable for use as a dwelling; and
2. grounds of up to one acre attaching to the house and, where the grounds attaching to the house exceed one acre, one acre of the total area which is most suitable for enjoyment and occupation with the dwelling house.

18.5.2   Clawback of Exemption

The exemption will cease to apply if:

1. The dwelling house is sold or otherwise disposed of before the death of the beneficiary and within the relevant period, unless the recipient was aged 65 years or more at the date of the gift or inheritance.

    If, however, the recipient sells or disposes of the dwelling house and invests some or all of the proceeds in a replacement house and continuously occupies both for a total period of six out of the seven years commencing on the date of the gift or inheritance, the clawback will be limited to the proportion of consideration not invested in the replacement dwelling house, e.g. if 90% of the proceeds are re-invested, then 90% of the exemption continues and 10% of the benefit is taxable.
2. The recipient ceases to occupy the dwelling house as their only or main residence during the relevant period, unless it is required that they cease to occupy the house as a result of any condition imposed by the employer of the beneficiary requiring them to reside elsewhere.

    There is, however, no clawback where the beneficiary ceases to occupy the dwelling house in consequence of a mental or physical infirmity. The infirmity must be certified by a doctor.
3. If the beneficiary subsequently inherits an interest in a dwelling house from the same disponer. Interest on the relief clawed back only applies from the valuation date for the second inheritance.

Example 18.7
Eoin inherits the family home from his mother on her death in January 2021 (the date of the inheritance and the valuation date). Eoin satisfies the conditions for dwelling house relief to apply. The residue of his mother's estate, which includes two rental apartments, is finally determined in July 2022 and the apartments are transferred to Eoin and his brother Jack.

As Eoin has inherited an interest in an additional residential property from his mother, the dwelling house exemption he qualified for on the inheritance in January 2021 is withdrawn. Eoin will be assessed to CAT on the inheritance of the family home and his share of the residual estate.

18.6   Exemption of Certain Receipts

There are a large number of exemptions, including:

1. Gifts/inheritances taken by charities.
2. The receipt, during the **lifetime** of the disponer, by:
    (a) a minor child of the disponer or of the civil partner of the disponer; or

(b) a child of the disponer or of the civil partner of the disponer who is older than 18 years but not older than 25 years and who is receiving full-time education at any educational establishment or undergoing training for a trade or profession for at least a two-year period; or

(c) a child of the disponer or of the civil partner of the disponer (of any age) who is permanently incapacitated by reason of physical or mental infirmity from maintaining himself or herself; or

(d) certain dependent relatives.

of sums from the disponer for normal support, maintenance or education. These sums must be reasonable having regard to the financial circumstances of the disponer.

3. **Post-death** support, maintenance or education is exempt where received by a minor child or a child who is either 18 years or over 18 but not older than 25 and in full-time education or training or permanently incapacitated (see (a) to (c) above) and the other parent of the child is also dead. These sums must be reasonable having regard to the financial circumstances of the deceased disponer.

4. Gift/inheritance taken exclusively for the purpose of discharging qualifying medical expenses of an individual who is permanently incapacitated by reason of physical or mental infirmity.

5. Bona fide compensation or damages for any wrong or injury suffered by the person or compensation for the death of another person.

6. Gifts or inheritances provided by the disponer to themself, e.g. from a trust created by the disponer.

7. Bona fide winnings from betting, lotteries, Sweepstakes or prizes from games.

8. Any benefit arising from the write-off of some or all of a debt under a debt relief notice, a debt settlement arrangement or a personal insolvency arrangement under the Personal Insolvency Act 2012 is not a gift or an inheritance.

18.7 Gifts and Inheritances taken Free of Tax

The law provides that where a gift or inheritance is taken by direction of the disponer free of CAT, the benefit taken is deemed to include the amount of tax chargeable on the gift or inheritance, but not the amount of tax chargeable on such tax.

Example 18.8

Brian receives a gift of €132,500, net of small gift exemption, from his sister Ann in July 2021. Ann has agreed to pay any tax due on the gift, i.e. the gift is free of tax. Brian is regarded as taking two benefits, i.e. the gift of €132,500 and the CAT on that amount. On the basis that Brian has received no previous gift or inheritance, the CAT on the gift is:

	€
Gift	132,500
Threshold amount	(32,500)
Taxable	100,000
Tax @ 33%	33,000
Tax on €33,000 @ 33%	10,890
Tax payable	43,890

Therefore the additional CAT due on the benefit as a result of it being free of CAT is €10,890. There is no further CAT due as a result of Ann paying this €10,890 of tax.

18.8 Relief in Respect of Certain Insurance Policies

There is a valuable relief under section 72 CATCA 2003 whereby the proceeds of **certain insurance policies are exempt from inheritance tax**, where the policy was taken out for the **sole purpose of paying inheritance tax** due in respect of dispositions made by the person insured. The relief, which originally applied to inheritances only, was subsequently extended and also covers *inter vivos* **dispositions (i.e. gifts)** provided that certain conditions are satisfied (see **Section 18.8.2**).

In the absence of this relief, the proceeds of a life insurance policy, whether taken out to pay inheritance tax or otherwise, are aggregated with the other assets of the deceased and itself subject to inheritance tax in the hands of the beneficiary. Indirectly, therefore, the insurance policy results in an increased tax liability.

18.8.1 Policies to Pay Inheritance Tax Only

To qualify for exemption, the assurance company gets its policy approved by Revenue to ensure Revenue conditions are satisfied. The premiums are payable annually. Obviously a person who is older or has an illness will find that they cannot get insurance or the premiums are too expensive. The policy can cover the life of one or both spouses/civil partners.

The **exemption available is limited to the proceeds of the insurance policy** which are **actually used to pay inheritance tax.** If, for example, the proceeds exceed the inheritance tax liability, then only the portion of the proceeds equal to the inheritance tax liability qualify for exemption. The balance of the proceeds would then become subject to inheritance tax in the normal manner.

Example 18.9
Mary died in June 2021. The inheritance tax liability of her estate amounted to €45,000. She held a qualifying life assurance policy which paid €50,000 to her estate on her death. As the proceeds exceed the inheritance tax liability, then only the portion of the proceeds equal to the inheritance tax liability of €45,000 qualifies for exemption. The balance of the proceeds, i.e. €5,000, would then become subject to inheritance tax in the normal manner.

This type of exempt policy can also be used to cover the income tax required to be deducted, in certain situations, from an approved retirement fund (commonly known as an ARF). Income tax at 30% must be deducted from assets in an ARF where the beneficiary of those assets is a child of the deceased who is aged 21 years or over.

The policy proceeds are payable on the death of the person insured. For people who are married or in a civil partnership, the policy can be taken out on the joint lives of the insured and his spouse/civil partner. In this case, the annual premiums are payable by either or both spouses/civil partners during their joint lives and the survivor of them during the life of the survivor. The proceeds of the policy are payable on the death of each survivor or the simultaneous death of both such spouses/civil partners. **Example 18.10** illustrates the operation of this exemption.

Example 18.10

Pat, a bachelor, died in November 2021 and in his will he left the following:

- a legacy of €30,000 to his housekeeper Mrs Brown, who is unrelated;
- a specific bequest of shares valued at €35,000 to his brother Bart; and
- the residue of his estate, valued at €120,000, equally between his two brothers, Bart and Cathal.

None of these three beneficiaries has taken any previous gift or inheritance since 5 December 1991.

Pat had taken out a qualifying insurance policy, the proceeds of which amounted to €20,000. Pat's will had specifically provided that all relevant CAT payable on his death was to be paid *pro rata* from this policy.

Note: the residue of €120,000 **does not** include the qualifying insurance policy.

The CAT in connection with Pat's death is calculated as follows:

(i) **Housekeeper Mrs Brown**

	€		€
Tax on threshold amount of	16,250		nil
Tax on	13,750	@ 33%	4,537
Total	30,000		4,537

(ii) **Brother Bart**

Bart takes the specific bequest of €35,000 and half of the residue, which will amount to €60,000, making a total inheritance of €95,000.

Tax on €95,000 is as follows:	€		€
Tax on threshold amount of	32,500		nil
Tax on	62,500	@ 33%	20,625
Total	95,000		20,625

(iii) **Brother Cathal**

Cathal takes half the residue valued at €60,000.

	€		€
Tax on threshold amount of	32,500		nil
Tax on	27,500	@ 33%	9,075
Total	60,000		9,075

It will be noted that the total of the CAT liability of the three beneficiaries is €34,237 (€4,537 + €20,625 + €9,075). As Pat directed in his will that the proceeds of the policy of €20,000 were to be paid *pro rata*, the CAT will be paid as follows:

(i) Mrs Brown's liability is paid out of the proceeds in the proportion of:

$$\frac{€4,537 \times €20,000}{€34,237} \text{ which amounts to } €2,650.$$

She pays the balance of tax of €1,887 from her own funds.

(ii) Bart's liability is discharged out of the policy proceeds in the proportion of:

$$\frac{€20,625 \times €20,000}{€34,237} \text{ which amounts to } €12,049.$$

Thus Bart pays the balance of tax of €8,576 from his own funds.

(iii) Cathal's liability is paid out of the policy proceeds in the proportion of:

$$\frac{€9,075 \times €20,000}{€34,237} \text{ which amounts to } €5,301.$$

The balance of €3,774 is paid by Cathal out of his own funds.

18.8.2 Inter Vivos *Dispositions*

There is a similar relief under section 73 CATCA 2003 (i.e. **exempts from CAT the proceeds of a qualifying policy**) when the policy is taken out to pay CAT arising on *inter vivos* dispositions made by the insured. The CAT which may be covered by the policy is the CAT payable in respect of a disposition made by the insured **within one year after the appointed day**. The appointed day is:

- a date not earlier than **eight years** after the date on which the policy is taken out; or
- the date on which the proceeds of the policy became payable either on the critical illness or the death of the insured.

Questions

Review Questions
(See Suggested Solutions to Review Questions at the end of this textbook.)

Question 18.1

Sarah and Enda are married with one son, Patrick, and all are Irish domiciled, resident and ordinarily resident. On 1 June 2021, Sarah died leaving the following estate:

	Market value at 1 June 2021 and date of retainer
	€
€18,000 stock of 10% Irish Government National Loan Stock	14,000
€20,000 stock of 12% Irish Government National Loan Stock	16,000

Both Government securities comprised in the estate qualify for exemption from Irish income tax when beneficially owned by individuals not domiciled or ordinarily resident. Sarah has owned these securities since December 2004.

Sarah's will contained the following provisions:

- the 10% National Loan Stock was left to Patrick;
- the 12% National Loan Stock was left to Harry, Sarah's cousin, who is domiciled and resident and ordinarily resident in the United States.

Patrick has received the following gifts:

- a gift of €15,000 from his aunt on 1 July 1989;
- a gift of €16,000 from his uncle, Sean, on 1 July 2006;
- a gift of 50 shares in Xbarn Ltd from his mother on 15 May 2016. For CAT purposes, the taxable value of these shares was €477,000 on that date. This figure was net of the small gift exemption.

Requirement

Compute the CAT liabilities, if any, in respect of:

(a) the benefits taken by Patrick under Sarah's will; and
(b) the benefits taken by Harry under Sarah's will.

Question 18.2

Shane Murray, a widower, died on 30 June 2021. Under the terms of his will he provided the following bequests:

	Value at 30 June 2021 and at the valuation date
	€
To his son John:	
100% of the shares in Murray Developments Ltd (Note 1)	1,500,000
Two investment properties (Note 2)	850,000
To his daughter Emily:	
His house (Note 3)	950,000
To his sister Sarah:	
An annuity of €10,000 for life (Note 4)	

The residue of his estate was left equally between John and Emily and was charged with the payment of funeral and testamentary expenses. The residue consisted of €146,000 in cash and €50,000 in quoted shares.

Shane had taken out a qualifying insurance policy in 2012 for the sole purpose of paying CAT on dispositions made by him under his will. The proceeds of the policy were €1,000,000 and Shane's will provided that all inheritance tax payable by John, Emily and Sarah on his death was to be paid *pro rata* from this policy.

The Murray family are all Irish domiciled and resident. In November 2002, Shane had transferred an investment property valued at €300,000, with a mortgage of €200,000 charged on the property, to John. This transfer gave rise to a gift tax liability to John of €3,800. In 2003 Emily inherited a house from her mother valued at €200,000. Emily has since let the house.

Notes:

1. Shane Murray established Murray Developments Ltd in 1999. It carries on a trade of buying and selling land. The company has employed John for the last five years.
2. The two properties transferred to John were valued at €400,000 and €450,000 with attaching mortgages of €150,000 and €75,000, respectively.
3. Emily, who is unmarried, had been living, and has always lived, with her father in his house when he died.
4. The annuity payable to Shane's sister is charged on the property valued at €400,000 inherited by John. This property yields an annual rental income of €30,000. Sarah was 63 at the date of Shane's death.
5. Funeral expenses and legal fees associated with the administration of his estate amounted to €3,500 and €8,500, respectively.

   (Ignore small gift exemption.)

Requirement

Compute the CAT liabilities, if any, payable by John, Emily and Sarah.

Question 18.3

Jerome Nutley, a widower, died on 26 October 2021. Under the terms of his will he provided the following bequests:

	Value at 26 October 2021 and at the valuation date
	€
To his nephew Declan:	
55% of the shares in Wiggies Wholesalers Ltd (Note 1)	350,000
To his son Jonathan:	
Property let to Wiggies Wholesalers Ltd (Note 2)	500,000
To his daughter Louise:	
His house (Note 3)	750,000

The residue of his estate was left equally between Jonathan and Louise, and was charged with the payment of funeral and testamentary expenses. The residue consisted of €65,000 in cash.

Jerome had taken out a life assurance policy some years previously and had nominated Louise as the sole beneficiary of the policy. Proceeds payable on his death amounted to €360,000.

The Nutley family are all Irish domiciled and resident. Declan had not previously received any taxable gifts or inheritances. Jonathan had previously received a gift of €10,000 from an aunt, an Irish domiciled and resident person, in March 2008. Louise had previously received an inheritance of €179,500 from her father-in-law in 2010.

Notes:
1. Wiggies Wholesalers Ltd carries on the trade of electrical wholesalers. The company was established by Jerome Nutley in 1995. However, he sold 45% of the shares to an unrelated party when he retired in September 2009. Jerome is a director of Wiggies Wholesalers Ltd. Declan has been working full-time for Wiggies Wholesalers Ltd for the past 10 years.
2. The property out of which Wiggies Wholesalers Ltd operates was acquired by Jerome Nutley in 1995 and has been let to the company by him for use in its trade since then.
3. Louise Nutley, a schoolteacher aged 50, had been living with her father in the house which he left to her since her husband died in 2007. Louise has no other interests in a dwelling house.
4. Funeral expenses and legal fees associated with the administration of Jerome's estate amounted to €2,500 and €4,000, respectively.

Requirement
Compute the CAT liabilities, if any, payable by Declan, Jonathan and Louise.

Credit for Certain CGT Liabilities

19.1 Credit for Certain CGT Liabilities

Certain events can result in the triggering of both a CGT liability and a CAT liability.

Typically, an inheritance will not trigger a CGT liability as assets passing on a death do not trigger CGT.

Gifts frequently trigger both CGT and CAT. If the asset gifted is a capital asset, then the disponer may have a capital gain liable to CGT and the donee receives a gift that may trigger a CAT liability. For instance, the gift of a farm by a father to a son is:

▪ a disposal of a chargeable asset by the father that may give rise to a CGT liability, computed by reference to the market value of the land transferred; and

▪ a gift received by the son that may give rise to a CAT liability, by reference to the market value of the land received.

Section 104 CATCA 2003 provides that where the **same event triggers both CAT and CGT liabilities and provided the CGT liability has been paid,** the amount of CGT may be **deducted** as a *credit* from the net CAT liability arising on the event. The **maximum amount of credit** deducted is **restricted to the lower of the CGT liability or the CAT liability arising on the same event**.

Example 19.1

On 5 October 2021, Michael gives his sister, Debbie, quoted shares worth €80,000. He had bought them for €10,000 on 1 August 1997. What are their CGT and CAT positions, ignoring small gift and annual exemptions? Debbie has not received any previous gifts or inheritances.

Under CGT rules, he is treated as disposing of the shares at their market value of €80,000. Therefore, ignoring annual exemption, Michael's CGT liability will be as follows:

continued overleaf

	€	€
Market value		80,000
Cost	10,000	
Index – 1997/98 @ 1.232		
Indexed cost		(12,320)
Gain		67,680
CGT @ 33%		22,334

Ignoring small gift exemption, Debbie's CAT liability is calculated as follows:

	€	€
Taxable value of gift		80,000
Group threshold amount		32,500
€32,500 @ Nil	Nil	
€47,500 @ 33%	15,675	
CAT liability	15,675	
Less: credit for CGT paid by Michael (restricted)	(15,675)	
CAT payable	Nil	

The maximum credit available is the lower of the CGT liability or the CAT liability, i.e. it is restricted to €15,675.

Example 19.2

Assume the same facts as the previous example except that Debbie had previously received €70,000 from Michael. Debbie's CAT liability is calculated as follows:

	€
Aggregate A	
Taxable value of gifts: €80,000 + €70,000	150,000
Group threshold amount	32,500
€32,500 @ Nil	Nil
€117,500 @ 33%	38,775
CAT on Aggregate A	38,775
Aggregate B	
Taxable value of previous gift	70,000
Group threshold amount	32,500
€32,500 @ Nil	Nil
€37,500 @ 33%	12,375
CAT on Aggregate B	12,375
CAT on current benefit = CAT on Aggregate A − CAT on Aggregate B	
= €38,775 − €12,375	26,400
Less: credit for CGT paid by Michael	(22,334)
CAT payable	4,066

A person's CAT liability is determined by their lifetime gifts and inheritances. The CAT arising on the current benefit exceeds the CGT because Michael had used his lifetime tax-free threshold when he received the prior gift of €70,000, meaning that the full amount of the current gift is taxable. As this current tax liability has arisen on an event whereby a CGT liability also arose, then credit relief is available up to a maximum of the lower of the CGT or CAT.

19.2 Clawback of CGT Credit

The credit for CGT will be clawed back if the beneficiary disposes of the property transferred within two years of the date of the gift or inheritance.

In **Examples 19.1** and **19.2**, if Debbie disposed of the shares within two years then the credit for CGT would be clawed back, i.e. she will have to pay €15,675 of CAT (in **Example 19.1**) and €22,334 of additional CAT in (**Example 19.2**).

19.3 Identification of CAT Liabilities where more than One Asset

The same event must trigger both the CGT and CAT liability. If the CAT relates to two different capital assets, then the CAT and CGT related to each asset must be established and the lower of the two is the creditable amount.

Prior to Finance Act 2012 the law required that, where benefits were taken on the same day, the CAT arising was apportioned between each asset taken on that day. As a result of the repeal of this legislation there is no guidance in law other than in section 104(1)(b) CATCA 2003, which states that the CAT is the amount equal to the CAT "attributable to the property which is that asset, or that part of that asset". Therefore the taxpayer may choose the approach that will minimise their tax liability (i.e. maximise the CGT credit to be deducted). Depending on the facts of the case regarding the CGT relating to an asset, the taxpayer will treat a particular asset as being received before another asset or that they were all received at the same time. This is illustrated in **Example 19.3** below.

Example 19.3

On 28 July 2021 Jack gifts his son, Shane, his principal private residence and quoted shares. Shane has received no prior benefits and does not live with his father. Information regarding these assets is as follows:

	House	Shares
	€	€
Market value	600,000	100,000
Cost	80,000	20,000
Indexation factor	3	1.5

Capital Gains Tax

House	Exempt as it is his principal private residence	
		€
Shares	Market value	100,000
	Indexed cost €20,000 × 1.5	(30,000)
	Gain	70,000
	Annual exemption	(1,270)
	Taxable gain	68,730
	CGT @ 33%	**22,681**

Capital Acquisitions Tax

		€
Taxable value: €600,000 + €100,000		700,000
Small gift exemption		(3,000)
		697,000
Group threshold	335,000	

continued overleaf

€335,000 @ 0%	–
€362,000 @ 33%	119,460
Less: credit for CGT (Note)	22,681
CAT payable	96,779

Note: the CAT relates to both the shares and the house, whereas the CGT only relates to the shares. Therefore, the **CGT** credit (in respect of the shares) **can only be offset against the CAT** attributable to the gift of **the shares**.

The CAT payable of €119,460 relates to both the house and the shares. How should it be apportioned between the house and the shares?

Option 1: Deemed to receive house first then shares

	House	Shares
	€	€
Value	600,000	100,000
Less: small gift exemption	(3,000)	
Threshold	(335,000)	
Taxable	262,000	100,000
CAT @ 33%	86,460	33,000

Option 2: Deemed to receive shares first then house

	Shares	House
	€	€
Value	100,000	600,000
Less: small gift exemption	(3,000)	
Threshold	(97,000)	(238,000)
Taxable	NIL	362,000
CAT @ 33%	NIL	119,460

Option 3: CAT apportioned between house and shares

CAT on house = €119,460 × 600,000/700,000	= €102,394
CAT on shares = €119,460 × 100,000/700,000	= €17,066

From Shane's perspective, he wishes to maximise the CAT associated with the shares as they carry a CGT credit. This is achieved by choosing the option that maximises the CAT arising on the shares (i.e. option 1). Therefore, the CAT re shares is €33,000.

The creditable CGT is the lower of:

(i)   CGT on shares €22,681; or
(ii) CAT on shares €33,000

   i.e. €22,681

If the shares are disposed of within two years, the CGT credit is clawed back, i.e. an additional €22,681 of CAT must be paid.

19.4 Other Matters

In certain circumstances, the entitlement to a CGT credit against a CAT liability may need to be apportioned between a number of beneficiaries and, in these circumstances, the Revenue Commissioners are empowered to make any necessary apportionments as appears to be "just and reasonable". There is, however, a right of appeal to the Appeal Commissioners if the method of apportionment is disputed.

The **CGT must be paid** in order for a credit against CAT to be allowed. If it has not been paid by the due date for payment of the CAT, the full CAT will have to be paid and a refund of CAT sought at a later stage when the CGT has been paid. However, where the due date for payment of CAT on a gift is before the due date for payment of CGT arising on the same event, in practice a credit may be claimed for the CGT payable.

Questions

Review Questions
(See Suggested Solutions to Review Questions at the end of this textbook.)

Question 19.1

You are a tax specialist in a firm of Chartered Accountants. A client of your firm, Mr O'Donovan, owns a substantial portfolio of investment properties. Mr O'Donovan has two daughters, Lorraine and Sheila. Mr O'Donovan is considering transferring an apartment currently valued at €350,000 to Lorraine and an apartment valued at €250,000 to Sheila.

You are given the following additional information:

1. Lorraine has been living rent-free in the apartment which her father intends to transfer to her since 1 April 2019. She intends to continue to live in the apartment. She may, however, be transferred by her employer to work in the UK for a six-month period in 2022. Her father also owns an identical apartment next to hers, which he has been letting out at €1,500 a month for the last five years. Mr O'Donovan had acquired the apartment that Lorraine occupies in November 1999 for €220,000. (Legal fees and stamp duty associated with the purchase amounted to €15,000.)
2. Sheila has been living at home with her father but intends to live in the apartment which her father has bought to give to her. A monthly rent of €1,200 could be charged if this apartment were let at arm's length to a third party. Mr O'Donovan had acquired this apartment in July 2019 for €240,000. (Legal fees and stamp duty associated with the purchase amounted to €28,000.)
3. Lorraine and Sheila had each inherited assets on the death of their mother in May 2012. Lorraine received €160,000. Sheila received €225,000. Sheila had also received a gift of Irish quoted shares valued at €20,000 from an uncle in June 2011. Apart from this, neither has previously received any taxable gifts or inheritances.
4. Neither Lorraine or Sheila has, or has ever had, any other interest in a residential property.
5. Mr O'Donovan has made no other disposals for CGT purposes during 2021.

Requirement

Write a letter to Mr O'Donovan advising him on the taxation consequences arising from the proposed property transfers to his daughters. (You should assume that the transfers take place on 1 December 2021 and that the transfers cannot be delayed and given as inheritances.) In your letter you should also advise Mr O'Donovan on any steps which might be taken by him to mitigate the tax liabilities arising. (Ignore small gift exemption.)

Question 19.2

Janet, a 58-year-old widow, made the following gifts during 2021.

1. 20 April 2021 – 100% of the shares in Fogarty Fabrics Ltd, a company involved in the manufacture of curtains and bed linen, to Janet's son, Adam. Fogarty Fabrics Ltd had been incorporated by Janet's husband in 1987 with a share capital of €100. Janet's husband died in March 1997 and Janet has been a full-time working director since then. The shares in Fogarty Fabrics Ltd were valued at €340,000 in March 1997.

   On 20 April 2021, the shares in Fogarty Fabrics Ltd were valued at €950,000. The company's net assets at 20 April 2021 were as follows:

	Market Value
	€
Factory premises	130,000
Goodwill	215,000
Investment property	350,000
Plant and machinery	70,000
Inventories	180,000
Receivables	80,000
Net liabilities	(75,000)
Net assets	950,000

   Adam has previously received a gift of €150,000 (net of small gift allowance) on 2 May 2012 from his mother.

2. 20 May 2021 – A house valued at €250,000 to her daughter, Julie, and Julie's husband, Nigel. Janet had acquired this house in December 1989 for €40,000. The house had been let by Janet since then.

   Julie has not previously received any taxable gifts or inheritances. Nigel had previously inherited Bank of Ireland shares valued at €10,000 from an aunt.

3. 30 September 2021 – Farmland valued at €1.25 million to her son, Kevin. Janet had inherited this land from her mother in August 1994, at which time the land was valued at €168,000. The land had always been leased out by Janet.

   Kevin has no other assets and has not previously received any taxable gifts or inheritances. Kevin intends to lease the land to a neighbouring farmer who will farm the land full-time.

   All persons mentioned above are Irish domiciled and Irish resident.

   Janet had capital losses forward of €10,000 at 31 December 2020.

Requirement

(a) Calculate Janet's CGT liability for 2021, assuming she made no other disposals in 2021 other than those listed above and that she has not previously disposed of any chargeable business assets.

(b) Calculate the CAT liabilities arising from each of the above gifts. You may ignore stamp duty.

Question 19.3

On 16 July 2021, on the occasion of his 56th birthday and in order to mark his early retirement, Ronnie Doyle made the following gifts:

		Market value on 16 July 2021
		€
1.	To his sister Janet:	
	€35,000 4.5% Government stock purchased by Ronnie	
	in December 2005 and which is exempt from income tax	
	where held by a foreign domiciled and ordinarily resident person	40,000
2.	To his son Jake:	
	His interest in a van rental business (Note 1)	1,280,000
	Cash	20,000
3.	To his son Brendan:	
	Two vans (Note 2): Van 1	15,000
	Van 2	25,000
	An office building (Note 2)	250,000
	Cash	50,000

Brendan and Jake had each inherited assets valued at €460,000 on the death of their mother in March 2008. Brendan had also inherited €120,000 on the death of his grandfather in 2002. Apart from this, none of the above had previously received any taxable gifts or inheritances.

Ronnie, Jake and Brendan are all Irish domiciled and resident. Janet is UK domiciled and UK resident and ordinarily resident.

Notes:

1. Ronnie purchased the van rental business as a going concern in January 2015 for €350,000. He has been involved in running the business on a full-time basis since then.

   The value of the business at the relevant dates is made up as follows:

	January 2015	July 2021
	€	€
Vans	175,000	650,000
Inventories of spare parts	30,000	150,000
Net receivables	10,000	180,000
Building	80,000	0
Goodwill	55,000	300,000
Total	350,000	1,280,000

   The cost of all vans exceeds their values outlined above. The vans given to Brendan are not included in the above figures.

2. Ronnie gave most of the assets of the business to Jake, but he gave two vans and the building to Brendan to help him establish his own office supplies business. The vans and building

transferred to him had been acquired by his father for his van rental business at the following costs:

	Date of acquisition	Cost
		€
Van 1	06/05/2016	20,000
Van 2	20/08/2017	45,000
Building	11/01/2015	80,000

Requirement

(a) Calculate the CGT liability, if any, arising from the above gifts.

(b) Calculate the CAT liability, if any, arising on the above gifts.

(Small gift exemption and annual exemption and stamp duty may be ignored.) It may be assumed that Ronnie has not disposed of any chargeable business assets since 1 January 2016.

Question 19.4

You are a tax specialist in a firm of Chartered Accountants. In June 2021, the tax director to whom you report has a telephone conversation with a client to whom your firm has provided tax advice occasionally in the past.

The client, Mr Mark Murphy, owns all the shares in an unquoted company, Murphy Electrical Wholesalers Ltd, which carries on a trade as electrical wholesalers. Mr Murphy inherited the shares in Murphy Electrical Wholesalers Ltd from his brother in June 1995. Mr Murphy has many other business interests and has **only been a non-executive director of the company**. Mr Murphy's son, Jake, works on a full-time basis for the company. Mr Murphy is considering gifting his shares in Murphy Electrical Wholesalers Ltd to Jake. Murphy Electrical Wholesalers Ltd has been valued recently at €3.5 million. The shares were valued at €2 million on the date of Mr Murphy's brother's death in 1995.

Mr Murphy has asked the tax director to advise him on the tax consequences of the proposed gift to his son.

Requirement

Draft a letter in the name of the tax director advising Mr Murphy on the tax consequences of the proposed gift of shares. Your letter should outline in particular the conditions that must be satisfied if any relief from CAT is to be availed of. (Annual exemption and small gift exemption may be ignored.)

Administration

20.1 Accountable Persons

The person accountable for payment of the CAT is the beneficiary. If a beneficiary is deceased, the CAT is recoverable from their personal representative.

20.2 Delivery of Returns

Self-assessment applies to CAT. A person who is accountable for CAT is obliged to **deliver a return** by 31 October (see **Section 20.3**). Any return involving claiming an exemption (other than small gift exemption) or a relief must be filed on ROS. All other returns may be filed using a paper tax return (short form IT38) provided the benefit received is an absolute interest without conditions and restrictions. If a paper return is filed, the taxpayer must calculate the CAT due. There are penalties if a return is not filed by the due date.

20.2.1 Obligation to File Returns for Capital Acquisitions Tax

The obligation to file self-assessment returns for CAT is imposed on persons who are accountable for CAT under CATCA 2003 where the **aggregate taxable values of all taxable benefits taken within the same group threshold exceeds 80% of the group threshold amount** that applies in the computation of CAT on that aggregate.

> **Example 20.1**
> In December 1995, €10,000 was received as a gift from a brother. In January 2021, €20,000 was received as a gift from a sister.
>
> The €32,500 group threshold applies to both of these gifts.
>
> The total aggregate is €30,000. Therefore, as the aggregate exceeds 80% of the group threshold amount, a return is required.

With effect from 1 January 2021, the accountable person must file a return if the gift/inheritance includes any agricultural property or relevant business property even if the 80% limit has not been exceeded. Even if no benefit has been received, a person is required to deliver a return if requested to do so by the Revenue Commissioners.

Forms 11 and 12 and CG50 (application for a CGT clearance certificate) all contain questions designed to act as prompts for the filing of CAT returns in relevant cases.

20.2.2 Content of a Return

1. The return must show:

    (a) every applicable gift or inheritance;
    (b) all property comprised in such gift or inheritance;
    (c) an estimate of the market value of the property; and
    (d) such particulars as may be relevant to the assessment of CAT in respect of such gift or inheritance.

2. The taxpayer must make on the return an assessment of the amount of CAT payable to the best of their knowledge, information and belief that ought to be charged and paid.
3. Finally, the person must pay any CAT calculated as due.

20.3 Payment of CAT and Interest, and Filing Returns

There is a fixed 'pay and file' date for CAT of 31 October. **All gifts and inheritances with a valuation date in the 12-month period ending on the previous 31 August will be included in the return to be filed by 31 October**. That means where:

1. the valuation date arises in the period from 1 January to 31 August, the pay and file deadline is 31 October in that year; and
2. where the valuation date arises in the period from 1 September to 31 December, the pay and file deadline is 31 October in the following year.

Similar to income tax and capital gains tax, where the taxpayer files the return and pays tax using ROS, the filing date is generally extended to mid-November.

A paper return may be filed where the beneficiary is not claiming any reliefs, exemptions, etc. other than the small gift exemption and the benefit received is an absolute interest without conditions or restrictions.

Where any other relief, etc. is being claimed, the return must be filed electronically through ROS.

Example 20.2
Ann receives a gift and it has a valuation date of 21 August 2021. The CAT due is €40,222 after claiming agricultural relief. Ann must file and pay €40,222 of CAT on ROS by 17 November 2021.

Terry receives an inheritance and it has a valuation date of 6 November 2021. The CAT due is €30,522. Terry is not entitled to any reliefs or exemptions.

As Terry is not entitled to any reliefs or exemptions, he can file a paper return if he wishes. That return (short form IT38) and payment are due by 31 October 2022. If he files and pays on ROS, the deadline will be some date (not yet known) in mid-November 2022.

Provided that CAT is paid by the due date, no interest is payable. However, if the CAT is not paid by the due date, simple interest of 0.0219% per day or part of a day is charged (equivalent to an annual rate of approximately 8%) from 1 November until the date of payment.

Provision is made whereby payments on account are applied first by the Revenue Commissioners in settlement of any outstanding interest charges and only then may the balance be set against the principal due.

There is a surcharge for the late filing of a return. The surcharge is calculated as follows:

1. 5% surcharge applies, subject to a maximum of €12,695, where the return is delivered within two months of the filing date (e.g. for the year ending 31 August 2021, any date between 1 November 2021 and 31 December 2021 inclusive);
2. 10% surcharge, up to a maximum of €63,485, applies where the tax return is not delivered within two months of the filing date.

Example 20.3

Anthony receives a gift on 1 August 2021 and the CAT due is €20,000. He files his form IT38 and makes a payment of €20,000 CAT on 1 December 2021. It was due on 31 October 2021. As a result of late filing, he is subject to a surcharge of 5% of €20,000, i.e. €1,000. He will also be liable to interest on €20,000 from 1 November to 1 December and on €1,000 from 31 October to the date of payment.

A person is deemed to have failed to deliver a return before the due date and will be liable to the surcharge where:

1. the person fraudulently or negligently delivers an incorrect return before the due date and does not correct the error in the return before the due date for filing the return;
2. the person delivers an incorrect return, but does not do so fraudulently or negligently, and it comes to the person's notice that the return is incorrect, but the person fails to correct the return without unreasonable delay; or
3. the person files a return before the due date but is served with a notice by the Revenue Commissioners, by reason of their dissatisfaction with the return, to deliver further evidence and that evidence is not provided within the time specified in the notice.

The accountable person must retain records for six years from the valuation date, or the filing date if the return is filed late. However, where the taxpayer has claimed a relief with conditions that needed to be satisfied for a period greater than four years (e.g. agricultural relief), supporting documentation must be retained for four years from the length of period for which the conditions to avail of the relief need to be satisfied.

20.4 Payment of CAT by Instalments

The accountable person may elect to pay CAT in respect of a taxable gift or inheritance by means of monthly instalments over a period not exceeding five years in such manner as may be determined by the Revenue Commissioners, the first of which becomes due on 31 October following the valuation date. Interest on the unpaid tax at 0.0219% per day must, however, be added to each instalment and paid at the same time as each instalment.

This option is only open where the taxable gift/inheritance comprises either of:

1. real property, e.g. freehold land and buildings; or
2. a limited interest, e.g. a life interest or interest for a period certain.

The CAT will be regarded as paid under self-assessment where the CAT due and payable is paid in instalments, by the payment of:

1. an amount which includes any instalment that is due prior to or on the date of the self-assessment; and
2. any further instalments of such CAT on the due dates as they fall due.

If a life tenant dies before all instalments have been paid, any instalments due after death cease to become payable. This applies whether or not instalment arrangements were entered into. Accordingly, where a life tenant dies and an instalment arrangement was not entered into, any instalments which would have not yet been paid had an instalment arrangement been entered into can be reclaimed.

If the property comprising a gift or inheritance is sold at any time prior to payment of all instalments, then the balance due becomes immediately payable, unless the interest of the donee or successor is a limited interest.

20.4.1 Agricultural and Business Property

If the gift or inheritance is property that is agricultural or business property (except quoted shares), then the daily interest rate is only three-quarters of the normal daily rate, i.e. 0.0164%. Also, the instalment arrangement can continue even if the property is sold or compulsorily acquired within the instalment period, provided that the proceeds are re-invested in other qualifying property within a year of the sale or compulsory acquisition or within six years in the case of the compulsory acquisition of agricultural property.

20.5 Overpayment of CAT

If CAT has been overpaid, the Revenue Commissioners will repay the excess CAT paid if a valid claim is made within four years, commencing on 31 October in the year in which the tax was due to be paid. Interest on CAT overpaid will accrue starting 93 days after the date on which a valid claim is made. In the case where the repayment arises due to a mistaken assumption on behalf of Revenue, interest will accrue from the date of payment of the excess CAT. Interest is payable at the rate of 0.011% per day or part of a day (equivalent to an annual interest rate of approximately 4%).

20.6 Surcharge on Undervaluation of Property

There is a surcharge to **penalise accountable persons who underestimate the market value of property** in returns for CAT purposes. The surcharge can be as high as 30% of the tax ultimately attributable to the property.

Questions

Review Questions
(See Suggested Solutions to Review Questions at the end of this textbook.)

Question 20.1

The managing partner of your firm of Chartered Accountants has asked you, as the CAT specialist, to advise him on each of the following matters:

(a) Who is an accountable person for CAT purposes?
(b) Under what circumstances is a return required from an accountable person and what is the time frame for the submission of each return?

(c) What details must be shown on a return and what must accompany a return?

(d) What action is required of an accountable person who becomes aware that a return that has been lodged is defective in a material respect?

(e) What are the consequences for the taxpayer of having made a return where the estimated value of the gift or inheritance is materially understated?

Requirement

Write a memorandum to the managing partner setting out your reply to the queries raised by him as outlined at (a) to (e) above.

Question 20.2

Robert Doyle died suddenly on 20 April 2021 without leaving a will. Under the laws of intestacy, his estate was inherited two-thirds by his wife Sheila, from whom he had been separated for the last 10 years, and one-third by his daughters, Ruth (21) and Angela (16).

Ruth and Angela had been living with their father when he died. Ruth has a full-time job and Angela is in full-time education and has no income of her own. Robert had taken out a life insurance policy and had nominated Ruth and Angela as the beneficiaries of this policy. The proceeds from the policy amounted to €140,000.

Apart from the insurance proceeds, Robert's assets at the date of his death consisted of the following:

	Value at 20 April 2021 and at the valuation date €
His house	600,000
50% share in a newsagents (Note 1)	900,000
€60,000 6% Exchequer Stock purchased by Robert in Nov. 2002	66,000
Cash	45,000
Holiday home in Co. Kerry	150,000
The following debts were outstanding:	
Income tax liabilities	15,000
Mortgage on his house	60,000

Notes:

1. Robert was a 50% owner in a thriving Dublin newsagents which he had established in 2001. Robert's partner will continue to manage the Doyles' 50% share in the newsagents on their behalf.

2. Funeral expenses and legal fees associated with the administration of his estate amounted to €3,000 and €6,000, respectively.

3. Neither Sheila, Ruth nor Angela had previously received any taxable gifts or inheritances. Sheila lives in the US but is Irish domiciled. The rest of the Doyle family are Irish domiciled and resident.

Requirement

(a) Compute the CAT liabilities, if any, payable by Sheila, Ruth and Angela.

(b) If the valuation date is 19 October 2021, outline the latest date by which CAT is payable if interest charges are to be avoided.

Part Four

Corporate Taxation

Corporation Tax: Residence and Administration

Chartered Accountants Ireland's *Code of Ethics* applies to all aspects of a Chartered Accountant's professional life, including dealing with corporation tax issues. As outlined at the beginning of this book, further information regarding the principles in the *Code of Ethics* is set out in **Appendix 2**.

Students should also be aware of the issues around tax planning, tax avoidance and tax evasion, and these are discussed in **Appendix 3**.

21.1 Overview

Irish corporation tax is levied on the worldwide income and gains of companies resident in Ireland and on the trading income of non-resident companies to the extent that it arises in Ireland. Under the Taxes Consolidation Act 1997 (TCA 1997), corporation tax is charged on the income and chargeable gains that together constitute the "profits" of companies. The period for which corporation tax is charged is the "accounting period". For corporation tax purposes, an accounting period cannot exceed 12 months.

As explained at CA Proficiency 1, when taxing the profits of a company it is essential that the total profits and expenses are correctly analysed between:

Case I	Trading income
Case II	Professions
Case III	Untaxed Irish income or foreign income
Case IV	Taxed Irish income and miscellaneous
Case V	Irish rental income

| Chargeable gains | Capital disposals (excluding development land) as adjusted for corporation tax purposes (i.e. chargeable gain $\times$ 33% $\div$ 12.5%) |
| Franked investment income (FII) | Distributions from Irish-resident companies, excluding Irish REITs. FII is exempt from Irish corporation tax. |

21.2 Charge to Corporation Tax

The question of whether, and how, a company is to be charged to corporation tax depends on whether or not it is resident in the State.

21.2.1 Resident Company

In the case of a **company resident in the State**, the charge to corporation tax is imposed on **all its income and chargeable gains** (excluding gains on development land) wherever arising and whether or not they are remitted to the State. Certain tax reliefs are only available to resident companies. Gains on disposals of development land are subject to CGT.

21.2.2 Non-resident Company

A **non-resident company** is chargeable to corporation tax only if it carries on a trade in the State through a branch or agency. Such a company is chargeable to corporation tax on any **income attributable to the branch or agency** and on any **chargeable gains on the disposal of specified Irish assets** used for the purposes of the trade or **attributable to the branch or agency**.

For example, if a German resident company sets up a factory in Ireland, the German company would be liable to Irish corporation tax on any income or gains attributable to the Irish factory.

A non-resident company with Irish source income not attributable to an Irish branch (e.g. Case V income) may be subject to Irish income tax, depending on the terms of the double tax treaty, if any.

A non-resident company is liable to CGT on chargeable gains on the disposal of:

- development land used for the purpose of an Irish branch; and
- specified Irish assets not used for the purpose of an Irish branch.

21.3 Residence of Companies

The residence of a company is normally located in the place from which it is managed and controlled. However, certain Irish-incorporated companies are also regarded as resident in the State.

21.3.1 Rules to Establish Residence of a Company

The chart below summarises the rules used to establish whether a company is resident or non-resident in Ireland for tax purposes.

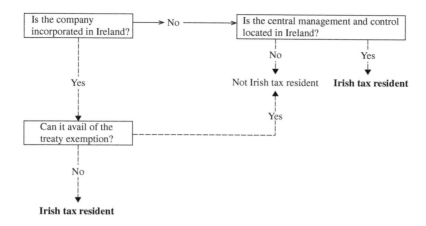

Companies Managed and Controlled in the State

The rules for determining the residence of a company have evolved from UK case law, which has been followed in Ireland. A company, irrespective of where it is incorporated, is Irish tax resident if it is "managed and controlled" in the State. Again, UK case law has provided guidance on what constitutes "managed and controlled". Based on these cases, the *key* factors that are taken into account in determining where a company is "managed and controlled" are:

- Where are the questions of important policy determined?
- Where are the directors' meetings held?
- Where do the majority of the directors reside?
- Where are the shareholders' meetings held?
- Where is the negotiation of major contracts undertaken?
- Where is the head office of the company?
- Where are the books of account and the company books (minute book, share register, etc.) kept?
- Where are the company's bank accounts?

As you can see, control is to do with where the directors hold their meetings and **"whether real decisions affecting the company are taken at those meetings"**. In each case, one needs to look at the facts of the case to determine where the company is actually managed and controlled.

Irish Incorporated Companies

As can be seen from the chart, Irish incorporated companies are tax resident in Ireland unless they can avail of the treaty exemption.

Treaty Exemption

The treaty exemption applies where the Irish incorporated company is regarded as resident in another country (generally managed and controlled in that other country) under the terms of the double taxation treaty (DTT) between Ireland and that country. The rules for determining where a company is managed and controlled are set out above.

Example 21.1

R Ltd is a UK incorporated company that manufactures clothes in England, France and Germany. It has a warehouse and offices in Ireland. All of its directors are Irish residents. All directors' and shareholders' meetings take place in Ireland. It has the following sources of income:

- UK profits;
- French profits;
- German profits;
- New Zealand deposit interest; and
- rental income in the USA.

Therefore, as its controlling body and management is located in Ireland, its place of residence is Ireland. **All** sources of profits are liable to Irish corporation tax.

21.4 Rates of Corporation Tax

21.4.1 Trading Rate of Corporation Tax

The trading rate of corporation tax is **12.5%** and applies to Schedule D Case I and II profits, capital gains as adjusted for tax and to certain foreign dividends (see **Chapter 22**, Section 22.2).

Example 21.2

Mary Ltd had total Case I profits of €700,000 in the year ended 31 December 2021. Corporation tax payable by Mary Ltd is €87,500 (€700,000 @ 12.5%).

21.4.2 Passive Rate of Corporation Tax

The passive rate of corporation tax of **25%** applies to the following income of companies:

1. **Case III** income, i.e. foreign income and untaxed Irish interest. Certain foreign dividends are, however, taxable at 12.5% (see **Chapter 22, Section 22.2.3**).
2. **Case IV** income, i.e. taxed Irish income and miscellaneous income not taxed under any other Case of Schedule D.
3. **Case V** income, i.e. Irish rental income.
4. Income from an "excepted trade" (which is beyond the scope of this textbook).

Example 21.3

John Ltd, a company involved in the construction of office buildings, has the following income for the year ended 31 December 2021:

	€
Case I – construction operations	800,000
Case III interest	20,000
Case V rental income	150,000
Total	970,000

The corporation tax payable by John Ltd is as follows:

	€
Case I: €800,000 @ 12.5%	100,000
Case III and Case V: €170,000 @ 25%	42,500
Total corporation tax payable	142,500

21.5 Reporting Requirements

A company, regardless of its size, is required to file its corporation tax return for an accounting period by the 23rd day of the ninth month after the end of the accounting period. For example, a company with an accounting period ended 31 December 2021 must pay the balance of corporation tax and file its corporation tax return by 23 September 2022.

The corporation tax return (Form CT1) is submitted electronically using ROS (Revenue Online Service).

21.5.1 Country-by-Country (CbC) Reporting

There is an additional filing requirement for an Irish-resident parent company of a large multinational enterprise (MNE), i.e. one where consolidated turnover exceeds €750 million in the preceding accounting period. The parent company is required to provide a country-by-country (CbC) report to Revenue within 12 months of the fiscal year end for each tax jurisdiction in which it does business.

The CbC report is based on guidance published in the OECD/G20 Action Plan on Base Erosion and Profit Shifting (BEPS). The report must contain details of the MNE's revenue, profit before income tax, income tax paid, income tax accrued, stated capital, accumulated earnings, number of employees and tangible assets in each tax jurisdiction. It also requires the tax identification numbers of all entities within the MNE, each company's tax residence and an indication of the business activities engaged in by each entity. Revenue will share the report with other tax administrations under mandatory automatic exchange of information provisions.

Revenue may impose a penalty for failure to make a return, or where an incorrect or incomplete return is filed. The penalty is €19,045, plus €2,535 for each day the failure continues.

21.6 Transfer Pricing

Corporation tax is charged on the total profits of a company for an accounting period contained in its financial statements. However, as previously noted, profits must be analysed and adjusted before inclusion in the corporation tax computation. Many of these adjustments were covered at CA Proficiency 1. As part of the analysis undertaken, transfer pricing rules need to be considered in respect of transactions between associated companies. Companies are 'associated' if one controls the other, or both are controlled by the same person.

Tax legislation sets out transfer pricing rules that apply the arm's length principle to trading and non-trading transactions between associated persons. In the absence of these rules, associated companies all over the world could supply and acquire goods, services, money, assets or anything else of commercial value from each other at prices that maximise their taxable profits in low-tax jurisdictions and minimise their profits in high-tax jurisdictions.

In Ireland, transfer pricing rules apply to trading transactions between associated companies that result in the understatement of Case I and Case II income for Irish corporation tax purposes. If the amount payable exceeds the arm's length amount, or the amount receivable is less than the arm's length amount, then the Case I and Case II profit must be adjusted to reflect the arm's length amount.

> **Example 21.4**
>
> Spruce Ltd sells goods to its subsidiary, Evergreen Ltd, at a price of €250 per unit. The arm's length price would have been €380 per unit. During the accounting period ended 31 December 2021, Spruce Ltd sold 1,000 of these items to Evergreen Ltd.
>
> A transfer pricing adjustment is made on the basis that the arm's length price was received. As a result, Spruce Ltd's taxable income for corporation tax is increased by €130,000 (1,000 × €130), as its profit was originally understated for tax purposes.
>
> Evergreen Ltd can adjust its allowable expenditure, reducing its taxable profit (or increasing its allowable loss) by €130,000 to reflect the arm's length price.

Finance Act 2019 extended the transfer pricing rules to non-trading activities, including the disposal and acquisition of assets (see **Chapter 24, Section 24.5.2**), with effect for accounting periods commencing on or after 1 January 2020. As a result, there may now be a potential charge to tax at 25% in respect of certain cross-border financing transactions, such as intragroup lending.

> **Example 21.5**
>
> Taragon Ltd, an Irish resident IT company makes an interest free loan of €1 million to its sister company, Turmeric Ltd, tax resident in Luxembourg.
>
> As Taragon Ltd is within the charge to Irish tax as regards the supply, the transaction is subject to transfer pricing rules. An adjustment will be required to Taragon Ltd's profits to align the transaction with arm's length principles.
>
> Assuming that an appropriate interest rate in respect of the arrangement is 4%, this would result in Taragon Ltd's profits increasing by €40,000, taxable at 25%, thus increasing the corporation tax liability by €10,000.

Currently, there is an exemption from the transfer pricing rules in respect of non-trading transactions where both parties are within the charge to Irish tax and the transaction is non-trading in nature. The exemption is only available to the supplier or acquirer where the transaction is assessed under Schedule D, Cases III, IV and V. Section 15 of Finance Act 2020 provides for significant amendments to this exemption, but the amended legislation is subject to a Ministerial commencement order and has not yet come into effect.

> **Example 21.6**
>
> Cupid Ltd and Hebe Ltd are both Irish resident companies and are associated for transfer pricing purposes. Hebe Ltd lets a commercial property for a below market value rent to Cupid Ltd for the purpose of its trade.
>
> As both companies are within the charge to Irish tax and Hebe Ltd is assessed under Schedule D, Case V on the rental income, transfer pricing rules should not apply to the computation of taxable profits for Hebe Ltd.

It is necessary to retain records that may reasonably be required to determine whether or not an arrangement exists for transfer pricing purposes and which support the arm's length nature of the arrangement. Small and medium enterprises (SMEs) are subject to reduced documentation requirements. Irish transfer pricing rules did not previously apply to SMEs. Finance Act 2019 extended the rules to SMEs, with the date of implementation subject to Ministerial Order and as yet does not apply.

A "small enterprise" is defined as employing fewer than 50 people with an annual turnover and/or balance sheet not exceeding €10 million. A small enterprise will be exempt from the documentation requirements whereas a medium enterprise will be obliged to have documentation for relevant arrangements with foreign counterparties to the extent that the aggregate consideration exceeds €1 million. A "medium enterprise" is an enterprise that is not small and:

▨ employs less than 250 employees; and
▨ have an annual turnover not exceeding €50 million; or
▨ total assets not exceeding €43 million.

The legislation contains anti-avoidance provisions to ensure that any transfer pricing adjustment is based on the substance rather than the form of the transaction. Revenue has the ability to disregard arrangements when, viewed in their totality, they differ from what would have been agreed by independent parties behaving in a commercially rational manner in comparable circumstances, thus eliminating any arrangements being used to avoid or exploit transfer pricing rules in an artificial manner.

Where an arrangement is disregarded by Revenue, the rules deny any tax deduction for the acquirer for the goods/services/assets. Alternatively, the transaction is replaced with an arrangement that achieves a commercially rational and expected result, with the arm's length consideration which is to be applied determined by reference to this alternative arrangement.

Questions

Review Questions
(See Suggested Solutions to Review Questions at the end of this textbook.)

Question 21.1

Overseas Ltd, a distribution company resident in Taxland and under the control of individuals resident in Taxland, has been trading in Ireland for many years through a branch.

The company has the following income during the year ended 31 December 2021:

	€
Trading profits (including branch trading profits of €600,000)	900,000
Interest income from surplus funds invested by branch (received gross)	20,000
Dividends received from Australian subsidiary	10,000

The Irish branch had chargeable gains, before adjustment, on the sales of premises out of which the branch traded of €32,000 in December 2021.

The company also owned development land in the State, not used for the purposes of the branch, which was sold in August 2021 to a manufacturer and realised a capital gain of €50,000. This land had been acquired in 1999.

Requirement
Calculate the relevant Irish tax liabilities of Overseas Ltd.

Double Taxation Relief

22.1 Introduction

It is common for the laws of two countries to levy tax on the same income and capital. This arises because a resident company is normally taxed on its worldwide profits and a non-resident company is taxed on its profits in that country only.

Example 22.1

An Irish resident company carries on business through a branch in a foreign country. The branch profits would be subject to corporation tax in Ireland as a resident company is liable to tax on its worldwide profits. The branch profits would also be subject to tax in the foreign country as the income arises in the foreign country.

If the foreign income is earned by an Irish tax resident company, then that income is liable to Irish tax. It may also be liable to tax in the foreign country in which it arises. This depends on the laws of that foreign country and the tax treaty between Ireland and the foreign country.

Alternatively, the Irish company may establish a wholly owned subsidiary in the foreign country or make an investment (e.g. 20% shareholding) in a foreign company. In this case, the foreign company typically will not be managed and controlled in Ireland and will not have Irish source income. Therefore, the foreign company has no Irish tax liability. The Irish parent or investor company will not receive any income from this foreign company until a dividend is paid to it. Therefore, the Irish parent/investor company does not have an Irish tax liability until it receives a dividend. Generally, this dividend will have been paid out of profits which have suffered foreign tax. When the dividend is actually paid, it may also suffer withholding tax in the foreign country.

When the Irish company receives the dividend, the dividend is taxable in Ireland. Generally there is a credit for foreign tax suffered, be it the withholding tax and/or an appropriate share of the tax on profits of the foreign company. Sometimes there is only relief by deduction – see **Section 22.3.1**.

22.2 Foreign Income: Rates of Corporation Tax

22.2.1 *Trading or Professional Services Income*

If the foreign income is trading income from a foreign branch of the Irish company, then provided the trade is not carried out wholly abroad – and, generally, this is the case – this income is assessed as Case I or Case II income and taxable at 12.5%.

If the trade is carried out wholly abroad, it is regarded as a foreign trade and the income therefrom is Case III income, subject to corporation tax at 25%.

22.2.2 *Interest or Rental Income*

If the income is interest or rental income from a foreign deposit or property, the income is taxable at 25%.

22.2.3 *Dividends*

Foreign dividends are assessed as Case III income. Previously, all foreign dividends were taxable at 25%. Currently, certain foreign dividends are taxable at 12.5%.

The 12.5% corporation tax rate will apply where an Irish company receives a dividend from a company resident in:

- an EU Member State;
- a country with which Ireland has signed a tax treaty;
- a company quoted on any stock exchange in the EU or a tax treaty country;

and either:

- the dividend is paid out of the trading profits of the non-resident company; or
- the dividend is received by a company that is a **portfolio investor** (i.e. holds no more than **5%** of the dividend-paying company).

However, if the dividend is partly paid out of the trading profits of the non-resident company, apportionment is required unless:

- 75% of its profits are trading profits (or dividends received from trading companies resident in EU or treaty countries); and
- 75% of the assets of the group must be trading assets.

All other foreign dividends are taxable at 25%.

22.3 Methods of Relief

Relief is given for double taxation in one of the following ways:

1. deduction;
2. credit; or
3. exemption.

In the absence of a double tax treaty (DTT) the deduction method will apply. If there is a DTT with the foreign country, then either the credit or exemption method will apply.

22.3.1 Deduction Method

If no other double tax relief (i.e. credit relief or an exemption) applies, under general Irish tax law foreign profits are reduced by the foreign tax borne on these profits for corporation tax purposes.

The deduction method applies, for example, in the case of other income (e.g. interest, rental income) if there is **no** DTT with the foreign country. There is no DTT with Argentina. The list of countries with which Ireland has a DTT is outlined in **Section 22.5**.

Example 22.2

X Ltd, an Irish resident company, was in receipt of the following income for the year ended 31 December 2021:

	€	€
Irish trading profits		500,000
Argentinian bank deposit interest	10,000	
Less: Argentinian withholding tax	(1,000)	9,000

There is no tax treaty between Ireland and Argentina, therefore the foreign income of €10,000 is reduced by the foreign tax of €1,000 for corporation tax purposes.

Corporation Tax Computation

	€
Schedule D Case I	500,000
Schedule D Case III	9,000
	509,000

Corporation tax
€500,000 @ 12.5% = €62,500
€9,000 @ 25% = €2,250
Corporation tax due   64,750

The effective rate of tax suffered on the Argentinian interest is:
(€1,000 + €2,250)/ €10,000 = 32.50%

22.3.2 Credit Method

Credit relief is allowed either because it is provided for **under a tax treaty** between Ireland and another country, or because Irish domestic tax law allows it (known as **unilateral credit relief**).

Example 22.3: Operation of credit relief

Ladder Ltd has a branch in a country with which Ireland has a tax treaty. In the year ended 31 December 2021, the branch had profits of €120,000 on which tax was paid at 10%. Ladder Ltd's total Case I profits, including the branch profit, for the year ended 31 December 2021 were €400,000.

	€
Irish corporation tax	
Schedule D Case I	400,000
Corporation tax @ 12.5%	50,000
Less: credit relief €120,000 @ 10%	(12,000)
Tax due	38,000

Irish effective rate of tax $\dfrac{50,000}{400,000} \times 100 = 12.5\%$

Note: branch profits are taxable under Case I rather than Case III where the trade is not carried out "wholly" abroad.

Credit relief is far more beneficial than relief by deduction as it can fully relieve any liability to Irish tax, e.g. if the foreign tax rate had been 12.5% or higher, then no Irish tax would have been payable on the foreign income. Under credit relief, the Irish company will suffer the higher of the Irish and the foreign rate.

If the foreign income is a dividend, credit relief is normally available not only for any foreign withholding tax but also in respect of **tax paid on the profits out of which the dividend has been paid (underlying tax)**. Under many of Ireland's tax treaties, there is a minimum shareholding requirement as a condition of obtaining credit relief for underlying tax on dividends. However, unilateral credit relief rules also apply and can be more beneficial in the case of dividends. (There is a formula for the calculation of underlying tax, but this is beyond the scope of this textbook.) The Irish corporation tax liability will be on the aggregate of the dividend received and the amount of credit relief.

There are other issues that arise when dealing with the credit for foreign tax, including unilateral credit relief, limit on credit relief and special provisions for dividends from EU and EEA countries with a tax treaty with Ireland. These issues are beyond the scope of this textbook.

22.3.3 Exemption Method

This simply exempts the profits from tax in one of the two countries. The most common example is that under many DTTs **interest is not liable to tax in the country of origin**, only in the country of residence.

Example 22.4

A Ltd, an Irish resident company, was in receipt of the following income for the year ended 31 December 2021:

	€
Irish trading profits	800,000
UK deposit interest	10,000

Under the terms of the Irish/UK DTT, UK deposit interest earned by an Irish resident company is only taxable in Ireland.

	€
Schedule D Case I	800,000
Schedule D Case III	10,000
	810,000
€800,000 @ 12.5%	100,000
€10,000 @ 25%	2,500
Corporation tax due	102,500

No UK tax paid as exempt in UK under Ireland–UK DTT.

22.4 Ireland as a Holding Company Location

Irish tax law contains provisions designed to make Ireland an attractive location for holding companies and, thereby, attract holding companies and the related headquarter activities to Ireland.

- There is the very low holding of 5% to avail of unilateral credit relief.
- There is on-shore pooling of excess foreign tax credits in relation to qualifying foreign dividends. This topic is beyond the scope of this textbook.
- There is the exemption from tax in the case of capital gains from the disposal of holdings in "subsidiaries" – this is dealt with in **Chapter 25, Section 25.3** on company capital gains.
- There is an exemption from the close company surcharge on dividends from these shareholdings, but only where they are shares in a foreign company. This is dealt with in **Chapter 26**.

22.5 Double Taxation Treaties

Ireland has concluded double taxation treaties with the following countries:

Albania	Estonia	Luxembourg	Serbia
Armenia	Ethiopia	Macedonia	Singapore
Australia	Finland	Malaysia	Slovak Rep.
Austria	France	Malta	Slovenia
Bahrain	Georgia	Mexico	South Africa
Belarus	Germany	Moldova	Spain
Belgium	Greece	Montenegro	Sweden
Bosnia & Herzegovina	Hong Kong	Morocco	Switzerland
	Hungary	Netherlands	Thailand
Botswana	Iceland	New Zealand	Turkey
Bulgaria	India	Norway	Ukraine
Canada	Israel	Pakistan	United Arab Emirates
Chile	Italy	Panama	United Kingdom
China	Japan	Poland	United States of America
Croatia	Kazakhstan	Portugal	
Cyprus	Korea (Rep. of)	Qatar	Uzbekistan
Czech Rep.	Kuwait	Romania	Vietnam
Denmark	Latvia	Russia	Zambia
Egypt	Lithuania	Saudi Arabia	

Given the possibility of delay in bringing treaties into force with relevant foreign countries, the treaty requirement has been relaxed to mere signing of the treaty, i.e. once the treaty has been signed with the country, companies dealing with that country may avail of its provisions as they impact on Irish tax.

For countries outside the EU, it is normal practice to advise a student in an exam as to whether Ireland has a treaty with a particular country.

Questions

Review Questions
(See Suggested Solutions to Review Questions at the end of this textbook.)

Question 22.1

Foreign Income Ltd is in receipt of the following sources of income for the year ended 31 December 2021:

	€
Trading income	800,000
Dividend from Treaty Ltd (Note 1)	88,000
Dividend from Non-treaty Ltd (Note 2)	80,000
Dividend from Irish Maniacs Ltd (Note 3)	75,000

Notes:

1. The dividend of €88,000 was received from its 100% subsidiary in a country with which Ireland has a tax treaty and the dividend was paid out of trading profits.
2. The dividend of €80,000 was received from an unquoted company in a country with which Ireland does not have a tax treaty.
3. Irish Maniacs Ltd is an Irish tax resident company.

Requirement
Calculate the corporation tax payable for the accounts year ended 31 December 2021.

Expenditure on Intangible Assets and Research & Development

Learning Objectives

After studying this chapter you will be able to:
- Advise on the relief for expenditure incurred on the provision of intangible assets for trade purposes.
- Advise on and calculate relief in respect of expenditure incurred on qualifying research and development activities.

23.1　Intangible Assets: Capital Allowances

(**Note:** the computations for capital allowance are beyond the scope of this textbook.)

There is tax relief for capital expenditure incurred by companies on the provision of intangible assets for the purposes of a trade. In summary, the legislation provides for capital allowances against taxable income on capital expenditure incurred by companies on the provision of intangible assets for the purposes of a trade. If the expenditure is incurred before trading commences, it will be allowed when the relevant trade commences.

The scheme applies to intangible assets that are recognised as such under generally accepted accounting practice and which are included in the specified categories listed in the legislation.

An asset may be recognised as an intangible asset in a company's financial statements only if:

- the cost of the asset can be reliably measured; and
- it is probable that future economic benefits attributable to the asset will flow to the enterprise.

The list of specified intangible assets includes: patents, registered designs, trade marks, brands, copyrights, domain names, customer lists, know-how and related goodwill to the extent that it relates to these categories of intangible property.

Companies are eligible for a writing-down allowance, which reflects the standard accounting treatment of intangible assets. However, companies can opt instead for a fixed write-down period of 15 years at a rate of **7% per annum and 2% in the final year**.

The normal rules in relation to balancing allowances/charges apply on the disposal of an intangible asset, with a significant exception. There is no clawback of allowances where an intangible asset that was acquired before 14 October 2020 is disposed of more than five years after the beginning of the accounting period in which the asset was first provided. If the disposal is to a connected company, then it can only claim capital allowances of the lower of what it paid and the allowances not claimed by the previous owner.

There are a number of restrictions applying to ensure that:

1. relief is targeted to business **activities** (amounting to the conduct of a **relevant trade**) in which the specified intangible assets are used;
2. the aggregate amount of capital allowances and related interest that may be claimed in any accounting period is limited to 80% of the trading income of the relevant trade where the asset is acquired on or after 11 October 2017. Where the asset was acquired before this date, the aggregate amount of capital allowances and related interest that may be claimed in any accounting period is limited to the trading income of the relevant trade. Related interest in this context is interest incurred as a trading expense on borrowings to fund expenditure on intangible assets for which capital allowances are claimed. Where the relevant trade relates to assets acquired before and after 11 October 2017, the trading income is deemed to consist of two separate income streams, with the income apportioned reasonably. This results in capital allowances on assets acquired before 11 October 2017 not being available for offset against income arising from assets acquired after 11 October 2017 and any related interest; and
3. the capital allowances may only be offset against income from a "relevant trade", i.e. a trade consisting of:
   (a) managing, developing or exploiting the intangible assets; or
   (b) activities which consist of the sale of goods or services that derive the greater part of their value from the intangible assets or whose value is increased by the use of the intangible assets.

Example 23.1		
	Accounting Period 1	**Accounting Period 2**
	€	€
Income from relevant trade before allowances	10 m	15 m
Capital allowances available under scheme*	11 m	9 m
Allowances carried forward from previous accounting period	NIL	3 m
Computation of income		
Income from relevant trade before allowances	10 m	15 m
Capital allowances (max. 80%)	8 m	12 m
Income chargeable	2 m	3 m
Allowances carried forward to next accounting period	3 m	NIL
* Intangible asset acquired after 11/10/2017.		

The definition for intangible assets is the same as that for stamp duty exemption for qualifying intellectual property (see **Chapter 11, Section 11.1**).

23.2 Research & Development Tax Credit

23.2.1 Overview

The research and development (R&D) tax credit is provided for by section 766 TCA 1997 and allows a qualified company engaged in qualifying R&D activities to avail of a 25% tax credit on qualifying expenditure. The various qualifying conditions are explained in detail below.

Essentially, the R&D tax credit operates by reducing the corporation tax liability in two ways:

1. by deducting qualifying expenditure when calculating the taxable income, in the normal manner; and then
2. by applying the 25% R&D tax credit to the corporation tax liability.

There is no minimum spend required and there is no maximum limit on the qualifying expenditure. The 25% credit can be used to reward key employees (excluding directors) and/or to reduce the company's corporation tax payable and possibly get a refund of corporation tax.

23.2.2 Qualified Company

The R&D tax credit is available to all companies falling within the charge to Irish corporation tax that undertake qualifying R&D activities within the European Economic Area (EEA) or the UK. In addition, the legislation specifies that "qualified company" is one that:

- carries on a trade itself, **or** is a 51% subsidiary of a trading company **or** is a member of a trading group (i.e. a 51% subsidiary of a holding company of a trading company);
- carries out R&D activities;
- maintains a record of its R&D expenditure; and
- maintains separate records if it has R&D activities in separate geographical locations.

As is evident from the first list item above, the legislation is drafted in terms applicable to groups of companies, a single company being treated as a group comprising one company. **Section 23.2.6** looks at groups in more detail.

23.2.3 Qualifying R&D Activities

The legislation defines R&D activities as "systematic, investigative or experimental activities in a field of science or technology", being one or more of the following:

- basic research;
- applied research; and
- experimental development.

Each of these is defined in tax law. In addition, activities will not be R&D activities unless they:

- "seek to achieve scientific or technological advancement; and
- involve the resolution of scientific or technological uncertainty."

However, the R&D does not have to be successful. Companies claiming the R&D tax credit are not required to hold the intellectual property rights resulting from the R&D work.

23.2.4 Qualifying R&D Expenditure

In general, expenditure incurred by a company on R&D activities carried out in an EU or EEA Member State or in the UK qualifies for the R&D tax credit. However, in the case of an Irish tax-resident company, the credit is available only if the expenditure on the R&D does not otherwise qualify for a tax benefit elsewhere. Also, this law does not apply to expenditure on a building or structure – see **Section 23.2.5** for the rules on buildings used for R&D.

For expenditure to be regarded as expenditure on R&D for the purposes of the tax credit, it must qualify for tax relief in the State under one of the following:

- as an allowable deduction of a trade (e.g. payroll) or as a charge on income (or would be but for accounting rules) – this does not include capital allowances;
- as capital allowances on plant or machinery, or
- as other expenditure that qualifies for scientific research allowance.

The expenditure must be incurred wholly and exclusively in carrying on the R&D activities. Accordingly, indirect overheads such as general administration costs are not included. Where plant or machinery will not be used wholly and exclusively for R&D activities, a proportionate allocation of the expenditure, as appears to be just and reasonable, will be made.

The cost of subcontracting or outsourcing R&D does not generally qualify for the tax credit. Where it does qualify, the amount of outsourced R&D expenditure qualifying for relief is restricted to the non-outsourced R&D expenditure up to a maximum of €100,000 or to 15% of the non-outsourced R&D expenditure in that accounting period, whichever is the higher. Where a company outsources R&D activities to a third party that is not a university or third-level educational institute, the company must notify the subcontractor, in advance of making the payment for the service, that the company will be making a claim under section 766 TCA 1997 in relation to that activity. The subcontractor is then not entitled make a claim, under section 766, for expenditure it incurs in relation to that same R&D activity.

Grants received from the State, the EU, EEA or the UK (or any agency of these) must be deducted from qualifying expenditure. Interest payments do not qualify as expenditure on R&D. Expenditure that is met by any EU, EEA or UK grant assistance is not considered to be expenditure incurred by the company and will therefore not be eligible for the credit. Expenditure incurred under cost sharing or pooling arrangements will qualify for the tax credit only to the extent that the expenditure is incurred by the qualified company in the carrying on by it of qualifying R&D activities. If the company carrying on the R&D in Ireland receives a cost-sharing contribution from another company in the international group, this receipt is ignored, i.e. it is the gross expenditure on R&D that is taken into account. Reimbursements or sharing of costs incurred by another company in the carrying on of R&D activities would not qualify.

Documentary evidence must be maintained in respect of the credit claim. This includes details of the technical aspects of the project, the skills of the R&D team, as well as the basis for the actual costs and time incurred on the project.

23.2.5 Buildings Used for R&D

A 25% credit is also available for capital expenditure on buildings or structures used for the purpose of carrying on an R&D activity where such a building also qualifies for industrial buildings capital allowances. Such expenditure can qualify provided that at least 35% of the use of the building, over a specified four-year period, is for R&D purposes (section 766A TCA 1997). Qualifying relevant expenditure includes construction, reconstruction, repair or renewal of a building, but not the cost of the site nor expenditure that has been met directly or indirectly by assistance (grant or otherwise) from the State, the EU/EEA or the UK, or any agency thereof. The expenditure will not qualify if it qualifies for tax relief in another EU/EEA country or in the UK.

Where only part of a building is used for R&D purposes, the relevant expenditure on the building will be restricted to the proportion used for R&D purposes (i.e. specified relevant expenditure). For example, if 50% of the building is to be used for R&D activities, then only 50% of the construction expenditure will be "specified relevant expenditure".

The tax credit is utilised in the same manner as set out in **Section 23.2.8**.

Example 23.2

Rev Ltd constructed a building in Kildare in the accounting period ended 31 December 2021 at a cost of €1 million, including site cost of €240,000. The R&D activities to be carried on by the company in that building over the specified relevant period will represent 40% of all activities carried on in the building or structure. The tax credit is calculated as follows:

	€
Building costs	1,000,000
Less: site cost	(240,000)
Relevant expenditure	760,000
Specified relevant expenditure	760,000 @ 40% = €304,000
Tax credit	304,000 @ 25% = €76,000

The full amount of the tax credit of €76,000 is used to reduce the corporation tax liability in respect of the accounting period ended 31 December 2021. If any excess remains, it may be carried back to reduce the corporation tax of the preceding accounting period. A refund of any unused credits may be claimed, as outlined at **Section 23.2.8**. Unused credits may be carried forward indefinitely.

23.2.6 Groups

The definition of a group is the same as that for loss relief purposes as outlined in **Chapter 24**, except that the shareholding requirement is only 51%, i.e. a parent and its 51% subsidiaries form a group. In addition, companies are treated as being in the same group, for the purposes of this credit, if they are under common control.

Those members of a group that incur R&D expenditure in the current period may allocate the expenditure between them as they wish. Any such allocation is to be specified in a written notice made jointly by the members of the group. If no allocation is made, the relief is allocated between the group members that incurred qualifying expenditure in the current period in the same proportion as the amount of total group expenditure the company incurred, i.e. if a group member incurred 50% of the group qualifying R&D expenditure in the current period, that group member will be allocated 50% of the relief available to the group.

Corporation tax of an accounting period of a company can be reduced by 25% of so much of the qualifying expenditure of the group on R&D as has been allocated to the company.

Where, in an accounting period, the amount of the credit exceeds the corporation tax against which it can be offset, the excess is to be carried back for offset against corporation tax payable in the preceding accounting period and a refund of any unused credits may be claimed, as outlined at **Section 23.2.8**. Unused credits can be carried forward indefinitely.

23.2.7 Reward Key Employees

The 25% R&D tax credit can be used to reward key employees working in the R&D activities of the company. To qualify, the employee must not be a director or own 5% or more of the company or an associated company. At least 50% of the employee's emoluments must qualify for the R&D tax credit and the employee must perform 50% or more of the duties of his or her employment in the conception or creation of new knowledge, products, processes, methods or systems. The employee can claim the R&D credit against their income tax payable. An employee's maximum claim is limited in that the employee's effective income tax rate cannot be reduced below 23%. Unclaimed credits can be carried forward by the individual. If the credit or some of it is given to the employee(s), then that part of the credit is not available to the company to offset against corporation tax.

Example 23.3

High Tech Ltd, a technology company, is an Irish subsidiary of a US multinational. It has had an R&D programme for a number of years. During 2021, it significantly expanded its R&D programme. Its R&D spend was as follows:

- new building, all of which is used for R&D, at a cost of €2 million, of which €200,000 was the cost of the site;
- €200,000 on new machinery; and
- €300,000 on salaries, overheads, etc.

High Tech Ltd has a cost-sharing agreement with its US parent company and fellow subsidiaries. As a result, it received a contribution of €350,000 from these companies towards the cost of its R&D programme. High Tech Ltd satisfies the conditions regarding genuine R&D (maintaining records, etc.). High Tech Ltd's corporation tax payable for the year ended 31 December 2021, before R&D credit, is €582,000.

What is the R&D tax credit due to High Tech Ltd for the year ended 31 December 2021 and what is the final corporation tax payable, assuming that €25,000 of the credits are surrendered to key employee(s) working in R&D?

	€
Tax credit due on qualifying R&D expenditure	
Machinery	200,000
Salaries, overheads, etc.	300,000
Qualifying for credit	500,000
R&D tax credit @ 25%	125,000
Less: surrendered to key R&D staff	25,000
Credit due against corporation tax	100,000
Tax credit due on R&D building	
Expenditure on building	2,000,000
Less: site cost	(200,000)
	1,800,000
Total credit due re. building @ 25%	450,000
Corporation tax payable	
Originally due	582,000
Less: R&D tax credits	(100,000)
R&D tax credit re. building	(450,000)
Corporation tax payable	32,000

23.2.8 *Reduce Corporation Tax*

Any credit not given to a key employee working in R&D can be claimed against corporation tax. Claims must be made within 12 months of the end of the accounting period.

- The credit is used to **first reduce** the liability to **corporation tax for that accounting period**.
- The company may then offset any unused portion of the credit against the corporation tax of the **preceding accounting period**.
- Where a company has offset the credit against the corporation tax of the preceding accounting period or where no corporation tax arises for that period, and an excess still remains, the company may make a claim to have the amount of that **excess paid** to it by the Revenue Commissioners in **three instalments**. The three instalments will be paid over a period of at least 33 months, from the end of the accounting period in which the expenditure was incurred. Students are required to do a computation involving claiming the credit against corporation tax payable, but are not required to do a calculation involving a repayment of the credit.
- There is a limit on the amount of tax credits payable to a company by Revenue. The limit refers to expenditure on R&D activities and on buildings which qualify for the credit. The amount cannot exceed the greater of:
  - the corporation tax payable by the company for the 10 years prior to the accounting period preceding the period in which the expenditure was incurred, or
  - the amount of PAYE, PRSI and USC the company is required to remit in the period in which the expenditure was incurred and in the previous accounting period, as adjusted for prior claims.
- Any credit that has not been offset against corporation tax or refunded is available to offset against corporation tax of future accounting periods.

Example 23.4
In the accounting period ended 31 December 2021, PQR Ltd incurred €400,000 of qualifying expenditure on R&D. The following shows the company's corporation tax liability:

	CT Liability
12 months ended 31/12/2020	€30,000
12 months ended 31/12/2021	€10,000
12 months ended 31/12/2022	€15,000
12 months ended 31/12/2023	€10,000

R&D tax credit due in respect of the accounting period ended 31/12/2021:
   €400,000 @ 25% = €100,000

Of this €100,000, €20,000 is surrendered to key employees working in R&D.

Offset remaining R&D tax credit as follows:

	CT Liability	Order	Tax credit
12 months ended 31/12/2021	€10,000	1	€10,000
12 months ended 31/12/2020	€30,000	2	€30,000

The unclaimed credit of €100,000 − €20,000 − €10,000 − €30,000 = €40,000 may be reclaimed from Revenue over the next three years or so, to the extent it has not been used to offset against corporation tax of subsequent accounting periods. This repayment assumes that the company has paid sufficient corporation tax, PAYE, PRSI and USC in 2021 and 2020.

23.2.9 Clawback

If the building or structure, expenditure on which qualified for a R&D credit, is sold or ceases to be used by the company for R&D activities or for the purpose of the same trade that was carried on by the company at the start of the "specified relevant period" within 10 years of being incurred for the purposes of R&D, no further credit is to be given and any credit given will be clawed back. The clawback is by way of a Case IV assessment of four times the credit granted, which is then taxed at 25% to equal the amount of the credit originally granted.

Legislation also provides for a clawback in the case of a claim for a repayment or surrender of credits found to be incorrect in any material particular. Again the clawback is by way of a Case IV assessment of four times the excess repayment claimed/surrendered, which is then taxed at 25% to equal the excessive amount originally claimed/surrendered. However, the clawback amount is equal to eight times the amount of the excess credit surrendered to key employees in the case of a claim that is found to be deliberately false or overstated. Where such an amount is charged to tax under Case IV, no loss, deficit, expense or credit shall be allowed to shelter the liability raised. In addition, this Case IV amount will not form part of the close company surcharge calculation (see **Chapter 26**).

Penalties and interest charges for late payment of tax will apply where a clawback occurs.

23.2.10 Micro-entities and Small Companies

Finance Act 2019 introduced an enhanced R&D regime for micro-entities and small companies, which is subject to enactment by ministerial commencement order. A micro-entity or small company is one that employs fewer than 50 persons and whose annual turnover and/or annual balance sheet total does not exceed €10 million.

Under the proposed provisions:

- the R&D tax credit rate is increased to 30% (excluding buildings);
- there is an additional method to determine the cap in calculating the payable credit to the company, being the aggregate of twice the payroll liabilities of the relevant accounting period in which the R&D expenditure is incurred;
- the R&D tax credit can be claimed on pre-trading expenditure (other companies can only claim once they have commenced trading), excluding expenditure on buildings;
- the pre-trading R&D tax credit may, after offsetting it against the corporation tax liability, be offset against income tax and USC or VAT liabilities in the same period; and
- the pre-trading R&D tax credit may not be surrendered to key employees nor can a claim for a repayment of the tax credit be made.

The credit may not be offset against payroll liabilities where emoluments to which the payroll liabilities relate remain unpaid three months after the end of the relevant accounting period. A claim must be submitted within 12 months of the end of the accounting period.

Questions

Review Questions
(See Suggested Solutions to Review Questions at the end of this textbook.)

Question 23.1

Grabbit Ltd acquired the trade and assets of Utopia Ltd, an unconnected Irish tax resident company, on 1 May 2021 for a total consideration of €7 million. €3 million of the purchase price relates directly to patents held by Utopia Ltd and the goodwill related to those patents. The amortisation policy of Grabbit Ltd is to amortise intangible assets over an 18-year period.

Requirement
Advise if any of the expenditure incurred by Grabbit Ltd is eligible for capital allowances, giving reasons for your conclusion. Your answer should include the options available to Grabbit Ltd to claim writing down allowances, if available.

Question 23.2

Global Fishing Ltd, an Irish trading company with annual turnover of €12 million, has incurred the costs listed below in the year ended 31 December 2021 in researching new fishing techniques using sonar technology.

	€
Staff costs (Note 1)	2,600,000
Plant and machinery expenditure (Note 2)	200,000
R&D payments made to subcontractors (Note 3)	155,000

Notes:
1. The company employs 58 people, of which two are engaged directly with R&D. Staff costs include the following:

	€
Two employees directly involved in R&D activities	156,000
Employer's PRSI contributions for employees directly involved in R&D activities	17,250
	173,250

2. During the year ended 31 December 2021, the company purchased plant and machinery that qualifies for capital allowances at a total cost of €200,000. The plant and machinery was used 50% of the time for research activities.
3. The R&D payments were made to unconnected third-party subcontractors to carry out research on the company's behalf.

Professional advice taken confirms that the research undertaken by Global Fishing Ltd is qualifying research and development activity for the purpose of the research and development tax credit.

Requirement
Calculate the R&D tax credit that can be claimed by Global Fishing Ltd in respect of expenditure incurred during the year ended 31 December 2021.

Group Relief

Learning Objectives

After studying this chapter you will be able to:

■ Determine when a company can make certain payments without deduction of income tax to another group company.
■ Determine when a company can surrender certain losses to another group company.
■ Implement efficient utilisation of trading losses, excess charges, non-trade losses, certain capital allowances and management expenses within a group of companies.
■ Advise on and calculate restrictions on loss relief following a change of ownership.

24.1 Introduction

A company is a separate legal entity for tax purposes. However, where certain conditions are met, companies can be considered to be members of a group that can then avail of reliefs that are not available to single entities. There are different definitions of groups depending on the type of relief claimed. Broadly speaking, these reliefs may be broken down under the following headings:

1. Payments relief.
2. Loss relief.
3. Relief from tax on capital gains (see **Chapter 25**).

24.2 Payments Relief

Certain payments made by companies are generally required to be made under deduction of income tax at the standard rate:

■ yearly interest;
■ annual payments; and
■ patent royalties.

A company making any of the above payments would, in the normal course of events, be required to deduct income tax at the standard rate from the gross amount due and pay this over to Revenue as part of its corporation tax payments. Under section 410 TCA 1997, such payments of interest and royalties can be made without the necessity to withhold 20% income tax, i.e. these payments can be made gross within a group provided certain conditions are satisfied.

24.2.1 Conditions to be Satisfied

1. Both the paying and the recipient company must be resident in a "relevant Member State", i.e. an EU Member State, an EEA country that has a tax treaty with Ireland, or the UK.
2. There must be a 51% (direct or indirect) shareholding relationship between paying and recipient company, i.e. more than 50% of its ordinary share capital is owned. In **Example 24.1** below, A Ltd indirectly owns 54% of D Ltd, while B Ltd owns 90% of C Ltd directly. The 51% relationship is also satisfied when both companies are 51% subsidiaries of another company. Shareholdings in share-dealing companies and companies not resident in a relevant Member State cannot be used to establish the 51% relationship.
3. If the recipient company is not resident in the State, the payment must be taxable in its country of residence.

Example 24.1: 51% test

Assuming all companies are Irish resident, interest paid by D Ltd to A Ltd will qualify for relief, as there is a 54% relationship between these two companies (i.e. 100% × 90% × 60% = 54%). Equally, interest paid by D Ltd to B Ltd or C Ltd will qualify for relief, as there is at least a 51% relationship between the companies.

Example 24.2

Qualifying payments from Z Ltd to H Ltd, or vice versa, would qualify for relief as both companies are 51% subsidiaries of another company, providing X Ltd, Z Ltd and H Ltd are resident in a relevant Member State and the recipient company is taxed on the interest/royalty in its country of resident.

If X Ltd is resident in, say, the USA, the conditions would not be met and relevant payments between them would be subject to 20% income tax being withheld at source.

24.3 Loss Relief

The legislation provides that, where a loss group exists, certain losses incurred by one group company can be used by another group company (sections 411–429 TCA 1997) **during the same accounting period**. The companies and the losses must satisfy the qualifying group requirements as outlined in **Sections 24.3.1** and **24.3.2**.

A formal claim for group relief must be made by the "profit maker" within two years of the end of the accounting period in which the loss arose, Formal consent must also be given by the 'loss-maker'. Any payments to the loss maker by the profit-maker for use of the losses are ignored for corporation tax purposes provided they do not exceed the amount of the loss surrendered, i.e. no tax deduction is available to the profit-maker in respect of the payment and the receipt by the loss-maker is not taxable.

As outlined at CA Proficiency 1, separate rules apply for each type of loss claimed by a company. Losses that can be surrendered within a group are:

- trading losses excluding pre-trading losses;
- excess charges;
- excess management expenses (**Chapter 27**); and
- excess Case V capital allowances.

The application of these losses for group relief purposes is outlined in **Section 24.3.3**. Losses incurred under Cases III, IV and V, capital losses, and losses from earlier or later accounting periods cannot be group relieved.

24.3.1 Qualifying Group – 75% Relationship

To avail of group loss relief, the profit-maker must be in the same "75% group" as the loss-maker. Under section 411 TCA 1997, this condition is satisfied in relation to two companies if one company holds, directly or indirectly, not less than 75% of the ordinary share capital of that company or both companies are 75% subsidiaries of a third company. In addition, the parent company must be entitled to 75% of the profits available for distribution and 75% of assets on a winding up. For the purposes of the 75% test, "ordinary share capital" is defined as meaning all the issued share capital (by whatever name called) of the company other than capital where the holders have a right to a dividend at a fixed rate but have no other right to a share in the profits of the company. It should be noted that this definition would include participating preference shares as "ordinary share capital".

In determining if one company owns 75% of another company, the following shareholdings must be ignored:

- shareholdings in share-dealing companies;
- shareholdings in companies not resident in the EU or in a country that has not signed a tax treaty with Ireland.

In addition, a company cannot be treated as a 75% subsidiary of another company unless the other company is resident in the EU or in a country that has signed a tax treaty with Ireland, or is quoted on a stock exchange in such a country or in one approved by the Minister for Finance.

A company may establish the 75% holding by aggregating any ordinary shares held directly in that company and also those held indirectly through a third company.

Example 24.3: 75% loss group

All companies are Irish tax resident unless otherwise stated.

1. The loss-maker is a 75% subsidiary of profit-maker or vice versa:

2. Both are 75% subsidiaries of a third company:

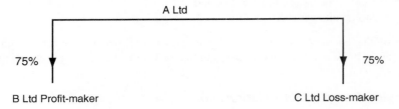

If A Ltd is resident in Germany (an EU country) or the USA (a country with which Ireland has a tax treaty), then B Ltd and C Ltd are in an Irish loss group.

If A Ltd is resident in Bolivia, a country with which Ireland does not have a tax treaty, then for a group to exist, A Ltd must be quoted on a recognised stock exchange in the EU or a country which has signed a tax treaty with Ireland, or a stock exchange which is approved by the Minister for Finance.

3. Establishing a 75% relationship through a third company:

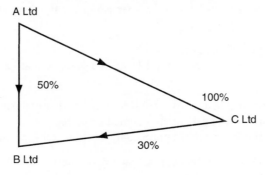

A, B and C Ltd are all members of the same 75% loss group.

continued overleaf

4. Non-qualifying group

A Ltd

↓ 100%

B Ltd

↓ 100%

C Ltd

A Ltd is an Irish unquoted company. A Ltd and C Ltd are Irish resident. B Ltd, an unquoted company, is resident in Peru (which does not have a tax treaty with Ireland). A Ltd and C Ltd are not in a group for loss relief purposes as A Ltd:

- does not hold the shares in C Ltd directly; and

- does not hold the shares indirectly through a company resident in the EU or a country with which Ireland has signed a tax treaty.

24.3.2 *Qualifying Group – Non-resident Company Losses*

In the past, all members of the group had to be Irish tax resident. Therefore, only Irish companies could be used to establish the 75% relationship and the loss must have been incurred by an Irish resident company and only surrendered for group relief to another Irish resident group company.

This rule was changed as a result of the decision of the European Court of Justice (ECJ) in 1998 in the case of *Imperial Chemical Industries plc v. Colmer* (Case C-264/96). As a result of this and subsequent legislation, Irish tax law was amended to provide that companies resident in an EU Member State or EEA State that has a tax treaty with Ireland (i.e. a relevant Member State) can be taken into account in:

- determining if the group relationship exists, i.e. 75% relationship (**Section 24.3.1**); and
- to allow losses to be surrendered between the Irish resident company and the Irish branch of a company resident in a relevant Member State.

While the TCA now provides that companies resident in a treaty country (excluding relevant Member States detailed above) or quoted on a recognised stock exchange can be used to establish the 75% relationship, losses of these companies may not be offset against Irish profits.

Following the ECJ decision in the *Marks & Spencer plc v. Halsey* (2005) (Case C-446/03) case, Irish law was amended to provide that trading losses incurred by its non-Irish subsidiaries resident in a relevant Member State can be group-relieved against profits of the Irish parent (for this purpose the definition of "relevant Member State" does not include the UK). It must be proven that the loss cannot be otherwise used by the foreign subsidiary, the 75% relationship must exist between the companies and the claim must be made within two years. Where these conditions are satisfied, such losses are only available for relief "vertically upwards" from the non-resident subsidiary to the Irish resident company.

24.3.3 Application of Losses for Group Relief

In a qualifying group, qualifying losses may be passed upwards, downwards or sideways so that any qualifying company (or Irish branch) in the 75% group may use the losses. Some or all of the loss may be used regardless of the percentage relationship. For example, even if A Ltd only owns 80% of B Ltd, all of B Ltd's loss may be used by A Ltd. In addition, two or more profit-makers can claim relief from any one loss-making company. However, before claiming group relief, the profit-maker must claim all its own losses, charges and capital allowances (except set-off of losses for a subsequent accounting period and terminal loss relief). Any claim for group relief will be restricted if the company fails to submit its corporation tax return by the due date. As with single entities, separate rules apply for each type of loss to be claimed under group relief:

1. **Trading losses** – the provisions for a company to claim relief for its own trading losses under section 396A and section 396B were covered at CA Proficiency 1. For group relief purposes, trading losses in the current accounting period incurred by a group company, excluding trade losses attributable to pre-trading expenses, can be offset against the trading income (section 420A), or reduce the corporation tax liability on a value basis (section 420B), of another group company in the same accounting period. There are other restrictions, but these arise infrequently.

Example 24.4

Parent Ltd has a trading profit of €100,000. Subsidiary Ltd is in a group for loss relief purposes with Parent Ltd. Subsidiary Ltd has a trading loss of €60,000. The trading loss of Subsidiary Ltd can be grouped against the trading profits of Parent Ltd, reducing Parent Ltd's taxable trading income to €40,000.

Example 24.5

New Company Ltd incurs qualifying pre-trading expenses of €50,000. It commenced to trade and earned income of €10,000. New Company Ltd's tax computation would show a Case I loss of €40,000 (i.e. €10,000 – €50,000). If New Company Ltd is a member of a group, that loss of €40,000 cannot be grouped, it can only be carried forward and offset against future trading income of New Company Ltd.

If a company incurs a trading loss, it must make a section 396A claim before it can make a claim under section 396B. A similar rule applies for group relief, whereby a claim must be made under section 420A before a claim can be made under section 420B.

Also, the company incurring the trading loss must make a claim for loss relief under section 396A in the current accounting period, if possible, before it surrenders it to another company under section 420B (i.e. use the surrendered loss on a value basis to reduce corporation tax of another group company). The company that incurred the trading loss does not have to claim relief under section 396B (i.e. reduce its own corporation tax on a value basis in the current accounting period or preceding period of same length) before it surrenders it to another company under section 420A (i.e. offset the surrendered loss against trading income of another group company) or section 420B.

Example 24.6

A Ltd owns 80% of B Ltd. The following are the results for the year ended 31 December 2021:

	A Ltd	B Ltd
	€	€
Relevant trading income/(loss)	10,000	(25,000)
Case III	8,000	6,400

Computation

B Ltd

Case I	–
Case III	6,400
Corporation tax @ 25%	1,600
Section 396B: relief on a value basis	(1,600)
Corporation tax payable	Nil

A Ltd

Case I	10,000
Group relief section 420A	(10,000)
Case I	Nil
Case III	8,000
Corporation tax:	
€8,000 @ 25%	2,000
Section 420B: group relief on a value basis	(275)
Corporation tax payable	1,725

Loss Memo

Relevant trading loss for y/e 31/12/2021	25,000
Utilised by way of:	
section 396B(3) against corporation tax of B Ltd	
€12,800 × 12.5% = €1,600	(12,800)
Utilised by way of:	
section 420A against trading income of A Ltd	(10,000)
section 420B against corporation tax of A Ltd	
€2,200 × 12.5% = €275	(2,200)
Loss forward to 2022	Nil

A claim must be made under section 420A (trading losses) against relevant trading income of A Ltd before a claim can be made under section 420B on a value basis.

A claim does not have to be made by B Ltd under section 396B before a claim can be made by A Ltd under section 420A or section 420B. However, a claim must be made by B Ltd under section 396A, if possible, before A Ltd can make a claim under section 420B.

2. **Excess charges paid** comprise:

   (a) ***Relevant trading charges paid*** (e.g. patent royalties). The relief given for a company's excess trade charges against its own corporation tax liability (section 243B) was considered at CA Proficiency 1. A group company can surrender its excess trade charges to another group company for offset against relevant trading income of another group member (section 420A) or claim against relevant corporation tax on a value basis (section 420B). Again, section 420A relief must be claimed against relevant trading income before a claim under section 420B against corporation tax on a value basis.

(b) ***Non-trade charges paid*** (e.g. protected interest) in an accounting period that are in excess of that period's total profits (before any deduction has been made in arriving at those total profits for losses, capital allowances or management expenses of other accounting periods) may be surrendered and set against the total profits of another group company under section 420.

Example 24.7

T Ltd owns 80% of Q Ltd. The following are the results for the year ended 31 December 2021:

	T Ltd	Q Ltd
	€	€
Case I	10,000	200,000
Adjusted chargeable gain	-	40,000
Trade charges paid	50,000	
Non-trade charges paid	8,000	

Computation: T Ltd

Case I	10,000
Deduct: section 243A trade charges paid	(10,000)
Taxable profits	NIL

Computation: Q Ltd

Case I	200,000
Deduct: section 420A group relief	(40,000)
	160,000
Chargeable gains	40,000
Total profits	200,000
Deduct: non-trade charges group relief	(8,000)
Taxable profits	192,000
Corporation tax @ 12.5%	24,000

Excess Trade Charges Memo

	€
Relevant trading charges paid for y/e 31/12/2021	50,000
Utilised by way of section 243A by T Ltd	(10,000)
Available to surrender to group	40,000
Utilised by way of section 420A against trading income of Q Ltd	(40,000)
Excess forward to 2022	NIL

Excess Non-trade Charges Memo

	€
Non-trade charges paid for y/e 31/12/2021	8,000
Utilised by group relief by Q Ltd	(8,000)
Excess forward to 2022	NIL

---

3. **Excess management expenses** (see **Chapter 27**) of the current accounting period (excluding those of a previous accounting period which have been carried forward and are deemed to be management expenses of the current accounting period) may be grouped against total profits of the other group company. It is not necessary for the other group company to be an investment company for group relief to be claimed.

4. **Excess Case V capital allowances**, as detailed at CA Proficiency 1, can be used to reduce the total profits of another group company.

Example 24.8

C Ltd owns 90% of D Ltd. The following are the results for the year ended 31 December 2021:

	C Ltd	D Ltd
	€	€
Relevant trading income/(loss)	(10,000)	30,000
Case III	5,000	6,000
Case V	8,000	
Case V capital allowances	15,000	

Computation

C Ltd

	€
Case I	–
Case III	5,000
Case V	–
Income	5,000
Excess Case V capital allowances (Note)	(5,000)
Taxable	nil

Note:	Case V	8,000
	Capital allowances	(15,000)
	Excess Case V capital allowances	7,000
	Utilised by C Ltd	(5,000)
	Available for grouping	2,000

D Ltd

	€
Case I	30,000
Section 420A	(10,000)
	20,000
Case III	6,000
	26,000
Excess Case V capital allowances from C Ltd	(2,000)
Taxable	24,000

	€
Corporation tax:	
€20,000 @ 12.5%	2,500
€4,000 (Note) @ 25%	1,000
Corporation tax payable	3,500

Note: the excess Case V capital allowances are claimed against the profits taxable at the highest rate, i.e. Case III at 25%.

It should be noted that the excess allowances available for group relief are those claimed for the current accounting period in excess of the Case V income for that period **before any reduction of that income for previous periods' capital allowances or losses forward.**

Example 24.9

Jammy Dodger Ltd is owned 100% by Biscuits Ltd. Its results for the year ended 31 December 2021 are below. Calculate the excess Case V capital allowances available for surrender to Biscuits Ltd for the year ended 31 December 2021.

	€
Current period Case V income	20,000
Current period Case V capital allowances	50,000

continued overleaf

Current period Case V balancing charge	5,000
Case V capital allowances forward	7,000
Case V losses forward from previous period	3,000
Computation	
Case V tax-adjusted income (current period)	20,000
Add: Case V balancing charge (current period)	<u>5,000</u>
	25,000
Deduct: current period Case V capital allowances	<u>(50,000)</u>
Excess Case V capital allowances available for group relief:	<u>(25,000)</u>

Excess Case V capital allowances which arise due to wear and tear allowances claimed on rented residential accommodation may not be surrendered by way of group relief.

24.3.4 Corresponding Accounting Periods

Group relief is only available where the accounting period of both the loss-maker and profit-maker corresponds wholly or partly. Where they correspond partly, the relief is restricted on a time apportionment basis.

Example 24.10

Group Limited has a wholly owned subsidiary, Sub Limited. In the year ended 31 December 2021, Group Limited incurs a Case I loss of €240,000. In the year ended 30 September 2021, Sub Limited has Case I income of €120,000.

The corresponding accounting period is the period 1 January 2021 to 30 September 2021, i.e. nine months. Therefore, the maximum group relief available is the lower of:

- loss of €240,000 × 9/12 = €180,000:
- profit of €120,000 × 9/12 = €90,000.

Sub Limited can make a claim to utilise €90,000 of the losses incurred by Group Limited, thereby reducing its taxable income in the year ended 30 September 2021 to €30,000. Group Limited will have unused losses of €240,000 less €90,000 = €150,000 and some of these losses may be available for group relief against Sub Ltd's trading income for the year ended 30 September 2022, i.e. the period 1 October to 31 December 2021.

Group relief is only given if the surrendering company and the claimant company are members of the same group throughout the whole of the surrendering company's accounting period and the claimant company's corresponding accounting period. Where a company joins or leaves a group, all of the companies in the group are deemed to end an accounting period at that date for the purposes of establishing any group relief due. The corresponding accounting period rules referred to above apply.

Example 24.11

Owner Limited acquired 100% of the share capital of Acquired Limited on 30 June 2021. Both companies make up their financial statements to 31 December. In the year ended 31 December 2021, Owner Limited has Case I income of €100,000, while Acquired Limited has a Case I loss of €60,000. Only losses incurred since 1 July 2021 may be grouped, i.e. the corresponding accounting period is the period 1 July 2021 to 31 December 2021, i.e. six months. Therefore, the maximum group relief available is the *lower* of:

continued overleaf

▨   profit of €100,000 × 6/12 = €50,000;
▨   loss of €60,000 × 6/12 = €30,000.

Owner Limited can make a claim to have €30,000 of the losses incurred by Acquired Limited to be offset against its trading income, thereby reducing its taxable income for the year ended 31 December 2021 from €100,000 to €70,000. Acquired Limited will have unused losses of €60,000 less €30,000 = €30,000.

Example 24.12

A Ltd owns 80% of B Ltd. The following are the results for each company:

	A Ltd y/e 31/12/2021	B Ltd y/e 30/06/2021
	€	€
Relevant trading income/(loss)	10,000	(50,000)
Case III	8,000	6,400

Computation

B Ltd

	€
Case I	–
Case III	6,400
Corporation tax @ 25%	1,600
Less: section 396B relief	(1,600)(1)
Corporation tax payable	Nil

A Ltd

	€
Case I	10,000
Less: group relief section 420A	(5,000)(2)
Case I	5,000
Case III	8,000
	13,000
Corporation tax:	
€5,000 @ 12.5%	625
€8,000 @ 25%	2,000
Less: section 420B group relief	(1,000)(3)
Corporation tax payable	1,625

Loss Memo

Relevant trading loss for y/e 30/06/2021	50,000
1 Utilised by way of section 396B against corporation tax of B Ltd (Note 1) €12,800 @ 12.5% = €1,600	(12,800)
2 Utilised by way of section 420A against trading income of A Ltd (Note 2)	(5,000)
3 Utilised by way of section 420B against corporation tax of A Ltd (Note 3) €8,000 @ 12.5% = €1,000	(8,000)
Loss forward to 2022	24,200

Notes:

1. Typically a company will make a claim under section 396B. However, there is no legal requirement to make a claim under section 396B for B Ltd before surrendering the loss to A Ltd to use under section 420A against relevant trading income of A Ltd. A claim must be made under section 420A against relevant trading income of A Ltd before a claim can be made under section 420B on a value basis.

continued overleaf

2. Section 420A claim is for lower of:
   - trading loss of surrendering company for overlap period, i.e. 6/12 × (€50,000) = (€25,000); or
   - trading income of claimant for overlap period, i.e. 6/12 × €10,000 = €5,000.
     Therefore, claim €5,000.
3. Section 420B claim – the unclaimed loss of the overlap period on a value basis – the unclaimed loss is €25,000 − €5,000 = €20,000; its value is €20,000 × 12.5% = €2,500. Relief may be claimed against the corporation tax on profits of the overlap period which have not already been relieved. All the Case I of the overlap period has been relieved, so it is the corporation tax on the Case III income of the overlap period (6/12 × €8,000 × 25% = €1,000).

24.4 Disallowance of Trading Losses following a Change of Ownership

Losses carried forward are potentially valuable – a company will not pay tax on profits until all losses carried forward are utilised. This fact would mean that companies with significant trading losses carried forward could become an attractive target for other (profitable) companies to acquire. By acquiring a company with trading losses and ensuring that it becomes profitable by, for example, transferring business from another company, corporation tax on the profits could be reduced by the original losses. Such tax planning strategies are prevented by anti-avoidance measures in TCA 1997.

Provisions in TCA 1997 disallow the carry forward of trading losses incurred prior to a substantial change of ownership of a company's shares. The disallowance will apply:

1. if "a major change in the nature or conduct of a trade" and the change in ownership both occur within any period of three years; or
2. where the activities of the trade have become small or negligible and there is a change of ownership before any considerable revival of the trade.

In applying the provisions to the accounting period in which the change of ownership occurs, the part of the period occurring before the change of ownership and the part occurring after the change are treated as separate accounting periods. Apportionments are to be made on a time basis.

A "major change in the nature or conduct of a trade" includes:

1. a major change in the property dealt in, services or facilities provided, in the trade; or
2. a major change in customers, outlets or markets of the trade.

It should be noted, however, that this definition is not exhaustive. Any such change will be regarded as occurring even if it is the result of a gradual process begun outside the three-year period.

There have been a number of legal cases that have dealt with the meaning of a "major change in the conduct of the trade" and which give some guidance on the meaning of the term.

Cases where it was held that there had been **no major change** in the nature or conduct of the trade include:

- A company that had sold its products direct to customers, mainly wholesalers, then commenced to do the same through distribution companies.
- A company that ceased to slaughter pigs and manufacture meat products and, for a temporary period of 16 months, distributed the same products manufactured by its parent company. After the 16-month period, it recommenced slaughtering and manufacturing meat products.

Cases where it was held that there had been a **major change** in the nature or conduct of the trade include:

▩ A company that carried on a business of minting coins and medallions from precious metals, purchased its principal supplier's entire inventories of gold and then purchased gold directly from wholesalers. This resulted in substantial increases in inventory levels.

▩ A company that operated a retail chain of shops changed its promotional policy by discontinuing the issue of trading stamps and reducing prices. The change resulted in a substantial increase in turnover.

There are rules for determining whether there has been a change in ownership and generally these are such as to ensure that if there is a new person or persons controlling the company, then there is a change of ownership.

Questions

Review Questions
(See Suggested Solutions to Review Questions at the end of this textbook.)

Question 24.1

B Ltd has the following results for the year ended 31 December 2021:

	€
Tax-adjusted trading profits (i.e. after current year capital allowance claim)	180,000
Interest on Government stocks (Case III)	4,000
Profit rent (Case V)	20,000

Unutilised trading losses forward from the year ended 31 December 2020 amount to €16,000.

Z Ltd is a 100% trading subsidiary of B Ltd. During the year ended 31 December 2021 it incurred tax-adjusted trading losses of €96,000. It also had taxable Case III income of €20,000.

Requirement

Compute B Ltd's corporation tax liability for the year ended 31 December 2021, after allowing for any group relief for losses of Z Ltd.

Question 24.2

A Ltd owns 80% of B Ltd's issued share capital and 75% of C Ltd's issued share capital. Results for the year ended 31 March 2021 were:

	A Ltd	B Ltd	C Ltd
	€	€	€
Tax-adjusted Case I profit/(loss)	(90,000)	56,000	48,000
Case III income	1,000	2,000	3,000

Case V income	20,000	25,000	2,000
Case I trading losses forward	(4,000)	–	(26,000)

A Ltd wishes to arrange its affairs to ensure that it pays no corporation tax, if possible, before it surrenders any loss relief to its subsidiaries.

Requirement
Calculate the tax payable by each company for the year ended 31 March 2021.

Question 24.3

Queen Ltd has two wholly owned subsidiaries, Pawn Ltd and Rook Ltd. All three companies are trading companies. Accounts for the year to 31 December 2021 show the following results:

	Queen Ltd	Pawn Ltd	Rook Ltd
	€	€	€
Gross operating profit	297,463	81,000	47,437
Less: depreciation	12,000	10,000	16,000
Entertaining (customers)	1,350	1,200	1,650
Administration	73,650	61,110	107,373
Interest	11,150	10,720	3,000
Capital grant release	(3,000)	–	–
	95,150	83,030	128,023
Net profit/(loss) before investment income	202,313	(2,030)	(80,586)

Additional information:

1. Rook Ltd was incorporated and commenced to trade on 1 January 2021.
2. (i) Interest is analysed as follows:

	Queen Ltd	Pawn Ltd	Rook Ltd
	€	€	€
Accrued 1 January 2021	(1,250)	–	–
Paid	10,000	9,000	2,750
Accrued 31 December 2021	2,000	1,750	250
Interest on overdue tax	400	–	–
	11,150	10,720	3,000

    (ii) Pawn Ltd has used its loan to purchase 7% of the share capital of Bridge Ltd, whose income consists mainly of rental income from commercial properties. None of the directors of Bridge Ltd is also a director of Pawn Ltd. Interest incurred by Queen Ltd and Rook Ltd were in respect of borrowings taken out for the purpose of their trades.

3. (i) Queen Ltd received dividends of €7,500 from other Irish resident companies. These dividends have not been included in the profit figures above.
    (ii) Queen Ltd also received deposit interest of €23,846, which was not subject to DIRT.

4. Capital allowances:

	Queen Ltd	Pawn Ltd	Rook Ltd
	€	€	€
Capital allowances	7,375	3,000	5,627

5. Pawn Ltd had trade losses brought forward of €80,000 at 1 January 2021.
6. The companies paid the following corporation tax on 2020 profits of:

	Queen Ltd	Pawn Ltd
	€	€
Corporation tax	55,000	10,000

Requirement

(a) Compute the corporation tax liabilities (if any) of each of the three companies for the year ended 31 December 2021, on the assumption that all available reliefs are claimed to the benefit of the group as a whole.
(b) State the amount of any losses available to carry forward at 1 January 2022 for each company.
(c) State the due date of payment of any tax payable.

Company Capital Gains

Companies can be liable to Irish tax on capital gains. In this chapter we will look at the rules that determine if the gain is actually liable, and whether it is liable to corporation tax (most commonly) or CGT. We also look at reliefs from tax on capital gains that are applicable to companies only. Note that a gain is either liable or not liable. There is no remittance basis for companies.

The tax residence status of a company is determined by where the **central management and control of the company is exercised**. However, certain Irish **incorporated** companies may be resident in the State even if the central management and control of the company is exercised abroad. See **Chapter 21, Sections 21.2** and **21.3** for a more detailed consideration of the concept of corporate residence.

25.1 Capital Gains Liable to Corporation Tax

25.1.1 Irish Resident Companies

Such companies are liable to corporation tax in respect of **all** capital gains wherever arising, excluding disposals of development land. Thus gains on disposal of foreign assets by an Irish resident company are liable to Irish corporation tax.

25.1.2 Non-resident Companies

A non-resident company is only liable to corporation tax on its capital gains if it is trading in the State through a branch or agency and it disposes of a specified Irish asset (see **Chapter 4, Section 4.3.1**), which it acquired for the purpose of its trade in the State.

Therefore, non-resident companies are not liable to corporation tax on most disposals, e.g. disposals of foreign assets, non-specified Irish assets.

25.2 Capital Gains Liable to Capital Gains Tax

25.2.1 Irish Resident Companies

Irish resident companies are liable to CGT on the disposal of development land only (see **Chapter 3, Section 3.3**).

25.2.2 Non-resident Companies

Non-resident companies are liable to CGT on the following disposals:

1. disposals of development land; and
2. disposals of specified Irish assets not used for the purpose of branch or agency in the State.

25.3 Method of Taxation

The rules for calculating the chargeable gain, as set out in **Chapter 3**, Section 3.2, apply regardless of whether a company is assessed to corporation tax or to CGT on a capital gain.

Where the disposal is subject to corporation tax, the gain, net of any allowable losses, is adjusted for inclusion in the corporation tax computation (as covered at CA Proficiency 1). The adjusted gain, and any tax attaching, may be further reduced for corporation tax purposes if the company has other reliefs available (e.g. excess Case V allowances; losses on a value basis). Any liability forms part of the company's corporation tax liability and is paid and filed accordingly.

Where the disposal is subject to CGT, normal rules regarding the rate of tax and dates for paying and filing the CGT return apply (see **Section 3.1**). Capital losses and other reliefs that are subject to corporation tax (e.g. excess Case V allowances) cannot be offset against gains subject to CGT.

Example 25.1

X Ltd prepares accounts to 31 December each year. Its corporation tax liability for the year ended 31 December 2020 was €3,000. In the year ended 31 December 2021 the tax-adjusted Case I profit was €20,000. During that year the company bought an asset for €10,000 and sold it for €17,000 in October 2021. The company had a capital loss forward of €1,000. It also sold a site for €155,000. The current use value of the site was €55,000 at date of disposal, 10 May 2021. It had acquired the site in July 2015 for €60,000.

	Year ended 31 December 2021 €
Schedule D Case I	20,000
Chargeable gain:	
current year €7,000	
loss forward (€1,000)	
Chargeable gain = €6,000 × 33% ÷ 12.5%	15,840
	35,840
Corporation tax due €35,840 @ 12.5%	4,480

X Ltd will pay preliminary tax of €3,000 at 23 November 2021 and the balance of corporation tax, €1,480, when it submits its corporation tax return by 23 September 2022.

continued overleaf

2021 CGT Computation

	€
Sales proceeds	155,000
Deduct: cost of acquisition 2015	(60,000)
Gain	95,000
CGT @ 33%	31,350

X Ltd will pay €31,350 CGT by 15 December 2021 and will include details of the gain in its corporation tax return (Form CT1) for the year ended 31 December 2021.

You have done this tax computation for X Ltd and are satisfied that you have done the calculations correctly. However, you are uncomfortable as you know that another client company, Dabble Ltd, bought a property for €80,000 from X Ltd on 1 February 2021, and there is no mention of this disposal in the information that was sent to your manager by the client. What should you do?

You should advise your manager of this purchase by Dabble Ltd and, therefore, disposal by the client, so that your manager can raise it with the client.

25.4 Exemption from Tax on Disposal of Certain Shareholdings (Participation Exemption)

Section 626B TCA 1997 provides for an exemption from corporation tax in certain circumstances, in the case of gains from the disposal of shareholdings by parent companies. While any such gains are not taxable, if there is a loss on disposal, there is no relief for the loss. A number of conditions must be met before a gain can be exempt:

- The company disposing of the shares, i.e. the investor company, must be a 'parent' company at the time of disposal, or had been a parent company not less than two years prior to the time of disposal. A 'parent' company must have a **minimum shareholding of at least 5% in the investee company**. That is:
  - it must hold not less than 5% of the company's ordinary share capital;
  - it must be beneficially entitled to not less than 5% of the profits available for distribution to equity holders of the company; **and**
  - on a winding up, it must be beneficially entitled to not less than 5% of the assets available for distribution to equity holders.
- The investor is required to have the minimum holding in the investee company for a **continuous period of at least 12 months**.
- The **investee company must carry on a trade**, or the business of the investor company, its investee company and their "5%" investee companies, taken as a whole, must consist wholly or mainly of the carrying on of a **trade** or trades.
- Finally, at the time of the disposal the **investee** company must be resident in a **Member State of the EU or a country** with which **Ireland has a tax treaty**.

The exemption continues to apply for two years after the parent company's minimum shareholding is no longer satisfied. **The exemption does not apply where the shares derive the greater part of their value from specified Irish assets**. A similar exemption applies to assets related to shares, e.g. options, but this is beyond the scope of this textbook.

> **Example 25.2**
> Owner Ltd owns 100% of Irish Ltd, a trading company, for the last 10 years. Acquisition Ltd wishes to acquire Irish Ltd. The disposal by Owner Ltd will generate a profit of €5 million. Due to the exemption, Owner Ltd will pay no tax on this gain.
>
> If Owner Ltd disposed of 99% of its shareholding in Irish Ltd in 2021 and the remaining 1% in 2022, both disposals would qualify for the exemption – because even though Owner Ltd did not own 5% at the time it disposed of its 1% interest, it was not more than two years since it had been a parent company.
>
> If the facts were the same except that it is shares in French Ltd, a French resident company, the exemption would be available also to Owner Ltd. However, if it were a disposal of shares in a Jersey company, then the gain would be fully taxable as the investee company is not resident in a Member State of the EU or a country with which Ireland has a tax treaty.

25.5 Capital Gains Group

A company may be part of a group for CGT purposes. This provides important benefits to companies within the group, namely assets can be transferred from one group company to another without triggering a capital gain.

25.5.1 Definition of a Capital Gains Group

Section 616 TCA 1997 provides that a **principal company and its effective 75% subsidiaries form a capital gains group and, where a principal company itself is a member of a group (as being itself an effective 75% subsidiary), that group comprises all of its effective 75% subsidiaries.** In this, CGT groups differ from loss groups, as illustrated in **Example 25.3** below.

A principal company means a company of which another company is an effective 75% subsidiary (directly or indirectly). A company is an effective 75% subsidiary of another company, the parent, if:

1. the company is a 75% subsidiary of the parent, i.e. the parent owns, directly or indirectly, not less than 75% of its ordinary share capital;
2. the parent is beneficially entitled to not less than 75% of any profits available for distribution; and
3. the parent would be beneficially entitled to not less than 75% of the assets of the company available for distribution on a winding up.

The definition of "company" above means a company resident in an EU Member State or resident in a country that has a tax treaty with Ireland. Accordingly, both Irish and non-Irish companies may be part of a capital gains group.

(In the examples that follow, it should be assumed that a company is entitled to the same % of profits and assets as its shareholding %, e.g. where the example indicates 75% shareholding, it should be assumed that there is an entitlement to 75% of profits and assets also.)

The distinction between a group for loss relief purposes and for CGT purposes is that where a principal company is itself an effective 75% subsidiary, it and all its effective 75% subsidiaries will be part of the same capital gains group as its parent.

Example 25.3

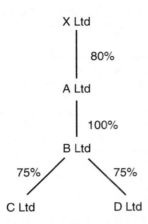

While X does not directly or indirectly own 75% of the ordinary share capital of C or D Ltd, all the companies, X, A, B, C and D, are members of the one capital gains group. This is because B, C or D are clearly 75% subsidiaries of A, and A itself is an effective 75% subsidiary of X.

All of the above companies do not form a single group for loss relief purposes, i.e. X, A, B and A, B, C, D groups form separate groups for loss relief purposes, as X does not have a 75% (direct or indirect) relationship with C or D.

Groups Incorporating Non-resident Companies

For many years the capital gains relief (transfer of assets without triggering a chargeable gain) for groups only applied to Irish resident companies.

The relief can also apply to an Irish branch of an EU resident company or of a company resident in a country that has a tax treaty with Ireland if it is a member of a group and the asset is used by the Irish branch, i.e. it is a chargeable asset. Therefore, any transfers between the branch and group members qualify for relief.

Example 25.4

A,B,C,D form a capital gains group.

If A, C and D are Irish resident and B is resident in France (but has no branch in Ireland), A, B, C and D still form a capital gains group but the reliefs applying on transfer of assets between group members only apply to transfers between A, C and D. However, if B had an Irish branch and if the asset were used by the Irish branch, then a transfer of the asset between B and A,C or D would qualify.

If A, C and D are Irish resident and B is resident in the USA, A, B, C and D still form a capital gains group, i.e. B can be taken into account to determine whether C or D are effective 75% subsidiaries of A, but not for actually claiming any relief in its own right, unless it has an Irish branch.

Example 25.5

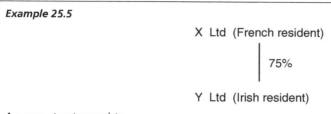

A group structure exists.

If the French resident company has an Irish branch operation, capital assets can be transferred between Y Ltd and the Irish branch of X Ltd without triggering a gain. However, if an asset was transferred by Y Ltd to the head office of X Ltd in France, then Y Ltd is liable to corporation tax on the gain.

Example 25.6

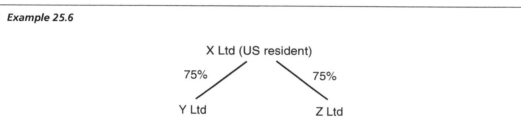

While X Ltd, Y Ltd and Z Ltd constitute a capital gains group, only transfers between Y Ltd and Z Ltd will qualify for relief, unless X Ltd has an Irish branch.

25.5.2 Disposal of Capital Assets within a Group

In general, a transfer of an asset from one member of the group to another is deemed to be for a consideration of such amount that neither a gain nor a loss accrues.

The group is effectively treated as one taxpayer so that a chargeable gain does not arise until the asset is sold outside the group or the company holding the asset leaves the group.

Example 25.7: Irish resident companies
X Ltd owns a building which it bought for €1 million, nine months ago. It disposes of it to its parent, Y Ltd, when it is worth €1.25 million. Therefore, a gain of €0.25 million arose. Normally this gain would be adjusted and included in the profits of X Ltd. However, this rule ensures that the asset moves at no gain/no loss, i.e. €1 million. So X Ltd has no chargeable gain and Y Ltd's base cost is €1 million.

Example 25.8: Transfers between an Irish resident company and an Irish branch of an EU resident company or a company resident in a country which has a tax treaty with Ireland

A Ltd, an Irish resident company, is owned by B Ltd, a French resident company that has a branch in Ireland. A Ltd owns a building which it bought for €1 million, nine months ago. It disposes of it to the Irish branch of its parent, B Ltd, when it is worth €1.25 million. Therefore, a gain of €0.25 million arose. Normally, this gain would be adjusted and included in the profits of A Ltd.

However, as the asset is being transferred to an Irish branch of an EU resident company and is, in any event, a specified asset, the asset continues to be a chargeable asset and, again, the rule ensures that the asset moves at no gain/no loss, i.e. €1 million. So A Ltd has no chargeable gain and B Ltd's base cost is €1 million.

If the sale were from the Irish branch of B Ltd to A Ltd, again the sale would be at no gain/no loss.

The same rule applies to transfers of capital assets between Irish branches of companies resident in the EU or in a country with which Ireland has a tax treaty. **Relief for sales between group companies is granted automatically and is compulsory**. There are no provisions for making elections or time limits.

Capital Losses

There are no provisions for transferring chargeable losses between group companies.

Planning: If one member of a group has a capital loss that it is unable to utilise, and another company in the group wishes to sell an asset (to a non-group company) which will realise a gain, then to utilise the loss the asset must first be sold to the group company holding the loss and then sold by that company to the non-group company.

Example 25.9

A Ltd has a capital loss of €100,000. L Ltd, its subsidiary, wishes to sell quoted shares in November 2021 which will generate a gain of €50,000. If L Ltd just sells the shares, it must pay tax on the gain of €132,000 @12.5%, i.e. include a chargeable gain of €50,000 × 33/12.5% in its corporation tax computation.

Alternatively, if L Ltd sold the shares to A Ltd, which then sold them to the third party:

- L Ltd would have no gain as it sold the shares to A Ltd, a member of the group; and
- A Ltd would have a gain of €50,000, but it would have a loss of €100,000 to offset. Therefore, it would have no gain and a reduced loss forward of €50,000.

Inventories

An asset may be held as a capital asset by one company and as inventory by another, e.g. a property could be held as an investment or as inventory by a property dealer. Because of this, there are special rules which apply where an asset is transferred within a group and one company holds it as a capital asset and the other holds it as inventory. These rules are beyond the scope of this textbook.

Transfer Pricing

Finance Act 2019 extended the transfer pricing legislation to capital transactions exceeding €25 million. The arm's length transfer price must be used when computing the chargeable gain or allowable loss on the disposal of an asset under an arrangement involving the supply and acquisition of an asset where, at that time, the supplier and acquirer are associated and the profits, gains or losses arising from the relevant activities are within the charge to Irish tax in the case of the supplier or acquirer or both. Furthermore, the acquisition cost of an asset acquired under an arrangement is to be determined by reference to the arm's length transfer price.

Although the market value principle applies to capital transactions already, this provision imposes a requirement to have full transfer pricing documentation to support the values attributable to capital transactions entered into with related parties.

Example 25.10

Dublin Design Ltd is a 100% subsidiary of Paris Tech Ltd. On 10 March 2021, Dublin Design Ltd transferred intellectual property to Paris Tech Ltd for €35 million (arm's length value is €40 million). As the companies are associated and Dublin Design Ltd is within the charge to Irish tax, transfer pricing rules apply.

An adjustment increasing the sales proceeds by €5 million is required by Dublin Design Ltd when computing the gain/loss.

There are certain circumstances where transfer pricing rules do not apply, including where:

- the market value of the asset does not exceed €25 million; or
- the asset is disposed under circumstances where it is treated as being disposed for no gain/no loss.

Anti-avoidance legislation prevents artificial arrangements, i.e. the splitting of transactions for the purpose of satisfying the €25 million test on a transaction-by-transaction basis.

Transfer pricing rules will not apply to capital transactions if it would result in a chargeable gain being lower, an allowable loss being higher, or the acquirer being treated as having acquired an asset for a consideration that is higher than it would have, but for the transfer pricing rules.

It should also be noted that Finance Act 2019 extends the transfer pricing legislation to SMEs, albeit with reduced documentation requirements, subject to ministerial commencement order that has yet to take effect.

25.5.3 Disposal of Capital Assets Outside the Group

If there is a disposal of an asset by a member of a group to a person outside the group, and the asset had been acquired by the company making the disposal from another group member, then **the period of ownership for the purpose of both indexation relief and determining the appropriate rate of tax to be applied to the gain (currently there is only one rate) is arrived at by reference to the length of time the asset had been owned by the group as a whole**. Of course, if the asset had originally been acquired prior to 6 April 1974, then the market value at that date will form the base cost for indexation purposes from 6 April 1974 to the date of sale.

Example 25.11

A Ltd and Y Ltd are Irish resident members of a capital gains group. Both companies prepare accounts to 31 December each year. Y Ltd acquired an asset on 13 February 1981 at a cost of €20,000 and transferred it to A Ltd in August 1999. On 31 December 2021 A Ltd sold the asset to a non-group company for €200,000. When the asset was disposed of by Y Ltd to A Ltd in 1999, no gain arose to Y Ltd.

A Ltd has a disposal in y/e 31 December 2021 of an asset with a base cost of €20,000, i.e. cost to Y Ltd on 13 February 1981.

Computation of A Ltd's liability	€
Proceeds	200,000
Base cost €20,000	
Indexed at 3.240	(64,800)
Gain	135,200

Re-gross to include in corporation tax computation:

$$€135,200 \times \frac{33}{12.5} = €356,928$$

25.5.4 Company Leaving Group – Anti-avoidance Measure

Where a company ceases to be a member of a group of companies (otherwise than because of a genuine liquidation), the CGT deferred on any **asset transferred** between the companies since 6 April 1974 and **within 10 years of the company ceasing to be a member of the group** shall become payable.

In effect, the asset is treated as sold and immediately re-acquired by the company leaving the group, at its market value at the time of its original acquisition from the other member of the group, i.e. **the gain arising on the original transfer between the group members is triggered**. Indexation relief is applied by reference to that date and not by reference to the date the company actually leaves the group. It should be particularly noted that the gain and corresponding **liability is that of the company leaving the group** and is included as part of the corporation tax due for the accounting period in which the company leaves the group. The cost of future disposals of the assets in question by the company leaving the group will, of course, be the market value attributed to the earlier transfer.

If the asset was acquired by the company more than 10 years prior to the date the company leaves the group, this anti-avoidance rule is not triggered.

Example 25.12

Groups Ltd has owned the €2 issued share capital of Feeley Ltd since its incorporation on 3 January 1999. Both are Irish resident companies. Feeley Ltd commenced to trade on 1 February 1999. On 1 March 2011, Groups Ltd sold Feeley Ltd its warehouse for €9,000.

Groups Ltd had purchased the warehouse for €1,000 on 3 January 1999. The market value of the warehouse at 1 March 2011 was €10,000.

On 3 January 2021, Groups Ltd sold its shareholding in Feeley Ltd for €100,000.

What are the chargeable gains arising in respect of the above transactions?

Groups Ltd

2011: no chargeable gain arises on the sale of the warehouse as it is sold to another group member.

2021: if Feeley Ltd is a trading company or the business of Groups Ltd and its 5% subsidiaries taken as a whole consists of trading, then the gain on the sale of the shares may be exempt, if all other conditions are satisfied, including that the shares do not derive the greater part of their value from land (which includes buildings) in the State.

Feeley Ltd

2011: acquired asset on a no gain/no loss basis.

2021: Feeley Ltd is leaving the group and, therefore, is treated as having sold and immediately re-acquired the warehouse at the market value at the time of its acquisition from Group Ltd.

	€	€
Market value on transfer at 1 March 2011		10,000
Cost 03/01/1999	1,000	
Index	1.212	
Indexed cost		(1,212)
Gain		8,788

Notes:

1. This would be taxable at the relevant rate in 2011.
2. When Feeley Ltd sells the warehouse, its base cost will be €10,000.
3. If Groups Ltd did not sell its shares in Feeley Ltd until March 2021, then no gain would arise on Feeley Ltd, as it would have held the warehouse for 10 years and, therefore, would be exempt from the anti-avoidance provisions.

25.5.5 Pre-entry Losses – Anti-avoidance Measure

In the past, companies who anticipated a future gain on the disposal of an asset would acquire a company with capital losses forward. The asset with the gain would be transferred intra-group at no gain/no loss to the company with the losses forward. This company would then sell the asset, realise the gain and the losses forward could be used to shelter the gain. The term "pre-entry losses" refers to losses accruing to the company before entry to the group as well as losses on the sale of assets brought in. Anti-avoidance provisions were introduced to prevent use of such pre-entry losses. While the provision ensures that these losses cannot be used subsequently by a group which had no previous commercial connection with the company when those losses accrued, that company will be allowed to use those losses itself in the same way that it could have had it never entered the group.

What is a Pre-entry Loss?

The term applies to:

- losses that have arisen in a company prior to it becoming a member of the group; and
- the pre-entry proportion of a loss arising on an asset held at the date a company became a member of a group (even though the loss is crystallised after it became a member).

Calculation of the Pre-entry Loss

The pre-entry loss is the smaller of:

- a loss calculated with reference to the market value at the date on which the company became a member of the group; or
- the amount of the loss which arose on disposal.

Pre-entry Loss before Joining Group: Gains from which it is Deductible

Pre-entry losses which actually accrued to the company before it joined the group can be set against:

- gains on assets disposed of after entry but which were held by the company before entry; or
- a gain arising on the disposal of an asset that was acquired from a non-group member and which has been used for the purpose of the company's trade.

Loss on Pre-entry Asset: Gains from which it is Deductible

The loss on a pre-entry asset must be split as between that which is pre-entry and can only be offset against the gains specified in the previous paragraph and that part which is post-entry and can be offset under the normal rules.

Questions

Review Questions

(See Suggested Solutions to Review Questions at the end of this textbook.)

Question 25.1

A client of yours, VC Holdings Ltd, has sent you an email seeking tax advice before closing the sale of one of its subsidiaries. The client hasn't involved you in the transaction to date, but now seeks your opinion in respect of any relevant tax matters. You have been tax advisor to the VC Holdings group for a number of years, and are familiar with most of the group's key tax issues.

VC Holdings Ltd owns two 100% subsidiaries – Irish Cable Installations Ltd and Fibre Optic Developments Ltd – both of which are Irish resident companies and have been owned by VC Holdings Ltd since they were incorporated.

Irish Cable will be sold for €20 million in the coming weeks to a third-party investor. The company has a successful cable trade, and also operates out of a high-specification factory unit based in Celbridge. The shares in Irish Cable are the subject matter of the sale. When Irish Cable was established in January 2019, VC Holdings Ltd contributed €500,000 for all its share capital.

Irish Cable took ownership of the factory premises in November 2019 from its previous owner, Fibre Optic. The value of the property in November 2019 was €4 million and all possible reliefs were claimed at that time. The property was originally purchased by Fibre Optic in 2016 at a cost of €3 million. It is currently valued at circa €4.5 million.

It is now 10 December 2021 and the sale of Irish Cable will close before 31 December. The group prepares its accounts annually to 31 December.

Requirement
Draft an email reply to VC Holdings Ltd addressing the tax implications of a sale of Irish Cable Installations Ltd before 31 December 2021 for it and/or its subsidiaries. Your email should consider CGT and stamp duty.

Question 25.2

A Ltd is an Irish holding company that holds shares in a number of trading companies. It owns:

- 90% of the share capital of B Ltd, which in turn owns 80% of the share capital of D Ltd; and
- 90% of share capital of C Ltd, which in turn owns 90% of the share capital of F Ltd.

All the companies are resident in Ireland for tax purposes, with the exception of C Ltd which is resident in France.

Requirement
Which of the above subsidiary companies form a group with A Ltd for the purposes of corporation tax loss relief and which for capital gains tax group relief? Explain why.

Question 25.3

Red Ltd is an Irish incorporated and tax resident trading company that manufactures and sells paint and painting products. The company was incorporated in 1998 by Simon Walsh. Red has grown significantly over the years and is now regarded as the leading manufacturer of paints in Ireland. In addition to its three wholly-owned subsidiaries (all of which are trading companies), in an attempt to increase market share Red has also invested in numerous other companies that operate in the same market.

Simon decided in 2021 that it was time to retire. His son, Jack, became managing director of the company on 1 September 2021. In the first few months, Jack closely monitored the performance of companies in which Red Ltd held an investment. On 30 November 2021 he decided, subject to your advice below, to dispose of the following investments as soon as possible:

1. 3% shareholding in Orange Ltd, an Irish resident trading company acquired on 1 October 2008.
2. 4% shareholding in Blue Ltd. Red Ltd acquired a 9% shareholding in Blue Ltd, an Irish resident paint distribution company, in June 2005. Red Ltd sold 5% of its 9% shareholding on 1 July 2021.
3. 11% shareholding in Pink Inc., a US incorporated and tax resident trading company. Red Ltd acquired its 11% shareholding in April 2018.
4. 3% shareholding in Black Ltd, a UK resident trading company acquired in November 2018. White Ltd, a 75% subsidiary of Red Ltd acquired in November 2020, also holds a 5% shareholding in Black Ltd. Black Ltd is a paint wholesaler.
5. 15% shareholding in Green Ltd, an Irish resident trading company acquired on 1 August 2021.
6. 12% shareholding in Purple Ltd, an Irish resident property investment company acquired in 2014. Purple Ltd's assets consist solely of Irish properties.

Requirement

Prepare a briefing paper for Jack, which addresses the following:

(a) Explain what is meant by "participation exemption" and the conditions that must be met by the investor company in order to qualify for the exemption.
(b) On the basis that Red Ltd meets the conditions for an investor company, state whether the participation exemption will be available to Red Ltd on the sale of each of the above investments 1.–6. Explain your conclusion in each case. Your answer should set out the conditions that must be met by an investee company.
(c) Jack thinks that a loss is likely to arise in November 2021 on the disposal of the remaining 4% shareholding in Blue Ltd by Red Ltd. He has asked for your advice regarding the timing of the disposal to ensure that any loss is allowed for tax purposes.

Question 25.4

AGA Ltd is the parent company of the AGA Group. Subsidiary companies in the group are:

- BGB Ltd, a 100% subsidiary of AGA Ltd;
- CGC Ltd, a 90% subsidiary of AGA Ltd; and
- DGD Ltd, an 80% subsidiary of AGA Ltd.

BGB plans to sell a property which will give rise to a significant chargeable gain. Both CGC and DGD have capital losses brought forward and AGA Ltd is wondering if there would be any way that the capital losses available in either CGC or DGD could be offset against the potential chargeable gain arising on the disposal of the property in BGB.

Requirement

Advise AGA Ltd on the most tax-efficient manner for BGB Ltd to dispose of its property, giving reasons for your answer and outlining any conditions that must be satisfied where you advise claiming a particular relief.

Close Companies

Learning Objectives

After studying this chapter you will be able to:

- Determine and advise on close company status for corporation tax purposes.
- Advise on and calculate the tax implications in respect of:
  - expenses of participators and their associates;
  - interest paid to directors and their associates;
  - loans to participators and their associates; and
  - repayment/write-off of loans to participators.
- Calculate the surcharge on undistributed estate and investment income of a trading company that is a close company.
- Calculate the surcharge on undistributed professional, estate and investment income of a professional service company that is a close company.
- Determine and advise on the tax implications of an election for a distribution not to be a distribution for close company surcharge purposes.

26.1 Meaning of Close Company

Most Irish private companies are close companies, whereas almost all publicly quoted companies are not close companies. Essentially, close company legislation is anti-avoidance legislation formulated to prevent a close company taking decisions so as to minimise tax in a way that would not be feasible for a publicly quoted company. The legislation is very widely defined to deter people finding a loophole and avoiding the rules.

Under section 430 TCA 1997, a **close company** is one that is resident in the State and:

- is under the control of:
  - five or fewer participators, or
  - participators who are directors; or
- if, on a full distribution of its income, more than 50% of it would be paid to:
  - five or fewer participators, or
  - participators who are directors.

26.1.1 *"Participator"*

A participator is a person having a share or interest in the capital or income of the company. The most common example would be a shareholder. However, the definition is very widely drafted so that a participator includes any person having a present or future share or interest in the capital, assets or income of the company; it also includes a "loan creditor" of the company, i.e. a creditor of the company, e.g. a debenture holder. Ordinary trade creditors are not included in the definition. A person carrying on a business of banking who has lent money to the company in the ordinary course of business is also not treated as a loan creditor.

26.1.2 *"Control"*

Under section 432 TCA 1997, a person is regarded as having control of a company if "such person exercises, or is able to exercise or is entitled to acquire, control, whether direct or indirect, over the company's affairs". The definition continues by making particular reference to whether "such person possesses or is entitled to acquire" more than 50% of the company's share capital, income if it were distributed, or assets in a winding up.

Importantly, in determining whether an individual satisfies any of these conditions, the rights and powers of such person's "associates", and any company over which they or their associates have control are also attributed to the individual.

26.1.3 *"Associate"*

An associate of a participator means:

1. a relative of the participator (i.e. spouse, civil partner, ancestor, lineal descendant, brother or sister), but it does not include an aunt, or uncle, or cousin;
2. a business partner of the participator; or
3. a trustee of a settlement established by the participator or a relative.

26.1.4 *"Director"*

In order to be regarded as a director, a person need not actually have the title of director. Section 433 TCA 1997 gives the meaning of "director" as:

"(a) any person occupying the position of director by whatever name called,
 (b) any person in accordance with whose directions or instructions the directors are accustomed to act, and
 (c) any person—
   (i) who is a manager of the company or otherwise concerned in the management of the company's trade or business and
   (ii) who is, either on his or her own or with one or more associates, the beneficial owner of, or able, directly or through the medium of other companies or by any other indirect means, to control **20 per cent or more** of the ordinary share capital of the company." (emphasis added)

Example 26.1
Shares in Alphabet Limited, an Irish resident company, are held as follows:

	Shareholding
Mr A (Director of company)	10%
Mrs A	2%
Mrs C (Mr A's aunt)	2%
Mrs B	10%
B Ltd (Shares in B Ltd held 50% each by Mr and Mrs B)	5%
Mr J (Mrs B's cousin)	4%
Mr D (Director of company)	10%
Mrs D	2%
Ms D (Mr and Mrs D's daughter)	2%
Mrs E (Mr D's sister)	2%
Mr F	6%
Mr G	5%
Other shareholdings (Unrelated parties all holding <5%)	40%
	100%

Is Alphabet Limited under the control of five or fewer participators?

Shares held by Mr A and his associates:		
Mr A	10%	
Mrs A	2%	12%
Shares held by Mrs B and her associates:		
Mrs B	10%	
B Ltd	5%	15%
Shares held by Mr D and his associates:		
Mr D	10%	
Mrs D	2%	
Ms D	2%	
Mrs E	2%	16%
Shares held by Mr F		6%
Shares held by Mr G		5%
		54%

In determining the shares controlled by each participator, shares held by associates are included. Spouses, civil partners, children, siblings and parents are included as associates; however, shares held by cousins or aunts/uncles are not included.

Alphabet Limited is under the control of "five or fewer participators" and is, therefore, a close company.

26.2   Consequences of Close Company Status

As a close company is controlled by relatively few persons, it could be perceived to be relatively easy for controlling participators to influence a company's decisions and so minimise their own, and the company's, tax liability. For example, the shareholders could choose to fund the company with loans rather than share capital, unlike a publicly quoted company with many shareholders where it would be quite infeasible. In the absence of the anti-avoidance rules applying to close companies, it would be more tax-efficient to pay shareholders interest, which is tax deductible for the company, rather than dividends, which are not tax deductible. However, close companies are subject to special anti-avoidance rules which have negative tax consequences for the company and/or its shareholders:

▓ Certain **expenses** for participators and their associates are treated as distributions, i.e. they are not tax deductible and are subject to DWT (**Section 26.2.1**).

▓ **Interest** paid to certain directors and their associates, which exceeds a prescribed limit, is treated as a distribution (**Section 26.2.2**).

▓ There is a tax penalty for close companies making **loans** to participators or their associates (**Section 26.2.3**).

▓ Loans to participators or their associates which are subsequently **written off** will be assessable to income tax in their hands (**Section 26.2.4**).

▓ A **surcharge** of **20%** is levied on the **distributable estate and investment income** of close companies, to the extent that it is not distributed (**Section 26.3**).

▓ In the case of **certain** closely held **service companies**, a **surcharge** of **15%/20%** is levied on:
  ● 50% of the distributable trading income; and
  ● 100% of the distributable estate and investment income (**Section 26.3.5**).

Obviously a publicly quoted company which is not a closely held company is not subject to these rules.

26.2.1 Certain Expenses for Participators and their Associates

Any expenses incurred by a close company in providing benefits or facilities of any kind for a participator or an associate of the participator will be treated as a distribution.

Where an item is treated as a distribution, there are three consequences:

1. the **expense** will be **disallowed** to the company, and is therefore added back when calculating corporation tax;
2. the company will have a dividend withholding tax (DWT) liability equal to 25% of the market value of the distribution. The company can recover this tax from the participator and, accordingly, the DWT is a cost to the participator. If the participator does not repay the DWT, the expense must be grossed up (the deemed distribution) when calculating corporation tax and DWT; and
3. the recipient will be **assessed** under **Schedule F** on the distribution, i.e. liable to income tax at the marginal rate (most likely 40%), liable to the Universal Social Charge (USC) at the marginal rate (up to 11%) and liable to PRSI at 4%.

The following expense payments are **not** treated as distributions:

▓ any expense repaid to the company by the participator;

▓ any expense incurred in providing benefits or facilities to directors or employees – as such expenses are already assessable as benefits in kind under Schedule E; and

▓ any expense incurred in connection with the provision for the spouse, civil partner, children or dependants or children of a civil partner of any director or employee of any pension, annuity, lump sum or gratuity to be given on his or her death or retirement.

The legislation also contains anti-avoidance measures to counter two or more close companies from arranging to make payments to one another's participators.

> **Example 26.2**
>
> Mr A holds 2% of the ordinary share capital of X Ltd, a close company. Mr A is not an employee or director of X Ltd.
>
> X Ltd pays the rent on Mr A's house of €3,000 per annum. The amount is charged each year in X Ltd's accounts under rental expenses.
>
> As X Ltd is a close company and Mr A is a participator, the expense will be treated as a distribution. Accordingly, the €3,000 will be disallowed to X Ltd in arriving at its profits assessable to corporation tax.
>
> X Ltd will be required to pay DWT of €750 (€3,000 × 25%) to Revenue within 14 days of the end of the month in which the rent is paid. X Ltd can recover this €750 from Mr A.
>
> Mr A will be assessed under Schedule F on €3,000, with a credit of €750 given against his total tax liability.
>
> However, if Mr A is not going to repay the DWT, the deemed distribution of €3,000 is grossed up, i.e. €3,000 is a receipt net of DWT at 25%. Therefore, the gross amount is €3,000/0.75 = €4,000. X Ltd will have to pay DWT of €4,000 × 25% = €1,000. Mr A will be taxable under Schedule F on €4,000, with credit for the DWT of €1,000.
>
> Whether or not Mr A repays the DWT due, he will be liable to income tax under Schedule F at his marginal rate – most likely 40%. He will also be liable to the USC, typically at 8% but up to 11% for self-employed taxpayers and others whose non-PAYE income is greater than €100,000, as well as to PRSI at 4%.

26.2.2 Interest Paid to Directors and their Associates

Generally, interest is an allowable deduction for corporation tax purposes if it is trade related. The company may be obliged to withhold income tax at the standard rate (20%) from the interest payment and pay it over to Revenue on behalf of the lender. The lender will be assessed to tax on the gross amount (Schedule D, Case IV) and will receive a tax credit for the income tax withheld.

However, close company anti-avoidance legislation restricts the amount of interest deductible by a close company where that interest is paid to a director, or associate of a director, of the close company or of any company that controls or is controlled by the close company, and who has a "material interest" in the close company or, where the company is controlled by another company, in that other company. The legislation is concerned with interest on loans in excess of a prescribed limit.

A person has a material interest if he, either on his own or with any one or more of his associates, or if any associate(s) of his with or without any such other associates, is the beneficial owner of, or is able to control, directly or indirectly, **more than 5%** of the ordinary share capital.

The **prescribed limit** is calculated in the first instance as an overall limit. The overall limit is then apportioned between the various directors affected according to the amounts of interest paid to them. The **overall limit** is **13%** per annum on the **lower** of:

1. the total of all **loans** on which interest to directors (or their associates) with a "material interest" was paid by the company in the accounting period. Where the total of the loans was different at different times in the accounting period, the average total is to be taken; or
2. the **nominal** amount of the issued **share capital** of the company plus the amount of any **share premium** account at the **beginning of the accounting period**.

If the total amount of interest paid to a director in the accounting period exceeds this limit, the excess will be treated as a distribution. This excess is added back for corporation tax purposes and the company will have a DWT liability equal to 25% of the distribution (the excess interest payment).

The director (or associate) will be **assessed** under **Schedule F** on the distribution at the marginal rate, with a tax credit for the DWT paid by the company.

Example 26.3

Zoey Ltd has an issued share capital of €100. It has two shareholders who are both directors and who each loaned the company €10,000 at an interest rate of 10% per annum.

The interest expense is €10,000 × 10% × 2 = €2,000. As both are directors with a material interest, then the limit on this interest is the *lower* of:

(a) 13% × €20,000 = €2,600; or
(b) 13% × €100 = €13.

Therefore, only €13 is a deductible expense to the company. As €2,000 has been expensed, €1,987 must be added back in the tax computation.

Zoey Ltd will be required to deduct DWT of €497 (€1,987 × 25%) from the interest paid and pay this amount to Revenue within 14 days of the end of the month in which the interest is paid. Also, assuming that the interest is annual interest, Zoey Ltd will have to withhold income tax from the interest, i.e. withhold €13 × 20% = €3.

From each director's perspective, they will be taxed on a gross distribution of 1/2 × €1,987, under Schedule F, and on interest income liable under Case IV of 1/2 × €13, with a credit for DWT of 1/2 × €497, and for income tax of 1/2 × €3, against his income tax liability.

Each will be liable to income tax at their marginal rate – most likely 40%. Each will also be liable to the USC, typically at 8% but as high as 11%, and to PRSI at 4%.

Not all interest payments by a close company to its directors (and their associates) are restricted; only those interest payments to directors with a "material interest", i.e. directors (including their associates), controlling more than 5% of the ordinary share capital.

Example 26.4

XYZ Ltd has an issued share capital of €30,000. The shares are held as follows:

	€
Mr A (Director)	3,000
Mr B (Director)	1,200
Mrs B	400
Mr C (Director)	1,500
Mr D (Director)	4,000
Mr E (Director)	3,500
Mr F (Director)	1,500
Mr G	1,000
15 unrelated shareholders each holding less than 1,000 shares	13,900
	30,000

The following loans were made to the company:

Mr A   €8,000 @ 20% per annum

Mr B   €7,000 @ 10% per annum for the first six months increased to €9,000 @ 10% per annum for the last six months of the year

continued overleaf

Mr C	€6,000 @ 15% per annum
Mr E	€5,000 @ 12% per annum for the first six months and @ 16% per annum for the last six months
Mr F	€5,000 @ 15% per annum
Mr G	€2,000 @ 15% per annum

The interest charge in XYZ Ltd's profit and loss account was made up as follows:

		€	€
Mr A	€8,000 @ 20%		1,600
Mr B	€7,000 @ 10% × 1/2	350	
	€9,000 @ 10% × 1/2	450	800
Mr C	€6,000 @ 15%		900
Mr E	€5,000 @ 12% × 1/2	300	
	€5,000 @ 16% × 1/2	400	700
Mr F	€5,000 @ 15%		750
Mr G	€2,000 @ 15%		300
			5,050

The share capital of the company was the same at the start of the year. There was no share premium account.

1. **Is the company close?**

    Yes, it is under the control of participators who are directors, i.e.:

	€	€
Mr A		3,000
Mr B	1,200	
Mrs B	400	1,600
Mr C		1,500
Mr D		4,000
Mr E		3,500
Mr F		1,500
		15,100

2. Identify **directors** who made loans to the company and who, together with their associates, **own more than 5%** of the shares.

	€
Mr A	3,000 (10%)
Mr B	1,600 (5.33%)
Mr E	3,500 (11.67%)

3. **Calculate the overall limit**

    The lower of:

    (a) 13% of share capital, i.e. 13% × €30,000 = €3,900; or

    (b) 13% × loans from directors with material interest.

continued overleaf

	€
Mr A	8,000
Mr B (average)	8,000
Mr E	5,000
	21,000

13% × €21,000 = €2,730
The overall limit is €2,730.

4. **Apportion limit** to relevant directors by reference to interest paid.

	Interest Paid	Limit	Excess treated as a Distribution
Mr A	€1,600	$\frac{€1,600}{€3,100}$ × €2,730 = €1,409	€191
Mr B	€800	$\frac{€800}{€3,100}$ × €2,730 = €705	€95
Mr E	€700	$\frac{€700}{€3,100}$ × €2,730 = €616	€84
	€3,100	€2,730	€370

€370 will be disallowed to XYZ Ltd in computing its profits for corporation tax. DWT @ 25% must be deducted from the portion of the interest treated as a distribution. Each of the directors will be assessed under Schedule F to income tax, USC and PRSI on the proportion of the excess referable to him with a credit given against their total tax liability for the DWT deducted.

5. The company paid €5,050 of interest, of which €370 is treated as distribution. The balance of the interest, i.e. €4,680, is deductible. However, as with any other annual payment, the company must deduct tax at the standard income tax rate when paying this interest and remit this tax to Revenue. Each of the directors will be assessed under Schedule D Case IV to income tax, USC and PRSI on the proportion of the €4,680 referable to them with a credit given against their total tax liability for the income tax deducted.

26.2.3 Loans to Participators and their Associates

In the absence of the close company anti-avoidance rules, companies would lend money to shareholders rather than pay a dividend – such a loan would not be income in the hands of the shareholder so, therefore, it would not be taxable. To prevent this type of planning, a close company is subject to a tax penalty if it makes a loan to a participator.

Where a close company makes a loan to an **individual** who is a participator or an associate of a participator, the company will be required to pay income tax in respect of the amount of the loan grossed up at the standard rate (i.e. 20%) as if that grossed-up amount were an annual payment. A close company is to be regarded as making a loan to any person who incurs a debt to the company or where a debt due from a person to a third party is assigned to the company. The income tax is paid to Revenue as part of the corporation tax payment for the accounting period. The deemed annual payment will not be a charge on the company's income for the purposes of corporation tax so that the company will not be entitled to a deduction for the net or gross amount.

There are **three exceptions** to the above, which means that the following are not treated as loans to participators:

1. Where the business of the company is, or includes, the lending of money and the loan is made in the ordinary course of that business.

2. Where a debt is incurred for the supply of goods or services in the ordinary course of the business of the close company, unless the credit given exceeds six months or is longer than the period normally given to the company's customers.

3. Loans made to directors or employees of the company (or an associated company) if:

   (a) the amount of the loan, together with all other loans outstanding made by the company (or its associated companies) to the borrower (or their spouse or civil partner), does not exceed €19,050;

   (b) the borrower works full-time for the company; and

   (c) the borrower does **not** have a "material interest" in the company or an associated company – a person has a material interest if, either on their own or with any one or more of their associates, or if any associate(s) with or without any such other associates, is the beneficial owner of, or is able to control, directly or indirectly, **more than 5%** of the ordinary share capital.

It should be noted that, in relation to 3(c), if the borrower subsequently acquires a material interest, the company will be required to pay income tax in respect of all the loans outstanding from the borrower at that time.

When the loan, or part of the loan, is repaid by the participator (or associate), the tax, or a proportionate part of it, will be refunded to the company provided a claim is made within four years of the year of assessment in which the loan is repaid. However, the tax will not be refunded with interest.

Example 26.5

ABC Ltd, a close company, made interest-free loans to the following shareholders in the accounting period to 31 March 2021.

	€
Mr A (full-time working director owning 10% of the share capital)	16,000
Mr B (full-time working director owning 4% of the share capital)	10,000
Mr C	8,000

What are the tax consequences for the company assuming that no other loans had been made to the three individuals in the past?

Solution

The company will be required to pay income tax in respect of the loans to Mr A and Mr C grossed up at the standard rate as if the grossed-up amount were an annual payment.

The tax penalty for the company is calculated as follows:

	€
Mr A	16,000
Mr C	8,000
	24,000 × 20/80ths = €6,000

The loan to Mr B is not subject to the annual payment as Mr B:

(i)   is a director who works full-time;
(ii) does not have a "material interest" in the company; and
(iii) the loan is less than €19,050.

This tax of €6,000 is added to the corporation tax on profits and must be paid over to the Collector General at the same time as the corporation tax on profits, i.e. preliminary tax due on/before 23 February 2021 and the balance due on/before 23 December 2021.

Revenue has confirmed that for the purposes of satisfying a company's preliminary tax obligations for an accounting period, Revenue will not require the company to take account of the income tax on loans to participators and their associates in circumstances where the participator or associate **repays the loan by the due date for filing of the company's corporation tax return**, i.e. within nine months of the end of the accounting period in which the loan was made.

The loan concerned must be undertaken in good faith and for purposes other than tax avoidance. The practice will not apply in the case of "bed and breakfast"-type arrangements where a new loan is taken out on, or shortly after, repayment of an existing loan. In such cases Revenue will insist that the income tax be taken into account for preliminary tax purposes. However, in circumstances where it is the practice of a director to operate a current account with the company and this account is cleared annually from the director's own resources (e.g. the director's remuneration), then such an arrangement will not be regarded as a "bed and breakfast" arrangement.

26.2.4 Write-off of Loans to Participators

Where a company makes a loan to a participator and subsequently releases or writes it off, the shareholder receives income at the time of writing off the loan, i.e. a debt is released. The participator will be assessed to tax on the amount released or written off grossed up at the standard rate of income tax. It is taxable under Case IV. The tax paid by the company can be claimed as a tax credit by the participator against their tax liability, but it can never generate a tax refund.

Example 26.6

Assume that in the previous example Mr A repays his loan of €16,000 on 31 December 2021 and at the same time the company writes off the loan to Mr C.

What are the tax consequences for the company and the shareholder?

Company

The company will be refunded the tax on Mr A's loan, i.e. €4,000 (20/80 × €16,000).
However, it will lose the tax paid on Mr C's loan, i.e. €2,000 (20/80 × €8,000).

Shareholders

There are no tax consequences for Mr A.

Mr C, however, will be assessed to tax under Case IV Schedule D on the grossed-up amount of the loan, i.e. €10,000 (8,000 × 100/80).

Assume Mr C has other income of €30,000, is liable to PRSI under Class A, has personal tax credits of €3,300, is single and the tax bands are as outlined below. The grossed-up loan of €10,000 would be taxed at current rates of tax as follows:

	€
Other income	30,000
Case IV loan	10,000
Taxable income	40,000
Tax: €35,300 @ 20%	7,060
€4,700 @ 40%	1,880
	8,940
Less: personal tax credits	(3,300)
	5,640
Less: €10,000 @ 20%	(2,000)
Tax payable (before PRSI and USC)	3,640

continued overleaf

```
USC:
        €12,012 @ 0.5%    = €60
         €8,675 @ 2%      = €173
        €19,313 @ 4.5%    = €869          1,102
   PRSI €40,000 @ 4%                      1,600
```

26.3 Close Company Surcharge

26.3.1 Introduction

Where a company has cash surplus to its trading requirements, it can invest the cash itself or dividend it to the shareholders. If the company invests the cash itself, it will be liable to corporation tax at 25% on most investment income. If, instead, it pays a dividend to its shareholders, the shareholder must pay tax – up to 55% (i.e. 40% income tax, plus up to 11% USC, plus 4% PRSI) – on the dividend and can only invest the dividend net of tax. Therefore, unless the shareholder needs the cash, it would generally be left in the company to avoid shareholder tax. The close company anti-avoidance rule, known as the surcharge, reduces some of the benefit of leaving cash in a company.

A surcharge of 20% is levied on a close company that does not distribute its after-tax estate (rental) and investment income. There is no surcharge on Case I trading income, but there is a surcharge of 15% on half the after-tax Case II income of professional services companies (see **Section 26.3.5**.)

Close company distributions (i.e. expenses for participators and associates and excess interest to directors and associates) can be taken into account to reduce the amount on which the surcharge is levied. The surcharge will not apply to any income that a company is by law precluded from distributing. If the amount liable to the surcharge is more than the accumulated undistributed income at the end of the accounting period, then the surcharge is levied on the lower accumulated undistributed income.

There will be no surcharge if the excess distributable income over the distributions is €2,000 or less. There will be marginal relief where the excess over the distributions is slightly in excess of €2,000, restricting the surcharge to four-fifths of the excess over €2,000. Where the accounting period is less than 12 months, the €2,000 will be reduced proportionately. If there are associated companies, the €2,000 will be reduced by dividing it by one plus the number of associated companies.

26.3.2 7.5% Trading Deduction

Revenue appreciates that a certain amount of undistributed income may be required within a company. Accordingly, trading and professional service companies are entitled to a 7.5% trading deduction when calculating "distributable estate and investment income" for close company surcharge purposes. This 7.5% trading deduction is not available to an investment company (see **Chapter 27**).

26.3.3 Trading Company: Basic Surcharge Calculation

In essence, the surcharge applies to after-tax non-trading income that has not been distributed to shareholders. It is a surcharge on undistributed estate and investment income, i.e. not trading income and not gains. However, it includes dividends received from Irish companies (franked investment income) that are exempt from corporation tax. The basic calculation of the surcharge for a trading company that has no trading losses, Case V losses, relevant trading charges or relevant charges is given below.

COMPUTATION – CLOSE COMPANY SURCHARGE

	€
Case III	X
Case IV	X
Case V (before capital allowances)	<u>X</u>
'Passive income'	Y
Franked investment income (FII)	<u>X</u>
Estate and investment income	X
Less: corporation tax (usually @ 25%) on 'passive income' ("Y")	(X)
After-tax estate and investment income	Z
Less: 7.5% trading deduction of "Z"	(X)
Distributable Estate and Investment Income (DEII)	X
Less:	
Dividends declared for or in respect of the accounting period and paid during or within 18 months of the end of the accounting period	X
All distributions made in the accounting period (other than dividends)	<u>X</u> (X)
Liable to surcharge	<u><u>X</u></u>
Surcharge @ 20%	<u>X</u>

Example 26.7

Shop Ltd, a close company, runs a shop in Dublin. It doesn't pay any dividends and had the following income in the year ended 31 December 2021:

Case I	€100,000
Case III	€2,000
Case V	€6,000

The close company surcharge is payable on distributable estate and investment income, to the extent that it is not distributed. Therefore:

	€
Estate and investment income (Note)	8,000
Corporation tax @ 25%	(2,000)
	6,000
Trading deduction 7.5%	(450)
DEII	5,550
Less: dividends paid/payable within 18 months	Nil
Liable to surcharge	5,550
Surcharge @ 20%	1,110

Note: as there are no dividends received from Irish companies (FII), 'passive income' in this example is the same as 'estate and investment income', i.e. Case III plus Case V (€2,000 + €6,000).

26.3.4 Trading Company Surcharge Calculation: Losses and Charges on Income

There is no deduction allowed for losses arising outside the current accounting period. Losses carried forward or back from other accounting periods are ignored.

Example 26.8

Trumps Ltd, a close company, has the following results for the year ended 31 December 2021:

	€
Trade income	480,000
Deposit interest	2,000
Rental income	40,000
Rental loss forward from 2020	(10,000)

Notes
1. The company had a loss forward relating to the trade of €20,000.
2. The company had chargeable gains in the accounting period of €2,000, after adjustment.
3. A cash dividend of €700 was received from another Irish company in the accounting period.
4. An interim dividend of €14,000 in respect of the accounting period was paid on 1 October 2022. A final dividend of €9,580 will be paid on 10 October 2023.

What is the amount of the close company surcharge (if any) arising in respect of the accounting period ended 31 December 2021?

Calculation of distributable estate and investment income

	€
Case III	2,000
Case V	40,000
Passive income	42,000
FII	700
Estate and investment income	42,700
Less: corporation tax @ 25% on €42,000	(10,500)
	32,200
Less: 7.5% × €32,200	(2,415)
Distributable estate and investment income	29,785

Note: any non-estate and investment income (e.g. Case I) and any losses forward and chargeable gains are ignored (i.e. only estate and investment income of the current accounting period is relevant).

Calculate amount on which surcharge is levied

	€
Distributable estate and investment income	29,785
Less: dividends paid within 18 months (Note)	(14,000)
Liable to surcharge	15,785

Surcharge @ 20% = €3,157

Note: the final dividend of €9,580, paid at 10 October 2023, is not deducted as it was paid more than 18 months after the end of the accounting period.

If the final dividend were paid on, say, 30 June 2023, the surcharge could have been as follows:

	€
DEII	29,785
Less: dividends paid within 18 months (€14,000 + €9,580)	(23,580)
Liable to surcharge	6,205
Surcharge @ 20%	1,241

When a company incurs trading and investment losses in an accounting period, such losses must be deducted when calculating the distributable income for close company surcharge purposes. Similarly, relevant trade charges and relevant charges (i.e. non-trade charges) paid in an accounting period reduce the amount of income available to be distributed by a company and must be deducted in calculating the amount liable to the surcharge. Therefore a more complex pro forma surcharge computation is required.

COMPUTATION – TRADING COMPANY
WITH LOSSES AND/OR CHARGES ON INCOME SURCHARGE

Step 1: Identify income for the accounting period

Income (i.e. Cases I, III, IV & V)	X
Less:	
current-year losses	(X)
current-year relevant trade charges	(X)
Income for accounting period	X

Step 2: Calculate 'passive income' (i.e. estate and investment income subject to corporation tax)

$$\text{Income for accounting period (from Step 1)} \times \frac{\text{(Total Cases III, IV and V)}}{\text{Income as per Step 1}}$$

Step 3: Calculate distributable estate and investment income

Passive income (from Step 2)	X
Less: relevant (non-trade) charges	(X)*
Net passive income	X
FII	X*
Estate and investment income	X
Less: CT on net passive income	(X)
	X
Less: 7.5% trading deduction	(X)
DEII	X

Step 4: Calculate surcharge

DEII (from Step 3)	X
Less: distributions paid/payable within	
18 months of the accounting period	(X)
Liable to surcharge	X
Surcharge @ 20%	X

* If relevant charges exceed passive income, deduct excess from FII.

Example 26.9: Trading loss
Loss Limited, a close company, runs a garage in Dublin. It pays no dividends and had the following income in the year ended 31 December 2021:

	€
Case I	(10,000)
Case III	2,000
Case V	16,000
FII	5,000

Close company surcharge calculation

1. Calculate income for accounting period:

	€
Case III	2,000
Case V	16,000
Income	18,000
Less: Case I current year	(10,000)
Income for AP	8,000

2. Calculate 'passive income':

€8,000 × €18,000/€18,000	8,000

3. Calculate DEII:

Passive income	8,000
FII	5,000
Estate and investment income	13,000
Less: CT @ 25% on passive income (€8,000)	(2,000)
	11,000
Less: 7.5% trading deduction	(825)
DEII	10,175

4. Calculate surcharge:

DEII	10,175
Less: dividends paid/payable within 18 months	NIL
Liable to surcharge	10,175
Surcharge @ 20%	2,035

Example 26.10: Trade charge
Patent Ltd, a close company, runs a manufacturing business in Dublin. It had the following income and charges in the year ended 31 December 2021:

	€
Case I	10,000
Trade charges paid	600
Case III	2,000
FII	17,000

On 9 January 2022, the company pays a dividend of €10,000 in respect of the year. How much close company surcharge is due?

Close company surcharge calculation

1. Calculate income for accounting period:

	€
Case I	10,000
Case III	2,000
Income	12,000
Less: trade charges	(600)
Income for AP	11,400

continued overleaf

2. Calculate 'passive income':

€11,400 × €2,000/€12,000	1,900

3. Calculate DEII:

Passive income	1,900
FII	17,000
Estate and investment income	18,900
Less: CT @ 25% on €1,900	(475)
	18,425
Less: 7.5% trading deduction	(1,382)
DEII	17,043

4. Calculate surcharge:

DEII	17,043
Less: dividends paid	(10,000)
Liable to surcharge	7,043
Surcharge @ 20%	1,409

Example 26.11: Non-trade charge

Interesting Limited, a close company, has a business in Dublin. It pays no dividend and had the following income and charges in the year ended 31 December 2021:

	€
Case I	100,000
Case III	2,000
Case V	16,000
FII	5,000
Non-trade charge paid	4,000

Close company surcharge calculation

1. Calculate income for accounting period:

	€
Case I	100,000
Case III	2,000
Case V	16,000
Income	118,000

2. Calculate 'passive income':

€118,000 × €18,000/€118,000	18,000

3. Calculate DEII:

Passive income	18,000
Less: non-trade charge	(4,000)
Net passive income	14,000
FII	5,000
Estate and investment income	19,000
Less: CT @ 25% on €14,000	(3,500)
	15,500
Less: 7.5% trading deduction	(1,163)
DEII	14,337

continued overleaf

4. Calculate surcharge:	
DEII	14,337
Less: dividends paid/payable	
within 18 months	NIL
Liable to surcharge	14,337
Surcharge @ 20%	2,867

26.3.5 Service Company Surcharge

A service company is a close company, the principal part of whose income chargeable under Cases I and II of Schedule D and Schedule E is derived from:

1. carrying on directly a profession or providing professional services or the having, or exercising, of an office or employment; or
2. providing services or facilities of any nature;
   (a) to a company within 1. above;
   (b) to an individual or partnership carrying on a profession;
   (c) to a person who holds or exercises an office or employment; or
   (d) to a person or partnership connected with any person in (a) to (c) above.

Services provided to an unconnected person or partnership are, however, ignored.

For a service company to be liable to the surcharge under this legislation, the main part of its income must come from a profession, provision of professional services, an employment or provision of the services or facilities to a connected person. Therefore, it is important to understand what is a profession. There is no definition in the law as to what is a profession. The UK case of *CIR v. Maxse* (1919) sets out the determining factors to be taken into account. A profession involves the idea of an occupation requiring either purely intellectual skill or of a manual skill controlled by the intellectual skill of the operator, e.g. painting or sculpture or surgery. This is distinguished from an occupation that is substantially the production or sale, or arrangement for the production or sale, of commodities, which would not be a profession.

The issue of whether an activity is a profession has been considered in a number of cases, particularly in the UK. Revenue has set out what, in its view, are and are not professions, taking into account case law. Activities considered as professions are:

- Accountant
- Actor
- Actuary
- Archaeologist
- Architect
- Auctioneer/estate agent
- Barrister
- Computer programmer
- Dentist
- Doctor
- Engineer
- Journalist
- Management consultant
- Optician
- Private school
- Quantity surveyor
- Solicitor
- Veterinary surgeon.

Revenue's guidance lists the following activities as, generally, **not considered** to be the carrying on of a **profession**:

- Advertising agent
- Auctioneers of livestock in a cattle mart
- Insurance brokers
- Operation of a retail pharmacy
- Public relations company
- Stockbrokers
- Bookkeeping.

The differences between this surcharge and the surcharge on trading companies is that **half the after-tax Case I/II income** is also liable to surcharge, but **a rate of only 15%** applies to this part of the income, in addition to the 20% surcharge applicable to distributable estate and investment income (net of 7.5%).

As with trading companies, there is no deduction for losses arising outside the current accounting period or for Case V capital allowances. Losses incurred in the accounting period, relevant trade charges and relevant charges paid in an accounting period must be deducted when calculating the distributable income for close company surcharge purposes. The computation is more complex as income from the trade is liable to a separate surcharge at a lower rate (15%). The distributable trading income must be identified and the distributions paid/payable must be allocated to minimise the surcharge payable. Hence, a more complex pro forma surcharge computation is required.

COMPUTATION – SERVICE COMPANY
WITH LOSSES AND/OR CHARGES ON INCOME SURCHARGE

Step 1: Identify income for the accounting period

Income (i.e. Cases II, III, IV & V)	X
Less:	
current-year losses	(X)
current-year relevant trade charges	(X)
Income for accounting period	X

Step 2: Calculate 'passive income' (i.e. estate and investment income subject to corporation tax)

Income for accounting period (from Step 1) $\times \dfrac{\text{(Total Cases III, IV and V)}}{\text{Income as per Step 1}}$

Step 3: Calculate distributable estate and investment income

Passive income (from Step 2)	X
Less: relevant charges	(X)*
Net passive income	X
FII	X
Estate and investment income	X
Less: CT on net passive income	(X)
	X
Less: 7.5% trading deduction	(X)
DEII	X

Step 4: Calculate distributable trading income (DTI)

Income for accounting period (from Step 1)	X
Less: passive income (from Step 2)	(X)
Trading income	X*
Less: CT on trading income 12.5%	(X)
Distributable trading income	X

Step 5: Calculate amount liable to surcharge

DEII (from Step 3)	X
DTI (from Step 4) × 50%	X
	X
Less: distributions paid/payable within	
18 months of the accounting period	(X)
Liable to surcharge	X

Step 6: Calculate surcharge

As DEII is taxed at 20% and DTI at 15%, the amount calculated at Step 5 needs to be divided between DTI and DEII. All distributions are treated as first offset against DEII.

DEII (from Step 3)	X
Less: distributions paid/payable within	
18 months of the accounting period	(X)**
DEII liable to surcharge	X
Surcharge @ 20%	X
Liable to surcharge (from Step 5)	X
Less: DEII liable to surcharge	(X)
	X**
Surcharge @ 15%	X
Total Surcharge:	
Surcharge @ 20%	X
Surcharge @ 15%	X
Total surcharge	X

    * If relevant charges (non-trade charges) exceed passive income, deduct the excess from trading income.

** If distributions paid/payable within 18 months exceed DEII, use excess to reduce the amount liable to surcharge at 15%.

Example 26.12

Good Advice Ltd, a closely held firm of management consultants, had the following income for the year ended 31 December 2021:

	€
Professional income	100,000
Interest on Government securities	30,000
Rental income	20,000
Irish dividend received (cash amount)	14,000

The company declared and paid an interim dividend of €50,000 for the accounting period on 6 July 2021.

As the principal part of the company's income is derived from carrying on a profession, the company is a service company.

continued overleaf

The amount on which the surcharge is levied is calculated as follows:

1. Calculate income for accounting period:

	€
Case II professional income	100,000
Case III interest	30,000
Case V rent	20,000
Income for AP	150,000

2. Calculate 'passive income':

$$€150,000 \times \frac{(€30,000+€20,000)}{€150,000}$$

	50,000

3. Calculate DEII:

Passive income	50,000
FII	14,000
Estate and investment income	64,000
Less: CT @ 25% on €50,000	(12,500)
	51,500
Less: 7.5% trading deduction	(3,863)
DEII	47,637

4. Calculate DTI:

Income for AP	150,000
Less: passive income	(50,000)
Trading income	100,000
Less: CT @ 12.5%	(12,500)
DTI	(87,500)

5. Liable to surcharge:

DEII	47,637
DTI x 50%	43,750
Less: dividend paid	(50,000)
Liable to surcharge	41,387

6. Calculate surcharge:

DEII	47,637
Less: dividend paid	(50,000)
Excess	2,363
Surcharge @ 20%	NIL
DTI x 50%	43,750
Less: excess dividend	(2,363)
Liable to surcharge	41,387
Surcharge @ 15%	6,208
Total surcharge	6,208

26.4 Other Matters

26.4.1 Case III Income

Foreign dividends are generally taxable under Case III. In relation to foreign dividends, there are two key points:

1. If the dividends are paid by a foreign company and a gain on disposal of whose shares would qualify for exemption (see **Chapter 25**, **Section 25.3**), then that dividend is exempt from the surcharge and will not be included in Case III income for the surcharge calculation.
2. Case III income is generally taxed at 25%. However, many foreign dividends are taxable at 12.5% (see **Chapter 22, Section 22.2**) and, therefore, for any such Case III income, the tax rate used in the surcharge computation will be 12.5%.

26.4.2   Election – Not a Distribution for Surcharge

A company making a distribution (e.g. dividend) and a company receiving a distribution may jointly elect that the distribution will not be treated as a distribution for the purposes of the surcharge calculation.

As a result, an Irish holding company and an Irish subsidiary that pays or makes a distribution to the holding company can elect not to treat the distribution as coming under the close company surcharge provisions. Where such an election is made, the distribution will be treated as not being a distribution received by the holding company and as not being a distribution made by the subsidiary.

Example 26.13: Impact on company receiving FII
Using the information provided in **Example 26.11**, the company agreed with its subsidiary to treat the FII as not a distribution for surcharge purposes. Therefore, the company does not include it when calculating DEII. The surcharge will be reduced as follows:

Calculate DEII:

	€
Passive income	18,000
Less: non-trade charge	(4,000)
Net passive income	14,000
FII	n/a
Estate and investment income	14,000
Less: CT @ 25% on €14,000	(3,500)
	10,500
Less: 7.5% trading deduction	(788)
DEII	9,712
Surcharge @ 20%	1,942

Example 26.14: Impact on company paying FII
Using the information provided in **Example 26.12**, the company agreed with its parent to treat the dividend paid by Good Advice Ltd as not a distribution for surcharge purposes. Therefore, it is not deducted when calculating the amount liable to the surcharge. The surcharge will increase as follows:

5. Liable to surcharge:

	€
DEII	47,637
DTI × 50%	43,750
	91,387
Less: dividend paid	–
Liable to surcharge	91,387

continued overleaf

6. Surcharge:		
DEII	47,637	
Less: dividend paid	–	
Liable to surcharge	47,637	
Surcharge @ 20%	9,527	
DTI × 50%	43,750	
Less: excess dividend	–	
Liable to surcharge	43,750	
Surcharge @ 15%	6,563	
Total surcharge:		
Surcharge @ 20%	9,527	
Surcharge @ 15%	6,563	
Total	16,090	

Such an election is beneficial where a company with only Case I income is required to pay a dividend to its parent company.

26.4.3 Payment of Surcharge

The surcharge is treated as corporation tax for the earliest accounting period that ends on or after a day which is 12 months after the end of the accounting period in which the investment or rental income arises.

Example 26.15

Again, using the information from **Example 26.12**. The accounting period to which the surcharge relates is the year ended 31 December 2021. If the company prepares the next accounts to 31 December 2022, the earliest accounting period that ends on a day which is 12 months after the year ended 31 December 2021 is the year ended 31 December 2022, so the surcharge of €6,208 will be added to the corporation tax liability for the year ended 31 December 2022. It will be included when calculating the preliminary tax payment(s) and the balance of tax for the year ended 31 December 2022.

However, if the company prepares the next accounts for the nine-month period ending 30 September 2022, this is not more than 12 months after the ending of the accounting period to which the surcharge relates. Therefore, the surcharge will not be added to the corporation tax liability for the period ended 30 September 2022. It will be added to the corporation tax liability for the first accounting period ending 31 December 2022 or later.

Questions

Review Questions
(See Suggested Solutions to Review Questions at the end of this textbook.)

Question 26.1

(a) State the tax effect on a close company arising out of a loan made to a participator in that company. Indicate the circumstances in which the loan would have no tax consequences for the company.
(b) Size Ltd is a close company and has the following adjusted profits for the year ended 31 December 2021:

	€
Trading profits	500,000
Rents	30,000
Deposit interest	3,000
	533,000

It has declared the following dividends payable out of the year ended 31 December 2021 profits and payable on the dates shown:

	€
30/01/2022	6,300
30/09/2022	3,000
10/07/2023	4,000

Requirement

Show Size Ltd's corporation tax liability for the year ended 31 December 2021 and the additional corporation tax payable for the year ended 31 December 2022 due to the surcharge.

Question 26.2

Close Ltd is a family-owned distribution company with no associated companies. Results to 31 December 2021 are as follows:

	€	€
Gross profit	50,000	
Other income	10,000	
		60,000
Depreciation	15,000	
Salaries	10,000	
Rent and rates	1,000	
Sundry	1,100	(27,100)
Net profit		32,900

The directors do not recommend the payment of a dividend.

Other Income	€
Interest on Government securities	8,500
Capital grants	1,500
	10,000

Sundry	
Miscellaneous office expenses	300
Expenses of majority shareholder's brother Y, who does not work for Close Ltd, paid to him on 01/07/2021	800
	1,100

Capital allowances due are €4,000.

Requirement
(a) Compute corporation tax payable.
(b) Compute surcharge arising.
(c) Indicate treatment of specific items.

Question 26.3

Servisco Ltd, a closely held company trading as management consultants, had the following income for the year ended 31 December 2021:

	€
Professional income	430,000
Rental income	100,000
Interest on Government stocks	50,000
Chargeable gains before adjustment (October 2021)	54,000

The company had a loss forward of €9,000 on its professional activities from the year ended 31 December 2020.

In the year ended 31 December 2022, the company sustained a loss on its professional activities of €10,000, all of which was claimed for set off against the 2021 income.

The company received Irish dividends of €7,500.

Dividends of €70,000 were paid within 18 months.

Requirement
Compute the company's corporation tax liability for the year ended 31 December 2021 and the surcharge that will be payable as part of the corporation tax liability for the year ended 31 December 2022.

Question 26.4

Machinery Ltd was incorporated in the Republic of Ireland on 1 June 2002 and since that date has been engaged in providing machinery to companies. The founder members of the company were Mr V. Duffy and his wife, Fanny. The company was formed to take over their existing business, which they had previously conducted in partnership. Mr and Mrs Duffy have actively encouraged members of their immediate family and other relatives to take up employment within the company and have endeavoured to ensure that the control of the company remains, as far as possible, within the family. The company's income statement for the year ended 31 December 2021 showed the following results:

	€	€
Sales		1,660,000
Inventories at 31/12/2021	450,000	
Inventories at 01/01/2021	360,000	90,000
		1,750,000
Purchases		(805,000)
		945,000

continued overleaf

Less:

Depreciation	59,790	
Rent	79,710	
Light and heat	17,500	
Distribution costs	39,000	
Bank and loan interest	65,000	
Motor expenses (all vans)	44,000	
Sundry expenses	13,000	(318,000)
Net profit from trading		627,000
Add:		
Bank deposit interest	10,000	
Rents from let property		
(after allowable deductions)	50,000	60,000
Profit for year		687,000

The shareholdings in, and loans made to, the company as at 31 December 2021 were:

	Ordinary €1 shares	Loans Made	Interest Paid
Mr V. Duffy (Director)	3,000	€4,000 @ 15%	€600
Mrs V. Duffy (Director)	1,250	€5,000 @ 12%	€600
G. Duffy (mother of V. Duffy)	2,900	€5,000 @ 15%	€750
S. Duffy (father of V. Duffy)	2,000	€5,000 @ 15%	€750
D. O'Connell (Director)	2,750	€5,000 @ 15%	€750
Mrs K. Moran (aunt of V. Duffy)	500	–	–
L.T. Smith (Director)	2,100	€10,000 @ 13.21%	€1,321
Louise Hare (Company Secretary and sister of Paul Hare)	3,000	€3,000 @ 12%	€360
Paul Hare (husband of V. Duffy's sister)	2,500	€3,000 @ 9.3%	€279
	20,000		€5,410

Notes:
1. The loan interest was paid in addition to bank interest of €59,590, thus reconciling with the amount shown in the income statement.
2. For the accounting period ended 31 December 2021, capital allowances were €10,700.
3. None of the shareholders is related, other than as shown above.
4. The share capital at 1 January 2021 was the same as at 31 December 2021.

Requirement
Compute the corporation tax liability of the company for the accounting year ended 31 December 2021 and the surcharge that will be payable as part of the corporation tax liability for the year ended 31 December 2022.

Question 26.5

Tax Advisors Ltd, a professional services company, had the following sources of income and charges for the year ended 31 December 2021:

	€
Case II income	100,000
Case III income	100,000
Trade charges paid during 2021	(60,000)
Non-trade charges paid during 2021	(50,000)

Tax Advisors Ltd paid an interim dividend on 1 December 2021 of €30,000.

Requirement
Calculate the surcharge payable by Tax Advisors Ltd in respect of the above figures.

Investment Companies

27.1 Introduction

After studying this chapter you will have developed the competency to understand that, up to now, we have dealt with companies that just held shares in another company, i.e. a holding company, and companies that carried on a trade.

A holding company does not trade and therefore is not entitled to claim the type of expense deductions that a trading company could. By its nature, a holding company merely holds investments.

This is in contrast to a subsidiary of, say, a bank, which actively trades shares and securities daily so as to derive a profit from share dealing. Such a company carries on a trade and, therefore, is entitled to a deduction for its trading expenses.

An "investment company", in practice, lies somewhere between a holding company and a share-dealing company.

An investment company can have Cases III, IV and V income as well as chargeable gains, but would be unlikely to have Cases I or II income. Franked investment income (FII), other than dividends from an Irish REIT, is exempt. Chargeable gains are grossed up in the usual manner. Investment companies are often established by individuals. By establishing an investment company, expenses, i.e. management expenses, which would not otherwise be deductible for an individual are deductible for a company.

27.1.1 Definition

Under section 83 TCA 1997, an "investment company" is any company:

■ whose business consists wholly or mainly in the **making** of investments; and
■ the principal part of whose income is derived therefrom; and includes a savings bank.

The key issue is that there is active involvement by the company in making investments. To ensure that a company is an investment company, a company should have more than one investment.

A certain level of activity on the company's part is required, as opposed to a single, once-off investment. A company that acquires a property and manages that property is not considered to be an investment company as it is not actively making investments.

There is no specific guideline as to what level of activity a company needs to engage in to establish its "investment company" status. One would, however, expect an "investment company" to have **regular meetings to review existing investments** and decide on possible new investments.

27.1.2 Relief for Management Expenses

An "investment company" resident in the State is entitled to deduct its expenses of management in computing its total profits (including chargeable gains) for corporation tax purposes.

27.2 Management Expenses

The term "management expenses" is not defined in law. The law allows a deduction for "… any sums disbursed as expenses of management … except any such expenses as are deductible in computing income for the purposes of Case V…".

The courts have either taken the broad view or the narrow view of what are "expenses of management". The **broad** view is that *any* expenses **incurred by** management are deductible, whereas the **narrow** view is that only **expenses of management** are deductible, i.e. only the expenses of management in shaping policy and in other matters of managerial decision.

In the most recent Irish ruling on the matter, the case of *Hibernian Insurance Company Ltd v. MacUimis* (2000), the Supreme Court supported the narrower view. The judge held that the very substantial costs incurred by the group in getting advisors to evaluate three investment opportunities did not constitute "expenses of management". He held that the expenditure was capital in nature and, therefore, was not management expenses. Therefore, monies spent on evaluating new investment opportunities are not deductible as management expenses. A more recent UK case, *Camas plc v. Atkinson* (2004) decided in favour of the broader view (i.e. all costs up to the time a company makes a definitive decision to acquire a business are allowable "expenses of management"), although this decision is not binding in Ireland as it is not an Irish ruling.

The list set out below mainly reflects case law and practice. Management expenses:

1. include lump sums paid under the Redundancy Payments Act 1967 or an employer's contribution under an approved superannuation scheme;
2. do not include expenses which are deductible in computing income from rents, etc. under Case V;
3. are to be reduced by any income not subject to tax other than FII (such income is relatively rare);
4. include rent, rates, interest on loans to finance day-to-day running of the company, stationery, accountancy, secretarial and audit fees;
5. include stockbrokers' fees, but not fees spent on new investments, as these would relate to capital expenditure;
6. include directors' fees subject to the limit outlined below (Revenue practice); and
7. include donations to charities, etc. and approved sports bodies, where the donation to the charity/sports body is at least €250 (for a 12-month accounting period).

27.2.1 Directors' Remuneration

Directors' remuneration is only deductible for corporation tax purposes to the extent that it is commensurate with the services provided. In practice, Revenue permit a deduction for directors' remuneration up to 10% of the company's gross income, including FII. The maximum allowable deduction is increased to 15% gross rental income plus 10% other income, including FII where the investment company has rental income and the directors devote a substantial part of their time to the management of those properties and there is not a separate management charge.

Example 27.1

Thornton Properties Limited is an investment company. It has been established that its directors devote a substantial part of their time to the management of the company's properties. The company's income is as follows:

		€
Gross rents		400,000
Loan interest		25,000
Deposit interest, received gross		15,000
Irish dividends		35,000
Chargeable gains		6,000
Maximum deduction for directors' remuneration:		
Gross rents	€400,000 @ 15%	60,000
Other income:		
Loan interest	25,000	
Deposit interest, received gross	15,000	
Irish dividends	35,000	
	75,000 @ 10%	7,500
Maximum deduction for directors' remuneration		67,500

If the actual amount paid to directors were only €59,000, then only €59,000 would be deductible.

27.2.2 Carry Forward of Unutilised Management Expenses

If the management expenses of an accounting period, together with any charges on income paid in the period wholly and exclusively for the purpose of the company's business, cannot be wholly allowed by way of a deduction in that period, the balance may be carried forward to the succeeding period and treated as management expenses of that period, qualifying for allowance in that period or, if needs be, in subsequent periods. The balance cannot be carried back, but it is available for group relief (see **Chapter 24, Section 24.3.3**).

SUMMARY CHART OF OFFSET OF MANAGEMENT EXPENSES

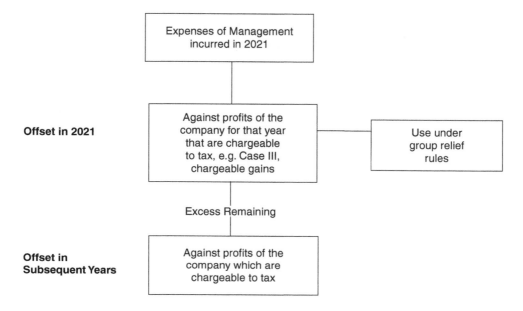

Questions

Review Questions
(See Suggested Solutions to Review Questions at the end of this textbook.)

Question 27.1

Equities Ltd, a company whose business is the making of investments, had the following income statement for the year ended 31 December 2021:

Income:	€
Dividends from other Irish companies	140,000
Interest on Irish Government security	15,100
	155,100

Expenditure:	
Accounting fees	1,000
Secretarial fees	2,000
Auditors' remuneration	6,000
Directors' remuneration	20,000
Stockbroker's charges for advice	3,000
	(32,000)

Net income	123,100

Requirement
Calculate the corporation tax liability for the period, claiming all possible reliefs.

Part Five

Income Tax

28

Territoriality Rules

Learning Objectives

After studying this chapter you will be able to:

- Explain the implications of residence, ordinary residence and domicile in the calculation of income liable to Irish tax.
- Explain the domicile levy.
- Explain the relief available for individuals entering or leaving the country during the year of assessment.
- Advise on the tax implications of paying rents to non-resident landlords.

28.1 Introduction

Income tax is assessed on individuals, trusts and certain non-resident companies (see **Chapter 21, Section 21.2.2**). A person's income is classified according to the various income sources in the same manner as occurs with a company for corporation tax (see **Section 21.1**).

The income tax year is a calendar year, assessed on the current year basis. Chargeable persons must submit an income tax return by 31 October in the year following the year of assessment (i.e. income for 2021 assessed in 2021 to be returned by 31 October 2022). In practice the 31 October deadline is extended to mid-November where tax is paid and returns are filed online via ROS. A person's entitlement to tax bands, tax credits and reliefs, as detailed at CA Proficiency 1, is determined by their personal circumstances.

The extent to which an individual's income is liable to Irish income tax depends on the individual's residence, ordinary residence and domicile (see **Chapter 2**). In simple terms, an Irish tax resident is liable to Irish income tax on their worldwide income. A non-resident is liable to Irish income tax on their Irish income only.

28.2 Impact of Residence, Ordinary Residence and Domicile

28.2.1 Resident and Domiciled

Individuals who are resident and domiciled are liable to Irish income tax on their **worldwide personal income**, irrespective of where it is earned and whether it is remitted to Ireland.

Example 28.1

Pat, a single man, has the following sources of income in 2021:

	€
Salary paid by Irish company	75,000
Dividends from Spanish company	10,000
Rent received from USA (not remitted)	5,200
Total income	90,200

Pat is resident and domiciled in Ireland. Therefore, he is liable to income tax on his worldwide income of €90,200, regardless of where it arises or whether it is remitted into Ireland.

28.2.2 Resident and Domiciled but Not Ordinarily Resident

An Irish domiciled individual who is resident but not ordinarily resident in Ireland (e.g. an Irish citizen who has been living abroad for many years and who has returned) is liable to income tax on their worldwide income.

Example 28.2

Patrick, an Irish domiciliary, returned to Dublin in May 2021 after a five-year secondment to his employer's parent company in Dubai. He has the following sources of income in 2021:

	€
Salary paid by Dubai parent company (to May 2021)	60,000
Salary paid by Irish company (June to Dec 2021)	40,000
Rent received on Dubai apartment (June to Dec) (remitted)	9,000
Dubai deposit interest (paid Oct 2021) (not remitted)	4,000

Patrick is domiciled and resident (>183 days) in Ireland for 2021 but is not ordinarily resident (as he was non-resident for 2020, 2019 and 2018). As Patrick qualifies for split-year residence (see **Section 28.4**), he is therefore liable to income tax on the following income:

	€
Salary paid by Irish company (June to Dec 2021)	40,000
Dubai rent	9,000
Dubai deposit interest	4,000

28.2.3 Resident but Not Domiciled

An individual who is resident but not domiciled in Ireland is liable to income tax on the remittance basis, being Irish income tax on:

1. any income arising in Ireland; *and*
2. other income (excluding employment income) arising outside of Ireland **but only** to the extent that it is **remitted into** Ireland; *and*
3. income from a foreign office or employment, insofar as that income relates to the performance, **in the State**, of the duties of that office or employment (irrespective of where it is paid or whether it is remitted into Ireland or not).

28.2.4 Not Resident and Not Ordinarily Resident

An individual who is not resident in Ireland is liable to income tax only on income arising in Ireland. In addition, a non-resident individual is not generally entitled to tax credits and reliefs (but see **Section 28.2.6**). The domicile of such a person is not relevant.

28.2.5 *Not Resident but Ordinarily Resident*

An individual who is not resident in Ireland but is ordinarily resident in Ireland is liable to Irish tax on their income as if they were resident **except for**:

1. income from a trade or profession, no part of which is carried on in Ireland;
2. employment that is carried on outside the State (incidental duties may be carried on in the State); and
3. other foreign income which in any year of assessment **does not exceed €3,810**.

Example 28.3

Mary Rose, an Irish domiciled individual, who is single, emigrated to Canada in May 2019. Apart from an annual two-week holiday she has not returned to Ireland. She has the following sources of income in 2021.

	€
Salary paid by her Canadian employer	90,000
Rent received from letting her house in Canada (not remitted)	15,000

She is non-resident for 2019 and 2020, but is still ordinarily resident for 2021. Therefore Mary Rose is liable to income tax on the Canadian rent, as it is in excess of €3,810, but not on her Canadian salary as the employment was exercised wholly outside Ireland.

28.2.6 *Non-resident Individual Entitlement to Tax Credits*

In general, non-resident individuals are not entitled to tax credits. However, there are two exceptions to this:

1. citizens or nationals of an EU Member State or the UK – full tax credits are granted on a cumulative basis if 75% of the worldwide income is taxable in Ireland. A portion of tax credits may be due if Irish income is less than 75%; or
2. citizens of a country with which there is a double taxation agreement – depending on the tax treaty, full tax credits are allowable on a cumulative basis where the person's only source of income is Irish. Where the person has non-Irish source income in addition to Irish income, a portion of tax credits may be due.

28.3 Domicile Levy

Section 531AA TCA 1997 introduced a levy, from 1 January 2010, to ensure that individuals who are domiciled in Ireland make a contribution to the Exchequer irrespective of their residence status. The individual is not required to be a "citizen of Ireland".

The domicile levy applies to an individual:

1. who is domiciled in Ireland in that tax year;
2. whose worldwide income for the tax year is greater than €1 million;
3. whose final Irish income tax liability (i.e. USC and PRSI paid is not taken into account) is less than €200,000; **and**
4. who has Irish property with a market value exceeding €5 million at 31 December.

The amount of the levy is **€200,000**. Irish income tax paid by an individual will be allowed as a credit against the domicile levy (i.e. no credit is given for USC and PRSI paid). However, taxes paid overseas on the worldwide income are not allowed as a credit. Irish property does not include shares in a company (or a holding company) **carrying on a trade**, but includes all property **situated in**

Ireland to which the individual is beneficially entitled in possession at 31 December. The market value is the price at which the property would sell on the open market and does not take into account any charges or mortgages taken out against the property.

The levy operates on an individual basis, i.e. if jointly assessed spouses both meet the conditions above, the levy is payable by both spouses. The tax is payable on a self-assessment basis on or before 31 October in the year following the valuation date, i.e. 31 December each year.

This section also empowers Revenue to request any person it believes to be a relevant person to deliver a full and true return of all particulars in relation to the determination of the domicile levy, together with payment of same within 30 days of the request.

28.4 Split-year Residence

An individual is Irish resident or non-resident, as the case may be, for a full tax year. Section 822 TCA 1997 provides that in certain circumstances an individual can be treated as Irish resident for **part** of a year only.

28.4.1 Year of Arrival

As far as **employment income** is concerned, an individual who:

1.   has not been resident in Ireland in the preceding tax year,
2.   arrives in Ireland in the current tax year,
3.   is resident in Ireland in the current tax year (i.e. 183 days or more), and
4.   satisfies Revenue that they are in Ireland with the intention of and in such circumstances that they will be Irish tax resident in the following tax year,

will be treated as Irish resident only from the date of arrival in the State. There is no apportionment of tax credits, allowances or tax bands.

Example 28.4

Simon, a single man, has lived in London all his life. His employer sends him on a three-year secondment to Ireland. He arrives on 1 June 2021. His salary from his UK employer is his only income. In 2021, his salary was €66,000 and was paid to him in the UK.

His basic personal tax credit was €1,650 and his employee tax credit was €1,650 for 2021. Will Simon qualify for split-year residence?

Q. Is he resident in 2020?	A. No.
Q. Did he arrive in 2021?	A. Yes.
Q. Is he resident in 2021?	A. Yes, under the 183-day rule.
Q. Does he intend to be resident in 2022?	A. Yes.

Simon therefore qualifies for split-year residence and, in calculating tax due on his employment income only, will be treated as resident from 1 June 2021. His Irish income tax liability will be as follows:

Schedule D Case III

€66,000 × 7/12ths		€38,500
Tax payable:		
€35,300 @ 20%		€7,060
€3,200 @ 40%		€1,280
		€8,340
Deduct: non-refundable tax credits:		
Basic personal tax credit	€1,650	
Employee tax credit	€1,650	(€3,300)
Net tax liability		€5,040

28.4.2 Year of Departure

For employment income only, an individual who is:

1. resident in the current tax year, **and**
2. satisfies Revenue that they are leaving the State, other than for a temporary purpose, with the intention and in such circumstances that they will not be resident in the next tax year,

will be treated as resident only up to the **date of departure**.

Example 28.5

Brian, a single man from Dublin, leaves to work in Boston on 1 May 2021. He has signed a three-year employment contract with a US firm.

His basic personal tax credit was €1,650 and his employee tax credit was €1,650 for 2021. His income in 2021 is as follows:

Irish salary (01/01/2021–30/04/2021)	€18,500
PAYE deducted	€3,950
US salary (01/05/2021–31/12/2021)	€44,000

Will Brian qualify for split-year residence?

Q. Is he resident in 2021?
A. Yes, under the 280-day rule.
Q. Is he leaving Ireland for other than a temporary purpose?
A. Yes.
Q. Does he intend and is it likely, given the circumstances of his departure to the USA, that he will not be resident in 2022?
A. Yes.

Brian therefore qualifies for split-year residence. His Irish income tax liability for 2021 will be as follows:

Schedule E

Irish salary		€18,500
Tax @ 20%		€3,700
Deduct: non-refundable tax credits:		
Basic personal tax credit	€1,650	
Employee tax credit	€1,650	(€3,300)
Net tax liability		€400
Less: PAYE deducted		(€3,950)
Tax refund due		(€3,550)

Brian is not taxed on his US employment income and receives full personal tax credits.

28.5 Rents Paid to Non-resident Landlords

Rents received in respect of property or land situate in the Republic of Ireland (the State) is assessed to tax under Schedule D, Case V (the specific rules were considered in detail at CA Proficiency 1). Individuals are assessed to income tax on the net rental income, regardless of whether or not they are Irish resident for tax purposes.

To ensure income tax is remitted to Revenue in respect of non-resident landlords, rents paid directly to a non-resident landlord (including payments of rent to a bank account in the name of the landlord) must be paid under deduction of tax at the standard rate (currently 20%), and the tax remitted to Revenue. Failure to deduct tax leaves the tenant liable for the tax that should have been deducted. While in strictness the tenant should make a return to the Revenue immediately after the tax is deducted and pay the tax, in practice an annual return made with the tenant's tax return for the tax year together with payment of the tax deducted is sufficient. The tenant should give the landlord a form R185 to show that the tax has been accounted for to Revenue. The landlord is chargeable on the gross rents less any allowable expenses in arriving at rental profit. Credit for the actual tax deducted from the rent by the tenant will be given.

If the rent is paid to an Irish agent acting on behalf of a non-resident landlord, then the agent becomes the one assessable on the rental income. The collection agent agrees to be responsible for submitting an annual income tax return detailing the rental income of the non-resident landlord. The collection agent also agrees to pay any tax liability due on the rents. Accordingly, rents paid to agents in Ireland are not paid under deduction of tax; in which case the rent can be paid gross, i.e. tax does not have to be deducted by the tenant. The agent will be assessed in the name of the non-resident landlord in the same manner as the non-resident would have been assessed if he were resident in Ireland. The agent need not be a professional person e.g. it can be a family member or other person prepared to take on the responsibility and who agrees to file annual tax returns and arrange payments as appropriate.

Questions

Review Questions
(See Suggested Solutions to Review Questions at the end of this textbook.)

Question 28.1

Aurore is a French woman who has been seconded from France to work in Ireland for three years. She arrives on 1 February 2018 and leaves on 10 January 2021. Her French employer continues to pay her salary in France of €3,000 per month and an additional €2,000 per month in Ireland.

Requirement
What is Aurore's residence status for each year? What advice would you give Aurore and her employer in connection with her residence status and salary payment?

Question 28.2

Mr Harris is married and has the following sources of income for 2021:

Irish rents	€37,000
US dividends	€4,000

Tax was deducted by the lessee of €7,400 on the gross rent received of €37,000 in 2021. Mr Harris is not Irish domiciled and is not resident or ordinarily resident in Ireland. Mr Harris is a US resident and citizen.

Requirement
Calculate Mr Harris's income tax liability for 2021.

29

Foreign Investment Income

Learning Objectives

After studying this chapter you will be able to:

- Advise on the scope and basis of assessment of Schedule D, Cases III and IV as they apply to foreign income.
- Determine the Irish tax payable on UK dividends and UK rental income.
- Advise on the tax treatment of interest received from EU and non-EU financial institutions.

29.1 Overview

Foreign-source income may be liable to Irish income tax when received by individuals who are resident or ordinarily resident in the State in the year of assessment, as outlined in **Chapter 28**, Section 28.2. In general, foreign income is assessed to tax under Schedule D, Case III (see **Section 29.2**) but in certain situations it is assessed under Case IV (see **Section 29.3**). This income may also be subject in tax in the other jurisdiction, but such consequences are not within the scope of this textbook.

29.2 Schedule D, Case III

Income assessed to tax under Schedule D, Case III, as outlined at CA Proficiency 1, is the actual income arising in the year of assessment. Case III income includes the following foreign-source incomes:

- Income arising to any member of the European Parliament (MEP) where the income is payable out of the money provided by the budget of the EU. (Where the income is payable out of money provided by the Irish State, it is chargeable to Irish tax under Schedule E).
- Non-EU deposit interest, being interest arising outside the EU that would be deposit interest subject to DIRT (deposit interest retention tax)if it were payable in the State.
- EU deposit interest if the taxpayer has not filed the tax return and paid the tax due on the deposit interest by the filing date of the year in question. Where the return is filed and the tax on the deposit interest is paid by the return filing date, EU deposit interest is assessed under Case IV (see **Section 29.3**).
- Income from foreign securities and possessions, such as:
  - UK dividends received by Irish resident shareholders.
  - UK interest received by Irish residents.

- Rent from foreign property.
- Income from foreign employments and businesses.
- Income from foreign securities.

29.2.1 Non-EU Deposit Interest

Interest arising outside the EU is taxable under Case III at the prevailing Irish DIRT rate of 33% for 2021 in the case of a standard-rate taxpayer, and at the higher rate of 40% for a non-standard-rate taxpayer. However, the 33% rate only applies where the taxpayer has discharged their tax liability by the return filing date for the year concerned. If there is an outstanding tax liability, the interest will be charged at the higher rate of 40%.

The extent to which the non-EU-sourced deposit interest is taxed at 33% rate is limited to the amount of the unutilised standard rate band available for offset against the non-EU-sourced deposit interest. Accordingly, if the non-EU-sourced deposit interest exceeds the unutilised standard rate band, the amount of the non-EU-sourced deposit in excess of the unutilised standard rate band will be taxed at the higher rate of 40%.

Example 29.1

Brian, who is single, works part-time in the local service station. In 2021 he had employment income of €25,000. During 2021 Brian also received interest of €1,000 from a Canadian deposit account. Brian pays his full tax liability for 2021 on or before 31 October 2022 (the due date for the filing of his 2021 income tax return). His tax credits are €3,300.

Income Tax Computation 2021

	€	€
Income:		
Schedule D Case III income	1,000	
Schedule E	25,000	
Taxable income		26,000
Tax Calculation:		
€25,000 @ 20%	5,000	
€1,000 @ 33%	330	5,330
€26,000		
Deduct: Non-refundable tax credits		
Personal tax credit		(1,650)
Employee tax credit		(1,650)
Tax payable 2021		**2,030**

29.2.2 UK Dividends and UK Interest

Irish resident individuals receiving a dividend from a UK company are liable to Irish tax under Case III on the actual amount of the dividend received.

Interest from UK securities is also assessable under Case III and subject to the terms of the Ireland/UK Double Taxation Agreement. The interest is only liable to Irish tax where the recipient is a resident of Ireland. Any UK tax deducted at source is therefore fully recoverable.

29.2.3 Foreign Rental Income

Income from immoveable property (e.g. rents) situated outside the State is assessed to tax under Case III. The rules for calculating the net rents from the property situated abroad are the same as the Case V rules (see CA Proficiency 1).

Foreign rental income may also be taxed in the country in which the property is situated. Relief may be given by allowing a credit against the Irish tax payable in respect of the tax payable in the other country where Ireland has a double tax treaty with that other country.

29.2.4 Deductions Available

Allowable deductions against Case III income for tax purposes are limited to:

- a deduction for foreign tax suffered at source where it is not available as a tax credit under a double taxation agreement;
- expenses allowable against foreign rental income (using the same eligibility criteria for expenses allowable against Case V rental income).

29.2.5 Case III Losses

Relief for losses incurred in a foreign trade is given in the same manner as relief for losses in an Irish trade, i.e. the losses may be offset against other income arising in the same year under section 381 TCA 1997 and carried forward for offset against future profits from the same trade under section 382 TCA 1997. Other Case III losses are only available against losses in a similar category and can only be carried forward against future profits in that category. For example, foreign rental losses are only allowable against foreign rental income.

29.3 Schedule D, Case IV

Case IV was originally a 'sweeping up' case to catch any profits or gains not falling under any other cases of Schedule D and not charged under any other Schedule. In recent years, legislation has tended to use Case IV for charging certain specific items, including EU deposit interest.

29.3.1 EU Deposit Interest

The tax treatment of interest earned on deposits held in Republic of Ireland banks, building societies and credit unions by Irish resident individuals was considered in detail at CA Proficiency 1. Such interest is subject to DIRT (deposit interest retention tax) at the current rate of 33% for 2021 and is paid net to the recipient. The recipient is taxed on the gross interest under Case IV and allowed a tax credit for the DIRT withheld. The DIRT is only refundable to individuals in certain limited situations.

EU deposit interest is also taxable as Case IV at the prevailing Irish DIRT rate of 33%, but only when the taxpayer has paid and filed their income tax return by the due date. Otherwise, the higher rate of 40% applies and the income is assessed under Case III (see **Section 29.2.1**).

While there is no further tax due on this interest and it is not liable to USC, it may be liable to PRSI at 4% if the recipient is a "chargeable person".

29.3.2 Basis of Assessment

The basis of assessment for income falling within Case IV is the actual income arising in the year of assessment, i.e. if the Case IV income arises in May 2021 then it is taxable in 2021.

29.3.3 Case IV Losses

While in practical terms Case IV losses are very rare, where they do occur they may be set against Case IV profits of the same year of assessment or, alternatively, of subsequent years.

Question

Review Questions
(See Suggested Solutions to Review Questions at the end of this textbook.)

Question 29.1

Colm and Dervla O'Rourke are married with two children. They are both resident and domiciled in Ireland. Details of their income for 2021 is as follows:

		€
Colm:	Salary	55,000
	Tax deducted under PAYE	(10,640)
	Bank of Ireland net deposit interest received	67
	Standard Life (UK) dividend received	900
	Kerry Group plc dividend received (net)	825
Dervla:	Salary	32,000
	Tax deducted under PAYE	(4,600)
	Dresdner Bank (Germany) gross deposit interest received	500
	Net rental income house in Belfast	9,000
	UK tax paid	(1,500)

Requirement
(a) Calculate Colm and Dervla's liability to income tax for 2021 under joint assessment. Their personal tax credits are €6,600.
(b) What are the implications if they pay the balance of tax and file their tax return on 30 November 2022?

Schedule E – Employment Income

Learning Objectives

After studying this chapter you will be able to:

■ Explain the rules regarding the assessment and computation of:
  ● the foreign earnings deduction (FED);
  ● relief arising under the Special Assignee Relief Programme; and
  ● income tax arising on termination payments and lump sums payable on retirement.

30.1 Introduction

Employment income is all income derived from employments, directorships and pensions arising in Ireland and, as detailed at CA Proficiency 1, is taxed under Schedule E. Employment income is usually, though not always, taxed at source under the PAYE system and is assessed on that actual income received in the year of assessment.

The following income is subject to tax under Schedule E:

■ emoluments from all offices and employments;
■ pensions and annuities;
■ benefits in kind and perquisites;
■ certain lump sum payments deriving from an office or employment, such as ex-gratia and compensation payments on retirement or dismissal (see **Section 30.4**);
■ taxable social welfare benefits;
■ treatment of flight crews;
■ payments made under restrictive covenants;
■ income arising to a member of the European Parliament (MEP) where the money is payable out of money provided by the Irish State (see **Chapter 29, Section 29.2**)

Sometimes an employee may be exempt or relieved from income tax on a portion of their Schedule E income, as detailed below.

30.2 Special Assignee Relief Programme

The Special Assignee Relief Programme (SARP) provides a relief from income tax for certain people who are assigned to work in Ireland from abroad.

Under section 825C TCA 1997, where a "relevant employee":

1. is resident in the State for tax purposes, **and**
2. performs in the State the duties of their employment with a "relevant employer" or "associated company", **and**
3. has "relevant income" from the relevant employer or associated company that is not less than €75,000,

then the relevant employee, on making a claim, will be entitled to claim for a **deduction** of a "**specified amount**" for the **first five years** from the income, gains or profit of the employment with the relevant employer or associated company.

The **specified amount** is calculated at **30% of employment income between €75,000 and €1 million (annualised)** and consequently **exempts this amount from income tax, but not from PRSI and USC**.

Employment income taken into account in calculating the specified amount is all income, profits and gains from the employment, excluding any amount not liable to tax in the State, and after deducting pension contributions and tax-deductible employment expenses.

30.2.1 Definitions

Relevant Employee

A "relevant employee" is a person who:

1. was a full-time employee of the "relevant employer" for the whole of the six months immediately before their arrival in the State and exercised their duties of employment for that relevant employer **outside** the State, *and*
2. arrives in the State in any of the tax years **2015–2022**, at the request of the relevant employer, to:
    (a) perform in the State the duties of their employment for that employer, *or*
    (b) to take up employment in the State with an associated company, *and*
3. performs their duties of employment in the State for a **minimum** period of **12 consecutive months** from the date they first performed those duties in the State; *and*
4. was **not resident** in the State for the **five tax years** immediately **preceding** the tax year in which they first arrive in the State for the purposes of the employment, *and*
5. in respect of whom the relevant employer certifies with Revenue the employee's compliance with conditions 1–3 above, within 90 days from the employee's arrival in the State.

Relevant Employer

"Relevant employer" is a company that is incorporated and tax resident in a country with which Ireland has a double taxation agreement, or an information-sharing agreement.

Associated Company

"Associated company" is a company associated with the relevant employer. Under section 432 TCA 1997, a company shall be treated as another company's associated company at a particular time if, at that time or at any time within the previous year, either company has control over the other, or both companies are under the control of the same person or persons.

Relevant Income

While all income and emoluments are subject to income tax, the "relevant income" definition assesses whether a person can **qualify** for SARP by having **relevant annual income of not less**

than €75,000. Relevant income includes all the relevant employee's income, profits and gains from the employment, but excludes the following:

1. benefits in kind and perquisites;
2. any bonus, commission or other similar payments (whether contractual or not);
3. termination payments;
4. shares or share-based remuneration; and
5. payments in relation to restrictive covenants.

In effect, **relevant income will be the base salary**. Note that the "relevant income" definition is **only** for the purposes of assessing whether the person can qualify for SARP and is **not relevant in calculating the actual relief**, i.e. the "specified amount".

Example 30.1

Mary Watson, an American citizen, was sent to work in the State in January 2021 by a relevant employer and had the following sources of income in 2021:

	€
Salary paid by US parent	150,000
Bonus paid by US parent	70,000
Benefit in kind	4,000
Total employment income	224,000

SARP relief:
(a) Relevant income ≥ €75,000 as Salary = €150,000 ⇨ eligible for SARP relief
(b) Calculation of **specified amount**:

Total employment income	224,000
Less: lower threshold	(75,000)
	149,000
Specified amount (30%)	**44,700**
Total income	224,000
Less: specified amount	(44,700)
Taxable income	179,300

Ms Watson will be entitled to tax relief of €17,880 (€44,700 @ 40%) for 2021.

Section 825C TCA 1997 requires the relevant employer to notify Revenue of an employee's entitlement to SARP within **90 days** of the employee's arrival in Ireland. Failure to meet this condition may mean that an employee cannot avail of the relief.

Relief may be granted through the payroll or by the employee making a claim for a repayment at the end of the tax year.

30.3 Foreign Earnings Deduction

Section 823A TCA 1997 provides for the foreign earnings deduction (FED), a special tax deduction for employees who carry out part of their employment duties in certain non-EEA foreign countries, i.e. "relevant states", which includes Russia, China and states in Africa, South America, Asia and Arabia. A full list is available on Revenue's website at www.revenue.ie.

30.3.1 Qualifying Conditions

The employee must have worked in one or more of the relevant states for a minimum period of 30 "qualifying days" within a period of 12 months. A "qualifying day" is one of at least three consecutive days devoted substantially to carrying out the duties of employment where, throughout the whole of each such day, the employee is present in a "relevant state".

Saturdays, Sundays and public holidays, where the employee is present for the whole day in a "relevant state" and which form an unavoidable part of a business trip to that state, may be counted as "qualifying days".

Days spent travelling directly from the State to a relevant state, from a relevant state to the State or between two relevant states, are treated as qualifying days, but only if the travel is direct, i.e. travelling via another destination would not qualify.

30.3.2 Relief Available

The FED available is the lesser of:

- €35,000, or
- the "specified amount", calculated as:

$$\frac{D \times E}{F}$$

where:

D is the number of "qualifying days" worked in a "relevant state" in the tax year;

E is all the income from the employment in the tax year **excluding** tax deductible expenses payments, benefits in kind, termination payments and payments payable under restrictive covenants but **including** any taxable share-based remuneration or share-option profits;

F is the total number of days that the relevant employment is held in the tax year (365 days in a full tax year).

The deduction is given by way of end-of-year review and must be claimed by the employee. The claim should be supported by a statement from the employer indicating the dates of departure and return to the State of the employee and the location at which the duties of the office or employment were performed while abroad.

Example 30.2

William Bryson is an Irish resident employee of Baby Gloop Ltd. In 2021, he spent 97 qualifying days in India developing new contacts with potential Indian customers. Mr Bryson was paid the following amounts in 2021:

	€
Salary 2021	120,000
Taxable share option profits	22,000
Benefit in kind	14,000

FED relief:

Specified amount = $\dfrac{97 \times €142,000}{365}$ = 37,737

Restricted to 35,000

Mr Bryson will be able to claim a reduction of €14,000 (€35,000 @ 40%) in his income tax liability for 2021.

30.3.3 Exclusions

The FED does not apply to public servants, nor does it apply to income to which the following reliefs apply:

▨ Special Assignee Relief Programme (SARP);
▨ the remittance basis of taxation (see **Chapter 28**, Section 28.2.3);
▨ key employee R&D relief (see **Chapter 23**, Section 23.2.7);
▨ split-year residence relief (see **Section 28.4**); or
▨ cross-border worker relief.

30.4 Termination Payments

30.4.1 Charge to Tax

Special taxation rules apply to lump sum payments made to employees after the termination of their employment. These are commonly referred to as 'golden boots' (compensation payments) or 'golden handshakes' (ex-gratia payments).

Section 123 TCA 1997 imposes a charge to tax under Schedule E on payments made after an individual has retired or been dismissed from office. The charge covers payments to holders of offices, or employments, whether made by the employer or by a third person, and includes payments to the executors or administrators of a deceased person.

The actual date(s) of payment of the lump sum(s) is irrelevant. The legislation deems the payment to have been made on the date of termination of the employment. Any assessment for income tax arises in the tax year in which the employment terminated.

The charge also extends to payments made to the spouse, civil partner or any relative or dependant of a person who holds or has held an office or employment, or to any person on his behalf.

Payments in kind are chargeable on their market value at the time they are given, e.g. a present of a company car, say, at a valuation of €4,000 would be included with the termination payment. Any contribution from the employee towards the cost may be deducted.

Pay in lieu of notice, which is payable under the terms of the employee's contract, is taxable as normal remuneration. If it is not provided for under the terms of the employee's contract, or by employment law, it is treated as a termination payment.

Holiday pay is treated as regular salary and does not form part of the termination payment.

30.4.2 Tax-exempt Termination Payment

Payments to which section 123 TCA 1997 applies come within the scope of Schedule E, but relief is given under section 201 and Schedule 3 TCA 1997, with the result that tax is charged only on the **excess of the payment** over the **higher** of:

1. the basic exemption; or
2. the increased exemption; or
3. the Standard Capital Superannuation Benefit (SCSB).

Basic Exemption
Section 201 TCA 1997 provides relief in the form of a **basic exemption of €10,160 plus €765 for each complete year of service** in the computation of the taxable portion of the lump sum received.

Increased Exemption

Schedule 3 TCA 1997 provides for an **increase in the basic exemption by an additional €10,000** where the taxpayer claiming relief has not lodged a claim for relief from taxation in respect of a lump sum payment (other than a claim for a basic exemption) received on the termination of an office or employment in the previous 10 years.

If, under a Revenue-approved superannuation scheme, the taxpayer receives or is entitled to receive a tax-free pension lump sum, then the **additional exemption** is **reduced** by the amount of the pension lump sum up to a maximum of €10,000.

Standard Capital Superannuation Benefit

A relief, known as the Standard Capital Superannuation Benefit (SCSB), may be deducted in computing the amount chargeable to income tax if it is greater than the basic exemption. It is calculated as follows:

$$\frac{A \times B}{15} - C$$

where: A = average of last three years' remuneration
B = number of complete years of service
C = tax-free lump sum from pension scheme.

The following meanings and conditions apply:

1. Last three years' remuneration is to the **date of the termination of the office or employment**, i.e. not the remuneration for the last three tax years.
2. Where the period of employment was **less than three years**, the amount of the last three years' remuneration is replaced by the **full remuneration** earned by an individual throughout the period of employment, and the average figure is computed based on that lesser period.
3. The SCSB calculated under the above formula **must be reduced** by any **tax-free lump sum received or receivable** under a Revenue-approved pension scheme (excluding refunds of personal contributions by the employee to such a scheme). Where an employee exercises their right to waive their entitlement to a pension tax-free lump sum, no reduction is necessary.
4. Only **full years** of service are taken into account, e.g. if an individual was employed for 10.5 years, only 10 years is used for the purpose of the fraction.
5. The definition of a tax-free lump sum received or receivable under a Revenue-approved pension scheme includes the **actuarial value** of any **future** lump sum which may be received from the pension scheme. This applies both for the increased basic exemption and for the SCSB.

Lifetime Tax-free Limit

Section 201 TCA 1997 provides for a lifetime aggregate tax-free limit of **€200,000** in respect of termination payments made on/after **1 January 2011**. The €200,000 limit is reduced by the aggregate of any prior tax-free payments (including basic exemption and SCSB deductions) that have been received, thus ensuring that the maximum lifetime tax-free termination payment cannot exceed €200,000.

Example 30.3

James Smith was an employee of Games Ltd for 30.5 years. He was made redundant by the company on 30 September 2021 and received €90,000 as a termination payment. Mr Smith is married and his spouse has no income. His credits include the married credit of €3,300 and the employee credit of €1,650.

James's salary from 1 January 2021 to date of redundancy (30 September 2021) was €45,750 gross (tax deducted: €7,940).

Mr Smith's last three years' remuneration as an employee was:

Y/E 30/09/2021	€52,250
Y/E 30/09/2020	€48,000
Y/E 30/09/2019	€39,500

Mr Smith has never received a termination payment before and will be entitled to a tax-free lump sum of €8,000 from an approved superannuation fund.

Basic Exemption Calculation

	€	€
Basic exemption		10,160
Years of service: 30 × €765		22,950
		33,110
Increase in basic exemption	10,000	
Less: tax-free pension lump sum	(8,000)	2,000
Total basic exemption		35,110

SCSB Calculation

$$\frac{€52,250 + €48,000 + 39,500}{3} \times \frac{30 \text{ years}}{15 \text{ years}} = \qquad 93,167$$

Less: tax-free pension lump sum	(8,000)
Total SCSB	85,167

The SCSB deduction is taken as it exceeds the increased basic exemption of €35,110 that would otherwise be available in this case.

Income Tax Computation 2021

	€	€
Schedule E income:		
Salary		45,750
Termination payment	90,000	
Less: SCSB	(85,167)	4,833
Taxable income		50,583
Tax (Married couple – one income):		
€44,300 @ 20%	8,860	
€6,283 @ 40%	2,513	11,373
Deduct: Non-refundable tax credits:		
Basic personal tax credit	3,300	
Employee tax credit	1,650	(4,950)
Net tax liability		6,423
Deduct: Refundable Tax Credits:		
Tax deducted under PAYE		(7,940)
Net tax refundable		(1,517)

The taxable portion of the termination payment (€4,833) is also liable to USC but is not liable to PRSI.

Example 30.4
Paddy Jayne was an employee of BCI Ltd for 19 years. He was made redundant by the company on 1 June 2021 and received the following redundancy package:

	€
Statutory redundancy	23,400
Non-statutory redundancy	190,000
Pay in lieu of notice	2,750
Company car	15,000
Total lump sum	231,150

Mr Jayne is also entitled to a lump sum of €215,000 from his pension fund of which €200,000 will be tax free. Mr Jayne's average salary over the past three years was €183,000.

Calculation of Exemption

	€
Basic exemption	10,160
Years of service: 19 × €765	14,535
	24,695
Increase in basic exemption*	NIL
Total basic exemption	24,695

* No increase in basic exemption as pension lump sum is greater than €10,000.

	€
SCSB: €183,000 × 19/15	231,800
Less: pension lump sum (restricted to €200,000)	(200,000)
Total SCSB	31,800

Calculation of Taxable Amount

	€
Statutory redundancy**	NIL
Non-statutory redundancy	190,000
Pay in lieu of notice***	2,750
Company car	15,000
Less: SCSB	(31,800)
Taxable lump sum	175,950

**Statutory redundancy is exempt from tax.
***Assuming Mr Jayne was not entitled to receive pay in lieu of notice under the terms of his contract of employment.

30.5   Retirement Lump Sum Benefits

Under certain Revenue-approved pension schemes, taxpayers can receive a retirement lump sum tax-free. Section 790AA TCA 1997 states that the maximum **lifetime** retirement **tax-free lump sum** will be **€200,000** in respect of benefits taken on or after **1 January 2011**. However, previous lump sum payments will count towards using up the maximum lifetime tax-free threshold of €200,000. Amounts in excess of this tax-free limit will be subject to tax in two stages. The portion between **€200,000 and €500,000** will be taxed (**under Schedule D Case IV**) at the **standard rate** of income tax in force at the time of payment, currently 20%, while any portion above that will be taxed (**under Schedule E**) at the recipient's **marginal rate of tax**.

The figure of €500,000 represents 25% of the **standard fund threshold of €2 million**. The standard rate charge is "ring-fenced" so that no reliefs, allowances or deductions may be set or made against that portion of a lump sum subject to that charge.

Example 30.5

John Bartlett retired in January 2021 and was paid a retirement lump sum from his pension of €800,000 on 31 January 2021. This is the first such lump sum he has received. He is charged to tax as follows:

- the first €200,000 is exempt;
- the next €300,000 is taxed at the standard rate for 2021; and
- the balance, i.e. €300,000, is taxed at his marginal rate of income tax and USC for 2021.

If John receives any future retirement lump sum, it will be subject to tax at the marginal rate in the year it is paid.

Example 30.6

David Murphy is paid a retirement lump sum on 1 July 2021 of €400,000. He had previously received a retirement lump sum of €220,000 on 1 January 2010. The earlier lump sum has 'used up' David's entire tax-free limit of €200,000, meaning that all the lump sum taken on 1 July is taxable. Even though the earlier lump sum is not taxable, it affects the rate of tax applying to the later lump sum. David is charged to tax on the following:

Lump sum received 1 January 2010	€220,000
Lump sum received 1 July 2021	€400,000
Total received	€620,000

The earlier lump sum has 'used up' the €200,000 tax-free limit, and €20,000 of the €300,000 standard rate.

	€
Lump sum taxable:	
At the standard rate – Case IV, Schedule D	300,000
Less: amount 'used up' in earlier lump sum	(20,000)
Amount taxable at standard rate	280,000
At the marginal rate – Schedule E	400,000
Less: amount taxable at standard rate	(280,000)
Amount taxable at the marginal rate	120,000

Note that the amount taxable is only the total of the lump sum received in 2021.

30.6   Lump Sum Payments on Account of Death or Disability

Section 201 TCA 1997 extended the **tax-free lifetime limit of €200,000** in respect of termination or ex-gratia payments to cover lump sum payments made on account of the death or injury or disability of an employee or office holder. Any amount where the non-statutory element of the payment exceeds €200,000 will be taxable in full under Schedule E. This €200,000 limit is in addition to the €200,000 which may be received tax free on the termination of an employment.

Questions

Review Questions
(See Suggested Solutions to Review Questions at the end of this textbook.)

Question 30.1

Mr Klaus, a German citizen, was sent to work in Ireland on 1 May 2021 by his company, Flow GmbH. He had the following sources of income liable to tax in Ireland in 2021:

Salary paid by German parent from 1 May 2021	€250,000
Benefit in kind	€2,500
Bonus payment	€20,000

Requirement
Calculate Mr Klaus's entitlement to relief under SARP, assuming that he satisfies all the conditions of the relief.

Question 30.2

Mr Houghton, a single person aged 60, retired from Liver Ltd on 30 June 2021 after 18 years service. As a token of its appreciation, the board of directors of Liver Ltd voted him a lump sum of €65,000.

Mr Houghton's remuneration for the three years prior to retirement was as follows and it accrued evenly throughout the year.

Year to 30 June 2019	€52,000
Year to 30 June 2020	€55,000
Year to 30 June 2021	€57,000

On 30 June 2021 Mr Houghton also commuted part of his pension to a tax-free lump sum of €3,000 and received an annual pension thereafter of €18,000. His tax deducted under PAYE for the tax year 2021 was €6,220.

Requirement
Calculate Mr Houghton's income tax liability for the tax year 2021. His personal tax credits are €3,300.

Question 30.3

Mr Lynch was made redundant by his employer, Tree Ltd, on 31 December 2021. He received a lump sum payment of €30,000 (excluding statutory redundancy). He also received a refund of his pension contributions of €5,600, from which income tax of €1,120 was deducted.

He had been employed by the company for 10 complete years and had not received a termination lump sum payment from any previous employer. Mr Lynch's remuneration for the three years prior to his redundancy was:

Year to 31 December 2021	€43,000
Year to 31 December 2020	€35,000
Year to 31 December 2019	€30,000

Tax deducted under PAYE from salary and lump sum payment in the tax year 2021 was €6,450.

Requirement

Calculate the balance of income tax payable (or repayable) in respect of Mr Lynch for the tax year 2021, assuming he is a widower with no dependent children and qualifies for a €3,840 tax credit.

Question 30.4

Terence Flynn, who is married, had been manager of a garage in Co. Monaghan for 15½ years until 30 September 2021. At that date, due to falling petrol sales and high taxes the garage closed and Mr Flynn was made redundant. His wife has no income.

You are given the following additional information regarding Mr Flynn:

1. He received an ex-gratia lump sum of €57,000 from his employer as compensation for loss of office. This was in addition to his statutory redundancy payments of €7,800. He also received holiday pay of €2,000 to which he was entitled. He has no entitlement to a tax-free pension lump sum payment.
2. On 1 October 2021, he moved to Dublin to take up a new job with a multinational oil company at a salary of €2,500 per month, together with a benefit in kind projected at €2,000 per annum.

His earnings for the last four years to 30 September were:

Year ended 30/09/2021	€47,000
Year ended 30/09/2020	€54,000
Year ended 30/09/2019	€52,000
Year ended 30/09/2018	€50,000

His pay accrued evenly from month to month. The total tax deducted under PAYE from both employments for the tax year 2021 was €3,030.

Requirement

(a) Calculate the amount of the lump sum that is liable to tax.
(b) Calculate the tax year 2021 income tax liability with a personal tax credit of €4,950.

Question 30.5

Dermot O'Donnell, a single parent with a five-year-old son, was an employee of Super McBurgers, a fast-food restaurant chain. He had been employed by the company for 15 years and 8 months, before being made redundant on 30 September 2021. You have the following information:

1. As part of the redundancy package he received:

Statutory redundancy	€8,000
Holiday pay	€1,200
Company car worth	€22,500
Ex-gratia payment	€40,500

2. In the period from 1 January 2021 to 30 September 2021, Dermot earned a salary (including benefit in kind on his company car) of €37,000. Tax deducted under PAYE was €5,418.
3. He commenced new employment in Burger Palace on 1 November 2021 and his earnings in the period to 31 December 2021 were €4,200 (tax deducted under PAYE was €100).
4. Dermot's salary was pensionable and, as part of the termination package, Super McBurgers made a special contribution of €11,700 into his Revenue-approved pension scheme. Dermot is

entitled to, and elects to receive, a tax-free lump sum payment under the terms of the pension scheme. The actuarial value of the lump sum entitlement on 1 October 2021 was €22,000.

5. His salary and benefit in kind for the prior tax years were as follows:

y/e 30/09/2021	salary	€46,000	BIK	€2,900
y/e 30/09/2020	salary	€36,000	BIK	€2,000
y/e 30/09/2019	salary	€39,000	BIK	€3,100

Requirement

(a) Calculate the tax-free termination payment that can be made to Dermot O'Donnell.

(b) Compute Dermot's final liability to income tax for the year 2021 with tax credits of €4,950.

Shares: Employment Incentive Schemes

Learning Objectives

After studying this chapter you will be able to:

- Understand the basic relief available to an investor under the Employment and Investment Incentive (EII) scheme.
- Advise on the tax treatment of employees who benefit from share option schemes.

31.1 Relief for Investment in Corporate Trades: Employment and Investment Incentive

The Employment and Investment Incentive (EII) is a tax relief incentive that provides income tax relief for individuals who invest in a qualifying company. The proceeds of the share subscription by the qualifying individual are to be used for the purpose of the qualifying trade and the creation and maintenance of employment. Provision is also made for tax relief to be available to individuals who make their EII investment in qualifying companies through designated funds.

31.1.1 The Relief

The maximum qualifying investment in respect of which an investor may claim relief is **€250,000 per annum** in each tax year from 2020 onwards. The shares must be held for four years (i.e. the relevant period). However, the maximum qualifying investment is increased to **€500,000** where the investor undertakes not to dispose of the those shares for a period of seven years. The relief is from income tax only; USC and PRSI will continue to apply.

For shares issued after 8 October 2019, a qualifying investor who makes a qualifying investment in a qualifying company shall be entitled to relief for the full amount subscribed, subject to the maximum limits above. The relief shall be given as a deduction from the investor's total income for the year of assessment in which the shares are issued.

Example 31.1

Jack works for an IT company and earned €150,000 in 2021 (PAYE deducted €49,640). He is single with no dependents. On 31 December 2021 he invested €50,000 in a qualifying EII company, receiving qualifying shares that he will hold until at least 1 January 2026.

Jack will be assessed to income tax in 2021 as follows:

	€
Schedule E	150,000
Less: EII investment	(50,000)
Taxable income	100,000
Taxed as:	
€35,300 @ 20%	7,060
€64,700 @ 40%	25,880
	32,940
Deduct: PAYE paid	(49,640)
Tax refund due*	(16,700)

*USC and PRSI will apply on his earnings of €150,000.

In respect of shares issued on or before 8 October 2019, the maximum qualifying investment was €150,000 per annum with the relief being given as:

1. 30/40ths of the amount subscribed as a deduction from the investor's total income for the year of assessment in which the shares are issued, and

2. 10/40ths of the amount subscribed as a deduction from the investor's total income for the year of assessment following the end of the four-year holding period, subject to the company achieving certain targets within the given timeframe.

A married couple/civil partnership can **each** obtain individual relief on investments up to the maximum permitted, provided each spouse/civil partner has sufficient taxable income to absorb the amount of their investment. Where relief cannot be obtained, either because the investment exceeds the maximum or due to an insufficiency of income, the unrelieved amount can be carried forward and claimed as a deduction in future years to 31 December 2021. There is no limit to the number of companies an investor can invest in, but tax relief is subject to the overall investment limit of €250,000/€500,000 per annum.

Example 31.2

Tara is a self-employed solicitor. In 2017 she invested €150,000 in a qualifying company, claiming 30/40ths of the investment against her total income in 2017. In 2021 she invested €100,000 in another qualifying company. What will Tara's EII claim be in 2021?

Tara will be able to claim:

10/40ths × €150,000 re 2017 investment	€ 37,500
100% 2021 investment	€100,000
Total EII claim 2021	€137,500

31.1.2 Qualifying Criteria for EII Relief

For the investment to qualify for relief, there are three main "qualifying" headings:

1. qualifying investor;
2. eligible shares;
3. qualifying company and its trade;
4. qualifying investment.

Qualifying Investor

A qualifying investor is an individual who subscribes on their own behalf, or via a designated fund, for eligible shares in a qualifying company and is not connected with the company, or with any member of the company's "RICT group", during the "compliance period". The compliance period is the period beginning two years before and ending four years after the subscription for the shares.

A company's RICT group consists of the company and its "partner" or "linked" businesses, as defined by EU regulations. Broadly, businesses are "partners" if one controls the other or if they are under common control; businesses are "linked" if one has at least at 25% interest in the other. Essentially, the investor should be a third-party investor with no prior connection with the company or its shareholders.

"Connected", in this context, includes situations where the individual, or a relative of the individual, is a partner, employee or director of the company, or any company in the RICT group, or has an interest in the capital of the company (other than a previous EII investment). The connected party rules are relaxed in the case of micro-enterprises that have no partner or linked businesses which have not been trading or carrying on a business for more than seven years. In such cases, relatives of shareholders can claim EII relief. A company with less than 10 employees and an annual turnover/balance sheet total of less than €2 million is a micro-enterprise. EII relief given in such circumstances is known as the Start-Up Capital Incentive.

The investor cannot claim relief until they receive a statement of qualification from the qualifying company (see below) or a certificate from the designated fund managers.

Eligible Shares

Eligible shares are newly issued shares forming part of the qualifying company's share capital. Shares issued on or after 1 January 2019 can carry preferential rights to dividends and to repayment of capital on a winding up. They can also be redeemable. The whole of the company's issued share capital must be fully paid up.

The proceeds of the subscription must be used to carry on relevant trading activities or, where the company has not yet commenced to trade, to carry on 'R&D+I' which is undertaken with a view to carrying on relevant trading activities. "Relevant trading activities" are trading activities taxed under Case I but excluding certain activities such as professional services, dealing in or developing land and financial services. R&D+I activities are R&D activities (as defined for the purpose of the R&D tax credit, see **Chapter 23**), plus innovation. Innovation is implementing new organisational methods or significantly improved production/delivery methods. The investment must contribute directly to the creation or maintenance of employment in the company.

The minimum investment in any one company is €250; the maximum investment in any one company or its associated companies is €15 million, subject to a maximum of €5 million in any one 12-month period.

Shares must be held by the investor for a period of four years after the shares have been issued. Where the investor has claimed the higher relief of up to €500,000 the shares must be held for seven years.

Qualifying Company and its Trade

A qualifying company is one that:

- is incorporated in the State or the EEA (i.e. EU Member States plus Norway, Liechtenstein and Iceland) and is resident in the State/EEA throughout the relevant period;
- is an SME or micro-enterprise and not a company in difficulty;
- is unlisted, and each company in the group is unlisted, with no arrangements to become a listed company;
- holds an appropriate tax clearance certificate;

- does not control (other than a qualifying subsidiary) or be controlled by another company throughout the relevant period;
- exists wholly for the purpose of carrying on "relevant trading activities" or is the holding company of such a qualifying subsidiary.

Relief may not be claimed by the investor until a statement of qualification is issued by the qualifying company.

Qualifying Investment

In order for an investment to be a qualifying investment the following conditions must be satisfied:

- the individual must invest in "eligible shares" in a "qualifying company";
- the investment must be based on a business plan;
- the RICT group must comply with conditions imposed by EU State Aid Regulations; and
- the funds raised must be used for a qualifying purpose, i.e. to carry on relevant trading activities or for R&D+I.

Business Plan

An investment will not be a qualifying investment unless it is based on a business plan. The business plan must be in writing and must contain details of products, sales and profitability development. It must establish the financial viability of the investment and should include quantitative and qualitative details of the activities that the investment will support

EU State Aid Regulations

Broadly, under EU state aid rules, a company can only raise EII funds if:

- it is the first time it has raised EII funds and it has been trading for less than seven years;
- it has been trading for more than seven years but it is raising the funds to expand into a new geographical market or produce a new product and the funds being raised are greater than 50% of the annual turnover for the last five years; or
- it had previously raised EII funds and the current fundraising was foreseen in the business plan prepared for the first EII fundraising.

31.1.3 Clawback

A clawback of the relief, **payable by the investor**, will be triggered by certain events, including:

- the investor ceasing to be a qualifying investor within the relevant period;
- the investor receiving value from the company during the compliance period;
- the shares being disposed of within the relevant period;
- raising the funds is part of a tax-avoidance scheme.

31.2 Share Option Schemes

Share options arise when employees or directors are granted an option to acquire shares in their employer's company or its parent company, at a fixed price, at some time in the future.

If the employee has been granted a share option by reason of their employment, under general Schedule E principles, a taxable emolument arises. Section 128 TCA 1997 contains the income tax rules that apply to share options granted to an employee or director. A person who realises a gain taxable by virtue of section 128 is deemed to be a **chargeable person** for self-assessment purposes for that year, unless an Inspector of Taxes has exempted them from filing a return.

Thus, a person whose income normally consists only of Schedule E salary and who pays all their tax under the PAYE system is required to file a return in accordance with the **self-assessment** system.

31.2.1 Relevant Tax on Share Options (RTSO)

Where share options are exercised, the employee or director must pay any tax, USC and employee PRSI **within 30 days** of the date of exercise by completing **Form RTSO1** and sending it along with **payment** to Revenue.

Income tax is due at the **marginal** rate (currently 40%). However, where a person's total income for the year is liable only at the standard rate of income tax (20%), an application may be made to Revenue to pay at the lower rate.

Share option gains are also **chargeable to USC and employee PRSI**, but not to employer PRSI. Like income tax, USC is paid at the highest rate in force for the tax year in which the share option is exercised (2021: 8%), unless advance approval is obtained for payment at the lower rate. Employee PRSI is paid at the rate applicable to the PRSI Class that applies to the employee for the particular tax year. Both USC and employee PRSI payable are included with the income tax payment and returned using Form RTSO1.

Employers' Obligations

Section 897B TCA 1997 makes it mandatory for employers to file returns regarding shares and other securities awarded to directors and employees before **31 March** of the year following the tax year (Form RSS1). This mandatory return must be made electronically through the Revenue Online Service (ROS).

31.2.2 Short Options – Less than Seven Years

Short options are options that must be exercised **within seven years** of being granted. Short options are charged to RTSO in the year the option is **exercised** on the difference between the price paid (the option price) for the shares and the market value of the shares at the **date of exercise** (date shares acquired). USC and employee PRSI are also payable on the difference.

Example 31.3

On 1 June 2015 James Doyle was granted an option, by reason of his employment, to acquire 5,000 shares in LoCo Ltd at €2 per share. The option must be exercised before 1 June 2021. No consideration was paid for the granting of the share option. James exercises his option on 1 May 2021 and acquires 5,000 shares at €2 each. The market values of the shares at the relevant dates are as follows:

1 June 2015 (5,000 × €2.50)	€12,500
1 May 2021 (5,000 × €3.50)	€17,500

Taxable Gain 2021:

	€
Market value of the shares on 1 May 2021	17,500
Less: option price paid (5,000 × €2)	(10,000)
Gain	7,500

This gain is chargeable to income tax, employee PRSI and USC in 2021.

31.2.3 Long Options – Longer than Seven Years

Long options are options capable of being exercised **more than seven years** after being granted. Long options are taxed:

▪ in the year the option was granted (on the difference between the market value of the shares at the date of grant and the option price), and

▪ in the year the option was exercised (as above) – but the shareholder is entitled to a credit for tax paid on the earlier charge on grant.

Example 31.4

Taking the same details from **Example 31.3** except that James has until 1 June 2024 to exercise his option, i.e. he has a long option. He decides to exercise his option on 1 May 2021, acquiring the 5,000 shares at €2 each. The market values are therefore as calculated above (1 June 2015: €12,500; 1 May 2021: €17,500).

To compute the tax payable in this instance, the gain in 2015 as well as 2021 must be calculated. James paid income tax at the marginal rate in 2015 and 2021.

	€	€
Income Tax Gain 2015		
Market value of the shares on 1 June 2015	12,500	
Less: option price	(10,000)	
Gain	2,500	
Taxed @ 40% (marginal rate 2015)	1,000	
USC @ 8%	200	
PRSI @ 4%	100	
Total due RTSO		1,300
Income Tax Gain 2021		
Market value of the shares on 1 May 2021	17,500	
Less: option price paid	(10,000)	
Gain	7,500	
Taxable @ 40% (marginal rate 2021)	3,000	
Less: income tax paid in 2015	(1,000)	
Tax payable 2021		2,000
USC @ 8%	600	
Less: USC paid 2015	(200)	
USC payable 2021		400
PRSI @ 4%	300	
Less: PRSI paid 2015	(100)	
PRSI payable 2021		200
Total due RTSO 2021		2,600

Income tax, USC and employee PRSI on each gain are payable within 30 days as RTSO.

31.2.4 Key Employee Engagement Programme

As outlined in **Chapter 5**, Section 5.5.2, the Key Employee Engagement Programme (KEEP) is a share option incentive scheme for unquoted companies to assist in the recruitment and retention of key employees. For qualifying share options granted between **1 January 2018** and **31 December 2023**, the KEEP provides for an exemption from income tax, USC and PRSI on any gain arising on the exercise of a qualifying share option by a qualifying individual in a qualifying company. Tax on such shares will be deferred until the shares are disposed of and CGT will be payable on the gain arising on the difference between the sales proceeds and the price paid on exercise of the option to acquire the shares.

Example 31.5

On 1 March 2019, Iseult Turner was granted an option under the KEEP to acquire 12,000 shares in HiCo Ltd at the current market value of €1 each. The options must be exercised before 1 March 2025. Iseult exercises her option on 1 August 2021 when the shares are worth €2.75 each. Iseult sells her shares on 20 February 2022 for €4 each.

Grant of option 01/03/2019:   No tax liability as the share options are at market value
Exercise of option 01/08/2021:   No tax liability under KEEP
Sale of shares 20/02/2022:

Sale price 12,000 @ €4	€48,000
Less: Consideration paid on exercise of option: 12,000 @ €1	(€12,000)
Gain on sale of shares	€36,000
Tax payable: CGT @ 33% (current rate)	€11,880

Example 31.6

Using the information in **Example 31.5** above, compare the tax treatment of the share option schemes between the KEEP option and non-KEEP short options. Assume Iseult pays tax at the higher rate and the applicable USC rate is 8%, the RTSO and CGT calculations would be as follows:

	KEEP option	Non-KEEP option
RTSO (Income tax, USC and PRSI)	€	€
1 March 2019 – Grant of Option		
No tax liability as the share options are at market value	Nil	Nil
1 August 2021 – Exercise of Option		
Market value of shares 12,000 @ €2.75 = €33,000		
Less: option price paid 12,000 @ €1.00 = (€12,000)		
Taxable gain on exercise of option €21,000		
Income tax @ 40%	Nil	8,400
PRSI @ 4%	Nil	840
USC @ 8%	Nil	1,680
Total RTSO payable on exercise of option	Nil	10,920
CGT		
20 February 2022 – Sale of Shares		
Sale price: 12,000 @ €4 = €48,000	48,000	48,000
Less: consideration paid on exercise of option	(12,000)	(12,000)
Less: gain already taxed	Nil	(21,000)
Chargeable gain on sale of shares	36,000	15,000
CGT payable @ 33%	11,880	4,950
Total tax payable:		
RTSO	Nil	10,920
CGT	11,880	4,950
	11,880	15,870
% tax payable on share gain	33%	44%

Questions

Review Questions

(See Suggested Solutions to Review Questions at the end of this textbook.)

Question 31.1

In 2017, Pharma Ltd granted Mandy a share option as part of her remuneration package. The share option allowed Mandy to purchase 2,500 shares at €2.85 per share (the market value of a share at that date was €3.00 per share). The share options must be exercised within seven years of being granted. No consideration was paid for the granting of the share option.

On 1 May 2021, Mandy exercised her option to acquire the 2,500 shares for €2.85 per share. The market value of a share at that date was €5.50 per share.

Requirement

(a) Outline the tax implications for Mandy and calculate any tax due (ignoring USC and PRSI) on:
   (i) the grant of the option; and
   (ii) the exercise of the option.
(b) State the due date for any income tax due on the exercise of a share option.
(c) Explain the tax treatment on the grant and exercise of options if it were a long option. Detailed calculations are not required.

Question 31.2

Charlotte and Fabio, aged 35 and 37 respectively, are an Irish resident couple who have been married for a number of years and are jointly assessed for income tax purposes.

Charlotte, an IT consultant, has her own business. Her Case II tax-adjusted profit is €150,000 for the year ended 31 December 2021. Charlotte pays 15% of her adjusted income into a Revenue-approved pension scheme. On 31 October 2021 she paid preliminary tax for 2021 of €30,000, being 100% of her 2020 liability.

Fabio is Irish resident for tax purposes but is Italian domiciled. He has been Irish resident for the past ten years. Fabio works for a large accountancy firm in Galway and earned an annual salary of €55,000 (gross) for 2021 (PAYE deducted of €16,200). Fabio pays 5% of his gross salary into a Revenue-approved pension scheme.

In addition to the main residence Fabio shares with Charlotte, he also owns two other properties that he lets out. One is a residential property in Italy and generates an annual net property income of €8,500, which he lodges into a bank in Galway. In previous years he had lodged this money into an account in Rome. His second rental property is an office in Athenry. The income and expenses associated with this property for 2021 are set out below:

	€
Rental income	12,000
Expenses:	
Rates	(920)
Insurance	(350)
Management fees	(610)
Interest on loan to acquire the property	(6,800)
	3,320

During 2021, Fabio subscribed €10,000 for eligible shares in an Employment and Investment Incentive qualifying company.

Requirement

Calculate the balance of income tax payable by Charlotte and Fabio for 2021. (Ignore PRSI and USC.)

Married Couples/Civil Partners: Years of Marriage, Death and Divorce

Learning Objectives

After studying this chapter you will understand:

■ The special rules that apply in the year of marriage and in the year of death of a spouse/civil partner.
■ The tax consequences of divorce, separation or dissolution of a marriage/civil partnership.

32.1 Introduction

Married couples and civil partners are treated in the same manner under the Taxes Acts and can be taxed, as outlined at CA Proficiency 1, under either:

1. joint assessment;
2. single assessment; or
3. separate assessment.

32.1.1 Joint Assessment

Under joint assessment the income **of each** spouse/civil partner is taxed as if it were the income of the assessable spouse or nominated civil partner. **Joint assessment is automatic**, i.e. it is provided in the legislation that a married couple or civil partners will be deemed to have elected for joint assessment **unless**, before the end of the year of assessment, **either** spouse/civil partner writes to Revenue indicating that they would prefer to be assessed as **single** individuals.

Joint assessment is generally only available where both individuals are Irish tax resident, although some exceptions may arise and would be examined on an individual basis. Under joint assessment, the tax credits and standard rate tax band can be allocated between spouses or civil partners in a way that suits their circumstances.

The **income bands** chargeable at the standard rate of tax are increased, depending on whether the married couple/civil partners have one or two incomes.

Tax Year 2021	Tax Rate	Joint Assessment (One Income)	Joint Assessment (Two Incomes)
Taxable income	20%	€44,300	€70,600*
	40%	Balance	Balance

*Transferable between spouses/civil partners up to a maximum of €44,300 for any one spouse/civil partner. The balance of €26,300 is available to the lower earning spouse only.

32.1.2 Single Assessment

If a married couple/civil partners wish to be assessed on the single assessment basis, then either spouse/civil partner must give notice to this effect to Revenue before the end of the year of assessment for which they wish to be assessed as single persons.

If an election for single assessment is made, then each spouse/civil partner will be assessed to income tax as if they were not married or in a civil partnership, i.e. they are effectively treated as single persons, and tax credits and reliefs are granted accordingly. In such cases, if either spouse/civil partner has tax credits or reliefs in excess of their assessable income, there is **no right to transfer** unutilised credits to the other spouse/civil partner.

32.1.3 Separate Assessment

A married couple/civil partners that are assessable on a joint basis may claim for separate assessment of their joint income tax liability. Either spouse/civil partner can make an election for separate assessment not later than 1 April in the year of assessment.

An election for separate assessment will result in the **same total income tax liability** as if the spouses/civil partners were jointly assessed, with each spouse paying their portion of the total tax liability. The amount of income tax payable by each spouse/civil partner is calculated by reference to their total income and the proportions of tax credits or reliefs to which they are entitled, as outlined at CA Proficiency 1. Separate assessment **does not diminish** or **increase** the total liability that would have arisen under normal joint assessment.

32.2 Tax Treatment in Year of Marriage

Each party to the marriage/civil partnership is initially taxed as a single person for the complete year of marriage/civil partnership. After the end of the year of assessment, they can elect to have their tax liability computed on a joint assessment basis as if they had been married/were civil partners for the whole of the tax year in which the marriage/civil partnership took place. If this election is made, the tax saving, if any, vis-à-vis the amount of their combined liabilities on a single assessment basis, is scaled down in the proportion that the period of marriage/civil partnership during the tax year bears to the full tax year, i.e.:

$$\text{Tax saving} \times \frac{\text{Number of income tax months from date of marriage/civil partnership to the end of the tax year *}}{12 \text{ months}}$$

* An income tax month is a calendar month, with part of a month being treated as a full month in the formula.

Example 32.1

John married Mary on 15 July 2021. John earned a gross salary of €45,000 in 2021 and paid income tax of €7,640. Mary earned a salary of €23,000 in 2021, on which she paid income tax of €1,300.

Assessment of John and Mary as Single Individuals for 2021

	John		Mary	
	€	€	€	€
Income: Schedule E	45,000		23,000	
Tax Calculation				
€35,300/€23,000 @ 20%	7,060		4,600	
Balance @ 40%	3,880		0	
	10,940		4,600	
Deduct: Non-refundable tax credits				
Basic personal tax credit	1,650		1,650	
Employee tax credit	1,650	(3,300)	1,650	(3,300)
Income tax liability		7,640		1,300
Deduct: Refundable tax credits				
Year of marriage relief (see below)		(769)		(131)
Tax paid under PAYE		(7,640)		(1,300)
Tax refund due		(769)		(131)

Notional Liability under Joint Assessment for 2021 and year of marriage relief

	€	€
Income: Schedule E		68,000
Tax Calculation:		
€67,300 @ 20% (€44,300 + €23,000)		13,460
Balance = €700 @ 40%		280
		13,740
Deduct: Non-refundable tax credits		
Basic personal tax credit	3,300	
Employee tax credit	3,300	(6,600)
Total liability under joint assessment		7,140
Total combined liability under single assessment		(8,940)
Saving under joint assessment		(1,800)

Saving restricted to:

$$\frac{\text{6 months (period of marriage in tax year)}}{\text{12 months}} \times €1,800 \quad = €900$$

$$\text{Split: John} \quad \frac{€7,640}{€7,640 + €1,300} \times €900 \quad = \underline{€769}$$

$$\text{Split: Mary} \quad \frac{€1,300}{€7,640 + €1,300} \times €900 \quad = \underline{€131}$$

32.3 Tax Treatment in Year of Death

The tax treatment of the surviving spouse/civil partner in the year of bereavement depends on how the surviving spouse/civil partner and the deceased were taxed **before** the bereavement.

32.3.1 Joint Assessment and Death of Assessable Spouse/Nominated Civil Partner

If the couple were assessed under joint assessment and if the **deceased** was the "assessable spouse" or "nominated civil partner", i.e. the person responsible for making a joint tax return, the **surviving spouse/civil partner** will be taxable in their **own right from the date of death** of the deceased. The surviving spouse/civil partner is entitled to the widowed person/surviving civil partner in the year of bereavement tax credit and the widowed person's/surviving civil partner's (without dependent children) tax band for this period (see **Section 32.3.4**). Any income of the couple **prior** to the death of the deceased is treated as the **income of the deceased** to the date of death.

Example 32.2

Mr Andrews, who was the assessable spouse under joint assessment, died on 1 November 2021. His salary from 1 January 2021 to the date of death was €46,000, from which tax of €8,240 was deducted.

Mrs Andrews was employed by a local wholesale company and earned €16,000 from 1 January to 1 November 2021 (tax deducted €490) and €3,500 from 2 November to 31 December 2021 (tax deducted €110).

Mr Andrews Deceased – Income Tax Liability Period 01/01/2021–01/11/2021

	€	€
Schedule E salary – self		46,000
Schedule E salary – spouse		16,000
Gross income		62,000
Tax calculation:		
€60,300 @ 20% (€44,300 + €16,000)	12,060	
€ 1,700 @ 40%	680	12,740
€62,000		
Deduct: Non-refundable tax credits		
Basic personal tax credit – married	3,300	
Employee tax credits: €1,650 × 2	3,300	(6,600)
Tax liability		6,140
Deduct: Refundable tax credits		
Tax paid under PAYE – self	8,240	
Tax paid under PAYE – spouse	490	(8,730)
Refund due		(2,590)

Mrs Andrews – Income Tax Liability Period 02/11/2021–31/12/2021

	€	€
Schedule E salary		3,500
Tax payable: €3,500 @ 20%		700
Deduct: Non-refundable tax credits		
Basic personal tax credit (year of bereavement)	3,300	
Employee tax credit (€3,500 @20%)	700	
Tax credits limited to the amount which reduces tax liability to nil		(700)
Tax liability		Nil
Deduct: Refundable tax credits		
Tax paid under PAYE		(110)
Refund due		(110)

32.3.2 Joint Assessment and Death of the Non-assessable Spouse or Non-nominated Civil Partner

If the couple were assessed under joint assessment and if the surviving spouse/civil partner was the "assessable spouse" or "nominated civil partner", i.e. the person responsible for making a joint tax return, the surviving spouse/civil partner will continue to receive the married person's/civil partner's tax credits and income tax bands for the remainder of the tax year. The surviving spouse/civil partner will be taxable on their own income for the full year of bereavement plus the deceased's income from the start of the tax year to the date of death.

Example 32.3

Jane Murphy died on 1 September 2021. Her salary from 1 January 2021 to the date of death was €36,000, from which tax of €7,490 was deducted.

Her civil partner, Ann Ward, is employed by a local company and earned €46,000 from 1 January to 1 September 2021 (tax deducted €9,015) and €13,500 from 2 September to 31 December 2021 (tax deducted €2,625). Ann is the nominated civil partner under joint assessment.

Ann Ward – Income Tax Calculation 2021

		€	€
Income: Schedule E			
– Ann Ward (total 2021)		59,500	
– Jane Murphy (to 01/09/2021)		36,000	95,500
Tax Calculation:			
(€44,300 + €26,300) @ 20%	€70,600	14,120	
Balance @ 40%	€24,900	9,960	24,080
	€95,500		
Deduct: Non-refundable tax credits			
Basic personal tax credit		3,300	
Employee tax credit (× 2)		3,300	(6,600)
Income tax liability			17,480
Deduct: Refundable tax credits			
Tax paid under PAYE:			
– Ann Ward (€9,015 + €2,625)		11,640	
– Jane Murphy		7,490	(19,130)
Tax refund due			(1,650)

32.3.3 Single Assessment and Death of a Spouse/Civil Partner

If the couple have been assessed as single persons, the deceased is taxed as a single person up to the date of death. The surviving spouse/civil partner is also taxed as a single person but is **entitled** to the widowed person/surviving civil partner in the year of bereavement tax credit (€3,300), instead of the single person's basic personal tax credit.

As can be seen from the above examples, where a couple have been jointly assessed and the **assessable spouse/nominated civil partner dies, extra tax credits** are given in the year of bereavement (i.e. widowed person/surviving civil partner in the year of bereavement personal tax credit to the surviving spouse/civil partner, the married/civil partner's personal tax credit and the couple, in effect, get an additional standard rate tax band).

Accordingly, a couple who have been assessed as single persons should consider electing for joint assessment in the year of death. An **election** can be made by the surviving spouse and the personal representative of the deceased and must be made **before the end** of the tax year in which the death occurs.

32.3.4 Tax Treatment of Surviving Spouse/Civil Partner for Subsequent Years

In the years following the year of bereavement, the surviving spouse/civil partner is entitled to the widowed person's/surviving civil partner's tax credit. If the surviving spouse/civil partner has dependent children, they will also be entitled to the Single Person Child Carer Credit and the widowed/surviving civil partner parent tax credit (for five years after the date of bereavement). The widowed person's/surviving civil partner's (without dependent children) income tax band or the one-parent family (with dependent children) tax band will also apply, depending on whether the surviving spouse/civil partner has dependent children.

Surviving Spouse/Civil Partner	With Dependent Children	Without Dependent Children
Year of Bereavement:		
Married Person/Civil Partner Tax Credit	€3,300	€3,300
Maximum Standard Rate Tax Band:		
Joint/Separate Assessment	€70,600	€70,600
Single Assessment	€39,300	€35,300
Subsequent Years:		
Widowed Person/Surviving Civil Partner Tax Credit	€1,650	€2,190
Single Person Child Carer Credit	€1,650	Nil
Maximum Standard Rate Tax Band	€39,300	€35,300
ADDITIONAL (years after year of bereavement)		
Year 1: Widowed Parent/Surviving Civil Partner Tax Credit	€3,600	Nil
Year 2: Widowed Parent/Surviving Civil Partner Tax Credit	€3,150	Nil
Year 3: Widowed Parent/Surviving Civil Partner Tax Credit	€2,700	Nil
Year 4: Widowed Parent/Surviving Civil Partner Tax Credit	€2,250	Nil
Year 5: Widowed Parent/Surviving Civil Partner Tax Credit	€1,800	Nil

32.4 Tax Treatment on Separation, Divorce or Dissolution

32.4.1 Recap – General Rule

The general rule is that in the case of separation, divorce or dissolution, spouses/civil partners are assessed to income tax as **single individuals**. The couple may elect for **joint assessment** only if:

- both individuals are **resident in Ireland** for tax purposes for the year of assessment;
- **legally enforceable maintenance payments** are made by one spouse/civil partner to the other; and
- **neither has remarried**.

If this election is made under section 1026 TCA 1997 the rules, as detailed at CA Proficiency 1, apply whereby:

- the payer **cannot deduct maintenance payments** made to the separated or divorced spouse/civil partner in arriving at their total income and the **separated or divorced spouse/civil partner is not assesse**d on the maintenance payments;
- the **married person's/civil partner's tax credits** and rate bands are granted; and
- if the separated or divorced spouse/civil partner has income in their own right, apart from maintenance payments received by them, the income tax liability applicable to each spouse's/civil partner's separate income is calculated using the separate assessment procedures.

32.4.2 Tax Treatment in Year of Separation, Divorce or Dissolution

In the year of separation, divorce or dissolution where **joint assessment** had been elected for under section 1026 TCA 1997, the tax treatment of the couple is similar to the tax treatment that applies in the year of death of the assessable spouse/nominated civil partner.

Treatment of Assessable Spouse/Nominated Civil Partner

1. They are assessable on their entire personal income for the year of separation and their spouse's/civil partner's income (applying appropriate basis of apportionment) for the proportion of the year up to the date of separation.
2. They are entitled to a **married person's/civil partner's basic personal tax credit**, €3,300 for the tax year 2021, and the benefit of the **married person's/civil partner's tax bands**.

Treatment of Non-assessable Spouse/Nominated Civil Partner

1. They are assessable as a single person on their own sources of income for the period of the year after the date of separation.
2. They are entitled only to a single person's basic personal tax credit and to the benefit of the rate bands applicable to a single person. If there are dependent children, they are entitled to the **one-parent family tax band** and, assuming they satisfy the conditions, a **Single Person Child Carer credit**.
3. Other allowances/reliefs, etc. available to them are given by reference to single person limitations.

Example 32.4

Mr and Mrs Doyle had been married for 10 years when they separated on 30 September 2021. Under the terms of the deed of separation drawn up on that day, Mr Doyle pays Mrs Doyle €300 per month, from 1 October 2021, which specifically includes €100 for the maintenance of their only child, Ruth, who lives with her mother.

Mr Doyle is the assessable spouse. He earned €49,000 in 2021, from which tax of €7,490 was deducted. Mrs Doyle earned €22,000 in 2021, from which tax of €1,100 was deducted. Mrs Doyle earned €16,500 (tax paid €825) for the period 1 January 2021 to 30 September 2021.

Mr Doyle – Income Tax Computation 2021

	€	€
Income:		
Schedule E – self	49,000	
Schedule E – spouse 01/01/2021–30/09/2021	16,500	65,500
Less: Charges		
Maintenance payments ((€300 – €100) × 3)		(600)
Total income		**64,900**

continued overleaf

Tax Calculation:		
€44,300 @ 20%	8,860	
€16,500 @ 20%	3,300	
€4,100 @ 40%	1,640	13,800
€64,900		
Deduct: Non-refundable tax credits:		
Basic personal tax credit (married)	3,300	
Employee tax credit (× 2)	3,300	(6,600)
Tax liability		7,200
Deduct: Refundable tax credits		
Tax paid under PAYE – self	7,490	
Tax paid under PAYE – wife 01/01/2021–30/09/2021	825	(8,315)
Net tax refundable		**(1,115)**

Mrs Doyle – Income Tax Computation 2021

	€	€
Income:		
Schedule D, Case IV	600	
Schedule E (01/10/2021–31/12/2021)	5,500	6,100
Tax Calculation:		
€6,100 @ 20%		1,220
Deduct: Non-refundable tax credits:		
Basic personal tax credit	1,650	
Single person child carer credit	1,650	
Employee tax credit (€5,500 @20%)	1,100	
	4,400	
Tax credits restricted to amount which gives a nil tax liability		(1,220)
Tax liability		NIL
Deduct: Refundable tax credits		
Tax paid under PAYE (01/10/2021–31/12/2021)		(275)
Net tax refundable		**(275)**

Questions

Review Questions

(See Suggested Solutions to Review Questions at the end of this textbook.)

Question 32.1

Peter and Paul married on 20 June 2021. The couple elected for joint assessment, with Peter as the assessable person. Peter is employed by a firm of auctioneers. His gross salary for 2021 was €50,000 (tax deducted €9,640). Paul is employed by a firm of stockbrokers. He earned €28,000 gross (tax deducted €2,300) during 2021.

Requirement

Compute Peter and Paul's tax liability for 2021 on the basis that they wish to minimise their total liability.

Question 32.2

Mr and Mrs Lynch separated on 30 June 2021. Under the terms of the deed of separation drawn up on that date, Mr Lynch pays Mrs Lynch €700 per month, of which €100 is specifically for their only child, Mary, who resides with her mother. The first monthly payment is made on 1 July 2021. He also pays the mortgage on the family home, where Mrs Lynch continues to reside.

Mr Lynch's salary for 2021 was €48,000 and Mrs Lynch's salary was €15,000. Mrs Lynch's payslip for the month ended 30 June 2021 showed cumulative gross salary of €7,000 for the period 1 January 2021 to 30 June 2021.

Mr and Mrs Lynch had been jointly assessed for all years up to the year of their separation.

Requirement
Calculate Mr and Mrs Lynch's tax liability for 2021 on the basis that:

(a) Joint assessment was claimed for the year of assessment in accordance with section 1026 TCA 1997.
(b) No election was made under section 1026 TCA 1997.

Question 32.3

Jane DuBlanc's husband, Matthew, died suddenly on 30 May 2021. They have three children, all aged under 18. Matthew was the assessable spouse and earned €60,000 until the date of his death (tax paid €19,680). Jane works as a design consultant and earned €72,000 in total for 2021 (tax paid €18,440). Her earnings to 30 May 2021 were €30,000 (tax €7,680).

Requirement
Calculate the couple's income tax liability for 2021 where:

(a) Matthew is the assessable spouse; and
(b) Jane is the assessable spouse at the date of death.

Part Six

Value Added Tax

Cross-border Transactions

Learning Objectives

After studying this chapter you will understand:

- The VAT rules for cross-border supplies of goods or services within the EU.
- The VAT rules for the supply of goods or services outside the EU.

33.1 Intra-EU Acquisition and Supply of Goods

The terms "intra-EU acquisition" and "intra-EU supply" relate to goods supplied by a business in one EU Member State to a business in another EU Member State where the goods have been dispatched or transported from the territory of one Member State to another.

Although the UK (i.e. Great Britain and Northern Ireland) is no longer a member of the EU, Northern Ireland continues to be subject to the same EU VAT rules on the acquisition and supply of goods as EU Member States under the Protocol on Ireland/Northern Ireland. Accordingly, the treatment of intra-EU acquisitions and supplies of goods outlined in **Sections 33.1.1** and **33.1.2** below also applies to the supply of goods between Northern Ireland and EU Member States.

33.1.1 VAT on Purchases from Other EU Member States and Northern Ireland

Where goods are imported from another EU Member State or Northern Ireland, the treatment for VAT on purchases varies, depending on the taxable status of the purchaser.

Accountable Persons

When an Irish accountable person purchases goods from a supplier in an EU Member State or Northern Ireland and these are dispatched to the State, they must provide the supplier with their Irish VAT number. Upon receipt and verification of this number, the supplier will zero-rate the goods in question. The accountable person then:

- becomes liable for VAT on the acquisition of the goods;
- declares a liability for the VAT in the VAT return;
- claims a simultaneous input credit, thus cancelling the liability (assuming they are entitled to full deductibility); and
- accounts for VAT on any subsequent supply of the goods in the normal manner.

Example 33.1
A shipment of wood is sold by a VAT-registered trader in France to a VAT-registered business in Ireland for €10,000, and delivered from France to Ireland by the supplier. The supply is charged at the zero rate out of France. The Irish company would then self-account for Irish VAT on the acquisition of the wood as follows:

VAT on sales €10,000 @ 23%	2,300
VAT on purchases @ 23%	(€2,300)

There is no net effect on the VAT liability since the VAT on the wood is recoverable by the trader.

If the Irish VAT-registered business were to buy the wood from a VAT-registered business in Northern Ireland, with delivery from NI to Ireland, the Irish company would self-account for Irish VAT in the same way.

Example 33.2
An Irish VAT-registered trader buys a motor car in France for €10,000 and it is delivered from France to Ireland by the supplier. The supply is charged at the zero rate out of France.

The Irish company would then self-account for Irish VAT on the acquisition of the car as follows:

VAT on sales €10,000 @ 23%	€2,300
VAT on purchases*	(€0)

*Assuming the car is not a "qualifying vehicle".

In this scenario, the trader is not allowed to claim VAT on motor cars and there is a VAT liability on the transaction as a result.

Unregistered Persons, Non-taxable Entities and Exempted Activities

In the case of persons not registered for VAT in the State, non-taxable entities (e.g. government departments) and exempted activities (e.g. insurance companies), VAT is payable in the Member State (including Northern Ireland) of purchase at the VAT rate applicable there. Where the threshold of **€41,000** in respect of intra-EU acquisitions **is exceeded**, the person or entity must register for VAT in Ireland and account for the VAT in the manner described above. However, as their activities are non-taxable/exempt, these entities **cannot claim input credits** and no Irish VAT is chargeable on a subsequent sale.

Purchases by Private Individuals

The private individual pays the VAT charged by the supplier in the Member State or Northern Ireland and no additional Irish VAT liability will arise. This does not apply to **new** means of transport, e.g. boats, planes, motor cars. These items are liable to VAT in the Member State of the **purchaser**.

Where a private individual purchases goods through **mail order**, they must pay the VAT applicable in the **place of purchase**. For example, goods purchased by mail order from a business in Germany will be subject to German VAT. However, such acquisitions may be subject to the distance sales rules (see **Section 33.1.3**).

33.1.2 VAT on Sales to Other EU Member States and Northern Ireland

The treatment for **VAT on supplies** varies depending on the **taxable status** of the customer.

VAT-registered Customers

Where a taxable person in Ireland **sells or supplies** goods to a VAT-registered person within the EU or Northern Ireland, the transaction will be **zero-rated** in Ireland and will be liable to foreign VAT in the country in which the purchaser is registered for VAT.

A VAT-registered person in the State may zero-rate the supply of goods to a customer in another EU Member State or Northern Ireland if:

- the customer is registered for VAT in the other EU Member State/Northern Ireland;
- the customer's VAT registration number (including country prefix) is obtained and retained in the supplier's records (the prefix for Northern Ireland is 'XI' for intra-EU transactions);
- this number, together with the supplier's VAT registration number, is quoted on the sales invoice; and
- the goods are dispatched or transported to that, or any other, EU Member State or Northern Ireland.

Where any of the above four conditions are not satisfied, the Irish supplier should charge Irish VAT at the appropriate Irish VAT rate (i.e. as if the sale had taken place between two Irish traders). If the conditions for zero-rating are subsequently established, the customer is entitled to recover the VAT paid from the supplier. The supplier can then make an adjustment in his/her VAT return for the period.

Unregistered Customers

Generally, subject to the 'distance selling' rules below, where the customer is unregistered the Irish supplier should charge Irish VAT. However, if the goods are to be installed or assembled by the Irish supplier in another EU Member State or Northern Ireland, Irish VAT will not be charged. Instead, the Irish supplier may be obliged to register for VAT in the customer's country and charge local VAT to its customers there.

33.1.3 Intra-EU Distance Sales

Distance sales covers mail-order and other distance sales of goods to **unregistered customers** where the supplier is responsible for delivering the goods.

Prior to 1 July 2021, where the value of distance sales into the State exceeded €35,000 in a calendar year, the supplier was obliged to register for VAT in the State and to charge Irish VAT on such sales. Irish businesses engaging in distance selling to unregistered customers in other EU Member States were required to register in each country in which the relevant threshold was exceeded (€100,000, €35,000 or £70,000) and to charge the appropriate VAT rate of that country. Suppliers could opt to register in any Member State, even if the annual threshold was not exceeded. If not VAT-registered in the other Member State, the Irish seller accounted for Irish VAT on the sale if its total sales exceeded the threshold for VAT registration in Ireland. VAT returns were required for each country of registration.

The EU's 'VAT e-commerce package' has implemented significant changes to the distance selling rules. With effect from 1 July 2021, the previous VAT distance sales registration thresholds were abolished and an EU-wide threshold of €10,000 now applies to intra-EU distance sales of goods. Where the supplier exceeds the threshold in a calendar year, they are obliged to charge local VAT in the Member State (or Northern Ireland) to which the goods are shipped. However, distance sellers dispatching their goods from a single country, are no longer required to register for VAT or to complete multiple VAT returns in EU Member States where they are selling. Instead, the VAT due on sales to customers in Member States in which the supplier does not have a VAT registration can be remitted through a single EU-wide VAT return, known as the One Stop Shop (OSS), alongside their regular domestic VAT return.

Where a supplier's annual intra-EU distance sales are below €10,000, the sales may remain subject to VAT in the Member State where the goods are located at the time their dispatch begins.

33.2 Intra-EU Supplies of Services

With effect from 1 January 2021, EU VAT rules in respect of intra-EU supplies of services no longer apply to the supply of services to/from the UK, including Northern Ireland. The supply of services to the UK, including Northern Ireland, is a non-EU supply of services (see **Section 33.5**).

33.2.1 Place of Supply of Services

The rules in relation to intra-EU supplies of services are more complicated than those applicable to the supply of goods. There are two general place of supply rules, depending on whether the recipient is a business or a consumer. To recap from CA Proficiency 1:

1. For supplies of business-to-business (B2B) services, the place of supply is the place where the recipient is established (reverse charge).
2. For supplies of business-to-consumer (B2C) services, the place of supply is where the supplier is established.

Businesses that receive services from a supplier **outside** Ireland will not be charged VAT by the supplier of those services, but the recipient will be required to **account** for Irish VAT unless the services concerned are exempt in Ireland.

TABLE 1

SUMMARY OF PLACE OF SUPPLY RULES FOR SERVICES (UNLESS SUBJECT TO EXCEPTIONS OR EFFECTIVE USE AND ENJOYMENT PROVISIONS)

Country of establishment of supplier	Country in which customer established	Place of supply	Person liable to account for Irish VAT
Business to business (B2B)			
Ireland	Other EU State	Other EU State	No Irish VAT
Other EU State	Ireland	Ireland	Customer
Business to consumer (B2C)			
Ireland	Other EU State	Ireland	Supplier
Other EU State	Ireland	Other EU State	No Irish VAT

It should be noted that financial services supplied by a supplier in the State to a private individual from outside the EU who avails of them here are deemed to be supplied in the State.

33.2.2 Exceptions to the General Rules

There are several exceptions to the general rules that more closely link the place of supply to where the service is performed. The implementation of the EU's VAT e-commerce package means that, with effect from 1 July 2021, EU and non-EU suppliers can use the One Stop Shop (OSS) to report all B2C services supplied to customers in the EU (see **Section 33.1.3**). (Prior to this the supplier was required to register and account for VAT in the Member State of supply, unless covered by a reverse charge arrangement.)

The following table summarises the exceptions and sets out the current place of supply rules.

TABLE 2
Exceptions to VAT Place of Supply of Services Rules

Supply	Place of Supply
Telecommunications, broadcasting and e-services, including e-gaming	Where the customer resides.
Provision of a cultural, artistic, sporting, etc., events	B2B – where the customer is established B2C – where the event takes place
Admission to cultural, artistic, sporting, etc., events	Where the event takes place
Supply of services connected with immovable goods (property) (B2B and B2C)	Place of supply is where the goods are located
Passenger transport services (B2B and B2C)	Where the passenger transport takes place
Intra-EU transport of goods B2C	The place of departure
Intra-EU transport of goods B2B	Where the customer is established
Ancillary transport services, valuations or work on movable property	Where the services are physically carried out (reverse charge for B2B)
Restaurant and catering services	Where the services are physically carried out
Restaurant and catering services for consumption on board ships, planes and trains	Point of departure
Hiring out of means of transport (B2B and B2C) (short-term ≤ 30 days)	Where the transport is put at the disposal of the customer
Hiring out of means of transport (B2B and B2C) (long-term >90 days)	Where the customer is established, has their permanent address or usually resides

33.3 Intra-EU Cross-border Reclaims of VAT

A trader that is VAT-registered in one EU Member State may incur VAT on goods and services purchased in another EU Member State. Under the EU's 8th and 13th VAT Directives, a VAT-registered trader engaged in business outside the State, and not engaged in business in the State, may claim a repayment of VAT on most business purchases in the State. An electronic VAT refund procedure was introduced across the EU for all VAT claims submitted by traders established within the EU.

33.4 Imports/Exports of Goods from/to Non-EU Countries

As a consequence of the UK's withdrawal from the EU in 2020, the UK (i.e. Great Britain and Northern Ireland) is now a non-EU country for VAT purposes, with effect from 1 January 2021. However, as Northern Ireland remains subject to the same EU VAT rules on goods as EU Member States (under the Protocol on Ireland/Northern Ireland, see **Section 33.1**), the rules outlined below relating to the import and export of goods from/to non-EU countries apply, for UK purposes, only to transactions with Great Britain (i.e. UK excluding Northern Ireland).

33.4.1 *Imports from Non-EU Countries*

For VAT purposes, "imports" are goods arriving from non-EU countries. VAT is payable at the **point of entry** on imports.

- VAT is charged at **the same rate** as applies to the sale of the particular goods within the State and is charged at the point of importation.
- VAT is payable **before** the imported goods are released by the Customs authorities, unless the importer is approved for the Deferred Payments Scheme.
- Eligibility under the **Deferred Payments Scheme** will permit payment of the VAT liability in respect of the goods on the **15th day** of the month **following** the month in which the VAT becomes due.
- The **value** of imported goods for the purposes of assessment to VAT is their **value for Customs purposes**, together with any taxes, duties and other charges levied inside the State on the goods, but not including VAT.
- A VAT-registered person who imports goods during a taxable period is entitled to **claim credit** in their VAT returns for the VAT paid or payable.
- VAT-registered persons who are in a **permanent repayment position** as a result of VAT paid at the point of importation may be permitted to make **monthly** returns.
- Goods imported into the Shannon customs-free zone and the Ringaskiddy free port from outside the State are not liable to VAT.
- Persons who **export 75%** or more of their produce are allowed to import raw materials and components **without** payment of VAT at the point of importation.

33.4.2 *Exports to Non-EU Countries*

For VAT purposes, "exports" are **goods** directly dispatched to a destination **outside the EU**.

The **zero rate** of VAT applies to **all exports**. Several export-type transactions and related services are also zero-rated, as are supplies of goods to VAT-registered traders in the Shannon Customs Free Airport.

A VAT-registered person who supplies goods to the domestic market and who **also** exports goods is entitled to an **input credit** or deduction for VAT invoiced on purchases for **both domestic and export sales**. The credit may be taken against the VAT liability on domestic sales.

33.5 Non-EU Supply of Services

As outlined in **Section 33.2**, the place of supply rules determine where a service is taxable. Therefore, unless covered by the exemptions described in **Section 33.2.2**, the position is as follows:

- Service suppliers in the State must **not charge** VAT when supplying services to a **business** customer (B2B) established **outside** the EU.
- Service suppliers in the State must **charge** VAT to **non-business** customers (B2C) **outside** the EU. However, Irish VAT is not chargeable on some services provided to non-business customers outside the EU. Such services include the transfer of intellectual property, consultancy, financial, advertising, the supply of staff and telecommunications. The Irish service provider must obtain and retain proof that the customer is established outside the EU.
- Businesses that receive services from a supplier **outside** the EU will not be charged VAT by the supplier of those services, but the recipient will be required to **account** for Irish VAT (reverse charge) unless the services concerned are exempt in Ireland. This includes services received from abroad by a Department of State, a local authority or a body established by statute in the State registered for VAT.

▨ Unregistered customers will **not be liable** for Irish VAT in respect of the receipt of the foreign services. The services should be taxed in the country from where they are supplied.

Table 3 below above summarises the place of supply rules for services.

TABLE 3
SUMMARY OF PLACE OF SUPPLY RULES FOR SERVICES (UNLESS SUBJECT TO
EXCEPTIONS OR EFFECTIVE USE AND ENJOYMENT PROVISIONS)

Country of establishment of supplier	Country in which customer established	Place of supply	Person liable to account for Irish VAT
Business to business (B2B)			
Ireland	Outside EU	Outside EU	No Irish VAT
Outside EU	Ireland	Ireland	Customer (reverse charge)
Business to consumer (B2C)			
Ireland	Outside EU	Depends on service	Supplier (if VAT occurs)
Outside EU	Ireland	Depends on service	Supplier (if taxable)

Questions

Review Questions
(See Suggested Solutions to Review Questions at the end of this textbook.)

Question 33.1

Hermes Ltd distributes pet food to domestic and foreign markets. The following transactions were undertaken by the company during the VAT period March–April 2021:

Sales invoiced to customers within the State	€250,000
Sales invoiced to customers in the US	€10,000

The above amounts are stated net of VAT. The VAT rate applicable to the company's sales is 23%.

During the same period, purchase invoices were received in respect of the following:

	Gross Invoice Value €	VAT Rate Applicable %
Stock purchased from suppliers in the State	233,700	23
Stock purchased from suppliers in Northern Ireland	50,000	23
Professional fees	6,150	23
Motor car repairs	1,135	13.5
Computer	9,225	23

The amounts stated include VAT where charged.

Requirement

Calculate the VAT due for the period March–April 2021. The computation of VAT return figures should be clearly laid out in your workings.

Question 33.2

Elixir Ltd operates an Irish-based business selling materials for the repair and maintenance of yachts and small boats. During the VAT period of two months ended 31 October 2021, it recorded the following transactions.

	€
Supplies (exclusive of VAT)	
Sales in Ireland	950,000
Sales to Spain (to Spanish VAT-registered customers)	320,000
Sales to non-VAT-registered customers in the UK	25,000
Sales to VAT-registered customers in the UK	135,000
Sales to non-VAT-registered customers in Northern Ireland	6,000

Purchases (inclusive of VAT where applicable)	**VAT Rate**	**€**
Purchase of materials from Irish suppliers	23%	369,000
Purchase of equipment from German supplier	23%	200,000
Purchase of machinery locally	23%	246,000
Rent of premises (Note)	23%	18,450
Repairs and maintenance of office and equipment	23%	14,145
Audit and accountancy fees	23%	11,070
Diesel for staff vehicles	23%	5,535
Electricity and gas	13.5%	2,400
Salaries and wages	n/a	167,000
Advertising costs	23%	30,750

Note: VAT at 23% is included in the amount of the rent paid on the company's premises.

All the above purchases of goods and services (except for wages, salaries and imports) are supplied by businesses that are registered for VAT in Ireland except for the equipment that was purchased from a VAT-registered business in Germany.

Requirement

Calculate the VAT payable by (or repayable to) Elixir Ltd for the VAT period ended 31 October 2021.

VAT and Property

Learning Objectives

After studying this chapter you will understand:

■ The VAT treatment of the supply of property in the State.
■ The interaction of VAT with stamp duty.

34.1 Introduction

There are a wide variety of transactions involving the supply of property in Ireland, including short-term lettings, assignments of leases and sales of freehold interests. In this context, property includes all land and buildings in the State. Only the sale of a freehold interest is to be considered at CA Proficiency 2. As such transactions generally carry a high value it is important to have a basic understanding and awareness of the rules to ensure the appropriate VAT treatment is implemented.

A significant reform of the VAT on property legislation was introduced with effect from 1 July 2008. The previous legislation is outside the scope of this book but be aware that those rules may still have an impact when dealing with VAT on property transactions in practice. VAT on property is a complex area of tax law and **specialist VAT on property advice should always be sought before a transaction is completed**.

34.2 Vatable Supplies of Property

Where property is supplied **for consideration in the course of business**, VAT at 13.5% applies to the following supplies:

■ Sale of a residential property by a developer or builder.
■ Supply of developed, but incomplete, property within 20 years of when the development ceased (referred to as the '20-year rule').
■ Supply of a developed completed property that is considered 'new' for VAT purposes.

Development, other than "minor development", essentially makes a property '**new**' for VAT purposes if it is either:

1. the first supply of a completed property supplied within five years of its completion (referred to as the 'five-year rule'); or
2. a second and subsequent supply of a property within five years of its completion if it has not been occupied for 24 months in total (the 'two-year rule').

Example 34.1

Eoin developed an office that was completed in August 2017. He sold it to Alan in November 2017 who occupied it immediately for his VAT-registered IT consultancy business.

This is a taxable supply as the first supply was made within five years of completion of the property. The sale is liable to VAT at 13.5%.

"Minor development" can be described as development that does not (and is not intended to) adapt the property for a materially altered use, provided that the cost of such development does not exceed 25% of the consideration for the (subsequent) supply of the property. For example, the conversion of a residential property for use as a medical clinic would be considered a materially altered use.

Example 34.2

James purchased a shop for €200,000 in 2017. In 2020 renovation works costing €100,000 were completed. James sold the shop to Kudos Ltd in 2021 for €500,000. Is the developed, completed property considered 'new' for VAT purposes?

No, the renovations are deemed to be minor development as the work did not adapt the property for a materially altered use and did not cost more than 25% of the sales price. Therefore, the sale is exempt from VAT.

If the renovation work had cost €150,000, the property would be considered 'new' for VAT purposes as the costs exceed 25% of the sales price. Accordingly, as the first supply is of a developed, completed property supplied within five years of its completion and considered 'new', the sale would be subject to VAT at 13.5%.

34.3 Exempt Supplies of Property

The following supplies of property are generally exempt:

- sale of undeveloped land;
- old, completed properties or buildings (greater than five years from completion);
- second-hand properties less than five years old and which have been occupied for more than two years; and
- sales of property not made in the course of a business, e.g. the sale of a private house by the homeowner.

Example 34.3

Following on from **Example 34.1**, Alan occupies the premises for three years until November 2020 when he decides to move to a larger premises. In March 2021 Alan sold the office to Paula, who runs a VAT-registered interior design service from the premises.

This is an exempt supply because although the sale was made within five years of completion of the property (August 2017), the property has been occupied for more than two years.

34.3.1 Option to Tax

Where a property is supplied when it is no longer considered new, the supply is exempt from VAT. The vendor is therefore not obliged to charge VAT. However, the seller and the purchaser may jointly **opt to tax** the supply if they are both carrying on businesses in the State. Where the option to tax is exercised, the purchaser must account for the VAT on the reverse charge basis.

> **Example 34.4**
>
> Following on from **Example 34.3** where the sale of the premises by Alan to Paula is exempt from VAT. If VAT is not charged on the sale, Alan may have to repay a significant portion of any VAT input credit he claimed when he purchased the property in 2017.
>
> If Alan and Paula jointly opt to tax the supply, as they are both carrying on businesses in the State, Alan will not have to repay any VAT claimed on the purchase of the premises. VAT will be charged at 13.5% on the sale and accounted for on the reverse charge basis by Paula thus having no impact on her cash flow.
>
> Therefore, in these circumstances, it is beneficial for Alan that he and Paula opt to tax the sale.

34.3.2 Letting of Property

The letting of property is not considered to be a supply of property. For VAT purposes, the letting of property is a service and is VAT-exempt.

34.4 Interaction with Stamp Duty

As outlined in **Chapter 10**, Section 10.4.2, where VAT is charged on the acquisition of a property, the **amount of consideration exclusive of VAT is liable to stamp duty**.

> **Example 34.5**
>
> In **Example 34.2**, Kudos Ltd purchased the shop in 2021 for €500,000. The stamp duty payable by on the purchase would be:
>
> | | |
> |---|---|
> | Consideration (excluding VAT) | €500,000 |
> | Stamp duty @ 7.5% | €37,500 |

Questions

Review Questions
(See Suggested Solutions to Review Questions at the end of this textbook.)

Question 34.1

Ciara Cawley bought a new house for €567,500, inclusive of VAT, from Doyle Construction Ltd on 11 September 2021.

Requirement
(a) Calculate the VAT charged by Doyle Construction Ltd.
(b) Advise Ciara as to the amount of stamp duty payable and the date by which it must be paid.

Question 34.2

Cosmos Ltd has recently agreed to purchase a warehouse in Dublin for €600,000 (exclusive of VAT) from Fuel Merchants Ltd. The warehouse was originally built in 2014 and used by Fuel Merchants Ltd and has not been developed since then. Cosmos Ltd has also agreed with a farmer in Dublin to buy an undeveloped field for €50,000 on which it intends to build a separate warehouse for use in its manufacturing business.

Requirement

(a) Advise Cosmos Ltd on the VAT implications arising on the purchase of the warehouse and the field, explaining your answer.

(b) Calculate the stamp duty arising on **both** acquisitions.

VAT: Advanced Aspects

Learning Objectives

After studying this chapter you will understand:

- The implications of a business making both taxable and exempt supplies.
- The concept and consequences of group registration for VAT.
- The availability of relief from VAT on the transfer of a business or business assets to an accountable person.

35.1 Partially Exempt VAT-registered Businesses

In general, a person who charges VAT on all of their supplies is entitled to reclaim VAT on expenses incurred in running the business. Conversely, a person who only makes VAT-exempt supplies is not entitled to recover any VAT incurred by them.

A VAT-registered business may be engaged in a variety of activities, some of which are liable to VAT and some of which are VAT-exempt. In such circumstances, the VAT input credits that such a business can claim will be restricted. The following rules are applied:

- VAT on purchases that are used solely for the VAT-registered business are available for full input credit.
- No VAT credit is available in respect of VAT on purchases used solely for exempt activities.
- For purchases relating to the general operation of the business, known as dual-use inputs, the taxpayer's turnover is used in the first instance to establish the VAT-apportionment rate. Where this method does not accurately reflect the use of inputs, the taxpayer may use another apportionment method.

Example 35.1

Variety Ltd had the following turnover:

Sale of taxable goods	€ 7m
Sale of exempt goods	€ 3m
Annual turnover	€10m

Variety Ltd's annual audit fee is €10,000 plus 23% VAT. The VAT payable = €10,000 × 23% = €2,300.

How much of the VAT paid on the audit fee can be recovered?

The audit fee is a dual-use input, so the input credit that can be claimed is:

Input credit recovery rate on dual-use inputs = €7m/€10m × 100% = 70%.
€2,300 × 70% = €1,610

35.2 Group Registration

Two or more persons can apply to Revenue to be included in a VAT group. This means that they are treated as a single taxable person for VAT purposes. In these circumstances, only one member of the group will submit VAT returns for the taxable period and that return will include **all activities** of all members of the group.

The granting of such an application is at the discretion of the Revenue Commissioners. Revenue will generally seek to ensure that the following conditions are satisfied before permitting VAT group registration:

- two or more persons established in the State and at least one of them is a taxable person;
- are closely bound by financial, economic and organisational links; and
- it is necessary or appropriate for the purposes of efficient and effective administration, including the collection of VAT.

As regards the parties to a VAT group, the following should be noted:

- a VAT group can contain individuals as well as corporate bodies;
- a VAT group may include a person involved in VAT-exempt activities;
- companies do not necessarily need to be in a legal group or corporation tax group to qualify;
- in rare situations, Revenue can oblige persons to form a VAT group.

Any persons wishing to form a VAT group must jointly apply in writing to the VAT section of their local Revenue district for approval. The approval must be formally granted and applies, generally, from the taxable period when granted. VAT group registration cannot be backdated. The issue of tax invoices in respect of inter-group transactions is not required.

35.2.1 Impact of Group Registration

The following points should be borne in mind when considering forming a VAT group as all are automatic once Revenue grants group registration:

- The group will nominate a single group remitter for VAT purposes who will be responsible for VAT compliance of the entire group. The remitter is the only entity in the group to file a VAT return.
- The group remitter must lodge all VAT returns and make all payments for the entire group with the Collector General.
- VAT invoices are not necessary in respect of transactions between individual group members. This facilitates cash flow within the group as it allows one member to pay another member without VAT arising. There is an exception in respect of issuing VAT invoices regarding supply of property within a VAT group (see below).
- All parties to the group are **jointly and severally liable** for all the VAT obligations of the other group members.
- All VAT invoices issued to third parties by a member of the group will show the VAT number of the group member making the supply.

> **Example 35.2**
>
> X Ltd and Y Ltd are both owned by Peter Jones. X Ltd is involved in VAT-exempt training, while Y Ltd is involved in providing consultancy services which are subject to VAT. Some administration work for X Ltd is carried out by Y Ltd and an invoice for €5,000 is issued every month to X Ltd by Y Ltd for the provision of these services.
>
> If X Ltd and Y Ltd are not in a VAT group, 23% VAT will apply to each invoice and X Ltd will not be able to recover the VAT as it is engaged in VAT-exempt activities. However, if both companies were in a VAT group, there would be no obligation to raise a VAT invoice resulting in a saving for X Ltd of €1,150 per month (€13,800 per annum).
>
> VAT group registration reduces the VAT recovery for the group as a whole. The members of the VAT group are deemed to be a single taxable person. Therefore, as X Ltd is VAT-exempt, Y Ltd's input VAT will be diluted.

35.2.2 Supply of Property within a VAT Group

The supply of property from one group member to another is excluded from the VAT group relief provisions. VAT must be charged on the intragroup supply of property if it is a vatable supply (see **Chapter 34**).

The member making the supply will issue a VAT invoice and the person purchasing the property will secure an input credit if appropriate. If the purchaser is entitled to 100% VAT recovery, no payment to Revenue should be required as the output VAT and input VAT will be recorded on the same VAT return. However, if the acquirer of the property is only entitled to 80% recovery, a payment will arise.

35.3   VAT and the Transfer of Business

When a VAT-registered business disposes of assets on which it has claimed a VAT input credit it must charge VAT to the purchaser. Transfer of business (TOB) is a relief from applying VAT on the transfer of a business or business assets to an accountable person as it deems no supply has taken place for VAT purposes. This is a useful relief on the transfer of an unincorporated business to a company (see **Chapter 7**).

VAT is **not** chargeable if all of the following conditions are satisfied:

- the purchaser is VAT registered, and
- the person acquiring the business is an accountable person, and
- the transfer must constitute an undertaking or part of an undertaking capable of being operated on an independent basis.

Where the conditions are satisfied, the transaction is deemed not to be a supply for VAT purposes. The relief is not optional – if the conditions are satisfied it is automatically applied. The relief applies even if the business or part of the business has ceased trading.

The third condition listed above, that the transfer is capable of being operated on an independent basis, refers to the fact that the trade and assets must be taken over:

- to carry on the same or a similar taxable business;
- for the purposes of the purchaser's own taxable business, following the cessation of the transferor's business; or
- to carry on a different taxable business in the premises using the assets acquired.

TOB relief is not available on the transfer of assets alone, e.g. the sale of stock-in-trade or a once-off sale of a fixed asset.

The transfer of a business by means of the transfer of **the shares in a company** is exempt from VAT in accordance with Schedule 1 of VATCA 2010.

Questions

Review Questions
(See Suggested Solutions to Review Questions at the end of this textbook.)

Question 35.1

Tom Clarke transferred a freehold commercial property to his trading company, Ekramot Ltd in January 2021. Both Tom and the company were in the same VAT group at the time. Tom owns 100% of the shares in Ekramot Ltd. Ekramot Ltd occupies the property for the purpose of its trade.

In October 2021, Tom is considering selling Ekramot Ltd and is approached by two potential buyers. Carla Hemmingway has offered to buy his shares while Sean Fitzhenry has offered to buy the assets in the company.

Requirement
Comment on the VAT issues arising.

Appendices

Taxation Reference Material for Tax Year 2021

Table of Contents

Income Tax, USC & PRSI

Table 1   Income Tax Rates 2021
Table 2   Non-refundable Tax Credits 2021
Table 3   Income Tax Allowances and Reliefs 2021
Table 4   Income Tax Exemption Limits for Persons Aged 65 and Over 2021
Table 5   Pension Contributions
Table 6   Preferential Loans
Table 7   Motor Car Benefit in Kind
Table 8   Motor Vehicle Category based on CO_2 Emissions
Table 9   Restricted Cost for Motor Lease Expenses
Table 10   Capital Allowances
Table 11   Civil Service Mileage and Subsistence Rates
Table 12   Universal Social Charge 2021
Table 13   PRSI 2021

Local Property Tax

Table 14   Valuation Table 2021
Table 15   Local Adjustment Factors 2021

Corporation Tax

Table 16   Corporation Tax Rates

Capital Gains Tax

Table 17   Rates and Annual Exemption
Table 18   Indexation Factors

VAT

Table 19   VAT Rates

Stamp Duty

Table 20   Rates 2021

Capital Acquistions Tax

Table 21   Rates
Table 22   Exemption Thresholds
Table 23   Limited Interest Factors

INCOME TAX, USC & PRSI

Income Tax Rates 2021

Single/Widowed/ Surviving Civil Partner with Qualifying Children	Rate	Single/Widowed/ Surviving Civil Partner without Qualifying Children	Rate	Married Couple/ Civil Partners	Rate
First €39,300	20%	First €35,300	20%	First €44,300/€70,600[1]	20%
Balance	40%	Balance	40%	Balance	40%

[1] Depending on personal circumstances of married couple/civil partners.

Non-refundable Tax Credits 2021

	Tax Credit
	€
Single person	1,650
Married couple/civil partners	3,300
Widowed person/surviving civil partner (year of bereavement)	3,300
Widowed person/surviving civil partner tax credit – no dependent children	2,190
Widowed person/surviving civil partner tax credit – with dependent children	1,650
Single Person Child Carer Credit (additional)	1,650
Widowed parent/surviving civil partner tax credit – with dependent children	
Year 1 after the year of bereavement	3,600
Year 2 after the year of bereavement	3,150
Year 3 after the year of bereavement	2,700
Year 4 after the year of bereavement	2,250
Year 5 after the year of bereavement	1,800
Employee tax credit	1,650
Earned Income Tax Credit	1,650
Fisher Tax Credit (maximum)	1,270
Age tax credit – single/widowed/surviving civil partner	245
Age tax credit – married/civil partners	490
Incapacitated child tax credit	3,300
Dependent relative – income limit €15,740	245
Home carer's credit – income limit €7,200 (lower)/ €10,400 (upper)	1,600
Blind person	1,650
Both spouses/civil partners blind	3,300
Third-level education fees[1]:	
Full-time course	800
Part-time course	1,100

[1] There is a maximum level of qualifying fees, per academic year, of €7,000 per student, per course, subject to the first €3,000 (full-time) or €1,500 (part-time) being disallowed (per claim, not per course). Relief is at the standard rate of tax on the amount of the qualifying fees.

Income Tax Allowances and Reliefs 2021

Deduction for employed person taking care of incapacitated person (maximum)	– €75,000
Provision of childcare services	– income limit €15,000
Rent-a-Room relief (maximum)	– €14,000

Income Tax Exemption Limits for Persons Aged 65 and Over 2021

	€
Single/widowed/surviving civil partner	18,000[1]
Married/civil partners	36,000[1]

[1] Dependent children: increase exemption by €575 for each of first two, and by €830 for each additional child.

Pension Contributions

The maximum amount on which tax relief may be claimed in 2021 in respect of qualifying premiums is as follows:

Age	% of Net Relevant Earnings[1]
Under 30 years of age	15%
30 to 39 years of age	20%
40 to 49 years of age	25%
50 to 54 years of age	30%
55 to 59 years of age	35%
60 years and over	40%

[1] The earnings cap for 2021 on net relevant earnings is €115,000.

Preferential Loans

The specified rates for 2021 are:

- 4% in respect of qualifying home loans;
- 13.5% in respect of all other loans.

Motor Car Benefit in Kind

Annual Business Kilometres	Cash Equivalent (% of OMV)
24,000 or less	30%
24,001–32,000	24%
32,001–40,000	18%
40,001–48,000	12%
48,001 and over	6%

Motor Vehicle Category Based on CO_2 Emissions

Vehicle Category	CO_2 Emissions (CO_2 g/km)
A, B and C	0g/km up to and including 155g/km
D and E	156g/km up to and including 190g/km
F and G	191g/km and upwards

Restricted Cost for Motor Lease Expenses

Restricted Cost of Passenger Motor Vehicle for Capital Allowances and Motor Leases Expenses Restriction Purposes

Specified Limit	€
From 1 January 2007	24,000

Restricted Cost for Motor Vehicles bought on/after 1 July 2008

Category	CO_2 Emissions	Restriction
A	0–120g/km	Use the specified amount regardless of cost.
B and C	121–155g/km	
D and E	156–190g/km	Two steps to calculate limit: 1. take the lower of the specified limit or cost; 2. limit is 50% of this amount.
F and G	191+g/km	No allowance available.

Capital Allowances

Plant and Machinery

Expenditure incurred on or after 4 December 2002:

Plant and machinery	12.5% straight-line
Cars other than those used as a taxi or in car-hire business	12.5% straight-line

Industrial Buildings

Expenditure incurred on or after 1 April 1992	4% straight-line

Civil Service Mileage and Subsistence Rates

Motor Car Travel Rates (effective from 1 April 2017)

Official Motor Travel in a calendar year	Engine Capacity		
	Up to 1,200cc	1,201cc–1,500cc	1,501cc and over
0–1,500km	37.95 cent per km	39.86 cent per km	44.79 cent per km
1,501–5,500km	70.00 cent per km	73.21 cent per km	83.53 cent per km
5,501–25,000km	27.55 cent per km	29.03 cent per km	32.21 cent per km
Over 25,001km	21.36 cent per km	22.23 cent per km	25.85 cent per km

Motor Cycle Travel Rates

Official Motor Travel in a calendar year	Engine Capacity			
	Up to 150cc	151cc to 250cc	251cc to 600cc	601cc and over
Up to 6,437km	14.48 cent per km	20.10 cent per km	23.72 cent per km	28.59 cent per km
Over 6,437km	9.37 cent per km	13.31 cent per km	15.29 cent per km	17.60 cent per km

Subsistence Rates

Overnight Allowances[1] (from 1 October 2018)			Day Allowances[2] (from 1 July 2019)	
Normal rate (up to 14 nights)	Reduced rate (next 14 nights)	Detention rate (next 28 nights)	10 hours or more	5 hours (but less than 10 hours)
€147.00	€132.30	€73.50	€36.97	€15.41

[1] Night allowance: the employee is at least 100km away from their home or place of work and covers a period of up to 24 hours from the time of departure, and any further period not exceeding five hours.

[2] Day allowance: the employee is at least 8km away from their home or normal place of work.

Universal Social Charge 2021

Employment Income

The rates of USC (where gross income is greater than €13,000 per annum) are:

Rate of USC	Annual Income	Monthly Income	Weekly Income
0.5%	First €12,012	First €1,001	First €231
2.0%	€12,013–€20,687	€1,002–€1,724	€232–€398
4.5%[1,2]	€20,688–€70,044	€1,725–€5,837	€399–€1,347
8.0%[1,2]	Balance	Balance	Balance

[1] Persons aged 70 years and over with income of €60,000 or less are not liable at the 4.5%/8% rates but instead pay at 2.0%.

[2] Persons who hold a full medical card and with income of €60,000 or less are not liable at the 4.5% or 8% rates but instead pay at 2.0%.

Exempt Categories

- Where an individual's total income for a year does not exceed €13,000.
- All Department of Social Protection payments.
- Income already subjected to DIRT.

Self-assessed Individuals

The rates of USC (where gross income is greater than €13,000 per annum) are:

	Aged under 70/Aged 70 and over with income >€60,000/Full medical card holder with income >€60,000	Aged 70 and over with income of €60,000 or less/Full medical card holder with income of €60,000 or less
First €12,012	0.5%	0.5%
Next €8,675	2.0%	2.0%
Next €49,357	4.5%	2.0% (max. €39,313)
Balance[1]	8.0%	N/A

[1] An additional USC charge of 3% is payable by individuals on self-assessed income (excluding employment income) in excess of €100,000 in a year, regardless of age.

Surcharge on Use of Property Incentives

There is also an additional USC surcharge of 5% on investors with gross income greater than €100,000 where certain property tax reliefs have been used to shelter taxable income.

PRSI 2021

Employees' and Employers' Rates

Employee's income	Employee rate	Employers' rate
Income of €38–€352 per week	Nil	8.8%
Income of €352–€398 per week	4%	8.8%
Income greater than €399 per week	4%	11.05%

Employee PRSI Credit

An employee PRSI credit of a maximum of €12 per week is available to Class A employees with gross earnings between €352.01 and €424 per week. The credit is reduced by one-sixth of gross earnings in excess of €352 per week. The reduced credit is then deducted from the employee PRSI liability calculated at 4% of gross weekly earnings.

Self-employed

Individuals in receipt of income of €5,000 or less in 2021 will not be subject to PRSI. Where income is greater than €5,000, PRSI at 4% is payable subject to a minimum contribution of €500. For those with an annual self-employed income of in excess of €5,000 but who have no net liability to tax, the minimum contribution is €300 for 2021.

LOCAL PROPERTY TAX

Valuation Table 2021

Valuation Band Number	Valuation Band €	Mid-point of Valuation Band €	LPT in 2021 (full-year charge) €
01	0 to 100,000	50,000	90
02	100,001 to 150,000	125,000	225
03	150,001 to 200,000	175,000	315
04	200,001 to 250,000	225,000	405
05	250,001 to 300,000	275,000	495
06	300,001 to 350,000	325,000	585
07	350,001 to 400,000	375,000	675
08	400,001 to 450,000	425,000	765
09	450,001 to 500,000	475,000	855
10	500,001 to 550,000	525,000	945
11	550,001 to 600,000	575,000	1,035
12	600,001 to 650,000	625,000	1,125

continued overleaf

Valuation Band Number	Valuation Band €	Mid-point of Valuation Band €	LPT in 2021 (full-year charge) €
13	650,001 to 700,000	675,000	1,215
14	700,001 to 750,000	725,000	1,305
15	750,001 to 800,000	775,000	1,395
16	800,001 to 850,000	825,000	1,485
17	850,001 to 900,000	875,000	1,575
18	900,001 to 950,000	925,000	1,665
19	950,001 to 1,000,000*	975,000	1,755

*Residential properties valued over €1 million will be assessed at the actual value at 0.18% on the first €1 million in value and 0.25% on the portion of the value above €1 million (no banding will apply).

Local Adjustment Factors 2021

The local adjustment factor (LAF) increasing or decreasing the basic LPT rate in operation for 2021:

Local Authority	LPT Rate Adjustment
Carlow County Council	5% increase
Cavan County Council	15% increase
Clare County Council	15% increase
Cork City Council	7.5% increase
Cork County Council	7.5% increase
Donegal County Council	15% increase
Dublin City Council	15% decrease
Fingal County Council	10% decrease
Kerry County Council	7.5% increase
Kildare County Council	7.5% increase
Kilkenny County Council	15% increase
Laois County Council	10% increase
Leitrim County Council	15% increase
Limerick City and County Council	15% increase
Longford County Council	15% increase
Mayo County Council	10% increase
Monaghan County Council	15% increase
Offaly County Council	15% increase
Roscommon County Council	15% increase
Sligo County Council	15% increase
South Dublin County Council	15% decrease
Tipperary County Council	10% increase
Waterford City and County Council	10% increase
Westmeath County Council	15% increase
Wexford County Council	10% increase

CORPORATION TAX

Rates of Corporation Tax

Trading Rate of Corporation Tax

The trading rate of corporation tax is **12.5**% and applies to the following income and gains:

- Schedule D, Case I and Case II profits;
- capital gains (as adjusted); and
- certain foreign dividends.

Passive Rate of Corporation Tax

The passive rate of corporation tax is 25% applies to the following sources of income:

- Case III income, i.e. foreign income and untaxed Irish interest (excluding certain foreign dividends taxable at 12.5%);
- Case IV income, i.e. taxed Irish income and miscellaneous income not taxed under any other Case of Schedule D;
- Case V income, i.e. Irish rental income; and
- income from an "excepted trade".

CAPITAL GAINS TAX

Rates and Annual Exemption

	Rate
Disposals on or after 6 December 2012	33%
Disposals on or after 7 December 2011 and before 6 December 2012	30%
Disposals on or after 8 April 2009 and before 7 December 2011	25%
Annual exempt amount for 2021 is €1,270	

Where revised entrepreneur relief applies:

Disposals on or after 1 January 2017	10%
Disposals on or after 1 January 2016 and before 1 January 2017 20%	20%

Indexation Factors

Year of Assessment in which Expenditure Incurred	5 April 1997	5 April 1998	5 April 1999	5 April 2000	5 April 2001	31 Dec 2001	31 Dec 2002	31 Dec 2003 et seq.
1974/75	6.017	6.112	6.215	6.313	6.582	6.930	7.180	7.528
1975/76	4.860	4.936	5.020	5.099	5.316	5.597	5.799	6.080
1976/77	4.187	4.253	4.325	4.393	4.580	4.822	4.996	5.238
1977/78	3.589	3.646	3.707	3.766	3.926	4.133	4.283	4.490
1978/79	3.316	3.368	3.425	3.479	3.627	3.819	3.956	4.148
1979/80	2.992	3.039	3.090	3.139	3.272	3.445	3.570	3.742
1980/81	2.590	2.631	2.675	2.718	2.833	2.983	3.091	3.240
1981/82	2.141	2.174	2.211	2.246	2.342	2.465	2.554	2.678
1982/83	1.801	1.829	1.860	1.890	1.970	2.074	2.149	2.253
1983/84	1.601	1.627	1.654	1.680	1.752	1.844	1.911	2.003
1984/85	1.454	1.477	1.502	1.525	1.590	1.674	1.735	1.819
1985/86	1.369	1.390	1.414	1.436	1.497	1.577	1.633	1.713
1986/87	1.309	1.330	1.352	1.373	1.432	1.507	1.562	1.637
1987/88	1.266	1.285	1.307	1.328	1.384	1.457	1.510	1.583
1988/89	1.242	1.261	1.282	1.303	1.358	1.430	1.481	1.553
1989/90	1.202	1.221	1.241	1.261	1.314	1.384	1.434	1.503
1990/91	1.153	1.171	1.191	1.210	1.261	1.328	1.376	1.442
1991/92	1.124	1.142	1.161	1.179	1.229	1.294	1.341	1.406
1992/93	1.084	1.101	1.120	1.138	1.186	1.249	1.294	1.356
1993/94	1.064	1.081	1.099	1.117	1.164	1.226	1.270	1.331
1994/95	1.046	1.063	1.081	1.098	1.144	1.205	1.248	1.309
1995/96	1.021	1.037	1.054	1.071	1.116	1.175	1.218	1.277
1996/97	-	1.016	1.033	1.050	1.094	1.152	1.194	1.251
1997/98	-	-	1.017	1.033	1.077	1.134	1.175	1.232
1998/99	-	-	-	1.016	1.059	1.115	1.156	1.212
1999/00	-	-	-	-	1.043	1.098	1.138	1.193
2000/01	-	-	-	-	-	1.053	1.091	1.144
2001	-	-	-	-	-	-	1.037	1.087
2002	-	-	-	-	-	-	-	1.049
2003 et seq.	-	-	-	-	-	-	-	1.000

Multiplier for Disposal in Period Ended

VAT

VAT Rate	Examples
Exempt	▪ Medical, dental and optical services ▪ Insurance services ▪ Certain banking services ▪ Educational services ▪ Funeral services ▪ Gambling and lotteries ▪ Transport of passengers (and their baggage) ▪ Certain lettings of immovable goods
Zero rate	▪ Supply of most foodstuffs (excluding those specifically liable at the standard rate) ▪ Printed books and booklets (excluding stationery, brochures, etc.) ▪ Most clothing and footwear for children under 11 years of age ▪ Oral medicine (excluding food supplements) ▪ Exported goods (i.e. despatched outside the EU) ▪ Sea-going ships (more than 15 tonnes) ▪ Fertilizer ▪ Animal feed, other than pet food
Standard rate (23%)	All goods and services that are not exempt or zero-rated, or are not liable at the other specific rates. Includes: ▪ Alcohol, soft drinks, bottled drinking water, juices ▪ Chocolate and confectionery, biscuits, crisps, ice cream and similar ▪ Adult clothing and footwear ▪ Office equipment and stationery
Reduced rate (13.5%)	▪ Fuel for power and heating (coal, peat, etc.) ▪ Supply of electricity and gas ▪ Waste disposal services ▪ Non-residential immovable goods, including supply and development ▪ Supply of concrete and concrete goods ▪ Repair and maintenance of movable goods ▪ General agricultural and veterinary services ▪ Short-term hire of cars, boats, caravans, etc. ▪ Food supplements ▪ Driving instruction ▪ Supply and hire of live horses and greyhounds
Second reduced rate (9%)	▪ Subscriptions for certain sporting activities ▪ Hairdressing services ▪ Printed newspapers, e-newspapers, magazines and periodicals and e-books ▪ Supply of hot food, including take-away food ▪ Hotel/holiday accommodation, including caravan parks and camping sites ▪ Admission to cinemas, theatres, certain musical performances, museums and fairground amusements
Farmer flat-rate addition (5.6%)	Supply of agricultural products and services by non-VAT-registered farmers to VAT-registered customers
Livestock rate (4.8%)	▪ Supply of livestock ▪ Supply of horses intended for foodstuffs

STAMP DUTY

Rates 2021

	Rate
Shares	1%
Residential property:	
Consideration up to €1m	1%
Excess over €1m	2%
10 or more houses/duplexes in 12 months*	10%
Non-residential property	7.5%

* With effect from 20 May 2021.

CAPITAL ACQUISITIONS TAX

Rates

	Rate
Benefits taken on or after 6 December 2012	33%
Benefits taken on or after 7 December 2011 and before 6 December 2012	30%
Benefits taken on or after 8 April 2009 and before 7 December 2011	25%

Exemption Thresholds

	Group Threshold		
	A	B	C
Benefits taken on or after 9 October 2019	335,000	32,500	16,250
Benefits taken on or after 10 October 2018	320,000	32,500	16,250
Benefits taken on or after 12 October 2016	310,000	32,500	16,250
Benefits taken on or after 14 October 2015 and before 12 October 2016	280,000	30,150	15,075
Benefits taken on or after 6 December 2012 and before 14 October 2015	225,000	30,150	15,075
Benefits taken on or after 7 December 2011 and before 6 December 2012	250,000	33,500	16,750
Benefits taken on or after 8 December 2010 and before 7 December 2011	332,084	33,208	16,604

Limited Interest Factors

Table A

1	2	3	4
Years of Age	Joint Factor	Value of an interest in a capital of €1 for a **male** life aged as in Column 1	Value of an interest in a capital of €1 for a **female** life aged as in Column 1
0	.99	.9519	.9624
1	.99	.9767	.9817
2	.99	.9767	.9819

continued overleaf

1	2	3	4
Years of Age	Joint Factor	Value of an interest in a capital of €1 for a **male** life aged as in Column 1	Value of an interest in a capital of €1 for a **female** life aged as in Column 1
3	.99	.9762	.9817
4	.99	.9753	.9811
5	.99	.9742	.9805
6	.99	.9730	.9797
7	.99	.9717	.9787
8	.99	.9703	.9777
9	.99	.9688	.9765
10	.99	.9671	.9753
11	.98	.9653	.9740
12	.98	.9634	.9726
13	.98	.9614	.9710
14	.98	.9592	.9693
15	.98	.9569	.9676
16	.98	.9546	.9657
17	.98	.9522	.9638
18	.98	.9497	.9617
19	.98	.9471	.9596
20	.97	.9444	.9572
21	.97	.9416	.9547
22	.97	.9387	.9521
23	.97	.9356	.9493
24	.97	.9323	.9464
25	.97	.9288	.9432
26	.97	.9250	.9399
27	.97	.9209	.9364
28	.97	.9165	.9328
29	.97	.9119	.9289
30	.96	.9068	.9248
31	.96	.9015	.9205
32	.96	.8958	.9159
33	.96	.8899	.9111
34	.96	.8836	.9059

continued overleaf

1	2	3	4
Years of Age	Joint Factor	Value of an interest in a capital of €1 for a **male** life aged as in Column 1	Value of an interest in a capital of €1 for a **female** life aged as in Column 1
35	.96	.8770	.9005
36	.96	.8699	.8947
37	.96	.8626	.8886
38	.95	.8549	.8821
39	.95	.8469	.8753
40	.95	.8384	.8683
41	.95	.8296	.8610
42	.95	.8204	.8534
43	.95	.8107	.8454
44	.94	.8005	.8370
45	.94	.7897	.8283
46	.94	.7783	.8192
47	.94	.7663	.8096
48	.93	.7541	.7997
49	.93	.7415	.7896
50	.92	.7287	.7791
51	.91	.7156	.7683
52	.90	.7024	.7572
53	.89	.6887	.7456
54	.89	.6745	.7335
55	.88	.6598	.7206
56	.88	.6445	.7069
57	.88	.6288	.6926
58	.87	.6129	.6778
59	.86	.5969	.6628
60	.86	.5809	.6475
61	.86	.5650	.6320
62	.86	.5492	.6162
63	.85	.5332	.6000
64	.85	.5171	.5830

continued overleaf

1	2	3	4
Years of Age	Joint Factor	Value of an interest in a capital of €1 for a **male** life aged as in Column 1	Value of an interest in a capital of €1 for a **female** life aged as in Column 1
65	.85	.5007	.5650
66	.85	.4841	.5462
67	.84	.4673	.5266
68	.84	.4506	.5070
69	.84	.4339	.4873
70	.83	.4173	.4679
71	.83	.4009	.4488
72	.82	.3846	.4301
73	.82	.3683	.4114
74	.81	.3519	.3928
75	.80	.3352	.3743
76	.79	.3181	.3559
77	.78	.3009	.3377
78	.76	.2838	.3198
79	.74	.2671	.3023
80	.72	.2509	.2855
81	.71	.2353	.2693
82	.70	.2203	.2538
83	.69	.2057	.2387
84	.68	.1916	.2242
85	.67	.1783	.2104
86	.66	.1657	.1973
87	.65	.1537	.1849
88	.64	.1423	.1730
89	.62	.1315	.1616
90	.60	.1212	.1509
91	.58	.1116	.1407
92	.56	.1025	.1310
93	.54	.0939	.1218
94	.52	.0858	.1132
95	.50	.0781	.1050
96	.49	.0710	.0972

continued overleaf

1	2	3	4
Years of Age	Joint Factor	Value of an interest in a capital of €1 for a **male** life aged as in Column 1	Value of an interest in a capital of €1 for a **female** life aged as in Column 1
97	.48	.0642	.0898
98	.47	.0578	.0828
99	.45	.0517	.0762
100 or over	.43	.0458	.0698

Table B

(Column 2 shows the value of an interest in a capital of €1 for the number of years shown in Column 1.)

1	2	1	2
Number of years	Value	Number of years	Value
1	.0654	26	.8263
2	.1265	27	.8375
3	.1836	28	.8480
4	.2370	29	.8578
5	.2869	30	.8669
6	.3335	31	.8754
7	.3770	32	.8834
8	.4177	33	.8908
9	.4557	34	.8978
10	.4913	35	.9043
11	.5245	36	.9100
12	.5555	37	.9165
13	.5845	38	.9230
14	.6116	39	.9295
15	.6369	40	.9360
16	.6605	41	.9425
17	.6826	42	.9490
18	.7032	43	.9555
19	.7225	44	.9620
20	.7405	45	.9685
21	.7574	46	.9750
22	.7731	47	.9815
23	.7878	48	.9880
24	.8015	49	.9945
25	.8144	50 and over	1.000

Taxation and the *Code of Ethics*

Under Chartered Accountants Ireland's *Code of Ethics*, a Chartered Accountant shall comply with the following fundamental principles:

(a) **Integrity** – to be straightforward and honest in all professional and business relationships.
(b) **Objectivity** – to not compromise professional or business judgments because of bias, conflict of interest or undue influence of others.
(c) **Professional Competence and Due Care** – to attain and maintain professional knowledge and skill at the level required to ensure that a client or employing organisation receives competent professional services based on current technical and professional standards and relevant legislation; and to act diligently and in accordance with applicable technical and professional standards.
(d) **Confidentiality** – to respect the confidentiality of information acquired as a result of professional and business relationships and, therefore, not disclose any such information to third parties without proper and specific authority, unless there is a legal or professional right or duty to disclose, nor use the information for the personal advantage of the professional accountant or third parties.
(e) **Professional Behaviour** – to comply with relevant laws and regulations and avoid any conduct that the professional accountant knows or should know might discredit the profession.

The Institute's "Five Fundamental Principles, Five Practical Steps" is a useful resource for members and students and is available at www.charteredaccountants.ie. As a Chartered Accountant, you will have to ensure that your dealings with the tax aspects of your professional life are also in compliance with these fundamental principles. You may be asked to define or list the principles and also be able to identify where these ethical issues might arise and how you would deal with them.

Examples of situations that could arise where these principles are challenged in the context of tax are outlined below:

Example 1

You are working in the Tax Department of ABC & Co and your manager is Jack Wilson. He comes over to your desk after his meeting with Peter Foley. He gives you all the papers that Peter has left with him. He asks you to draft Peter's tax return. You know who Peter is as you are now living in a house that your friend, Ann, leased from Peter. As you complete the return, you note that there is no information regarding rental income. What should you do?

Action

As a person with integrity, you should explain to your manager, Jack, that your friend, Ann, has leased property from Peter and that he has forgotten to send details of his rental income and expenses. As Peter sent the information to Jack, it is appropriate for Jack to contact Peter for details regarding rental income and related expenses.

Example 2

You are working in the Tax Department of the Irish subsidiary of a US-owned multinational. You are preparing the corporation tax computation, including the R&D tax credit due. You have not received some information from your colleagues dealing with R&D and cannot finalise the claim for R&D tax credit until you receive this information. Your manager is under pressure and tells you to just file the claim on the basis of what will maximise the claim. He says, "It is self-assessment, and the chance of this ever being audited or enquired into is zero." What should you do?

Action

You should act in a professional and objective manner. This means that you cannot do as your manager wants. You should explain to him that you will contact the person in R&D again and finalise the claim as quickly as possible.

Example 3

Anna O'Shea, Financial Controller of Great Client Ltd, rings you regarding a VAT issue. You have great respect for Anna and are delighted that she is ringing you directly instead of your manager. She says that it is a very straightforward query. However, as you listen to her, you realise that you are pretty sure of the answer but would need to check a point before answering. What should you do?

Action

Where you do not know the answer, it is professionally competent to explain that you need to check a point before you give an answer. If you like, you can explain which aspect you need to check. Your client will appreciate you acting professionally rather than giving incorrect information or advice.

Example 4

The phone rings, and it is Darren O'Brien, your best friend, who works for Just-do-it Ltd. After discussing the match you both watched on the television last night, Darren explains why he is ringing you. He has heard that Success Ltd, a client of your Tax Department, has made R&D tax credit claims. Therefore, you must have details regarding its R&D. Darren's relationship with his boss is not great at present, and he knows that if he could get certain data about Success Ltd, his relationship with his boss would improve. He explains that he does not want any financial information, just some small details regarding R&D. What should you do?

Action

You should not give him the information. No matter how good a friend he is, it is unethical to give confidential information about your client to him.

Example 5

It is the Friday morning before a bank holiday weekend and you are due to travel from Dublin to west Cork, after work, for the weekend. Your manager has been on annual leave for the last week. He left you work to do for the week, including researching a tax issue for a client. He advised you that you were to have an answer to the issue, no matter how long it took. It actually took you a very short time and you have it all documented for him.

Your friend who is travelling with you asks if you could leave at 11am to beat the traffic and have a longer weekend. You have no annual leave left, so you cannot take leave. You know that if you leave, nobody will notice, but you have to complete a timesheet. Your friend reminds you that the research for the client could have taken a lot longer and that you could code the five hours to the client. What should you do?

Action

It would be unprofessional behaviour and would show a lack of integrity if you were to charge your client for those five hours.

Tax Planning, Tax Avoidance and Tax Evasion

The global financial and economic crash of 2008 and the ensuing worldwide recession led to a fall in tax collected by many governments and moved tax and tax transparency higher up the agenda. Subsequent events further increased the focus and attention of the wider public – as well as governments – on both tax avoidance and the evasion of taxes: the revelations in the 'Paradise Papers' and the 'Panama Papers', the EU's state aid decision against Ireland and Apple Inc., coupled with the 'tax-shaming' of many multinational brand names and famous people has led to tax, and tax ethics, appearing in media headlines almost on a daily basis. As a result, a number of international and domestic initiatives have dramatically changed the tax planning and tax compliance landscape and brought tax transparency to the fore in many businesses and boardrooms.

The tax liability of an individual, partnership, trust or company can be reduced by tax planning, tax avoidance or tax evasion. Although the overriding objective of each is to reduce the taxpayer's tax bill, the method each adopts to do so is different. Each is also vastly different from an ethical and technical perspective.

Tax receipts are used to fund public services such as education, hospitals and roads. Individuals and businesses in a country benefit from these services directly and indirectly and it is therefore seen as a social and ethical responsibility for them to pay their fair share of taxes. Evading or avoiding paying your taxes is viewed as unacceptable as a result.

Tax Planning

Tax planning is used by taxpayers to reduce their tax bill by making use of provisions within domestic tax legislation. For example, any company with good tax governance will seek to minimise its tax liability by using the tools and mechanisms – allowances, deductions, reliefs and exemptions for example – made available to them by the government.

Planning can also take the form of simple decisions, such as delaying disposal of an asset when a fall in the rate of capital gains tax is expected so that the person pays a lower rate of tax on its taxable profits. Or a taxpayer may consider what type of assets to buy to maximise capital allowances. Any tax planning decision should work, not just from a tax planning and legislative perspective, but it should also be commercially feasible.

The Irish government accepts that all taxpayers are entitled to organise their affairs in such a way as to mitigate their tax liability – as long as they do so within the law and within the spirit in which government intended when setting the law. Tax planning is both legally and ethically acceptable.

Tax Avoidance

Tax avoidance is often viewed as a grey area because it is regularly confused with tax planning. Tax avoidance is the use of loopholes within tax legislation to reduce the taxpayer's tax liability. Although tax avoidance may seem similar to tax planning, as the taxpayer is using tax law to reduce their overall tax burden, the taxpayer is using tax legislation in a way not intended, or anticipated, by government.

TCA 1997 section 811C provides general anti-avoidance legislation. A transaction shall be a tax avoidance transaction if it would be reasonable to consider that the transaction gives rise to a tax advantage and it was not undertaken primarily for purposes other than to give rise to a tax advantage. These provisions are designed to counteract certain transactions which have little or no commercial reality but are carried out primarily to create an artificial tax deduction or to avoid or reduce a tax charge.

In addition, TCA 1997 sections 817D–817T provide mandatory disclosure of certain transactions that could result in a tax advantage. The regime seeks to force advisors, promoters and taxpayers who implement schemes designed to procure a tax advantage, to inform Revenue of the details of such schemes. The mandatory disclosure regime also has penalties for advisers who do not comply. The users of such schemes are also required to notify Revenue that they have used a particular scheme by including the scheme notification number on the relevant tax return or submission.

While tax avoidance is arguably legal, it is generally viewed as ethically unacceptable behaviour. Tax avoidance behaviour that is successfully challenged by Revenue will lead to the original tax saving being paid, in addition to interest and penalties.

Tax Evasion

At the extreme end of the spectrum is tax evasion. Tax evasion involves breaking the law deliberately and either not paying any of the taxes that fall due or underpaying the taxes that fall due when the law clearly states that they must be paid. Tax evaders intend to deliberately break rules surrounding their tax position in order to avoid paying the correct amount of tax they owe.

A tax evader illegally reduces their tax burden, either by a misrepresentation to Revenue or by not filing tax returns at all, thereby concealing the true state of their tax affairs. Tax evasion can include onshore (within the State) and offshore deliberate behaviour.

Examples of tax evasion include, *inter alia*:

- failure to file a tax return and pay the relevant tax arising;
- failure to declare the correct income;
- deliberately inflating expenses, which reduces taxable profits or increases a loss;
- hiding taxable assets;
- wrongly claiming a tax refund or repayment by being dishonest;
- not telling Revenue about a source of income;
- not operating a PAYE scheme for employees/pensioners;
- not registering for VAT when required to do so; and
- deliberate submission of incorrect or false information.

In all cases the Exchequer suffers a loss of tax. This is known as tax fraud. Tax evasion, and the tax fraud that flows from this behavior, is a criminal offence prosecutable by Revenue. It is viewed as ethically unacceptable behaviour. The error will generally fall into the "deliberate behavior" resulting in the original tax saving being paid, in addition to interest and penalties.

Suggested Solutions
to Review Questions

Chapter 1

Question 1.1

Dear Glen and Ursula,

I refer to our conversation regarding your recent discovery of an understatement of the company's corporation tax liability as filed with Revenue. Please see my comments below.

As directors of the company you have a duty to disclose the error to Revenue. I would recommend that you contact Revenue as soon as possible to advise of the error and to pay the additional tax liability, the interest chargeable on that amount and any penalties arising. In doing so you will be making an unprompted qualifying disclosure, which will mitigate any penalties that may arise.

With regard to the penalties that may be applied, there are two possibilities:

1. Revenue could deem the underpayment to be an 'innocent error'. In such situations, where the tax default was not deliberate and not attributable to a failure to take reasonable care to comply with a company's tax obligations, then no penalty will be payable. In deciding this, Revenue would look at other factors, such as whether your tax files are in order, your other tax obligations are up to date and your previous tax compliance.

   Although no penalty would be charged in this situation, the company would still be liable to the interest owing on the underpayment of tax. The interest would be calculated from the day the tax was originally due until the day the liability is cleared.

2. If not deemed an innocent error, a penalty would be applied. Penalties are tax geared with the penalty being expressed as a percentage of the tax payable. Revenue's penalty regime uses the following categorisation:
   - careless behaviour – penalty calculated as 20% of the tax amount owing;
   - careless behaviour with significant consequences – penalty calculated as 40% of the tax amount owing; or
   - deliberate behaviour – 100% of the tax amount owing is charged as the penalty.

These penalties can be mitigated by informing Revenue of the error, i.e. making an unprompted or prompted disclosure, and by your level of co-operation. Informing Revenue before they bring the matter to your attention would be an unprompted disclosure. If the matter was considered to be only careless behaviour, and if you were to fully co-operate with the investigation, the penalty could be reduced to 3% of the tax owing (instead of 20%).

If Revenue discover the error before you inform them, you will be issued an audit notice and asked if you would like to make a disclosure (a prompted disclosure). In which case, if it was only careless behaviour, and again if you fully co-operated, the penalty could be reduced to 10% of the tax owing.

As Revenue has not issued an audit notice into any aspect of the return, an unprompted disclosure could still be made by the company, which would maximise the mitigation of any penalties that might be imposed.

If I can be of any further assistance, please let me know.

Yours sincerely,

Chapter 2

Question 2.1

(a) **2019**
    TEST 1: Did Hank spend more than 30 days in Ireland in 2019?
        ANSWER: Yes, 226 days. Therefore, go to Test 2.
    TEST 2: Did Hank spend 183 days or more in Ireland in 2019?
        ANSWER: Yes; therefore, Hank is Irish resident for 2019.

(b) **2020**
    TEST 1: Did Hank spend more than 30 days in Ireland in 2020?
        ANSWER: Yes, the full year. Therefore, go to Test 2.
    TEST 2:Did Hank spend 183 days or more in Ireland in 2020?
        ANSWER: Yes, the full year. Therefore, Hank is Irish resident in 2020.

(c) **2021**
    TEST 1:Did Hank spend more than 30 days in Ireland in 2021?
        ANSWER: Yes, 122 days. Therefore, go to Test 2.
    TEST 2: Did Hank spend 183 days or more in Ireland in 2021?
        ANSWER: No. Therefore, go to Test 3.
    TEST 3: Did Hank spend more than 30 days in Ireland in 2020?
        ANSWER: Yes, the full year. Therefore, go to Test 4.
    TEST 4: Did Hank spend at least 280 days in Ireland in 2021 and 2020?

Number of days in Ireland in 2021	121
Number of days in Ireland in 2020	<u>366</u>
Total days in Ireland in current and previous years	487

        ANSWER: Yes. Therefore, Hank is Irish resident in 2021.

Question 2.2

(a) **2018**
    TEST 1: Did Kenji spend more than 30 days in Ireland in 2018?
        ANSWER: No, 15 days. Therefore, Kenji is not Irish resident for 2018.

(b) **2019**
    TEST 1: Did Kenji spend more than 30 days in Ireland in 2019?
        ANSWER: Yes, the full year. Therefore, go to Test 2.
    TEST 2: Did Kenji spend 183 days or more in Ireland in 2019?
        ANSWER: Yes. Therefore Kenji is Irish resident in 2019.

(c) **2020**
 TEST 1: Did Kenji spend more than 30 days in Ireland in 2020?
  ANSWER: Yes, the full year. Therefore, go to Test 2.
 TEST 2: Did Kenji spend 183 days or more in Ireland in 2020?
  ANSWER: Yes. Therefore Kenji is Irish resident in 2020.
(d) **2021**
 TEST 1: Did Kenji spend more than 30 days in Ireland in 2021?
  ANSWER: No, 16 days. Therefore, Kenji is not Irish resident in 2021.

Question 2.3

Tax Year	Resident	Ordinarily Resident
2018	Yes ≥ 183 days	No
2019	Yes ≥ 183 days	No
2020	Yes ≥ 183 days	No
2021	No – fails 30-day test	Yes, as resident for three preceding years

Chapter 3

Question 3.1

		€	
Painting:	Proceeds	40,000	
	Cost 1985/86 = €1,000		
	Indexed cost @ 1.713	(1,713)	
	Gain	38,287	
	Annual exemption	(1,270)	
	Taxable gain	37,017	
	CGT @ 33%	12,216	(Payable 15 Dec. 2021)
Table:	Proceeds	12,000	
	Deemed cost 2004	(10,000)	(No indexation post-1 Jan. 2003)
	Gain	2,000	
	Gain March 2021	38,287	
	Annual exemption	(1,270)	
	Taxable gains	39,017	
	CGT @ 33%	12,876	
	Less: CGT paid 15/12/2021	(12,216)	
	CGT payable 31/01/2022	660	

Question 3.2

Disposal of 4 acres	€
Proceeds: 4 × €50,000	200,000

Cost: base cost = 20 acres at €600 per acre (1974) = €12,000

Part disposal:

$$\text{Original cost} \times \frac{\text{Proceeds}}{(\text{Proceeds} + \text{Market value of remainder})}$$

$$€12,000 \times \frac{€200,000}{(€200,000 + €160,000^*)} = €6,667$$

Indexed cost: €6,667 @ 7.528	(50,187)
Chargeable gain	149,813
CGT @ 33%	49,438

* Market value of remainder = 16 acres at €10,000 per acre.

Chapter 4

Question 4.1

(a) **Disposal of shares in French company**

Gain is taxable when remitted.

Gain

	€	€
Proceeds		65,000
Cost 1994/95:		
$\dfrac{8,000}{16,000} \times €60,000$	30,000	
Indexation factor 1994/95: 1.309		
Indexed cost		(39,270)
"Gain"		25,730

Proceeds remitted to Ireland = portion of gain taxable in 2021, i.e. €10,000. Gain is deemed to be remitted first.

(b)   **Sale of UK rental property**

	€
Proceeds	200,000
Cost	(180,000)
Renovations	(30,000)
Loss	(10,000)

Note: no indexation as there is a monetary loss. UK property is taxed on a remittance basis and losses are not allowable.

(c)   **Sale of H Plc shares**

	€	€
Proceeds		24,000
Cost	8,025	
Indexation factor 1998/99: 1.212		
Indexed cost		(9,726)
Gain		14,274

Jacques' Capital Gains Tax Liability 2021

	€
Gain on disposal of shares – amount remitted	10,000
Gain on disposal of H Plc shares	14,274
Total	24,274
Annual exemption	(1,270)
Taxable gains	23,004
CGT @ 33%	7,591

Note: no relief is available for the loss incurred in 2020 as the loss arose on the disposal of an asset only liable on the remittance basis.

Question 4.2

Rio Hernandez is resident but not ordinarily resident or domiciled in Ireland, therefore he is liable to all gains on the disposal of Irish assets as well as the remittance of foreign gains to Ireland. The following tax treatment will apply to each disposal:

1.   The gain on the disposal of the Irish holiday home will be taxable.
2.   The loss on the Spanish commercial property will not be allowable against Irish gains. No tax is payable on the proceeds remitted to Ireland as no gain has arisen.
3.   Proceeds of €20,000 were remitted to Ireland. The gain on the disposal of the UK shares of €18,000 will be subject to CGT in Ireland as the gain is deemed to be remitted first.

Question 4.3

(a)   CGT liability – because Mark is resident (but not domiciled) in Ireland he will be taxable on all Irish gains and on foreign gains to the extent they are remitted into the State.

Wicklow cottage

The disposal of the cottage in Wicklow is an Irish gain so Mark will be liable to CGT on it. (In any event, regardless of resident status he would be liable as it is an Irish specified asset).

	€	€
Proceeds		250,000
Less: incidental costs		
Auctioneer fees	2,000	
Solicitor fees	3,000	(5,000)
Net proceeds		245,000
Less: base cost		
Market value at date of inheritance		(200,000)
Gross chargeable gain		45,000

UK shares

The disposal of the UK shares is an Irish remittance and so will be liable to CGT.

	€	€
Proceeds		35,000
Less: incidental costs		
Stockbroker fees	(350)	(350)
Net proceeds		34,650
Less: base cost		
Purchase price	70,000	
Stockbroker fees	700	
Indexation	Nil	(70,700)
Capital loss		(36,050)

Mark's loss is not an allowable loss as he is only taxable on the disposal on the remittance basis.

Share of Spanish apartment

The disposal of his share in the Spanish apartment is not an Irish gain, nor were there any proceeds remitted to Ireland, therefore he is not liable to CGT on this disposal. (In any event even if there were proceeds which were remitted, principal private residence relief may apply.)

Share of Spanish site

As Mark remitted the proceeds of the disposal of the Spanish site to Ireland, this will be liable to CGT.

	€	€
Proceeds		50,000
Less: incidental costs		
Legal and professional fees	(3,000)	(3,000)
Net proceeds		47,000
Less: base cost		
Purchase price	42,000	
Indexation	Nil	42,000
Chargeable gain		5,000
Mark's share of gain @ 50%		2,500

CGT computation – initial period 01 January 2021 to 30 November 2021

	€
Chargeable gain – Wicklow cottage	45,000
Less: annual exemption	(1,270)
Net taxable	43,730
CGT @ 33%	14,431

CGT computation – later period 01 December 2021 to 31 December 2021

	€	€
Chargeable gain:		
Wicklow cottage	45,000	
Spanish site	2,500	47,500
Less: annual exemption		(1,270)
Net taxable		46,230
CGT @ 33%		15,256
Less paid under initial period		(14,431)
Net payable		825

(b) CGT payment and filing dates:

	Due date	Payment
Initial period 1 Jan. 2021 to 30 Nov. 2021	15 Dec. 2021	€14,431
Later period 1 Dec. 2021 to 31 Dec. 2021	31 Jan. 2022	€825

Filing date – Mark must file a return in respect of his 2021 gains on or before 31 October 2022.

Chapter 5

Question 5.1

	Shareholding	Cost
		€
July 2006 purchased	4,000	6,000
October 2007 1-for-2 bonus	2,000	–
	6,000	6,000
		€
Proceeds		15,000
Cost:		
$6,000 \times \dfrac{5,000}{6,000}$		(5,000)
Gain		10,000
Less: exemption		(1,270)
		8,730

€8,730 @ 33% = €2,881 CGT due

Note: no indexation as acquired after 1 January 2003.

Question 5.2

	Shareholding	Cost	
		€	
Acquired 01/07/1972	6,000	1,320	(MV 06/04/1974)
Rights issue 01/11/1983	12,000	4,080	
	18,000		
		€	
Deemed proceeds		16,800	
Less:			
$1,320 \times \dfrac{10,000}{18,000} = 733 \times 7.528 = 5,518$			
$4,080 \times \dfrac{10,000}{18,000} = 2,267 \times 2.003 = 4,541$		(10,059)	
Gain		6,741	
Less: exemption		(1,270)	
		5,471	

€5,471 @ 33% = €1,805 CGT due

Question 5.3

	Shareholding	Cost
		€
Acquired May 1973	4,000	3,000 (market value 06/04/1974)
Rights issue 06/01/1988	2,000	6,000
	6,000	

Sale to Orla

No CGT due on inter-spouse transactions.

Sale to Gerry

		€
Deemed proceeds		9,000

Less:

$$3,000 \times \frac{900}{6,000} \times 7.528 = 3,388$$

$$6,000 \times \frac{900}{6,000} \times 1.583 = 1,425 \qquad \underline{(4,813)}$$

Gain		$\underline{4,187}$

Sale on open market

	€
Deemed proceeds	43,200

Less:

$$3,000 \times \frac{3,600}{6,000} \times 7.528 = 13,550$$

$$6,000 \times \frac{3,600}{6,000} \times 1.583 = 5,699 \qquad \underline{(19,249)}$$

Gain	$\underline{23,951}$

Summary

	€
Sale to Orla	-
Sale to Gerry	4,187
Sale on open market	$\underline{23,951}$
	28,138
Less: exemption	$\underline{(1,270)}$
	26,868 @ 33% = €8,866 CGT due

Chapter 6

Question 6.1

Carmel's disposal of the workshop in Cork would qualify for revised entrepreneur relief as:
- her business is a qualifying business;
- the warehouse is a chargeable business asset used in the business;
- the warehouse has been owned for 3 of the last 5 years; and
- Carmel's lifetime limit of €1 million on gains since 1 January 2016 is not exceeded.

Carmel's CGT liability is as follows:

	€
Proceeds	120,000
Cost	(85,000)
Gain	35,000
Annual exemption	(1,270)
Taxable gain	33,730
CGT @ 10%	3,373

Question 6.2

Simon's gift of shares to Dan will give rise to the following CGT liability:

	€
Proceeds (market value)	1,220,000
Cost	(60,000)
Gain	1,160,000
Less: annual exemption	(1,270)
Taxable gain	1,158,730

The gift will qualify for revised entrepreneur relief as the company is carrying on a qualifying business and Simon:
- owned at least 5% of the shares issued (a 30% shareholding);
- owned the shares for 3 continuous years;
- has been a working director of the company in a managerial capacity for 3 of last 5 years; and
- has spent at least 50% of his time working for the company in those 3 years.

However, the revised entrepreneur rate of 10% will only apply to the first €1 million of the taxable gain; the remainder will be charged at the 33% rate. Simon's CGT liability is therefore:

Taxable gain	€1,158,730
CGT @ 10%	€ 100,000
CGT @ 33%*	€ 52,381
Total CGT liability	€ 152,381

*The annual exemption of €1,270 is set against the gain liable at the higher rate.

Chapter 7

Question 7.1

(a) **2021 CGT Liability**

The transfer of a business to a company is treated as a disposal for CGT purposes. However, if the business is transferred as a going concern together with all the assets, other than cash, in exchange for shares in the new company, then the gain may be rolled over against the cost of the shares issued. Only partial rollover relief is available where the consideration is only partly satisfied by shares, as in this case.

Chargeable gains arising

(i)   Incorporation of Business

	€	€
Warehouse (Working 1)		269,560
Goodwill		130,000
Gain		399,560
Deferred (Working 2)		342,480
Chargeable in tax year 2021		57,080

(ii) Disposal of Shares

	€
Sale proceeds	5,000
Cost (no indexation as there is a monetary loss)	(10,000)
Loss	(5,000)

(iii) Capital Gains Tax

Initial period to 30 November:

	€
Incorporation of business	57,080
Less: loss relief – loss forward	(10,000)
Less: annual exemption	(1,270)
	45,810
CGT @ 10% (Note 1)	4,581

Later period:

	€
Incorporation of business	57,080
Less: loss relief re shares	(5,000)
Less: loss relief – loss forward	(10,000)
Less: annual exemption	(1,270)
	40,810
CGT @ 10% (Note 2)	4,081
Less: paid re initial period	(4,581)
CGT refund due	(500)

Notes:
1. The conditions for revised entrepreneur relief are satisfied, therefore CGT is payable at 10% on the gain.
2. The losses and annual exemption are offset first against the gain taxable at 33%. As they exceed that gain, they are then offset against the gain taxable at 10%.

Workings
1. Chargeable gains

	€	€
Warehouse		
Market value		400,000
Cost – May 2001	120,000	
Indexation factor: 1.087		
Indexed cost		130,440
Chargeable gain		269,560
Goodwill		
Market value		130,000
Cost		Nil
Chargeable gain		130,000

Plant and Machinery – no capital loss can arise in respect of the plant and machinery as capital allowances will have been claimed on this expenditure.

Inventories and receivables are not chargeable assets.

2. Deferred gain

The amount deferred is restricted as follows:

$$\text{Maximum deferred} = \text{chargeable gains} \times \frac{\text{value of shares received}}{\text{value of total consideration}}$$

Value of Total Consideration	€
Warehouse	400,000
Plant and machinery	40,000
Goodwill	130,000
Inventories	48,000
Receivables	117,000
Total consideration	735,000
Less: Loan	(50,000)
Payables	(55,000)
Value of shares	630,000

Deferred gain:

$$(€269,560 + €130,000) \times \frac{630,000}{735,000} \qquad 342,480$$

(b) **CGT Payable**

The CGT of €4,581 is payable by 15 December 2021.

(c) **Base Cost of Shares**

The base cost of shares in O'Dowd Ltd for a future disposal is:

	€
Cost of shares	630,000
Less: deferred gain	342,480
	287,520

Chapter 8

Question 8.1

(a) **CGT Computation (August 2021)**

Disposal of shares in family company on 1 August 2021:	€
Proceeds (market value)	800,000
Market value 01/12/1994 = €40,000 indexed @ 1.309	(52,360)
	747,640 @ 10%* = €74,764

*Qualifies for revised entrepreneur relief.

No CGT is payable on this gain on the assumption that it is a "family company", as defined for the purposes of the relief, and that no restriction in the relief arises out of the underlying assets of the company.

(b) **CGT Computation December 2021**

	€
Sale of shares by Paul	900,000
Cost (deemed – market value)	(800,000)
Gain	100,000
Annual exemption	(1,270)
	98,730
CGT @ 33%	32,581

In addition, Paul has to pay the tax relieved on the transfer of the shares to him – €25,000. This is calculated as follows:

The additional CGT payable by Paul is the CGT which would have been payable by his father if he had not qualified for full relief from CGT on a disposal to his son.

If his father had not qualified for this relief, he could have qualified for the relief available for a disposal of qualifying assets to **a person other than a "child"**.

If the proceeds had been less than €750,000, Jim would have qualified for full relief, so no additional CGT would have been payable by Paul on the subsequent sale. He would only have paid the €32,581. In this case, as the proceeds on the disposal by Jim exceeded €750,000, Jim would only have qualified for marginal relief. Marginal relief in this case would have restricted

Jim's liability to €25,000, i.e. €800,000 − €750,000 = €50,000 × 50%, which would have been the amount payable by Paul in addition to the €32,581.

Total CGT payable by Paul for 2021 = €32,581 + €25,000 = €57,581.

Question 8.2

(a) Eligibility for Retirement Relief

Sean should qualify for retirement relief on the disposal of his shares in Tara Foods Limited as he meets the conditions as follows:

- he has reached the age of 55 years, but not 66 years;
- the shares are in Sean's trading "family" company and are held for at least 10 years;
- Sean has been a working director of the company for at least 10 years, during which period he has been a full-time working director for at least five years.

However, full relief is not available to Sean as his shares derive some of their value from quoted investments, which are not chargeable business assets.

The amount qualifying for retirement relief is determined by the formula:

$$\frac{\text{Chargeable Business Assets}}{\text{Total Chargeable Assets}}$$

$$\frac{(600,000 + 50,000)}{(600,000 + 50,000 + 120,000)} = \frac{650,000}{770,000}$$

Note: inventory and trade receivables are not chargeable assets.

The premises qualifies for retirement relief as it falls within the definition of "qualifying assets" for the purposes of the relief, i.e. a building which the individual has owned for a period of not less than 10 years ending with the disposal and which was used throughout that period for the purposes of the company's trade and is disposed of at the same time and to the same person as the shares in the family company.

(b) Capital Gains Tax Computation

	€	€
Deemed sale proceeds		800,000
Cost 1987/88	100	
Index factor: 1.583		
Indexed cost		(158)
Gain		799,842
Retirement relief:		
€799,842 × 650,000/770,000		(675,191)
Gain liable to CGT		124,651
CGT @ 10% (Note)		12,465

Note: The 10% rate of CGT applies as the conditions for revised entrepreneur relief (see **Chapter 6**) are also satisfied.

Premises

The gain on the premises is not taxable.
No annual exemption is due.

(c) **Retirement Relief Withdrawn?**

The retirement relief at (b) in respect of the shares will be clawed back if the shares in Tara Foods Limited are disposed of by Michael within six years of the date of transfer by Sean, and the retirement relief claimed at (b) in respect of the property will be clawed back if the property is sold by Michael within six years of the date of transfer by Sean. The relief granted to Sean will, in effect, be withdrawn.

(d) **Revenue's CGT Recovery**

The relief is withdrawn not from Sean, who had the benefit of the relief, but by way of Michael paying the CGT relieved, i.e. Michael will have to pay the difference between the CGT already paid and the amount which would have been payable by Sean if the retirement relief were not available.

Question 8.3

(a) **Disposal of shares in Crawford Sportswear Ltd**

This disposal does not qualify for retirement relief as **Colin did not own the shares for at least 10 years**. The period of ownership of the trade prior to its transfer to the company is not taken into account, as **Colin would not have qualified for relief on transfer of a business to a company**. Relief on transfer of a business to a company would not have applied, as **not all of the assets of the business were transferred to the company**, i.e. the premises were not transferred.

The **premises let to the company does not qualify for retirement relief**, as it was not used for the purposes of the **company's business for 10 years**.

The cost of the shares for CGT purposes is their market value at 1 January 2013, i.e. the market value of the net assets taken over. Net assets transferred were:

	€	Market Value €
Fixtures and fittings		50,000
Goodwill		80,000
Inventories		120,000
Receivables		25,000
Payables		(110,000)
Net assets transferred		165,000
Gain on disposal of shares:		
Market value		500,000
Market value January 2013		(165,000)
Gain		335,000
Gain on disposal of premises:		
Market value		250,000
Cost June 1990	20,000	
Indexation factor 1990/91: 1.442		
Indexed cost		(28,840)
Gain		221,160

(b) **Disposal of holiday cottage**

	€
Market value	120,000
Less: Market value 10 October 2003	(25,000)
Gain	95,000

Colin's CGT Liability 2021

	€
Gains:	
Shares	335,000
Premises	221,160
Holiday cottage	95,000
	651,160
Annual exemption	(1,270)
	649,890
CGT @ 10% of €335,000 (Note)	33,500
CGT @ 33% on balance	103,914
Total CGT payable	137,414

Note: The 10% rate of CGT applies to the sale of the shares as the conditions for revised entrepreneur relief are satisfied.

Chapter 9

Question 9.1

(a) When an Irish resident company redeems its own shares at a premium, in this case €590,000, the premium is, on first principles, liable to income tax under Schedule F.

However, if it can be shown that:

(i)   the company is a trading or holding company;
(ii)   the vendor is resident (and ordinarily resident in the case of an individual) in the State;
(iii) the buyback is not part of a scheme or arrangement the purpose of which is to enable the shareholder to participate in the profits of the company;
(iv)   the share redemption benefits the trade of the company;
(v)   the shares have been held for five years;
(vi)   the shareholding is substantially reduced; and
(vii) the shareholder, post-redemption, is no longer connected with the company (shareholding less than 30%).

Therefore the proceeds of €600,000 can be regarded as a capital receipt.

(b) Provided all tests are met, Alan's liability to CGT is as follows:

	€
Proceeds	600,000
Cost €10,000 @ 1.442	(14,420)
Gain	585,580
Less: annual exemption	(1,270)
Taxable	584,310
CGT @ 33%	192,822

Alan may qualify for retirement relief, but we do not have sufficient information to establish whether he does. In addition, if Alan has worked full-time in a managerial or technical capacity for at least three continuous years in the five years before the buyback of his shares and has not disposed of any chargeable business assets giving rise to gains in excess of €414,420 (i.e. €1,000,000 – €585,580) since 1 January 2016, revised entrepreneur relief would apply so that the relevant rate of CGT would be 10%.

(c) If Alan fails the tests, he will be liable to income tax under Schedule F.

	€
Schedule F	590,000
@ 40%	236,000

The company will be obliged to deduct DWT of 25% from the payment, and Alan will be entitled to a credit for the DWT. Alan will also be liable to the USC and PRSI.

Chapter 10

Question 10.1

(a) Purchase of shares in an Irish Plc is liable to Irish stamp duty at 1%. Therefore, stamp duty payable is €30,000 × 1% = €300.
(b) Purchase of shares in a US Plc is not liable to Irish stamp duty. (Shares in a company not registered in the State and not related to property situated in the State.)
(c) The purchase of land in Galway will be liable to Irish stamp duty at 7.5%. Therefore, stamp duty payable is €80,000 × 7.5% = €6,000.
(d) The purchase of an apartment in Kilkenny will be liable to Irish stamp duty at 1% (less than €1m). Therefore, stamp duty payable is €120,000 × 1% = €1,200.

Question 10.2

(a) The purchase of an apartment is liable to stamp duty at 1%, if the value does not exceed €1 million. Therefore, stamp duty payable is €200,000 × 1% = €2,000. This is due within 44 days of 1 September, i.e. by 14 October 2021, and will be payable by Ann Murphy.
(b) A transfer by way of gift is chargeable the same way as a transfer on sale, with the market value of the shares being substituted for the consideration. Shares are liable to stamp duty at a rate of 1%. Therefore, stamp duty payable is €300,000 × 1% = €3,000. This is due within 44 days of 5 September, i.e. by 18 October 2021, and will be payable by either Frank Gibbons or his brother, depending on what has been agreed between them.

Chapter 11

Question 11.1

(a) Gift of Irish land is liable to Irish stamp duty at 7.5%. Therefore, stamp duty payable is €100,000 × 7.5% = €7,500.
(b) A transfer of property between spouses is exempt.
(c) Gift of Irish land would normally be liable to stamp duty at 7.5%. However, the recipient is a charity, so it is exempt.
(d) Gift of shares in a private Irish company is liable to stamp duty at 1%. Therefore, stamp duty payable is €200,000 × 1% = €2,000.
(e) Gift of UK land is not liable to Irish stamp duty (not related to property situated in the State and normally the transfer would not be executed in the State).

If, alternatively, he does not gift these assets and leaves them under his will, no stamp duty will arise as transfers under a will are exempt from stamp duty.

Question 11.2

Transactions between "associated companies" are taxed at 0% stamp duty. In order to be an associated company, there must be a 90% relationship, direct or indirect, between the two companies. Holdings Limited has that relationship with Private Limited (100%) and Major Limited (95%). Therefore, no stamp duty arises on the transfers to those companies. However, if either of them ceases to be a 90% subsidiary of Holdings Limited within two years, the stamp duty becomes payable, i.e. €1 million × 7.5% = €75,000 for Private Limited, and €1 million × 1% = €10,000 for Major Limited.

There is stamp duty due on the residential property worth €1.5 million transferred to Free Limited.

First €1,000,000 @ 1%	€10,000
Balance of €500,000 @ 2%	€10,000
Stamp duty payable	€20,000

The patent worth €3 million transferred to Free Limited is exempt from stamp duty as it is intellectual property.

Chapter 12

Question 12.1

The transfer of the business from Jack to the company will not trigger any CGT. He can claim transfer of a business to a company relief as he satisfies the conditions, i.e. he is transferring all of the assets of the business to the company. All of the CGT can be deferred as he is only receiving shares and having the trade payables taken over.

If there is a contract, stamp duty is payable by the new company on the assets which are conveyed (land and buildings) and also those that pass under the contract, but excluding the assets which are goods and merchandise, i.e. machinery and inventories are not liable but goodwill and receivables are liable.

The new company will be liable to stamp duty as follows:

	€
Land and buildings	500,000
Goodwill	180,000
Receivables	40,000
Total subject to stamp duty	720,000
Stamp duty @ 7.5%	54,000

If there is no contract, only the land and buildings will be liable to stamp duty. Therefore the stamp duty will be €500,000 @ 7.5% = €37,500.

Chapter 13

Question 13.1

John is the disponer as he instructs Mary to make the payment to Peter (the beneficiary).

Question 13.2

The date of the disposition is when the mother agrees to the future transfer. The beneficiary (daughter) does not become beneficially entitled in possession until she has her first child and this will be the date of the gift.

Question 13.3

Paddy gets a gift of €1,000,000, less consideration of €100,000, and Nora gets a gift of €100,000, both from Joyce.

Question 13.4

Memorandum

To :
From :
Date :
Re : **Capital Acquisitions Tax Queries**

I refer to the matters recently raised by you.

(a) Disposition

For capital acquisitions tax (CAT) purposes, a gift or inheritance is deemed to be taken where a disposition is made by a person, the disponer, as a result of which another person, the donee, becomes beneficially entitled in possession, see (c) below, to any benefit otherwise than for full consideration.

"Disposition" is the method by which ownership of the benefit provided is transferred. A simple example of a disposition is where a person transfers a property to another person. The deed of transfer in this case is the disposition.

The term disposition is very broadly defined in CATCA 2003 and includes the following:

(1) Any act by a person as a result of which the value of his estate is reduced, e.g. the transfer of property otherwise than for full consideration.

(2) Any trust, covenant, agreement or arrangement.

(3) An omission or failure to act by an individual, as a result of which the value of his estate is reduced.

Example:
This includes the passing of a resolution by a company which results directly or indirectly in one shareholder's property being increased in value at the expense of the property of any other shareholder, if that other shareholder could have prevented the passing of the resolution by voting against it.

(4) The payment of money.

(5) The allotment of shares in a company.

(6) The grant or creation of any benefit.

(7) The transfer of any property or benefit by will or on an intestacy.

(b) Date of the disposition

CATCA 2003 defines the date of the disposition as:

(1) The date of death of the deceased in the case of a benefit taken by will or on an intestacy.

(2) The date of the death of the deceased in the case of benefits derived under the Succession Act 1965.

(3) The latest date when the disponer could have exercised the right or power which has been waived, where the disposition consisted of a failure or omission to exercise a right of power.

(4) In any other case, the date of the disposition is the date on which the act or, where more than one act is involved, the last act of the disponer was done by which he provided, or bound himself to provide, the property comprised in the disposition.

(c) Beneficially entitled in possession

"Entitled in possession" is defined in CATCA 2003 as meaning, "having a present right to the enjoyment of property as opposed to having a future such right". CAT only arises where a person obtains the current enjoyment of a property as opposed to being entitled to enjoyment of the property at some time in the future.

A person has a "beneficial interest" in property if he is entitled to the benefits arising from a property without necessarily having legal ownership of the property. For example, X by deed appoints Y, his son, as trustee of a fund of investments the income from which is to be paid to X's wife, Mrs X, for the duration of her life. After Mrs X's death the fund is to be transferred into the ownership of X's son. Y is the legal owner of the investments. However, as the income from the investments is paid to Mrs X for her life, as soon as the deed is executed giving her the life interest, she is said to have a beneficial interest in the investments. Y also has a beneficial interest in the fund as he is entitled to the benefits from the fund in the future. Mrs X is said to be beneficially entitled in possession to the fund. However, her son Y, while having a beneficial interest in the fund, is not "entitled in possession" as he has a future interest rather than a current interest.

(d) Date of the gift

The date of the gift is defined as the date upon which the recipient of the gift becomes beneficially entitled in possession to the benefit (i.e. the date the recipient receives an immediate benefit).

Chapter 14

Question 14.1

1.	Group A	€335,000
2.	Group B	€32,500
3.	Group B €32,500. Group A €335,000 does not apply as uncle did not control company.	
4.	Group A – favourite nephew/niece	€335,000
5.	Group C	€16,250
6.	Group B – although father is deceased, grandson is not a minor, so Group A does not apply.	€32,500
7.	Group C	€16,250
8.	Group B	€32,500
9.	Group C	€16,250
10.	Group A – favourite nephew/niece	€335,000
11.	Group B	€32,500
12.	Group A – "child" includes stepchild	€335,000
13.	Group B – surviving spouse	€32,500
14.	Group B – not favourite nephew/niece as did not work for previous five years	€32,500
15.	Group A	€335,000
16.	Group B – surviving spouse	€32,500
17.	Group B – lineal ancestor	€32,500
18.	Group B – "child" of brother, includes adopted child	€32,500
19.	Group C – not a child of a brother or sister	€16,250
20.	Group A – minor child of the civil partner of a deceased child of the civil partner of the disponer.	€335,000

Question 14.2

Aggregate A	€
Inheritance from father	350,000
Previous gift from father	100,000
Previous inheritance from mother	30,000
Total gifts and inheritances (Note)	480,000
Less: tax-free threshold (Group A)	(335,000)
Taxable	145,000
CAT @ 33%	47,850

Aggregate B

Previous benefits €100,000 + €30,000   €130,000

Less: tax-free threshold (Group A)   €335,000

Therefore, no tax on Aggregate B as benefits received are less than threshold.

CAT payable:

Tax on Aggregate A – Tax on Aggregate B = €47,850 – €nil   <u>47,850</u>

Note: the gift from his father in 1990 is not aggregated as it is pre-5 December 1991. The inheritance from his uncle is ignored as it is a Group B benefit.

Chapter 15

Question 15.1

CATCA 2003 does not include rules for determining where property is situated. General law determines where property is located. The main rules are as follows:

1. *Land and buildings*
   Situated where they are physically located.
2. *Debts*
   (i) A simple contract debt is situated where the debtor resides.
   (ii) A speciality debt, i.e. a debt payable under a sealed instrument, is situated where the instrument happens to be.
   (iii) A judgment debt is situated where the judgment is recorded.
3. *Securities/shares*
   Situated where the share register is kept, if the securities/shares are registered. Bearer securities/shares are situated where the security/share certificate is physically located.
4. *Tangible property, e.g. cars, furniture, moveable goods*
   Situated where they are physically located.
5. *Cash or currency of any kind*
   Situated where they are physically located. Bank balances are located in the country of the bank branch at which the account is kept.

Question 15.2

(a) A gift or inheritance taken during the year ended 31 December 2021 will be a taxable gift or inheritance if:
   (1) Regardless of whether the gift or inheritance consists of Irish or foreign property,
       (i) the date of the disposition is on or after 01/12/1999 and the **disponer** is resident or ordinarily resident in the State at the date of the disposition; or
       (ii) the date of the disposition is on or after 01/12/1999 and the **donee/successor** is resident or ordinarily resident in the State at the date of the gift/ inheritance,

   provided that, in the case of a non-Irish domiciled person, such a person will only be regarded as resident or ordinarily resident in the State on the relevant date if he has been resident in the State for the previous five tax years and is resident or ordinarily resident on the relevant date, i.e. date of the disposition for the disponer and the date of the gift/inheritance in the case of the beneficiary.

(2) The gift or inheritance consists of Irish property (even though none of the rules under 1 above is satisfied).

(b) (1) As the disponer is Irish domiciled and Irish resident, both the Irish and the UK property are taxable inheritances. Rule (1)(i) above applies. (In any event, as the donee is also Irish domiciled and resident at the date of the inheritance, it would be a taxable inheritance even if the disponer had not been Irish domiciled and resident.)

(2) The date of the disposition, i.e. the date of Gordon's death, is after 01/12/1999. The property inherited is not Irish property. As the successor, Dermot, is Irish resident and domiciled at the date of the inheritance, the inheritance is a taxable inheritance. Rule (1)(ii) above applies.

(3) Neither the disponer nor the successor is Irish resident or ordinarily resident at the relevant dates. The property inherited is Irish property. The inheritance is a taxable inheritance. Rule (a)(2) above applies.

(4) The property inherited is not Irish property. The disponer is neither resident nor ordinarily resident in the State at the date of the disposition and the successor, Nevin, although Irish resident, is not Irish domiciled. Therefore, he is only taxable if he has been resident in the State for the preceding five tax years and resident or ordinarily resident on 16/09/2021. As he is, the inheritance is a taxable inheritance.

(5) The disponer is Irish domiciled and resident in the State at the date of the disposition. This is, therefore, a taxable inheritance. Rule (1)(i) above applies. It is irrelevant that one of the successors is not resident in the State. (In any event, as the entire property consists of Irish property, even if neither the disponer nor the successors were Irish resident at the relevant dates, the inheritance would still be a taxable inheritance.)

(6) As the donee, Darren, is Irish domiciled and is ordinarily resident in the State (he only ceased to be resident in Ireland in 2020 and, therefore, is still ordinarily resident), the gift is a taxable gift. Rule (1)(ii) above applies.

(7) As the disponer is Irish domiciled and Irish resident at the date of the disposition, the gift is a taxable gift. Rule (1)(i) above applies. (In any event, the donee is also Irish domiciled and Irish resident at the date of the gift, which means that even if Rule (1)(i) was not satisfied, the gift would be a taxable gift by virtue of Rule (1)(ii).)

(8) The disponer is Irish resident and ordinarily resident but not Irish domiciled. For Rule (1)(i) to apply, however, Jean must also have been resident for the last five years and be resident/ordinarily resident, as she is foreign domiciled. Since Jean is so resident and ordinarily resident, the gift of both the Irish and the foreign shares is taxable. (Had Jean not triggered a liability, Amelie would not be taxable on the French shares as she has not been resident for the last five years. Clearly, she would be taxable on the Irish shares.)

Question 15.3

(a) **Michael**
This is a taxable gift as the disponer, Michael, is Irish domiciled and resident. The relevant group threshold is €335,000 – gift from parent to a child.

Total gifts/inheritances received from persons within the same group threshold:

	€
Gift from father on 01/01/2021	40,000
Less: small gift exemption	(3,000)
Jewellery inherited from mother	20,000
Total	57,000

As this is less than the group threshold of €335,000, no CAT is payable.

(b) **Bridget**

This is a taxable inheritance as the disponer, Bridget's uncle, was Irish domiciled and resident at the date of his death.

Gifts and inheritances previously received from persons within the same group threshold include the inheritance from an aunt in March 2008 and the inheritance from Bridget's grandmother in September 1990. The inheritance in 1990 is ignored as it was taken before 5 December 1991. Accordingly, the only taxable gift/inheritance taken into account in calculating the CAT on the current inheritance is the inheritance of Irish quoted shares.

CAT on Aggregate A:	€
UK property	120,000
Irish quoted shares	50,000
	170,000
Group threshold: €32,500 @ Nil	
Balance: €137,500 @ 33%	45,375
CAT on "Aggregate A"	45,375

CAT on Aggregate B:	
Irish quoted shares	50,000
Group threshold: €32,500 @ Nil	
Balance: €17,500 @ 33%	5,775
CAT on "Aggregate B"	5,775

CAT on Aggregate A − CAT on Aggregate B = €45,375 − €5,775

CAT payable in respect of inheritance of UK property   €39,600

Chapter 16

Question 16.1

Memorandum

To	:	
From	:	
Date	:	
Re	:	**Capital Acquisitions Tax Agricultural Relief**

I refer to your recent query regarding the relief from CAT available on the transfer of land by a client to his son.

(a) Nature of the Relief

Where an individual qualifies for agricultural relief in respect of a gift of agricultural property, the value of the property is reduced by 90% for CAT purposes.

The taxable value of a gift is calculated by deducting from the market value of the property comprised in the gift any consideration given and any liabilities, costs and expenses payable out of the gift. Where an individual qualifies for agricultural relief in respect of a gift of property, the amount of any consideration given or liabilities, costs and expenses payable are also reduced by 90%.

For example, a father gifts land valued at €1 million to his son. The land is subject to a mortgage of €20,000, which is taken over by the son. Normally stamp duty would be payable at 7.5%. However, if the son intends to farm the land for at least six years and either has an agricultural qualification as specified in the legislation or will spend at least 20 hours a week farming the land, stamp duty at 1% of the value of the land, i.e. €10,000, will be payable on the transfer. If the son does not satisfy these conditions, stamp duty at 7.5%, i.e. €75,000, will be payable. The son may also qualify for the reduced rate of stamp duty if he intends to lease the farm to a person who will farm the land and satisfy the qualifications/working time requirements. (Also, if the son qualified for the young trained farmer stamp duty relief, he would be exempt from stamp duty. In this solution, it is assumed that stamp duty is paid at 1%.)

If the gift qualifies for agricultural relief, the taxable value of the gift received will be as follows:

	€
Market value	1,000,000
Agricultural relief (90%)	(900,000)
Agricultural value	100,000
Stamp duty €10,000 @ 10%	(1,000)
Mortgage €20,000 @ 10%	(2,000)
Taxable value	97,000

(b) Agricultural Property

Agricultural relief applies to gifts or inheritances of "agricultural property". Agricultural property is:

"Agricultural land, pasture and woodland in the EU and UK, including crops, trees, and underwood growing on such land and including such farm buildings, farm houses and mansion houses as are of a character appropriate to the property, and farm machinery, livestock and bloodstock thereon and entitlements under the EU Single Farm Payment Scheme."

(c) Definition of "Farmer"

In order for a gift to qualify for agricultural relief, the recipient of the gift must be a "farmer" on the "valuation date".

"Farmer" is defined by the legislation as an individual who satisfies the "asset test" and the "activity" test, as explained below.

Asset test – where an individual in respect of whom not less than **80% of the market value of all property to which he is beneficially entitled in possession (taking the current gift or inheritance into account) is represented by the market value of agricultural property in the EU and UK**. In this context, an individual is deemed to be beneficially entitled in possession to any assets which are the subject of a discretionary trust of which he is a settlor and an object, and also to any future interests in property to which the individual is currently entitled.

For the purpose of the 80% test, the gross value of assets are taken, ignoring any liabilities or charges. There is one exception, i.e. borrowings used to purchase, repair or improve an off-farm principal private residence are deductible for the 80% test.

Continuing with the example at (a) above, if, after the gift, the son's only other asset consists of a house valued at €120,000 with a mortgage of €100,000 attaching to it and a car valued at €20,000, the son will satisfy the asset test as after taking the gift his assets will be made up as follows:

	€	%
Agricultural property	1,000,000	96
House (net of mortgage)	20,000	2
Car	20,000	2
Total assets	1,040,000	100

Activity test – the beneficiary must:

- farm the agricultural property for a period of not less than six years commencing on the valuation date; or
- lease the agricultural property for a period of not less than six years commencing on the valuation date.

In addition, the beneficiary (or the lessee, where relevant) must either:

- have one of the agricultural qualifications set out in tax legislation; or
- farm the agricultural property for not less than 50% of his or her normal working time.

Revenue will accept working 20 hours per week on average as satisfying the condition of farming for not less than 50% of his or her normal working time. The agricultural property must also be farmed on a commercial basis and with a view to the realisation of profits.

The farmer test does not have to be satisfied to the extent that the gift consists of trees or underwood.

(d) Withdrawal of the Relief

The agricultural relief will be withdrawn if, within six years after the date of gift or inheritance, the property is sold or compulsorily acquired and is not replaced with other agricultural property within a year, in the case of a sale, or within six years in the case of a compulsory acquisition.

If part of the proceeds on the disposal of agricultural property are reinvested, then a similar fraction of the relief is clawed back.

There is no withdrawal of the relief to the extent that the property which qualified for agricultural relief consists of crops, trees or underwood.

Where a donee, successor or lessee ceases to satisfy the activity test (otherwise than on death) within the period of six years commencing on the valuation date of the gift or inheritance, the agricultural relief granted will be clawed back.

Question 16.2

Inheritances – breakdown

	Margaret	Liam	Eva
	€	€	€
Holiday home	180,000		
Stocks and shares	230,000		
Irish Government stock	101,500		
Shares in Fine Arts Ltd			960,000
Agricultural property		1,090,000	
Cash		50,000	
Mortgage		(120,000)	
Creditors		(15,000)	
Funeral expenses		(20,000)	
	511,500	985,000	960,000

CAT Calculations

€

Margaret

		€
Taxable value of inheritance		511,500
CAT payable:		
Group threshold:	€32,500 @ Nil	Nil
Balance:	€479,000 @ 33%	
CAT payable		158,070

Liam

Taxable value of inheritance (Working 1)		125,500
Tax payable:		
Group threshold:	€32,500 @ Nil	Nil
Balance:	€93,000 @ 33%	30,690

Eva

Market value of shares	960,000
Value attributed to investment property	(360,000)
Value excluding investment property	600,000
Business relief	(540,000)
	60,000
Value attributed to investment property	360,000
Taxable value	420,000

continued overleaf

Group threshold @ Nil		(335,000)
Balance		85,000
CAT @ 33%		28,050

Working 1 – Taxable value of inheritance

	€	€
Market value of agricultural property		1,090,000
Less: agricultural relief at 90%		(981,000)
		109,000
Less: mortgage €120,000 @ 10%		(12,000)
Less: farm creditors €15,000 @ 10%		(1,500)
Taxable value of agricultural property		95,500
Cash	50,000	
Funeral expenses	(20,000)	30,000
Taxable value of total property inherited by Liam		125,500

Clearly Liam qualifies as a "farmer".

Value of agricultural property	€1,090,000
Value of total property	
(€1,090,000 + €30,000* + €200,000 − €130,000)	€1,190,000

Agricultural property as percentage of total property = 92% (greater than the required 80%).

He also satisfies the activity test as he intends to spend not less than 50% of his normal working time farming the land for at least six years.

*As the funeral expenses will have been paid by the valuation date, the residue will be €50,000 − €20,000 = €30,000.

Question 16.3

(a) **James**

	€
Assets inherited:	
Investment property: €520,000 @ 50%	260,000
Shares: €1 million @ 20% (Note 1)	200,000
Business relief relating to shares (Note 2)	(135,000)
Share of residue (Note 3)	74,000
Taxable	399,000
Aggregate A	
Current benefit	399,000
Gift from mother in 2008	167,000
	566,000
Group threshold: €335,000 @ nil	Nil
€231,000 @ 33%	76,230
Tax on Aggregate A	76,230

Aggregate B

Gift from mother in 2008   167,000

Tax on Aggregate B = nil as €167,000 is less than the group threshold amount of €335,000.

Tax on Aggregate A – Tax on Aggregate B = Tax on inheritance
Tax on inheritance is therefore €76,230

(b) **John**

As the inheritance was taken from his wife, the benefits under the will are exempt from inheritance tax **and** are not taken into account (for aggregation purposes) in calculating CAT on later gifts or inheritances from other sources.

Notes:

1. Tyrex Ltd is a private company, which after the receipt of the shares by James is under the control of his relatives. Therefore, the value of the 20% shareholding in Tyrex Ltd inherited by James is valued as if it were part of a controlling holding, i.e. the value of a 20% shareholding is taken to be 20% of the market value of the company as a whole. No discount is given for the fact that a 20% interest is a minority (non-controlling) interest.

2. Business relief

	€	€
Total value of Tyrex Ltd		1,000,000
Value attributable to non-business assets:		
House	300,000	
Less: mortgage	(50,000)	
		(250,000)
Value attributable to relevant business property (balance)		750,000

Accordingly, 75% of the value of the shares in Tyrex Ltd is attributable to relevant business property.

	€
Value of shares inherited by James	200,000
Value attributable to relevant business property (75%)	150,000
Business relief @ 90%	135,000

3. Residue

	€
Bank accounts	60,000
Policy	104,000
Expenses	(16,000)
	148,000
50% share to James	74,000

Chapter 17

Question 17.1

(a) **Tom**

This is a taxable gift as the donee, Tom's mother, is Irish domiciled and resident.

Value of the annuity
In order to produce an annual income of €10,000, €200,000 of the 5% Government bond would have to be purchased, i.e. €10,000 ÷ 5%. At 92c per €1 of stock, €200,000 of this stock would cost €184,000. The value of a life interest in €184,000 received by a 59-year-old woman is €121,955, i.e. €184,000 × 0.6628.

The relevant group threshold is €32,500, a gift from a lineal descendant. Tom's mother previously received an inheritance of €30,000, from her sister, also within the €32,500 group threshold.

CAT payable in respect of the current gift is therefore:

CAT on Aggregate A:	€
Value of gift	121,955
Less: small gift exemption	(3,000)
	118,955
Inheritance from sister	30,000
	148,955
Group threshold: €32,500 @ Nil	
Balance: €116,455 @ 33%	
CAT on Aggregate A	38,430

CAT on Aggregate B:	
Inheritance from sister: €30,000	
Group threshold: €32,500	
CAT on Aggregate B	Nil

CAT on Aggregate A – CAT on Aggregate B = €38,430 − €Nil	
CAT payable in respect of gift of annuity from Tom	38,430

(b) **Jason/Mark**

UK Property
The inheritance of the UK property is a taxable inheritance. Although it is foreign property, it is taxable because the disponer, Martha, was Irish resident.

The relevant group threshold is €32,500. Although the property passes to Mark on the death of his father, the disponer is Martha, his aunt. Jason has not previously received any taxable gifts or inheritances from a person within the €32,500 group threshold (an inheritance from a nephew belongs to the €16,250 group threshold).

CAT payable in respect of the UK property is, accordingly:

	€
Value of inheritance	300,000
Group threshold: €32,500 @ Nil	
Balance: €267,500 @ 33%	
CAT liability	88,275

Cash

This is a taxable inheritance as both the disponer and successor are Irish resident and, in any event, consists of Irish property.

The relevant group threshold is €335,000. As Mark has previously received a taxable inheritance from a person within this group threshold, i.e. his mother, his CAT liability on the current inheritance is as set out below.

CAT payable in respect of the inheritance:

	€
Cash	260,000
Savings certificates from mother	190,000
	450,000
Group threshold: €335,000 @ Nil	
Balance: €115,000 @ 33%	
CAT liability	37,950

As the previous inheritance received was less than the Group A threshold of €335,000, €37,950 is now payable in respect of the inheritance of the cash and shares.

Total CAT payable by Mark:

	€
CAT on UK property	88,275
CAT on Irish cash	37,950
Total CAT payable	126,225

Question 17.2

(a) **Martin**

Taxable value of Dermot's inheritance:	€
Grocery business and premises	600,000
Business relief (90%) (assumed owned two years)	(540,000)
	60,000
House and contents	150,000

continued overleaf

Bank accounts	15,000
Funeral costs	(8,000)
Incumbrance-free value	217,000
Discount factor for life interest: 0.8204	
Taxable value of life interest €217,000 × 0.8204	178,027

(b) **Jack**

Taxable value of Margaret's inheritance:

	€
"Slice" of premises and business:	
€600,000 × $\dfrac{€15,000}{€150,000}$	60,000
Less: business relief (90%)	(54,000)
	6,000
Discount factor for 10-year interest: 0.4913	
Taxable value of 10-year interest €6,000 × 0.4913	2,948

Taxable value of John's inheritance:

	€
Premises and business	600,000
Less: Margaret's "slice"	(60,000)
	540,000
Business relief (90%)	(486,000)
	54,000
Residue	50,000
Costs: €20,000 + €9,000	(29,000)
Taxable value	75,000

(c) **David**

A taxable gift arises on the cessation of the payment of the annuity to Larry. David is taxable on the "slice" of the property returned to him.

The value of the "slice" is calculated by reference to the relative values at the date the payments cease, i.e. April 2021.

$$\text{Taxable value} = \text{"Slice"} = €375,000 \times \frac{€10,000}{€30,000} = €125,000$$

(d) **Alan**

Taxable value of gift of covenant = capitalised value of the annuity × discount factor for life interest of 65-year-old woman.

The capitalised value of the annuity is reached by calculating the amount which would have to be invested in the most recently issued Government bond, not redeemable within

10 years, in order to produce an annual income equal to the annuity. In order to produce an annual income of €10,000, €250,000 of a 4% Government bond would have to be purchased, i.e. €10,000 ÷ 4%. At 89c per €1 of stock, €250,000 of this stock would cost €222,500 = capitalised value of annuity.

Discount factor for life interest of 65-year-old woman = 0.565.

Taxable value of annuity = 0.565 × €222,500 = €125,712.

(e) **Tom**

Taxable value of Emer's inheritance:

	€
"Slice" of farmland and farm assets:	
€1,070,000 × $\dfrac{€15,000}{€50,000}$	321,000
Discount factor for life interest: 0.8683	
Taxable value of life interest €321,000 × 0.8683	<u>278,724</u>

Note: Emer is not entitled to agricultural relief in respect of her "slice" as she fails the asset test to qualify as a farmer, i.e. €321,000 ÷ (€321,000 + €120,000) = 73%.

Taxable value of Fintan's inheritance:

	€
Market value of farmland and assets	<u>1,070,000</u>
Agricultural value (Note) @ 10%	107,000
Less: Emer's "slice" × 10%, i.e. €321,000 × 10%	(32,100)
Less: proportion of costs:	
€9,500 × $\dfrac{€1,070,000 - €321,000}{€1,145,000 - €321,000}$ = €8,635	
Reduced for agricultural relief, i.e. €8,635 × 10%	<u>(863)</u>
	74,037
Stocks and shares	50,000
Cash	25,000
Remainder of costs: €9,500 − €8,635	<u>(865)</u>
Taxable value of Fintan's inheritance	<u>148,172</u>

Note: Fintan's agricultural asset percentage is calculated on the valuation date after receiving the inheritance (net of funeral expenses). As Fintan had no assets before the inheritance, the calculation is as follows:

$$\frac{€950,000 + €120,000}{€950,000 + €120,000 + €50,000 + €25,000 - €9,500} \times 100 = 94\%$$

The land is leased to a full-time farmer. Therefore Fintan is a farmer for agricultural relief. The agricultural relief will be clawed back if the farm is not leased to a full-time farmer or farmed full-time by Fintan for six years from the valuation date.

Question 17.3

(a) **Gift 6 August 2021**

	Total	25%
	€	€
300 acres	660,000	165,000
Farm buildings	28,200	7,050
Machinery	15,600	3,900
Livestock	24,400	6,100
Agricultural property		182,050
Cash in bank		126,000
Total assets		308,050

As agricultural property accounts for less than 80% of David's assets, he does not qualify as a farmer and so does not qualify for agricultural relief. However, business relief does apply.

	€
Market value of property gifted	182,050
Less: business relief @ 90%	(163,845)
	18,205
Small gift exemption	(3,000)
Taxable value	15,205

Group threshold amount of €335,000. Therefore, no tax payable.

(b) **Inheritance 25 November 2021**

	€
Farmland	1,080,000
Buildings	33,600
Machinery	19,300
Livestock	31,700
Total agricultural property	1,164,600
Agricultural property inherited 75%	873,450
Own agricultural property (25% previously received from father)	291,150

Agricultural property purchased	150,000
Total agricultural property	1,314,600
Other assets – investments	95,000
Total assets	1,409,600

As David's agricultural property accounts for in excess of 80% of the value of his total assets (i.e. 93.3%), and he is a full-time farmer, he qualifies as a farmer and so qualifies for agricultural relief.

Inheritance Tax computation

	€	€
Agricultural property: 10% $\times$ €873,450		87,345
Less: costs $\times$ 10% $\times$ €25,000 $\times \dfrac{€873,450}{€968,450 \text{ (Note 1)}}$		(2,255)
Taxable value of property		85,090
Investments	95,000	
Less: costs $\times$ €25,000 $\times \dfrac{€95,000}{€968,450}$	(2,452)	
Less: annuity (Note 2)	(59,375)	
Taxable value of investments		33,173
		118,263
Prior benefits (Group A)	15,205	
Deduct: Group threshold	(335,000)	
Unutilised group threshold		(319,795)
Taxable benefit		Nil

Notes:

		€
1.	Agricultural property	873,450
	Other property	95,000
	Total inheritance	968,450

2. Deduction for annuity payable out of income from investments.

Total value of investments	€95,000

Appropriate part inherited by Rachel:

$$€95,000 \times \frac{€5,000}{€8,000} \qquad €59,375$$

Note: do not apply table factor!

Question 17.4

(a) **CGT liability**

No CGT liability arises on the transfer to Stephen as the conditions necessary for Peter to qualify for retirement relief are satisfied.

(b) **CAT liability**

(i) Is Stephen entitled to agricultural relief?

Farmer test:

	Agricultural Property €000	Other Property €000	Total €000
Farmland gifted	5,000		5,000
House (less mortgage)		250	250
Car		20	20
Farmlands in Antrim	500		500
Site inherited from mother		450	450
Total	5,500	720	6,220

€5.5 million ÷ €6.22 million = 88.42%. As Stephen satisfies the asset and the activity tests, he is a farmer and is entitled to agricultural relief.

(ii) Taxable value of gift

	€
Agricultural value of property: €5,000,000 @ 10%	500,000
Less: stamp duty and legal fees: €165,000 @ 10%	(16,500)
Less: annuity payable: €540,000 @ 10% (Note)	(54,000)
Taxable value	429,500

Note: calculation of value of annuity

The capitalised value of the annuity is reached by calculating the amount which would have to be invested in the most recently issued Government bond, not redeemable within 10 years, in order to produce an annual income equal to the annuity. In order to produce an annual income of €30,000, €600,000 of 5% Government bond would have to be purchased, i.e. €30,000 ÷ 5%. At 90c per €1 of stock, €600,000 of this stock would cost €540,000.

(iii) CAT payable

Relevant threshold is Group A €335,000. Previous gifts/inheritances received from persons within this group include the site inherited from Stephen's mother. (The farmland inherited from Stephen's uncle is Group B.)

	€
Aggregate A	
Current benefit	429,500
Small gift exemption	(3,000)
	426,500
Inheritance from mother	10,000
Cumulative gifts/inheritances within Group A threshold	436,500
Group threshold taxed @ Nil	(335,000)
Balance taxable	101,500
CAT @ 33% on Aggregate A	33,495

Aggregate B

Inheritance from mother	10,000
CAT on Aggregate B	nil

Tax on current benefit = tax on Aggregate A – tax on Aggregate B, i.e.:

CAT payable on transfer to Stephen = €33,495

Chapter 18

Question 18.1

(a) **Patrick**

		€
Assets inherited:		
Government stock		14,000
Aggregate A		
Current benefit		14,000
Gift from mother in 2016		477,000
		491,000
Group threshold:	€335,000 @ nil	Nil
	€156,000 @ 33%	51,480
Tax on Aggregate A		51,480
Aggregate B		
Gift from mother in 2016		477,000
Group threshold:	€335,000 @ nil	Nil
	€142,000 @ 33%	46,860
Tax on Aggregate B		46,860

Tax on Aggregate A – Tax on Aggregate B = Tax on inheritance

Tax on inheritance is therefore €51,480 – €46,860	4,620

(b) **Harry**

The inheritance received by Harry is exempt because:

- he was not domiciled or ordinarily resident at the date of the inheritance; and
- the inheritance comprised of Irish Government securities, which qualify for exemption from Irish income tax when beneficially owned by persons who are not domiciled or ordinarily resident in the State; and,
- Sarah owned the securities for more than 15 years.

Question 18.2

John's CAT liability

Inheritance from father – CAT payable:

	€
Shares in Murray Developments	1,500,000
Investment properties	850,000
Part of investment property attributable to Sarah (Note 2)	(133,333)
Mortgages charged on properties	(225,000)
Residue (Note 3)	92,000
Taxable value of inheritance	2,083,667
Previous gift within same group threshold (Note 4)	100,000
Cumulative gifts/inheritances within Group A threshold	2,183,667
Group threshold taxed @ Nil	(335,000)
Balance taxable	1,848,667
CAT payable @ 33% (Note 5)	610,060

Notes:

1. Business relief does not apply as the trade is buying and selling land.
2. The inheritance received by Sarah is the "appropriate part" of the entire investment property on which the annuity payable to her is charged, i.e.:

$$\text{Entire property} \times \frac{\text{Gross annual value of annuity}}{\text{Gross annual value of property}}$$

$$€400,000 \times \frac{€10,000}{€30,000} = 133,333$$

3. Residue:

	€
Cash	146,000
Shares	50,000
Funeral expenses	(3,500)
Legal expenses	(8,500)
	184,000
50% each	92,000

4. Previous gift of property:

	€
Gross value	300,000
Less mortgage	(200,000)
Total	100,000

5. Previous gift is less than Group A threshold for 2021, so no CAT is attributed to this gift.

Emily's CAT liability

	€
House (Note 1)	950,000
Residue	92,000
Taxable value of inheritance	1,042,000
Previous inheritance with same group threshold	200,000
Cumulative gifts/inheritances within Group A threshold	1,242,000
Group threshold taxed @ Nil	(335,000)
Balance taxable	907,000
CAT @ 33%	299,310
CAT attributed to previous gift (Note 2)	Nil
CAT payable	299,310

Notes:
1. Emily does not qualify for exemption in respect of the house as she had an interest in another dwelling house at the date of the inheritance.
2. Previous gift was less than Group A threshold, so no CAT is attributed to this gift.

Sarah's CAT liability

	€
Value of inheritance (see Note 2 under John)	133,333
Factor for life interest for 63-year-old: 0.6	
Taxable value	80,000
Relevant group threshold @ Nil	(32,500)
Balance taxable	47,500
CAT payable @ 33%	15,675

Qualifying insurance proceeds (section 72 policy)

Total CAT payable:

	€
CAT – John	610,060
CAT – Sarah	15,675
CAT – Emily	299,310
Total	925,045
Proceeds from policy	1,000,000
Excess subject to CAT	74,955

Excess falls into the residue and is split evenly between John and Emily.

	Total	John	Emily
	€	€	€
Excess	74,955	37,477	37,477
CAT @ 33%	24,735	12,367	12,367

Proceeds of policy are used to pay €925,045 above. Balance of €24,735 payable separately.

Question 18.3

Declan's CAT liabilities

Declan qualifies for business relief in respect of the shares inherited from Jerome, as he satisfies the necessary share ownership requirements after receiving the inheritance. (The company is also a trading company and Jerome had owned the shares for at least two years prior to the date of the inheritance.)

The relevant group threshold is Group A €335,000 as Declan qualifies as a "favourite nephew", i.e. the inheritance is of shares in a private trading company controlled by the disponer (Jerome having held at least 50% of the shares). Jerome was a director and Declan has worked on a full-time basis for the company for the last five years.

	€
Market value of shares	350,000
Less: business relief (90%)	(315,000)
Revised taxable value	35,000

As the revised taxable value of the inheritance is less than the relevant group threshold and Declan had not previously received any taxable gifts or inheritances, no CAT is payable.

Jonathan's CAT liabilities

Jonathan does not qualify for business relief in respect of the property owned by his father and let to Wiggies Wholesalers as he only got the property and did not get any shares. In order for the property to qualify for business relief, the property and the disponer's interest in the company would have had to be given to the same beneficiary.

	€
Property	500,000
Residue (Note)	29,250
Taxable value of inheritance	529,250
Group A threshold taxed @ Nil	(335,000)
Balance taxable	194,250
CAT payable @ 33%	64,102

Note:

Residue: €65,000 − €2,500 − €4,000 = €58,500 × 50% = €29,250.

Previous gift from aunt is ignored as it belongs to the Group B €32,500 threshold.

Louise's CAT liabilities

The house is exempt from CAT, as the donor, Jerome, lived in the house at the date of death and Louise has lived in the house for at least three years prior to the date of the inheritance and owns no other dwelling house.

	€
Life insurance proceeds	360,000
Residue	29,250

Taxable value of inheritance	389,250
Previous inheritance with same group threshold (Note 1)	179,500
Cumulative gifts/inheritances within Group A threshold	568,750
Group threshold taxed @ Nil	(335,000)
Balance taxable	233,750
CAT @ 33%	77,137
CAT attributable to previous gift (Note 2)	Nil
CAT payable	77,137

Note:
1. The €335,000 Group A threshold applies to this inheritance as Louise's husband was dead at the time of the inheritance to her from her father-in-law.
2. As the previous inheritance is less than the group threshold, no CAT attributed to this inheritance.

Chapter 19

Question 19.1

ABC & Co.
Chartered Accountants

17 November 2021

Mr O'Donovan
3 New Street
Dublin

Re: Proposed Property Transfers

Dear Mr O'Donovan,

You asked me to advise you on the taxation consequences of the proposed property transfers to your daughters on 1 December next.

Stamp Duty
Lorraine and Sheila will have the following stamp duty liabilities:
Lorraine: €350,000 @ 1% = €3,500
Sheila: €250,000 @ 1% = €2,500

Capital Gains Tax
You will be treated as disposing of both properties at market value for CGT purposes. Stamp duty and other legal fees incurred in connection with the properties are deductible in calculating the taxable gains. Accordingly, although the property to be transferred to Sheila has increased in value since you acquired it, taking account of your stamp duty and legal fees, overall a capital loss arises.

I have estimated, however, that a CGT liability of approximately €22,564 will arise on the deemed disposal of the property to Lorraine (see Appendix 1).

Capital Acquisitions Tax

Both your daughters will be treated as receiving a taxable gift from you equal to the market value of the property transferred to them. An individual may receive gifts or inheritances up to a total value of €335,000 from parents over their lifetime (since 5 December 1991) without giving rise to any CAT liability. Total gifts and inheritances in excess of €335,000 are subject to CAT at 33%.

I understand both Lorraine and Sheila have previously inherited assets valued at €160,000 and €225,000, respectively, from their mother in 2012. (Sheila also previously received a gift of shares from an uncle, however this is ignored for the purposes of this calculation.) In addition, as Lorraine has been living rent-free in an apartment owned by you for the last few years, she is treated as receiving a taxable gift from you each year equal to the market rent that would have been payable by her in respect of the apartment.

Taking account of the above, I have estimated that the transfer will give rise to a CAT liability of approximately €72,435 for Lorraine and €45,375 for Sheila (see Appendix 2). Your CGT liability of approximately €22,564 relates to the disposal of the property to Lorraine and therefore may be offset against Lorraine's CAT liability, thereby reducing the CAT payable by Lorraine to approximately €49,871. However, if Lorraine disposes of the apartment within two years, the CGT credit will be clawed back.

There is an exemption from CAT for gifts or inheritances of residential property provided certain conditions are met. A key condition for gifts is not met as neither of your daughters is a dependent relative.

If you have any queries on the above or wish to discuss further any of the issues raised, please do not hesitate to give me a call.

Yours sincerely,

APPENDIX 1

Capital Gains Tax Liability on Transfer of Properties

Transfer to Lorraine O'Donovan

	€	€
Market value of property		350,000
Cost in November 1999	220,000	
Legal fees and stamp duty	15,000	
Total cost	235,000	
Indexation factor: 1.193		
Indexed cost of property		(280,355)
Capital gain		69,645
Annual exemption		(1,270)
Taxable gain		68,375
CGT @ 33%		22,564

Transfer to Sheila O'Donovan

	€	€
Market value of property		250,000
Cost in July 2019	240,000	
Legal fees and stamp duty	28,000	
Total cost		(268,000)
Capital loss		(18,000)

The loss arising on the property transferred to Sheila may not be offset against the gain arising on the transfer of the property to Lorraine as the loss arose on a **disposal to a connected person**.

APPENDIX 2
Capital Acquisitions Tax Liability on Transfer of Properties

Transfer to Lorraine O'Donovan

	€	€
Cumulative gifts/inheritances received from parents:		
Inheritance from mother		160,000
Gift of rent-free apartment from father:		
2019 €1,500 × 9 months	13,500	
2020 €1,500 × 12 months	18,000	
2021 €1,500 × 11 months	16,500	48,000
Gift of property from father:		
Market value	350,000	
Less: stamp duty	3,500	346,500
Total		554,500
Tax-free amount		(335,000)
Taxable		219,500
CAT @ 33%		72,435
Less: CGT credit		(22,564)
CAT payable		49,871

Transfer to Sheila O'Donovan

	€	€
Cumulative gifts/inheritances received from parents:		
Inheritance from mother		225,000
Gift of property from father:		
Market value	250,000	
Less: stamp duty	(2,500)	247,500

continued overleaf

Total	472,500
Tax-free amount	(335,000)
Taxable	137,500
CAT @ 33%	45,375

Question 19.2

(a) **Janet's CGT liability 2021**

1. Shares in Fogarty Fabrics Ltd

	€	€
Market value		950,000
Cost – market value March 1997	340,000	
Indexed cost (indexation factor: 1.251)		(425,340)
Gain		524,660

Exempt due to retirement relief:

$$\text{Proportion} = \frac{\text{Chargeable business assets}}{\text{Chargeable assets}}$$

$$= \frac{€130,000 + €215,000 + €70,000}{€130,000 + €215,000 + €70,000 + €350,000} = 54.25\%$$

Exempt portion of gain €524,660 × 54.25%		(284,628)
Taxable gain		240,032

As the conditions for revised entrepreneur relief have been satisfied, this gain is taxable at 10% (assuming Janet has not disposed of any other chargeable business assets on or after 1 January 2016).

2. House

	€	€
Market value		250,000
Cost	40,000	
Indexed cost (indexation factor: 1.503)		(60,120)
Gain		189,880

3. Farmland

	€	€
Market value		1,250,000
Market value August 1994	168,000	
Indexed cost (indexation factor: 1.309)		(219,912)
Gain		1,030,088

CGT liability for Janet 2021

	€
Shares	240,032
House	189,880
Farmland	1,030,088
Total	1,460,000
Losses forward	(10,000)
Taxable gain	1,450,000
CGT @ 10%/33%:	
€240,032 @ 10%	24,003
€1,450,000 – €240,032 = €1,209,968 @ 33%	399,289
Janet's CGT liability 2021	423,292

Note: no annual exemption is available as retirement relief applied.

(b) **CAT liabilities**

1. Shares in Fogarty Fabric Ltd (received by Adam)

	€
Market value of shares	950,000
Value attributed to investment property	(350,000)
Value excluding investment property	600,000
Business relief (90%)	(540,000)
	60,000
Value attributed to investment property	350,000
Taxable value	410,000
Small gift exemption	(3,000)
	407,000
Previous gift from mother	150,000
	557,000
Group threshold @ Nil	(335,000)
Balance	222,000
CAT @ 33%	73,260
CGT attributable to gift of shares:	
Less: CGT credit re shares	(24,003)
Adam's CAT liability	49,257

2. House

	€
Received by Julie €250,000 @ 50%	125,000
Received by Nigel €250,000 @ 50%	125,000

continued overleaf

Julie

Taxable value	125,000
Less: small gift exemption	(3,000)
Taxable	122,000

Julie has not previously received any taxable gifts or inheritances and, as the taxable gift less annual exemption is less than the Group A threshold of €335,000, no CAT liability arises in respect of the gift to her.

Nigel	€
Market value of gift	125,000
Small gift exemption	(3,000)
	122,000
Group C threshold @ Nil	(16,250)
Balance	105,750
CAT @ 33%	34,897

CGT attributable to gift of half-share in house:

$$€399,289 \times \frac{€189,880}{€1,209,968} = €62,660 \times 50\% \quad (31,330)$$

Nigel's CAT liability	3,567

Note: the previous gift from his aunt is ignored as the Group B, €32,500, threshold applies.

3. Farmland

	€
Market value	1,250,000
Agricultural relief (90%)	(1,125,000)
Taxable value	125,000
Less: small gift exemption	(3,000)
Taxable	122,000

He satisfies the asset test (100% agricultural property) and the activity test (lease to a full-time farmer), so he qualifies for agricultural relief. He must lease the land or farm it himself for at least six years to avoid a clawback.

Kevin has not previously received any taxable gifts or inheritances and, as the taxable gift is less than the Group A threshold of €335,000, no CAT liability arises in respect of the gift to him.

Note: the credit for CGT will be clawed back on any beneficiary who disposes of the asset within two years of the date of the gift.

Question 19.3

(a) **CGT liability**

Disposal to Janet

Government stock – exempt from CGT.

Disposal of business to Jake

Van rental business – no capital gain (loss relieved via capital allowance system).

Inventories, receivables – non-chargeable asset.

Goodwill:

	€
Market value 16/07/2021	300,000
Cost January 2015	(55,000)
Gain	245,000

Disposals to Brendan

Vans – no capital gain (loss relieved via capital allowance system).

Building

	€
Market value 16/07/2021	250,000
Cost January 2015	(80,000)
Gain	170,000

Cash – non-chargeable asset

CGT liability

Gains	€
Goodwill	245,000
Building	170,000
Total	415,000
CGT €415,000 @ 10%	41,500

Note: retirement relief does not apply as the business was only owned for six years, but revised entrepreneur relief does apply as the conditions have been satisfied.

(b) **CAT liability**

Janet

No CAT liability arises as Ronnie had owned the securities for 15 years and Janet is not Irish domiciled or ordinarily resident.

Jake

Taxable value of gift:

	€
Business	1,280,000
Less: business relief @ 90%	(1,152,000)
Taxable value	128,000
Cash	20,000

continued overleaf

Total taxable value	148,000
Inheritance from mother	460,000
Total gifts/inheritances within Group A threshold	608,000
Group A threshold taxed @ Nil	(335,000)
Balance taxable	273,000
CAT @ 33%	90,090
CAT attributed to previous inheritance (Note 1)	(41,250)
CAT in respect of current gift	48,840
Credit for CGT (Note 2)	(9,900)
CAT payable	38,940

Notes:
1. €460,000 − €335,000 = €125,000 @ 33% = €41,250
2. Credit for CGT:

CGT on disposal of business = goodwill of €245,000 @ 10% = €24,500
CAT attributable to goodwill – as the CGT relates only to the goodwill, the CGT can only be credited against CAT re goodwill, i.e. CAT re goodwill only is:

$$€48,840 \times \frac{€30,000 \text{ (i.e. } 300,000 \times 10\%)}{€148,000} = €9,900 \text{ (or } €30,000 \times 33\%)$$

Credit limited to lower of CGT or CAT, i.e. €9,900.
The credit for CGT will be clawed back if the goodwill of the van business is disposed of within two years.

Brendan

Taxable value of gift:	€
Vans	40,000
Building (Note 1)	250,000
Cash	50,000
Total taxable value	340,000
Inheritance from mother	460,000
Total gifts/inheritances	800,000
Group A threshold taxed @ Nil	(335,000)
Balance taxable	465,000
CAT @ 33%	153,450
CAT attributed to previous inheritance (Note 2)	(41,250)
CAT in respect of current gift	112,200
Credit for CGT (Note 3)	(17,000)
CAT payable	95,200

Notes:
1. Business relief does not apply to the gift of vans and office buildings as the relief only applies to gifts of business interests not business assets.
2. €460,000 – €335,000 = €125,000 @ 33% = €41,250
3. Credit for CGT:
    CGT on disposal of building = €170,000 @ 10% = €17,000

    CAT attributable to building = €112,200 $\times \dfrac{€250,000}{€340,000}$ = €82,500

    Credit limited to lower of CGT or CAT, i.e. €17,000.
    The credit for CGT will be clawed back if the building is disposed of within two years.

Question 19.4

XYZ Chartered Accountants
Main Street

4 June 2021

Mr Mark Murphy
Director
Murphy Electrical Wholesalers Ltd
Church Street

Re: Proposed transfer of shares to Jake Murphy

Dear Mark,

I refer to our recent telephone conversation in which you asked me to advise you on the tax consequences of the transfer of your entire shareholding in Murphy Electrical Wholesalers Ltd to your son, Jake.

Background

My understanding is that you inherited all the shares in Murphy Electrical Wholesalers Ltd on the death of your brother in June 1995. At that time the shares were valued at €2 million. The shares are now valued at €3.5 million and you are considering transferring your entire shareholding to your son, Jake.

Taxation consequences of transfer of shares

1. Capital Gains Tax
The gift of shares will be treated as a sale by you of your shares at market value for CGT purposes. I have estimated that the CGT arising will be €312,180 (see Appendix 1).

2. Stamp Duty
Stamp duty of 1% of the value of the shares will be payable by Jake, i.e. €35,000.

3. Capital Acquisitions Tax
Assuming your son has not previously received any taxable gifts from you or your wife, CAT will be payable at the rate of 33% on the excess of the taxable value of the shares received from you over €335,000. The taxable value of a gift is normally calculated as the market value of the property which is the subject of a gift less any consideration given and any liabilities payable out of the gift. However, if the property which is gifted consists of business assets or shares in certain unquoted

companies, the taxable value is further reduced by 90%. This relief is known as business relief. The conditions which must be satisfied if business relief is to apply to the transfer of shares to your son are outlined in Appendix 2.

Assuming the only cost payable by Jake is stamp duty, if your son qualifies for business relief, the taxable value of the shares for CAT purposes will be €346,500, and his CAT liability will be nil, calculated as follows:

	€
Market value of shares	3,500,000
Less: stamp duty @ 1%	(35,000)
	3,465,000
Business relief @ 90%	(3,118,500)
Taxable value	346,500
Less: tax-free amount	(335,000)
Taxable	11,500
CAT @ 33%	3,795
Less: CGT credit (lower of €3,795 or €312,180)	(3,795)
CAT liability	Nil

If, however, business relief does not apply, Jake's CAT liability will be as follows:

	€
Market value of shares	3,500,000
Less: stamp duty @ 1%	(35,000)
	3,465,000
Tax-free amount	(335,000)
Taxable	3,130,000
CAT @ 33%	1,032,900
Less: CGT payable	(312,180)
CAT liability	720,720

As can be seen from these computations, Jake's CAT liability may be reduced by the CGT payable by you on the transfer of the shares to him. This credit for CGT will only apply if your son does not dispose of the shares within two years after the date of the gift.

Conclusion

As outlined, if Jake qualifies for business relief, a substantial CAT liability can be avoided. Accordingly, it is important that before any decision is taken to transfer the shares to Jake that we meet to go through these conditions to make sure that they are satisfied.

In making a decision to transfer the shares to Jake, you should also bear in mind that if he were to inherit the shares from you rather than by receiving them as a gift, **there would be no CGT liability**, and Jake's CAT position, before CGT credit, would be unchanged.

Accordingly, bearing in mind the significant CGT cost associated with the transfer, you might decide ultimately to wait a few years to gift him the shares or, alternatively, leave him the shares in your will. We can, however, discuss this aspect further when we meet as there are rules to be satisfied before full retirement relief applies.

Yours sincerely,

APPENDIX 1

Capital Gains Tax Liability on Transfer of Shares by Mr Mark Murphy to Mr Jake Murphy

	€	€
Market value of shares		3,500,000
Market value in June 1995	2,000,000	
Indexation factor 1.277		
Indexed value of €2 million		(2,554,000)
Capital gain		946,000
CGT @ 33%		312,180

Note: Mark Murphy does not qualify for retirement relief as he did not work as a full-time director for at least five years; nor does he qualify for revised entrepreneur relief as he did not work for the company for not less than 50% of his time for three of the last five years.

APPENDIX 2

Business Relief – Conditions to be Satisfied

In order for a gift of shares in an unquoted company to qualify for business relief for CAT purposes the following conditions must be satisfied:

(1) The recipient of the gift must, after receiving the gift of shares, either:

  (a) control more than 25% of the voting shares in the company;

  (b) together with his relatives, control the company; or

  (c) hold at least 10% of the issued share capital and have worked full-time in the company for the five years prior to the gift or inheritance.

(2) The company's business must not consist wholly or mainly of:

  (a) dealing in currencies, securities, stocks or shares, land or buildings; or

  (b) making or holding investments.

  In determining whether a company's business consists wholly or mainly of one of (a) or (b) above, wholly or mainly can be taken as more than 50%. Each case is looked at separately, but broadly it can be taken that if more than 50% of a company's assets and more than 50% of its income is derived from business activities other than (a) or (b) above, the company will satisfy this test.

(3) The shares must have been owned by the person making the gift, or by him and his spouse, for at least five years prior to the gift.

(4) To the extent that the value of the shares is attributable to any non-trade assets owned by the company, that portion of the shares will not qualify for business relief. For example, a company valued at €5 million on an assets basis owns an investment property valued at €1 million. Only 80% of the value of any shares in this company transferred by way of gift or inheritance will qualify for business relief.

(5) To the extent that the value of the shares is attributable to any business assets which were not being used wholly or mainly for the business for a continuous period of two years prior to the

date of the gift, or if acquired less than two years ago for the period since acquisition, must also be left out of account. An asset is not regarded as being used wholly or mainly for the purpose of the trade where it was used wholly or mainly for the personal benefit of the owner of the shares or any of his relatives. This provision is aimed at significant assets which have an impact on the value of the shares, e.g. a private yacht or a large house provided to a director/shareholder. Assets such as the typical company car while used for the personal benefit of a director/shareholder would not normally impact upon the value of the shares in a company.

(6) The company need not be incorporated in Ireland. It can be incorporated anywhere.

Chapter 20

Question 20.1

MEMORANDUM

To	:	
From	:	
Date	:	
Re	:	Capital Acquisitions Tax Queries

I refer to the matters recently raised by you.

(a) Accountable Persons
The person accountable for payment of the tax is the donee or successor, as the case may be.

(b) Delivery of Returns
A person who is accountable for CAT is obliged to deliver a return where the benefit comprises agricultural property or relevant business property or when the aggregate taxable value of all taxable benefits taken by a donee or successor which have the same group threshold exceeds 80% of the group threshold amount. Even if the 80% threshold has not been exceeded, a person must deliver a return if required to do so by notice in writing from the Revenue Commissioners. They must comply within the time set out in the notice.

If the valuation date arises in the period from 1 January to 31 August, the pay and file deadline is 31 October in that year; if the valuation date arises in the period from 1 September to 31 December, the pay and file deadline is 31 October in the following year. If the return is filed using ROS, the filing date is extended, generally to mid-November.

(c) Return Details
   (i) The return must show:
      (I) every applicable gift/inheritance;
      (II) all property comprised in such gift/inheritance;
      (III) an estimate of the market value of the property; and
      (IV) such particulars as may be relevant to the assessment of tax in respect of such gift.
   (ii) Also, the taxpayer must make on the return an assessment of such amount of tax, as to the best of his knowledge, information and belief, ought to be charged and paid.
   (iii) Finally, he must pay any tax which he calculates is due.

(d) Defective Return

Where an accountable person, who has made a return becomes aware, at any time, that the return is defective in a material respect, by reason of anything contained or omitted from it, he shall, without being asked by the Revenue Commissioners:

(i) deliver to them an additional return;

(ii) make an amended assessment; and

(iii) pay the outstanding tax.

The above action is required within three months of becoming aware of the defect in the original return.

(e) Undervaluation of Property

A surcharge ranging from 10% to 30% will be levied where the market value of property is underestimated in returns for CAT purposes. The legislation contains a table setting out the percentage surcharge to be levied depending on the extent to which the property was undervalued.

The surcharge applies to the total amount of tax ultimately attributable to the property. In addition, interest penalties will apply to the tax underpaid as well as to the surcharge.

Question 20.2

Before computing the CAT liabilities, it is necessary to calculate the split of the estate for each beneficiary.

	Total	Sheila(^{2}/$_3$)	Ruth(^{1}/$_6$)	Angela(^{1}/$_6$)
	€	€	€	€
House	600,000	400,000	100,000	100,000
Mortgage thereon	(60,000)	(40,000)	(10,000)	(10,000)
	540,000	360,000	90,000	90,000
Newsagents	900,000	600,000	150,000	150,000
Government Stock	66,000	44,000	11,000	11,000
Holiday home	150,000	100,000	25,000	25,000
Residue:				

Cash	45,000				
Income tax liabilities	(15,000)				
Legal expenses	(6,000)				
Funeral expenses	(3,000)				
Net cash		21,000	14,000	3,500	3,500

Ruth and Angela also received the insurance proceeds of €140,000.

(a) CAT liabilities

Sheila

Sheila has no liability to CAT as she was the spouse of Robert. The fact that they had been separated for 10 years is irrelevant. They are still legally married.

Ruth

	€	€
Newsagents	150,000	
Business relief @ 90%	(135,000)	15,000
Life insurance €140,000 × 50%		70,000
House less mortgage (Note)		90,000
Government stock		11,000
Holiday home		25,000
Net cash		3,500
Taxable value of inheritance		214,500
Group A threshold taxed @ Nil		(335,000)
CAT payable		Nil

Note:
House does not qualify for exemption from CAT as Ruth had an interest in another dwelling house at the date of the inheritance, i.e. the holiday home in Kerry.

Ruth has not previously received any taxable gifts or inheritances and the current benefit is below the threshold, so no CAT is payable in respect of the current inheritance.

Angela

	€	€
Newsagents	150,000	
Business relief @ 90%	(135,000)	15,000
Life insurance €140,000 × 50%		70,000
House less mortgage (Note)		90,000
Government stock		11,000
Holiday home		25,000
Net cash		3,500
Taxable value of inheritance		214,500
Group A threshold taxed @ Nil		(335,000)
CAT payable		Nil

Note:
House does not qualify for exemption from CAT as Angela had an interest in another dwelling house at the date of the inheritance, i.e. the holiday home in Kerry.

As Angela has not previously received any taxable gifts or inheritances and the current benefit is below the threshold, no CAT is payable in respect of the current inheritance.

(b) **Payment of tax**
If interest charges are to be avoided, CAT must be paid by 31 October 2022.

Chapter 21

Question 21.1

Overseas Limited

1. Corporation tax

		€
	Case I: Branch trading profits	600,000
	Case III: Branch interest income	20,000
		620,000
	Chargeable gains	
	Gain on branch assets: €32,000 @ 33% ÷ 12.5%	84,480
		704,480
	Corporation tax:	
	€684,480 @ 12.5% = €85,560	
	€20,000 @ 25% = €5,000	90,560
2.	Capital gains tax	
	Sale of land – €50,000 @ 33%	16,500

Chapter 22

Question 22.1

Foreign Income Limited
Accounts Year ended 31 December 2021
Corporation Tax Computation

	€
Case I	800,000
Case III (€88,000 + €80,000)	168,000
Income	968,000
Corporation tax:	
€800,000 @ 12.5% = €100,000	
€88,000 @ 12.5% = €11,000 (Note)	
€80,000 @ 25% = €20,000	
Corporation tax	131,000

Note: As the dividend of €88,000 is received from a company resident in a country with which Ireland has a tax treaty and it is paid out of trading profits, it is taxed at 12.5%.

The dividend from Irish Maniacs Limited is exempt.

Chapter 23

Question 23.1

Capital allowances may be claimed on intangible assets used for the purpose of the trade, which includes patents and the related goodwill. The expenditure of €3 million paid by Grabbit Ltd for patents and related goodwill will qualify for capital allowances.

Grabbit could claim the writing down allowance based on its accounting treatment of intangible assets, i.e. in accordance with its policy of amortising over 18 years. Alternatively, it could opt for a fixed write down period of 15 years at a rate of 7% per annum plus 2% in final year.

The 15-year fixed period would be preferable for Grabbit as it is the shorter of the two options.

As Grabbit acquired the asset after 11 October 2017, the aggregate amount of capital allowances and related interest that may be claimed in any accounting period is limited to 80% of the trading income of the relevant trade.

Question 23.2

Global Fishing Ltd – R&D Tax Credit:

	€
Staff costs (Note 1)	173,250
Plant and machinery (Note 2)	100,000
Subcontracted R&D (Note 3)	100,000
Total qualifying costs	373,250
R&D Tax credit @ 25%	93,312

Notes:
1. Only staff costs for employees undertaking R&D activities qualify for the R&D tax credit.
2. Plant and machinery restricted to 50% based on usage for R&D.
3. Subcontracted R&D restricted to the amount of the non-outsourced R&D expenditure up to a maximum of €100,000 or 15% of the non-outsourced R&D expenditure. Therefore:

Outsourced R&D expenditure	€155,000
Non-outsourced R&D:	
Staff costs	€173,250
Plant and machinery	€100,000
	€273,250

Allowable outsourced R&D limited to **greater** of:

€100,000 (as €273,250 exceeds the €100,000 limit)

or

15% of non-outsourced R&D expenditure = €273,250 × 15% = €40,988

Therefore, maximum claim for outsourced R&D is **€100,000**.

Chapter 24

Question 24.1

Corporation Tax Computation Period Ended 31/12/2021 – Z Ltd

	€
Case I	Nil
Case III income	20,000
Total profits	20,000
Corporation tax @ 25%	5,000
Less: loss relief on a value basis	(5,000)
Corporation tax	Nil

Corporation Tax Computation Period Ended 31/12/2021 – B Ltd

		€
Case 1	Adjusted trading profit	180,000
	Deduct: Case I losses forward	(16,000)
	Deduct: group relief surrendered by Z Ltd	(56,000)
		108,000
Case III	Interest	4,000
Case V	Rents	20,000
Profit liable to corporation tax		132,000
Corporation tax:		
€108,000 @ 12.5% = €13,500		
€24,000 @ 25% = €6,000		19,500

Loss Memo

	€
Loss	96,000
Used on a value basis in Z Ltd: €40,000 @ 12.5% = €5,000	(40,000)
Claim section 420A balance of loss	(56,000)
Loss available	Nil

It should be noted that Z Ltd could have opted not to claim section 396B relief and instead surrender losses of €96,000 to B Ltd.

Question 24.2

A Ltd – Corporation Tax Computation Period to 31/03/2021

	€
Case I profits	Nil
Case III income	1,000

continued overleaf

Case V income	20,000
Liable to corporation tax	21,000
Corporation tax @ 25%	5,250
Less: loss relief on a value basis	(5,250)
Corporation tax payable	Nil

B Ltd – Corporation Tax Computation Period to 31/03/2021

	€
Case I	56,000
Less: group loss surrendered by A Ltd	(48,000)
	8,000
Case III	2,000
Case V	25,000
Liable to corporation tax	35,000
Corporation tax:	
€8,000 @ 12.5%	1,000
€27,000 @ 25%	6,750
Corporation tax payable	7,750

C Ltd – Corporation Tax Computation Period to 31/03/2021

	€
Case I	48,000
Less: Case I loss forward	(26,000)
	22,000
Case III	3,000
Case V	2,000
Liable to corporation tax	27,000
Corporation tax:	
€22,000 @ 12.5%	2,750
€5,000 @ 25%	1,250
Corporation tax payable	4,000

Loss Memo	
Loss	90,000
Used on a value basis in A Ltd	
€42,000 @ 12.5% = €5,250	(42,000)
Claim section 420A balance of loss to B Ltd	(48,000)
Loss available	Nil

Alternatively, part of the loss could have been surrendered to C Ltd to reduce its Case I income to nil.

The loss forward of €4,000 in A Ltd is carried forward to be used against trading income of the same trade in A Ltd.

Question 24.3

(a) **Corporation Tax Computation**

Queen Group

	Queen Ltd	*Pawn Ltd*	*Rook Ltd*
	€	€	€
Profit/(loss) per accounts	202,313	(2,030)	(80,586)
Disallow:			
Depreciation	12,000	10,000	16,000
Entertainment	1,350	1,200	1,650
Interest (Note 1)	400	10,720	–
	216,063	19,890	(62,936)
Less: grant release	(3,000)	–	–
	213,063	19,890	(62,936)
Capital allowances	(7,375)	(3,000)	(5,627)
Case I loss forward	–	(80,000)	–
	205,688	(63,110)	(68,563)
Group relief re trading losses (Note 2)	(68,563)	–	68,563
Case I	137,125	–	–
Case III deposit interest	23,846	–	–
	160,971	–	–

Corporation tax payable:

Pawn Ltd	Nil
Rook Ltd	Nil

Queen Ltd:

Profit for period	160,971

€137,125 @ 12.5% = €17,141

€23,846 @ 25% = €5,961

Corporation tax	23,102

Notes:

1. The interest paid by Pawn Ltd is not allowed as 'a charge on income', as there is no common director. The amount charged in arriving at the profit is disallowed, as it is not a trading expense.
2. The trading loss of Rook Ltd can be offset against the trading income of Queen Ltd. Pawn Ltd has no income for this period, as it is covered by losses forward and these cannot be grouped.

(b) **Losses Forward to 2022**

	Losses Forward
Pawn Ltd	€63,110
Rook Ltd	Nil
Queen Ltd	Nil

(c) **Payment of tax**

As Queen Ltd is a small company (its prior period corporation tax did not exceed €200,000), preliminary tax is the lower of €55,000 × 100% or €23,102 × 90%, i.e. €20,792. The preliminary tax of €20,792 is due on or before 23 November 2021. The balance of €2,310 is due on/before 23 September 2022, at the same time as the tax return.

Chapter 25

Question 25.1

Dear Client,

I refer to your recent query in respect of the tax implications of Irish Cable Installations Ltd being sold in the coming weeks.

I assume the following to apply:

- Fibre Optic Developments Ltd purchased the property in 2016 at a cost of €3 million.
- The property was transferred to Irish Cable in November 2019, at a time when the property was valued at €4 million.
- Stamp duty and CGT group relief were claimed in November 2019, and as such no tax arose on the transfer of the property between both companies.
- Irish Cable is due to leave the VC Holdings Group before 31 December.
- The property is currently valued at €4.5 million.

It is now circa 25 months since the property was transferred to Irish Cable.

CGT and stamp duty must be considered in advance of the share sale closing.

Group Relief – Chargeable Gains

CGT group relief was claimed on the transfer of the property to Irish Cable and as such no CGT arose for Fibre Optic on the disposal in November 2019.

There is, however, provision that where Irish Cable leaves the VC Holdings CGT group within 10 years of the transfer, there will be a clawback of CGT relief provided for in November 2019. Irish Cable is due to leave the group before 31 December 2021.

The factory, on the event of the group relationship being broken, will be deemed to be sold and immediately re-acquired by the company leaving the group (i.e. Irish Cable) at its market value at the time of original acquisition by that company (i.e. €4 million in November 2019).

This, in effect, means that the gain on the original transfer from Fibre Optic to Irish Cable is triggered.

Indexation relief, if available, will be applied by reference to that date and not by reference to the date that Irish Cable actually leaves the group. In this case, however, as the property was acquired in 2016, no indexation relief will be available.

It is important to note that the liability in respect of this clawback rests with Irish Cable and is due to be paid with its corporation tax liability for the year ended 31 December 2021. The company may be required to make a top-up payment of preliminary tax on or before 31 January 2022 to meet its preliminary tax obligations. The clawback can be computed as follows:

Deemed market value consideration	€4,000,000
Less: cost (no indexation relief)	(€3,000,000)
Chargeable gain	€1,000,000
Tax payable:	
Taxed at effective rate of 33%	
€1,000,000 @ 33%*	€330,000

*The rate that applied when the asset was transferred, i.e. 33% in November 2019.

The base cost of the property will be €4 million on the event of a future disposal.

Disposal of Shares in Irish Cable by VC Holdings

VC Holdings is due to receive consideration of €20 million on the disposal of its 100% shareholding in Irish Cable.

VC Holdings acquired the share capital in Irish Cable for €500,000 in 2019.

A chargeable gain will arise as follows on disposal:

Proceeds	€20,000,000
Less: base cost	(€500,000)
Chargeable gain	€19,500,000

VC Holdings would ordinarily be liable to an effective rate of 33% on the chargeable gain arising on the disposal of its shares in Irish Cable.

There is, however, an exemption from tax on the disposal of certain shareholdings. This relief is known as the "participation exemption". The relief exempts a chargeable gain from tax in certain circumstances. The conditions for the relief are:

1. VC Holdings must be the parent company of Irish Cable at the time of disposal. This means that VC Holdings must have held a minimum shareholding in Irish Cable at the time of disposal or within two years prior to the disposal. This minimum holding must be at least 5% of the following:

    - the ordinary share capital of Irish Cable;
    - entitlement to distributable profits; and
    - assets available for distribution on winding up of the company.

    As VC Holdings owns 100% of the share capital, the minimum shareholding condition is met.

2. VC Holdings is required to have held the minimum holding for a continuous period of 12 months over the last 24 months. This condition is also satisfied.
3. Irish Cable must have carried on a trade, which it has.
4. Irish Cable must be resident in a Member State of the EU or a country with which Ireland has signed a tax treaty. Irish Cable is an Irish resident company, so this condition is met.
5. Irish Cable must not derive the greater part of its value from land and minerals in the State. We will need to ensure that this condition is satisfied.

If all of the above required conditions have been met, the chargeable gain of €19,500,000 will be exempt from Irish tax.

This results in a tax saving to VC Holdings of €6,435,000 (i.e. €19,500,000 @ 33%).

Stamp Duty

Stamp duty relief was claimed in November 2019 as both companies were 100% associated at the time of transfer. This effectively reduced the level of stamp duty arising to nil.

Companies are associated with one another if there is a minimum 90% direct or indirect relationship between them in terms of ordinary share capital, profits available for distribution and assets available for distribution on a winding up.

If both companies cease to be associated within two years of the date of the conveyance or transfer of the property, full stamp duty will become payable.

The property was transferred to Irish Cable in November 2019. It is now 25 months since the transfer and on this basis, a clawback of stamp duty will not arise in the event of Irish Cable being sold (and the association being broken).

Should you have any further queries, please do not hesitate to contact me.

Kind regards,

Question 25.2

The structure of the group can be shown as:

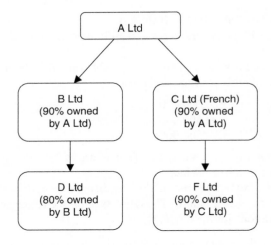

Corporation Tax Group

A corporation tax loss group exists if one company holds, directly or indirectly, not less than 75% of the ordinary share capital of the other company, or both are 75% subsidiaries of a third company.

A Ltd and B Ltd are in a group, because A Ltd owns directly 75% of the share capital of B Ltd. D Ltd is **not** in a group with A Ltd as A Ltd owns indirectly only 72% of its share capital.

As C Ltd is resident in the EU or an EEA country that has a tax treaty with Ireland (i.e. France), then provided it has a branch in Ireland, it can be in the group. Also, in determining whether F Ltd is in a corporation tax group with A Ltd, the holding via C Ltd is taken into account as it is resident in the EU or an EEA country which has a tax treaty with Ireland. Therefore, as A Ltd holds indirectly 81% of F Ltd, F Ltd is in the group.

Capital Gains Group

A capital gains group consists of a principal company and its 75% subsidiaries, and its subsidiaries 75% subsidiaries.

A Ltd is in a group with its 75% subsidiaries and its subsidiaries 75% subsidiaries. Both B Ltd and D Ltd are in the capital gains group with A Ltd, because B Ltd is a 75% subsidiary of A Ltd and D Ltd is a 75% subsidiary of B Ltd.

C Ltd and F Ltd are in a capital gains group with A Ltd (and therefore with B Ltd and D Ltd) as both are an Irish resident company (F Ltd) or a company resident in a country with a tax treaty with Ireland (C Ltd). The holding through C Ltd may be taken into account in determining if a capital gains group exists, but assets can only be transferred at 'no gain/no loss' to C Ltd if they continue to be chargeable assets (e.g. used for the purposes of an Irish branch of C Ltd).

Solution 25.3

(a) The "participation exemption" is an exemption from corporation tax on gains from the disposal of shareholdings by a parent company. Although a gain on disposal is not taxable, this also means that there no relief for a loss on such a disposal.

The conditions that the **investor company** (the company disposing of the shareholding) must satisfy are:

- The company disposing of the shares, i.e. the investor company, must be a 'parent' company at the time of disposal, or had been a parent company not less than two years prior to the time of disposal. A 'parent' company must have a **minimum shareholding of at least 5% in the investee company**. That is:
  - it must hold not less than 5% of the company's ordinary share capital;
  - it must be beneficially entitled to not less than 5% of the profits available for distribution to equity holders of the company; **and**
  - on a winding up, it must be beneficially entitled to not less than 5% of the assets available for distribution to equity holders.
- The investor is required to have the minimum holding in the investee company for a **continuous period of at least 12 months.**

The exemption continues to apply for two years after the parent company's minimum shareholding is no longer satisfied. **The exemption does not apply where the shares derive the greater part of their value from specified Irish assets.**

(b) An investee company must satisfy the following conditions:

- It must **carry on a trade**, or the business of the investor company, its investee company and their "5%" investee companies, taken as a whole, must consist wholly or mainly of the carrying on of a trade or trades.
- At the time of the disposal the investee company must **be resident in a Member State of the EU or a country with which Ireland has a tax treaty**.

Availability of PE on Red Ltd's disposal of companies:

1. **Orange Ltd** – PE is not available as Red Ltd did not hold a substantial (i.e. at least 5%) holding.
2. **Blue Ltd** – PE is available as:
   - Blue Ltd is a trading company, and
   - although the % shareholding in Blue Ltd no longer constitutes a substantial shareholding, the exemption is still available for disposals in the 24 months following 1 July 2021, as at least a 5% stake has been held for 12 months.
3. **Pink Inc** – PE is available on the sale as:
   - Red Ltd holds a substantial shareholding in Pink Inc,
   - Pink Inc is a trading company,
   - Pink Inc is resident in a double tax treaty country,
   - the shareholding was held for more than 1 year.
4. **Black Ltd** – The shareholding of Red Ltd and White Ltd can be aggregated in order to determine whether the substantial shareholding requirement is satisfied.
   PE is available on the sale as:
   - Red Ltd has a substantial shareholding in Black Ltd (3% + 3.75% (75% × 5%) = 6.75%). As Red Ltd controls 75% of White Ltd, the shares held through White Ltd are treated as though they are held by Red Ltd,
   - Black Ltd is a trading company both before and after the disposal by Red Ltd,
   - the shareholding was held for more than 1 year.
5. **Green Ltd** – PE is not available on the sale as Red Ltd has not held the shares throughout a 12-month period.
6. **Purple Ltd** – The shares in Purple Ltd derive their value from land in the State. The PE is therefore not available.

(c)   Red Ltd owns 4% of Blue Ltd. Red Ltd sold 5% of its 9% shareholding, acquired in June 2005, on 1 July 2021. To qualify for the minimum shareholding test for PE, Red Ltd must have held a minimum shareholding of 5% in Blue Ltd for a continuous period of at least 12 months ending within two years of the date of disposal. Therefore, Red Ltd meets the minimum holding test for PE until 1 July 2023. Accordingly, if the disposal of Blue Ltd's remaining shareholding is **expected to realise a gain**, Red Ltd should dispose of the shares on or before 1 July 2023 (i.e. within two years of the previous sale of Blue Ltd's shares) to avail of the PE and the gain will be exempt.

However, If Red Ltd were to dispose of the 4% shareholding before 1 July 2023 and in doing so crystallised a loss, the loss would not be allowable for corporation tax purposes.

Therefore, if Red Ltd is **expected to make a loss** on disposal it should wait until after 1 July 2023 to sell the shareholding, at which time Red Ltd will not have held a minimum 5% stake in the last two years. The PE will therefore not apply and the loss will be allowable.

Question 25.4

Capital Gains Tax

Capital gains group relief is available to the AGA group on transferring the property of BGB to other group companies, providing the following conditions are met:

1.   The companies are 75% subsidiaries (or greater) of the parent company. As all three companies are owned at least 80% by AGA this condition is satisfied.
2.   The parent company is entitled to at least 75% of the profits available for distribution and assets available on a winding up of the subsidiaries. Again, all three companies are owned at least 80% by AGA so this condition is also met.
3.   The subsidiary companies are Irish resident. As they have not indicated that they are resident elsewhere, it is assumed that all companies are Irish resident and so this condition is also met.

The AGA group therefore qualifies as a CGT group and the property can be transferred from BGB to either CGC or DGD before it is sold, thereby utilising the capital losses.

Stamp Duty

Group relief on stamp duty is available to the AGA group on transferring the property to other group companies if the following conditions are met:

1.   The companies are 90% subsidiaries (or greater) of the parent company. Only BGB (100%) and CGC (90%) satisfy this condition, so stamp duty relief would only apply to them. DGD is an 80% subsidiary and would not qualify for the relief.

2. The parent company is entitled to at least 90% of the profits available for distribution and profits available on a winding up of the subsidiaries. Again, as in 1. above, only BGB and CGC satisfy this condition. DGD would not qualify for the relief.

Therefore, the most tax-efficient manner for BGB to transfer the property is to transfer it to CGC where it can avail of both CGT and stamp duty relief. This would enable CGC to acquire the property without a stamp duty liability and to claim its capital losses brought forward against the gain on disposal of the property when it sells it.

Chapter 26

Question 26.1

(a) **Tax effect on close company from loan**
TCA 1997 provides that the company must account for tax as if the loan were a net annual payment after deduction of tax. For example, if the loan amounted to €8,000 in the accounts to 31 December 2021, then the calculation would be:

	€
Grossed-up loan	10,000
Income tax @ 20%	(2,000)
Loan	8,000

A return of these figures must be included in the company's annual corporation tax return (form CT1) for the year ended 31 December 2021. The tax due of €2,000 is collected as part of the corporation tax for that year and, therefore, assuming the company is a "small" company, unless preliminary tax is based on 100% of the previous year, €1,800 (90%) is payable on or before 23 November 2021 and the balance of €200 is payable on or before 23 September 2022 in order to avoid interest.
If and when the loan is repaid, the company may claim a refund of the sum of €2,000.

Exemption from this tax charge is, however, available where:

- the business of the company is, or includes, the lending of money, and the loan is made in the ordinary course of that business;
- a debt is incurred for the supply of goods or services in the ordinary course of the business of the close company, unless the credit given exceeds six months or is longer than the period normally given to the company's customers; or
- the borrower satisfies the following conditions:
  - total loans to borrower or spouse or civil partner do not exceed €19,050; and
  - the borrower works full-time for the close company or any of its associated companies; and
  - the borrower and/or his associates is not the beneficial owner of, or able to control more than 5% of, the ordinary shares of the company or an associated company.

(b) **Corporation tax liability year ended 31/12/2021**

	€
€500,000 @ 12.5%	62,500
€33,000 @ 25%	8,250
Corporation tax liability	70,750

continued overleaf

Surcharge:		€
Case III and Case V		33,000
Less: corporation tax @ 25%		(8,250)
		24,750
Less: 7.5%		(1,856)
		22,894
Less: dividends paid within 18 months		(9,300)
		13,594

€13,594 @ 20% = €2,719 surcharge due

Question 26.2

(a) **Corporation tax computation year ended 31/12/2021**

	€	€
Net profit per accounts		32,900
Add: depreciation	15,000	
Sundry (Note 1)	800	15,800
		48,700
Less: interest on:		
Government securities	8,500	
Capital grants	1,500	(10,000)
		38,700
Less: capital allowances		(4,000)
Case I income		34,700
Case III income:		
Interest on Government securities		8,500
Total income		43,200
Corporation tax:		
€34,700 @ 12.5%	€4,337	
€8,500 @ 25%	€2,125	
Corporation tax payable		6,462

(b) **Surcharge**

	€
Case III	8,500
Less: tax @ 25%	(2,125)
	6,375
Less: 7.5% relief	(478)
	5,897
Less: distribution	(800)
	5,097
Surcharge @ 20%	1,019

(c) **Specific Items**

Note 1: the expense payment is treated as a "distribution" and added back in the Case I computation.

Close Ltd will be required to deduct DWT at 25% from the payment of €800 to Y, who will be assessed to income tax, USC and PRSI as follows (assume Y's marginal income tax rate of tax is 40%, USC is 8% and PRSI is 4%):

	€
Additional income tax payable:	
Schedule F: €800 @ 40%	320
Less: DWT €800 @ 25%	(200)
	120
Add: USC €800 @ 8%	64
Add: PRSI €800 @ 4%	32
	216

Close Ltd is entitled to recover the DWT of €200 from Y. However, if Y is not going to repay the DWT to Close Ltd, the deemed distribution of €800 must be grossed up and the DWT payable will be €267, i.e. €800/0.75 – €800. Y will then be subject to income tax under Schedule F and USC and PRSI on €1,067 instead of €800 and will be entitled to a credit for DWT of €267 instead of €200.

Question 26.3

Servisco Ltd
Corporation Tax Computation
year ended 31 December 2021

	€
Case II professional income	430,000
Less: loss forward	(9,000)
Less: loss carried back (Note 1)	(10,000)
	411,000
Case III interest on Government stocks	50,000
Case V rents	100,000
	561,000
Chargeable gains: €54,000 × 33/12.5	142,560
	703,560
Corporation tax:	
€553,560 @ 12.5% = €69,195	
€150,000 @ 25% = €37,500	106,695

Note 1: loss carried back of €10,000 is offset against trading income taxed @ 12.5%.

Surcharge Computation

1. "Income for the accounting period" is:

		€
Case II	Professional income (Note 1A)	430,000
Case III	Interest on Government stocks	50,000
Case V	Rents	100,000
Total income for the accounting period (Note 1B)		580,000

Notes:

1A. income of the current period, i.e. ignore loss forward and loss back.

1B. as there are no current-year losses or current-year trade charges, income for the accounting period is the same as total income.

2. Distributable estate and investment income of the company is:

	€
Passive income	150,000
FII	7,500
	157,500
Less: corporation tax @ 25% of passive income	(37,500)
	120,000
Less: trading deduction (7.5%)	(9,000)
Distributable estate and investment income	111,000

3. Distributable trading income of the company is:

	€
Trading income	430,000
Corporation tax @ 12.5%	53,750
Distributable trading income	376,250

4. Surcharge is therefore calculated as:

		€
(a)	50% distributable trading income: €376,250 @ 50%	188,125
(b)	Distributable estate and investment income (DEII)	111,000
		299,125
Dividend paid		(70,000)
Liable to surcharge		229,125

	€
DEII	111,000
Dividends	(70,000)
Liable @ 20%	41,000

Balance of €229,125 – €41,000 = €188,125, will be liable @ 15%. Therefore, surcharge is:

	€
€41,000 @ 20%	8,200
€188,125 @ 15%	28,219
	36,419

Question 26.4

Machinery Ltd
Corporation tax computation for year ended 31 December 2021

	€	€
Net profit from trading		627,000
Add: depreciation	59,790	
Loan interest treated as a distribution	2,171 (Note)	61,961
		688,961
Less: capital allowances		(10,700)
Case I		678,261
Case III bank interest		10,000
Case V rents		50,000
		738,261
Corporation tax:		
€678,261 @ 12.5% = €84,783		
€60,000 @ 25% = €15,000		99,783
Add income tax (Note)		648
Total due		100,431

Note:
Interest limit is lower of:
  (a) 13% @ €20,000 = €2,600
  (b) 13% @ €34,000 = €4,420

Therefore, interest limit = €2,600.

Loans from directors (and/or associates) with material interest:

	€
V. Duffy	4,000
Mrs V. Duffy	5,000
G. Duffy	5,000
S. Duffy	5,000
D. O'Connell	5,000
L.T. Smith	10,000
	34,000

continued overleaf

Interest on above loans = €4,771.

Distribution: €4,771 − €2,600 = €2,171. DWT at 25% (€543) must be deducted from this.

Income tax deducted from:	€
Interest of €2,600 @ 20%	520
Interest on other loan (€5,410 − €4,771) @ 20%	128
	648

Surcharge Computation

	€
Estate and investment income: €10,000 + €50,000	60,000
Less: corporation tax @ 25%	15,000
	45,000
Less: 7.5% × €45,000	(3,375)
	41,625
Less: distributions made	(2,171)
Excess	39,454
Surcharge @ 20%	7,891

Question 26.5

1. Identify income for the accounting period

	€
Income (Cases II & III)	200,000
Less: trade charges (section 243A)	(60,000)
Income for accounting period	140,000

2. Calculate 'passive income'

$$€140,000 \times \frac{€100,000}{€200,000} = €70,000$$

3. Calculate distributable estate and investment income

	€
Passive income	70,000
Less: non-trade charges	(50,000)
Net passive income	20,000
FII	NIL
Estate and investment income	20,000
Less: corporation tax @ 25%	(5,000)
	15,000
Less: 7.5% trading deduction	(1,125)
DEII	13,875

4. Calculate distributable trading income (DTI)

	€
Income for accounting period	140,000
Less: passive income	(70,000)
Trading income	70,000
Less: CT on trading income @ 12.5%	(8,750)
Distributable trading income	61,250

5. Calculate amount liable to surcharge

	€
DEII	13,875
DTI × 50%	30,625
	44,500
Less: distributions paid/payable within 18 months of the accounting period	(30,000)
Liable to surcharge	14,500

6. Calculate surcharge

All taxable at 15% as distributable estate and investment is less than dividend paid.

Surcharge @ 15% = €2,175

Chapter 27

Question 27.1

Equities Ltd

	€	€
Case III		15,100
Less: Management expenses:		
Accounting fees	1,000	
Secretarial fees	2,000	
Auditor's remuneration	6,000	
Directors' remuneration: €155,100 @ 10%	15,510	
Stockbroker's charges	3,000	(27,510)
Excess		(12,410)

The company can carry forward the excess of €12,410 to offset against profits of future accounting periods or to offset against total profits of another group member, if it is a member of a loss group.

Chapter 28

Question 28.1

Tax Year	Resident	Ordinarily Resident
2018	Yes ≥183 days	No
2019	Yes ≥ 183 days	No
2020	Yes ≥ 183 days	No
2021	No – fails 30-day test	Yes, as resident for three preceding years

For the years 2018–2020, Aurore is resident in Ireland and will be taxed on both her Irish salary and her salary paid in France, if the latter is paid in respect of the performance of her duties as an employee in Ireland. The salary paid in France does not have to be remitted to be liable to tax in Ireland; it must be connected to the performance of Aurore's employment duties in the State. Any other foreign income will only be taxed to the extent that it is remitted to the State.

For the tax year 2021, Aurore will be taxed on her Irish income, and on other income paid into the State, but will not pay tax on her French salary or other non-Irish income where it does not exceed €3,810 in the year. (In any event, as Aurore is domiciled in France she would only be within the charge to Irish tax on foreign income exceeding €3,810 if it were remitted to the State. In practice, it is likely that the terms of the Ireland/France DTA would take her non-Irish income out of the charge to Irish tax.) Aurore will continue to be ordinarily resident in Ireland until she has been non-resident for three years, i.e. until 2024.

Question 28.2

As Mr Harris is neither Irish resident nor Irish domiciled he is liable only on income arising in Ireland. He is not entitled to the married persons tax bands and has a reduced entitlement to any tax credits.

	€
Schedule D, Case V	37,000
Tax:	
€35,300 @ 20%	7,060
€ 1,700 @ 40%	680
€37,000	7,740
Less: tax deducted at source from rent paid	(7,400)
Tax payable	340

Chapter 29

Question 29.1

(a)

Income Tax Computation 2021 for Colm and Dervla O'Rourke

			€	€
Income				
Schedule D:	Case III	UK dividends (Note 1)	900	
		UK rent (Note 1)	9,000	9,900
	Case IV	Irish bank interest (Note 2)	100	

continued overleaf

	German bank interest (Note 2)	500	600
Schedule E:	Salary (Colm)	55,000	
	Salary (Dervla)	32,000	87,000
Schedule F:	Irish dividend (Note 3)		1,100
Total taxable income			98,600

Tax Calculation

	€	€
€600 @ 33%	198	
€70,600 @ 20% (Note 4)	14,120	
€27,400 @ 40%	10,960	25,278
Deduct non-refundable tax credits:		
Personal tax credits	6,600	
DIRT paid (€100 @ 33%)	33	
UK tax	1,500	(8,133)
Net tax liability		17,145
Deduct refundable tax credits:		
PAYE paid (€10,640 + €4,600)	15,240	
DWT (€1,100 @ 25%)	275	(15,515)
Net tax payable		1,630

Notes:
1. Schedule D, Case III income:

UK dividend – taxed amount received	900
UK rent (taxed net of expenses but incl. UK tax)	9,000

2. Schedule D, Case IV income:

Irish bank interest – received net but gross taxed:	
€67 × 100/(100 – 33)	100
German bank interest – received gross	500

3. Schedule F income:

Irish dividend – received net but gross taxed:	
€25 × 100/(100 – 25)	1,100

4. As both incomes exceed €26,300, the full marriage tax band of €70,600 is available to the O'Rourkes.

(b) Implications of filing return at 30 November 2022 – As the due date to file the return was 31 October 2022, the German deposit interest will be assessed to income tax under Schedule D, Case III at the rate of 40%, thereby increasing the tax payable by €35 (€500 × 7%) to €1,665.

In addition, the O'Rourkes will have to pay interest and surcharge on the late payment of income tax.

Chapter 30

Question 30.1

SARP Relief 2021:

Is relevant income > €50,000 (€75,000 × 8/12ths)?

Salary €250,000 > €50,000 (€75,000 × 8/12ths), therefore eligible for SARP relief.

Calculation of specified amount:

	€
Total income	272,500
Less: lower threshold (€75,000 × 8/12ths)	(50,000)
	222,500
Specified amount (30%)	66,750
Total income	272,500
Less: specified amount	(66,750)
Taxable income	205,750

Note: Mr Klaus will either obtain relief at source under the payroll or, if not, he will need to make a claim for a tax repayment of €66,750 @ 40% = €26,700 at the end of the tax year.

Question 30.2

Tax-free Element of Lump Sum

	€	€
Basic exemption: €10,160 + (€765 × 18)		23,930
Plus: Increased exemption	10,000	
Less: Tax-free lump sum from pension scheme	(3,000)	7,000
Increased basic exemption		30,930
Or, SCSB can be applied if greater.		

$$SCSB = \frac{(A \times B)}{15} - C$$

A = average of last three years' emoluments = (€52,000 + €55,000 + €57,000)/3 = €54,667
B = number of complete years of service = 18 years
C = tax-free lump sum from pension scheme = €3,000

$$SCSB = \frac{(€54,667 \times 18)}{15} - €3,000 = €62,600$$

As SCSB results in the highest figure, the tax-free element of the lump sum is €62,600. Therefore the taxable element is €2,400 (€65,000 − €62,600).

Income Tax Liability 2021 – Mr Houghton

	€	€
Schedule E income:		
Salary €57,000 × 6/12		28,500
Pension €18,000 × 6/12		9,000
Termination payment	65,000	
Less: SCSB	(62,600)	(2,400)
Total/taxable income		39,900
Tax payable		
€35,300 @ 20%	7,060	
€4,600 @ 40%	1,840	
€39,900		8,900
Deduct: Non-refundable tax credits		(3,300)
Net tax liability		5,600
Deduct: Refundable tax credits: tax paid under PAYE		(6,220)
Net tax refundable		(620)

Question 30.3

Income Tax 2021 – Mr Lynch

	€	€
Schedule E income:		
Salary		43,000
Termination payment (Note)	30,000	
Exempt (Note)	(27,810)	2,190
Total/taxable income		45,190
Tax payable		
€35,300 @ 20%	7,060	
€9,890 @ 40%	3,956	
€45,190		11,016
Deduct: Non-refundable tax credits		(3,840)
Net tax liability		7,176
Deduct: Refundable tax credits: tax paid under PAYE		(6,450)
Income tax payable		726

Note:

Lump sum:	€30,000
Exemption: €10,160 + (€765 × 10)	€17,810
Increased basic exemption	€10,000
Total	€27,810

continued overleaf

Or, SCSB:

$$= \frac{(\text{€}43{,}000 + \text{€}35{,}000 + \text{€}30{,}000)}{3} \times \frac{10}{15} = \frac{(\text{€}108{,}000)}{3} \times \frac{10}{15} = \text{€}24{,}000$$

As SCSB is lower than the increased basic exemption, the taxable element is €30,000 less increased exemption of €27,810 = €2,190.

Pension contributions refund: these have been taxed at 20% under the usual arrangement and the figures do not impinge upon the computation of liability.

Question 30.4

(a) **Taxable Element of Lump Sum**

	€
Basic exemption €10,160 + (€765 × 15)	21,635
Plus: Increased exemption	10,000
Less: Tax-free lump sum from pension	Nil
Increased basic exemption	31,635

May be further increased to SCSB if greater.

$$\text{SCSB} = \frac{(A \times B)}{15} - C$$

A = average of last three years' salary

Year ended 30/09/2021	€47,000
Year ended 30/09/2020	€54,000
Year ended 30/09/2019	€52,000
	€153,000
Average (total ÷ 3)	€51,000

B = number of complete years of service = 15 years
C = tax-free lump sum from pension scheme = Nil
SCSB = €51,000 × 15/15 = €51,000

As SCSB is greater than the increased basic exemption, the taxable element of the lump sum is: €57,000 − €51,000 = €6,000

(b)

Income Tax 2021 – Mr Flynn			
		€	€
Schedule E income:			
Salary from old job	€47,000 × 9/12	35,250	
Holiday pay		2,000	
Salary from new job		7,500	

continued overleaf

Benefit in kind	€2,000 × 3/12	500	45,250
Lump sum		57,000	
Less: SCSB exempt amount		(51,000)	6,000
Taxable income			51,250

Tax payable

€44,300 @ 20%	8,860	
€6,950 @ 40%	2,780	
€51,250		11,640
Deduct: Non-refundable tax credits:		
Personal tax credits		(4,950)
Tax liability		6,690
Deduct: Refundable tax credits: tax paid under PAYE		(3,030)
Net tax payable		3,660

Question 30.5

(a) **Tax-free Termination Payment**

Basic exemption: €10,160 + (€765 × 15) = €21,635
Increased basic exemption not available as tax-free pension lump sum of €22,000 receivable exceeds €10,000.

Or, SCSB:

$$SCSB = \frac{(A \times B)}{15} - C$$

A = (€48,900 + €38,000 + €42,100)/3 = €43,000
B = 15 years
C = €22,000

$$SCSB = \left(€43,000 \times \frac{15}{15}\right) - €22,000 = €21,000$$

As the basic exemption is higher than the SCSB, €21,635 is the tax-free termination payment that can be made to Dermot O'Donnell.

Calculation of the lump sum:

	€
Compensation payment	40,500
Car	22,500
Lump sum	63,000
Less: basic exemption	(21,635)
Taxable lump sum	41,365

(b)

	Income Tax Computation 2021 – Dermot O'Donnell		
		€	€
Schedule E income:			
Salary to September		37,000	
Holiday pay		1,200	
Salary to year-end		4,200	
Taxable lump sum		41,365	
Taxable income			83,765
Tax payable			
€39,300 @ 20%		7,860	
€44,465 @ 40%		17,786	
€83,765			25,646
Deduct: Non-refundable tax credits			(4,950)
Net tax liability			20,696
Deduct: Refundable tax credits: tax paid under PAYE			
(€5,418 + €100)			(5,518)
Tax payable			15,178

Note: statutory redundancy is not taxable.

Chapter 31

Question 31.1

(a) (i) As it is a short option, i.e. it must be exercised within seven years, at the date of the granting of the option there is no charge to tax.

   (ii) When the option is exercised income tax becomes payable, as follows:

2,500 shares × (€5.50 – €2.85)	€6,625
Income tax @ 40%	€2,650

(b) Due date for income tax (RTSO) to be paid on the exercise of a share option is within 30 days of the date on which the share option is exercised, i.e. by 31 May 2021.

(c) If the option granted was a long option, i.e. it could have been exercised more than seven years after it was granted, tax would be charged at the date of the grant of the option on the difference between the market value of the shares at the date of grant and the option price. In addition, tax is also charged at the date of the exercise of the option on the difference between the market value of the shares at the date of exercise and the option price, with a credit for the tax paid at the date of the grant.

Question 31.2

Tax Computation for Charlotte and Fabio for 2021

		Charlotte €	Fabio €	Total €
Schedule D	Case II	150,000		
	Less: pension	(22,500)		127,500
	Case III		8,500	8,500
	Case V		3,320	3,320
Schedule E	Salary		55,000	
	Less: pension		(2,750)	52,250
Total		127,500	64,070	191,570
EII			(10,000)	(10,000)
Taxable income		127,500	54,070	181,570

Tax Calculation (Joint Assessment)

	€	€
€70,600 @ 20%	14,120	
€110,970 @ 40%	44,388	58,508

Deduct: Non-refundable tax credits:		
Married persons	3,300	
Earned income	1,650	
Employee	1,650	(6,600)
Tax liability		51,908
Deduct: Refundable tax credits:		
PAYE paid	16,200	
Preliminary tax paid	30,000	(46,200)
Net tax payable		5,708

Chapter 32

Question 32.1

Peter and Paul – Income Tax Computation 2021: Assessment as Single Persons

		Peter €	Paul €	Total €
Income: Schedule E		50,000	28,000	
Tax payable:				
Peter:	Paul:			
€35,300 @ 20%	€28,000 @ 20%	7,060	5,600	

continued overleaf

€14,700 @ 40%	5,880	–
€50,000	12,940	5,600
Deduct: Non-refundable tax credits:		
Basic personal tax credit	(1,650)	(1,650)
Employee tax credit	(1,650)	(1,650)
Initial tax liability	**9,640**	**2,300**	**11,940**
Deduct: Refundable tax credits:		
Year of marriage relief (Note)	(688)	(164)	(852)
Tax paid under PAYE	(9,640)	(2,300)	(11,940)
Net tax refund	**(688)**	**(164)**	**(852)**

Note: notional liability under joint assessment for 2021 (see below).

Peter and Paul – Income Tax Computation 2021: Notional Liability under Joint Assessment

	Peter	Paul	Total
	€	€	€
Income: Schedule E	50,000	28,000	78,000
Tax payable:			
€44,300 @ 20%			8,860
€26,300 @ 20%			5,260
€7,400 @ 40%			2,960
€78,000			17,080
Deduct: Non-refundable tax credits:			
Basic personal tax credit (married/civil partners)			(3,300)
Employee tax credits (× 2)			(3,300)
Notional tax liability			**10,480**
Total under single assessment			**11,940**
"Saving"			**1,460**
Saving restricted to: €1,460 × 7/12 (months)			852
Year of marriage relief (Note)	**688**	**164**	**852**

Note: "Saving" is split as follows:
Peter: €852 × €9,640 / €11,940 = €688
Paul: €852 × €2,300 / €11,940 = €164

Question 32.2

(a) Claim for joint assessment made for year of separation – as Mrs Lynch has income other than the maintenance payments, the separate assessment rules are used.

Mrs Lynch Income Tax Computation 2021	€	€
Income: Schedule E		15,000
Tax payable:		
€15,000 @ 20%		3,000
Deduct: Non-refundable tax credits:		
Basic personal tax credit	(1,650)	
Employee tax credit	(1,650)	(3,300)
Excess tax credits transferred to Mr Lynch		**(300)**
Tax liability		**0**

Mr Lynch Income Tax Computation 2021	€	€
Income: Schedule E		48,000
Tax payable (married):		
€44,300 @ 20%	8,860	
€3,700 @ 40%	1,480	
€48,000		10,340
Deduct: Non-refundable tax credits:		
Basic personal tax credit	(1,650)	
Employee tax credit	(1,650)	
Excess tax credits transferred from Mrs Lynch	(300)	(3,600)
Tax liability		**6,740**
Combined tax liability		**6,740**

(b) No claim made for joint assessment for year of separation

Mrs Lynch Income Tax Computation 2021	€	€
Income:		
Schedule E (01/07/2021 – 31/12/2021)	8,000	
Schedule D, Case IV (€600 × 6)	3,600	
Total income		11,600
Tax payable:		
€11,600 @ 20%		2,320
Deduct: Non-refundable tax credits:		
Basic personal tax credit	(1,650)	

continued overleaf

	€	€
Single person child carer credit	(1,650)	
Employee tax credit (€8,000 @ 20%)	(1,600)	(4,900)
Tax credits restricted to amount needed to reduce tax liability to NIL		(2,320)
Tax liability		**0**

Mr Lynch Income Tax Computation 2021	€	€
Income:		
Schedule E – self	48,000	
Schedule E – Mrs Lynch (01/01/2021 – 30/06/2021)	7,000	55,000
Less: maintenance payments (€600 × 6)		(3,600)
Net income		51,400
Tax payable (married):		
€44,300 @ 20%	8,860	
€ 7,000 @ 20%	1,400	
€ 100 @ 40%	40	
€51,400		10,300
Deduct: Non-refundable tax credits:		
Basic personal tax credit (married)	(3,300)	
Employee tax credit Mr Lynch	(1,650)	
Employee tax credit Mrs Lynch (€7,000 @ 20%)	(1,400)	(6,350)
Tax liability		**3,950**
Combined tax liability		**3,950**

Note: as the assessable spouse in the year of separation, Mr Lynch is entitled to a married person's tax credits and tax bands.

Question 32.3

(a) Income Tax Computation 2021 – Assessable Spouse Matthew (deceased)

Matthew DuBlanc (deceased) – Income Tax Liability 01/01/2021–30/05/2021	€	€
Income: Schedule E		
Matthew	60,000	
Jane (to 30/05/2021)	30,000	
Total income		**90,000**

continued overleaf

Tax payable (married):

€70,600 @ 20%	14,120	
€19,400 @ 40%	7,760	
€90,000		21,880
Deduct: Non-refundable tax credits:		
Basic personal tax credit (married)	(3,300)	
Employee tax credits (× 2)	(3,300)	(6,600)
Tax liability		15,280
Deduct: Refundable tax credits:		
Tax paid under PAYE (€19,680 + €7,680)		(27,360)
Tax refund due		**(12,080)**

Jane DuBlanc – Income Tax Liability 31/05/2021–31/12/2021

	€	€
Income: Schedule E		42,000
Taxable income		**42,000**
Tax payable (widowed):		
€35,300 @ 20%	7,060	
€6,700 @ 40%	2,680	
€42,000		9,740
Deduct: Non-refundable tax credits:		
Basic personal tax credit (year of bereavement)	(3,300)	
Employee tax credit	(1,650)	(4,950)
Tax liability		4,790
Deduct: Refundable tax credits:		
Tax paid under PAYE		(10,760)
Tax refund due		**(5,970)**
Total refund 2021		**(18,050)**

(b) Income Tax Computation 2021 – Assessable Spouse Jane

Jane DuBlanc – Income Tax Liability 01/01/2021–31/12/2021

	€	€
Income: Schedule E		
Jane	72,000	
Matthew	60,000	
Total income		**132,000**

continued overleaf

Tax payable (married):

€70,600 @ 20%	14,120	
€61,400 @ 40%	24,560	
€132,000		38,680
Deduct: Non-refundable tax credits:		
Basic personal tax credit (married)	(3,300)	
Employee tax credits (× 2)	(3,300)	(6,600)
Tax liability		32,080
Deduct: Refundable tax credits:		
Tax paid under PAYE (€19,680 + €18,440)		(38,120)
Tax refund due		**(6,040)**

Jane would receive an extra €12,010 tax refund if Matthew was the assessable spouse at the date of his death.

Chapter 33

Question 33.1

HERMES LTD
VAT Liability for March–April 2021

	Net of VAT	VAT Payable/Claimable
	€	€
VAT on Sales		
Supplies in Ireland	250,000	57,500
Supplies to US	10,000	0
Purchases from NI (Note 1)	50,000	11,500
Total VAT payable on sales		69,000
VAT on Costs		
Purchase of stock from Irish suppliers		
(€233,700 × 100/123)	190,000	43,700
Purchase of stock from NI suppliers (Note 1)	50,000	11,500
Professional fees (€6,150 × 100/123)	5,000	1,150
Motor car repairs (€1,135 × 100/113.5)	1,000	135
Computer (€9,225 × 100/123)	7,500	1,725
Total VAT claimable on purchases		58,210

	€
VAT on sales	69,000
VAT on purchases	(58,210)
VAT payable	10,790

Notes:

1. Where goods are purchased for business purposes from another EU Member State or Northern Ireland, the supplier will not charge VAT, provided they are given the VAT registration number of the purchaser.

    The purchaser must account for a notional amount of VAT in the sales (reverse charge) and the purchases on their VAT return.

Question 33.2

ELIXIR LTD
VAT Payable for September–October 2021

	Net of VAT	VAT
	€	€
VAT on Sales (output VAT)		
Supplies in Ireland (@ 23%)	950,000	218,500
Supplies to Spain (to Spanish registered customers) @ 0%	320,000	0
Exports to non-VAT-registered customers in the UK @ 0%	25,000	0
Exports to VAT-registered customers in the UK @ 0%	135,000	0
Supplies to non-VAT-registered customers in NI @ 23%	6,000	1,380
		219,880
VAT EU acquisitions	200,000	46,000
Total VAT on sales		265,880

	VAT-inclusive	VAT
	€	€
VAT on Costs (input VAT)		
Purchase of materials from Irish suppliers		
(€369,000 × 23/123)	369,000	69,000
Purchase of machinery locally (€246,000 × 23/123)	246,000	46,000
Rent of premises (€18,450 × 23/123)	18,450	3,450
Repairs and maintenance of office and equipment		
(€14,145 × 23/123)	14,145	2,645
Audit and accountancy fees (€11,070 × 23/123)	11,070	2,070
Diesel for staff vehicles (€5,535 × 23/123)	5,535	1,035
Electricity and gas (€2,400 × 13.5/113.5)	2,400	285
Salaries and wages	167,000	N/A
Advertising costs (€30,750 × 23/123)	30,750	5,750
Total VAT on costs		130,235
EU acquisitions (€200,000 net of VAT)		46,000
Total VAT on costs		176,235
Net VAT payable		89,645

Chapter 34

Question 34.1

(a) VAT on property is charged at 13.5%.

Consideration including VAT	€567,500
VAT charged by Doyle Construction Ltd: €567,500 × 13.5%/1.135	€67,500
Consideration excluding VAT	€500,000

(b) Stamp duty is charged on the VAT-exclusive consideration. As the value of the property does not exceed €1 million, the rate of stamp duty is 1%. Therefore, the stamp duty payable by Ciara is €500,000 @ 1% = €5,000. This is due within 44 days of 11 September, i.e. by 24 October 2021.

Question 34.2

(a) The following VAT implications arise for Cosmos Ltd:

- The warehouse was built in 2014 and thus is not 'new' for VAT purposes – the purchase of this building would be exempt from VAT.
- As an exempt property, the vendor is not obliged to charge VAT on the transaction. However, as both parties are carrying on business in Ireland, they could opt to tax the supply of the property if they jointly agree to do so.
- If this option is exercised, Cosmos Ltd would have to account for the VAT on the reverse charge basis. Meaning, Cosmos Ltd would be liable to pay VAT of €81,000 (€600,000 @ 13.5%) but can claim a simultaneous VAT credit.
- No VAT arises on the purchase of the field as it is undeveloped land.

(b) The stamp duty liability is charged on the VAT-exclusive prices, and the amounts payable are:

Warehouse €600,000 @ 7.5% = €45,000
Field €50,000 @ 7.5%   =   €3,750

Chapter 35

Question 35.1

There are three separate VAT issues to be considered: the transfer of the commercial property, the potential sale of shares and the potential sale of assets.

Transfer of Freehold Property
Generally, transactions between members of a VAT group can be ignored for VAT purposes. However, this does not apply to the supply of property. If the property is a vatable supply (e.g. it is 'new'), then VAT at 13.5% will be charged on the transfer of the property to the company. As the company will be using the property for the purpose of its business it will be entitled to recover any VAT charged on the acquisition of the property if it is carrying on a taxable business.

Potential Sale of Shares to Carla Hemmingway

The sale of shares is a VAT-exempt activity, therefore no VAT would arise on the transaction. Tom would not be able to recover any VAT incurred on the costs associated with the sale.

Potential Sale of Assets to Sean Fitzhenry

If Ekramot Ltd were to sell the assets of the business individually, the VAT treatment of each asset would need to be considered.

However, the sale of the company's entire assets would likely qualify for transfer of business relief for VAT purposes. The transfer would therefore be outside the scope of VAT, providing the following qualifying conditions are met:

1. the purchaser (Sean Fitzhenry) is VAT registered;
2. the acquirer (Sean Fitzhenry) is an accountable person; and
3. the transfer constitutes an undertaking or part of an undertaking capable of being operated on an independent basis.

The company is entitled to recover the VAT on any costs incurred in connection with the transaction (e.g. legal or other professional fees) if it is a taxable person for VAT purposes.

Index

accountable persons
    capital acquisitions tax, 169
    capital gains tax, 21
    stamp duty, 83
accounting periods, 208–10
acquisitions of own shares
    capital gains tax
        benefit of the trade test, 74, 75, 76–7
        and the close company surcharge, 76
        conditions to be satisfied for CGT
            treatment, 74–5
        overview, 73
        for purpose of paying inheritance tax, 75–6
        quoted companies, 73–4
        returns, 76
        Tax and Duty Manual guidance, 76–7
        treasury shares, 76
        unquoted companies, 74–6
    stamp duty, 85
activity test (farmers), 127–8, 133
ad valorem stamp duty, 82
agency assets, 26, 178
agricultural property: capital acquisitions tax
    definition for agricultural relief, 127
    interest on instalment payments, 172
    see also farmland; land and buildings
agricultural relief
    additional considerations, 132
    and business relief, 132, 137, 139
    calculation of taxable value, 126
    cessation of farming within six years, 133
    clawback of relief on disposal, 132–3
    computation of relief, 128–32
    definitions, 127–8
    overview, 126–7
    restriction of deductions, 130–32
allowable deductions
    capital acquisitions tax
        consideration paid by donee or successor,
            125–6

        deductions allowed against taxable value,
            125–6
        deductions prohibited against taxable
            value, 126
        restrictions for agricultural relief, 130–32
    income tax
        deductions against foreign investment
            income, 267
annual exemption: capital gains tax, 21, 46, 56
annuities
    cessation of, 145
    charged or secured on property, 143–4
    not charged or secured on property, 144
    valuation, 122, 143–4
anti-avoidance measures
    capital acquisitions tax
        gift splitting, 110
    capital gains groups
        companies leaving the group, 221–2
        pre-entry losses, 223
        transfer pricing, 221
    capital gains tax
        'bed and breakfast' share transactions,
            36–7
        disposals by temporary non-residents, 26,
            28
        disposals outside the state by non-
            domiciled individuals, 26
    corporation tax
        close companies, 226–47
        transfer pricing, 183, 221
appeals
    Appeal Commissioners hearings, 2
    conditions for valid appeal, 2
    court hearings, 2–3
    overview, 1–2
    settlements, 3
approved retirement funds (ARFs), 156
aspect queries, 3
asset test (farmers), 127

associated companies
  definitions, 91, 270
  stamp duty relief on transfers between,
    90–92
  transfer pricing rules, 181–3
associates
  definition for acquisition of own shares, 75
  definition for close companies, 227
assurance checks, 3
audit notification, 4–5

Base Erosion and Profit Shifting (BEPS)
    Action Plan, 181
'bed & breakfast' transactions, 36–7
benefit of the trade test, 74, 75, 76–7
bonus issues, 35
branch assets, 26, 178
business relief
  and agricultural relief, 132, 137, 139
  calculation of taxable value, 133–4
  clawback of relief on disposal, 137–8
  minimum ownership period, 136
  overview, 133
  relevant business property, 134
  valuation of property, 136–7
business transfers *see* transfer of a business
buy-backs *see* acquisition of own shares

capital acquisitions tax (CAT)
  accountable persons, 169
  anti-avoidance measures, 110
  computation of tax payable
    aggregation, 111
    basic computation, 111
    examples, 112–15
    group thresholds, 106–10
    overview, 106
  credit for certain capital gains tax liabilities,
    161–5
  exemptions and reliefs
    agricultural relief, 126–33
    business relief, 133–8
    exemption for certain dwelling houses,
      152–4
    exemption for certain government
      securities, 152
    exemption for certain inheritances taken
      by parents, 152

exemption for certain receipts, 154–5
exemption for gifts/inheritances taken by
    spouse/civil partner, 108, 150–51
gifts and inheritances taken free of
    tax, 155
relief for certain insurance policies,
    156–8
small gifts exemption, 103, 150
on gifts *see* gifts: capital acquisitions tax
on inheritances *see* inheritances: capital
    acquisitions tax
interest on late payment, 171
late filing penalties, 171
on limited interests, 143–5
overpayments, 172
overview, 99
payment dates, 123, 170–71
payment by instalments, 171–2
returns, 123, 169–71
self-assessment, 169–70
special relationship situations, 107–9
spouses/civil partners
  divorced spouses/dissolved civil
      partnerships, 151
  exemption for gifts/inheritances taken by,
      108, 150–51
  separated couples, 151
  surviving spouse/civil partner of
      deceased person, 109
surcharge for undervaluation of property, 172
taxable value
  allowable deductions, 125–6
  calculation where there is agricultural
      relief, 126
  calculation where there is business relief,
      133–4
  general principles, 121
  market value, 122–3, 143–5
  valuation date, 123–5
territoriality rules, 117–19
capital allowances
  group relief for excess Case V allowances,
      206–8
  intangible asset expenditure, 190–91
capital gains groups
  anti-avoidance measures, 221–3
  capital losses, 220
  companies leaving the group, 221–2

capital gains groups – *contd.*
  definition, 217
  disposal of capital assets outside the
      group, 221
  disposal of capital assets within the group,
      219–21
  inventories, 220
  non-resident companies, 218–19
  pre-entry losses, 223
  75% relationship, 217
  transfer pricing, 220–21
capital gains tax (CGT)
  acquisitions of own shares
      benefit of the trade test, 74, 75, 76–7
      and the close company surcharge, 76
      conditions to be satisfied for CGT
          treatment, 74–5
      overview, 73
      for purpose of paying inheritance tax,
          75–6
      quoted companies, 73–4
      returns, 76
      Tax and Duty Manual guidance, 76–7
      treasury shares, 76
      unquoted companies, 74–6
  anti-avoidance measures
      'bed and breakfast' share transactions,
          36–7
      disposals by temporary non-residents,
          26, 28
      disposals outside the state by non-
          domiciled individuals, 26
  certain liabilities credited against capital
      acquisitions tax, 161–5
  chargeable assets, 21
  chargeable persons, 21
  company capital gains liable to, 215–17
  computation of gain or loss, 22
  development land, 23
  exemptions and reliefs
      annual exemption, 21
      overview, 23–4
      retirement relief, 56–70
      revised entrepreneur relief, 42–5
      transfer of a business to a company,
          47–53
  loss relief, 23
  overview, 21

  payment dates, 21
  rates of tax, 21
  returns, 21
  shares
      acquisition within four weeks of
          disposal, 36
      bonus issues, 35
      disposal within four weeks of acquisition,
          36–7
      employee share options, 37–40
      overview, 32–3
      rights issues, 33–5
  spouses/civil partners
      exemption for transfer of assets
          between, 23
      sale and re-acquisition of shares, 37
  territoriality rules, 25–9
capital losses
  pre-entry losses, 223
  transfer within capital gains groups, 220
careless behaviour penalties, 6
cash: location of assets, 17
chargeable business assets
  definition for retirement relief, 56–7
  definition for revised entrepreneur
      relief, 43
chargeable persons
  capital gains tax, 21
  stamp duty, 83
charges on income
  group relief for excess charges, 205–6
  non-trade charges, 206
  trading charges, 205
  treatment for close companies, 238–42
charities
  capital acquisitions tax exemption, 154
  stamp duty exemption, 88
chattels
  capital gains tax exemptions, 24
  non-wasting chattels, 23, 24
  restriction of loss relief on disposal, 23
  wasting chattels, 24
children
  capital acquisitions tax
      definition of a child, 107
      exemption for maintenance payments,
          154–5
      minor child of deceased child, 107–8

children – *contd.*
  capital gains tax
    definition of a child for retirement
      relief, 66–7
    disposal of a site to a child, 23
    retirement relief on disposals to, 66–8
civil partners *see* spouses/civil partners
close companies
  anti-avoidance measures, 226–47
  certain participator expenses treated as
    distributions, 229–30
  close company surcharge, 76, 236–47
  definitions, 226–8
  foreign dividends, 245–6
  interest paid to directors, 230–32
  loans to participators, 233–5
  service company surcharge, 242–5
  write-off of loans to participators, 235–6
close company surcharge
  and acquisitions of own shares, 76
  basic surcharge calculation, 236–7
  calculation with losses and charges on
    income, 238–42
  election not to treat distributions as such for
    purposes of, 246–7
  overview, 236
  payment, 247
  service company surcharge, 242–5
  7.5% trading deduction, 236
*Code of Practice for Revenue Audit and other
  Compliance Interventions*, 3
company capital gains
  capital gains groups, 217–23
  gains liable to capital gains tax, 215
  gains liable to corporation tax, 214–15
  overview, 214
  participation exemption, 216–17
  taxation method, 215–16
compensation (personal damages), 155
consanguinity relief, 89–90
control, definition for close companies, 227
conveyance or transfer on sale
  definition, 84
  mixed-use property, 86
  non-residential property, 86
  overview, 84
  residential property, 85–6
  stocks and securities, 84–5

corporation tax
  anti-avoidance measures
    close companies, 226–47
    transfer pricing, 183, 221
  charge to tax, 178
  close companies
    anti-avoidance measures, 226–47
    certain participator expenses treated as
      distributions, 229–30
    close company surcharge, 76, 236–47
    definitions, 226–8
    foreign dividends, 245–6
    interest paid to directors, 230–32
    loans to participators, 233–5
    service company surcharge, 242–5
    write-off of loans to participators, 235–6
  company capital gains
    capital gains groups, 217–23
    gains liable to capital gains tax, 215
    gains liable to corporation tax, 214–15
    overview, 214
    participation exemption, 216–17
    taxation method, 215–16
  country-by-country reporting, 181
  exemptions and reliefs
    double taxation relief, 184–8
    group relief, 201–10
    management expenses relief (investment
      companies), 253–5
    participation exemption, 216–17
    payments relief (groups of companies), 199–200
    R&D tax credit, 192–7
  foreign income, 185
  groups of companies
    company capital gains *see* capital gains
      groups
    disallowance of trading losses
      following change of ownership, 210–11
    loss relief, 201–10
    overview, 199
    payments relief, 199–200
    R&D tax credit, 194
  investment companies, 252–5

corporation tax – *contd.*
   non-resident companies
      capital gains groups, 218–19
      charge to tax, 178
      company capital gains, 215
      qualifying for group relief, 203
   overview, 177–8
   payment dates, 181
   rates of tax, 180, 185
   resident companies
      charge to tax, 178
      company capital gains, 214–15
   returns, 181
   small and medium enterprises (SMEs)
      definitions, 182–3
      R&D tax credit, 197
      transfer pricing rules, 182–3
   territoriality rules, 178–80
   transfer pricing, 181–3, 220–21
country-by-country (CbC) reporting, 181

death or disability lump sum payments, 277
debts: location of assets, 17, 25, 82
deliberate behaviour penalties, 6
deposit interest retention tax (DIRT)
   on EU deposit interest, 267
   on non-EU deposit interest, 266
   rates of tax, 266
desk audits, 4
development land: capital gains tax, 23
directors
   definition for close companies, 227
   full-time working directors, definition, 57
   interest paid to, 230–32
   remuneration, 254
disposals
   of chattels, 23, 24
   deemed disposals, 28
   outside capital gains groups, 221
   on retirement *see* retirement relief
   of shares *see* shares
   of a site to a child, 23
   of specified Irish assets, 26–7
   to a spouse/civil partner, 23
   by temporary non-residents, 26, 28
   within capital gains groups,
      219–21
distance sales (intra-EU), 303

distributions
   close companies
      certain participator expenses treated as,
         229–30
      election not to treat distributions as such
         for purposes of surcharge, 246–7
   foreign dividends, 185, 245–6, 266
   income tax, 73, 229, 236
   UK dividends, 266
   USC and PRSI, 73, 229, 236
dividend withholding tax (DWT), 229,
   230–31
dividends *see* distributions
divorced spouses/dissolved civil partnerships
   capital acquisitions tax, 151
   income tax, 294–6
   stamp duty, 88
domicile
   domicile levy, 261–2
   domicile of choice, 16
   domicile of dependence, 17
   domicile of origin, 16
   and income tax, 259–61
   overview, 16
   see also territoriality rules
domicile levy, 261–2
double taxation relief
   credit method, 186–7
   deduction method, 186
   double taxation treaties, 179, 188
   exemption method, 187
   holding companies, 187–8
   overview, 184
   rates of tax for foreign income, 185
double taxation treaties, 179, 188
dwelling house exemption
   clawback of exemption on disposal, 154
   definition of dwelling house, 154
   gifts of dwelling houses, 152
   inheritances of dwelling houses, 152–4
   overview, 152

e-stamping, 83–4
employee share options
   capital gains tax
      general tax treatment, 37
      Key Employee Engagement Programme,
         38–40

employee share options – *contd.*
  income tax
    Key Employee Engagement Programme,
      286–7
    overview, 284–5
    relevant tax on share options, 285
    long options, 286
    short options, 285
  USC and PRSI, 285
Employment and Investment Incentive (EII)
  clawback of relief, 284
  overview, 281
  qualifying criteria, 282–4
  relief available, 281–2
employment income: income tax
  foreign earnings deduction, 271–3
  lump sum payments on account of death or
    disability, 277
  overview, 269
  retirement lump sum benefits, 276–7
  Special Assignee Relief Programme,
    269–71
  termination payments, 273–6
EU deposit interest, 267
EU State Aid regulations, 284
exemptions and reliefs
  capital acquisitions tax
    agricultural relief, 126–33
    business relief, 133–8
    exemption for certain dwelling houses,
      152–4
    exemption for certain government
      securities, 152
    exemption for certain inheritances taken
      by parents, 152
    exemption for certain receipts, 154–5
    exemption for gifts/inheritances taken by
      spouse/civil partner, 108, 150–51
    gifts and inheritances taken free of
      tax, 155
    relief for certain insurance policies,
      156–8
    small gifts exemption, 103, 150
  capital gains tax
    annual exemption, 21
    overview, 23–4
    retirement relief, 56–70
    revised entrepreneur relief, 42–5

    transfer of a business to a company,
      47–53
  corporation tax
    double taxation relief, 184–8
    group relief, 201–10
    management expenses relief (investment
      companies), 253–5
    participation exemption, 216–17
    payments relief (groups of companies),
      199–200
    R&D tax credit, 192–7
  income tax
    Employment and Investment Incentive,
      281–4
    foreign earnings deduction, 271–3
    Key Employee Engagement Programme,
      286–7
    Special Assignee Relief Programme,
      269–71
    tax-exempt termination payments,
      273–6
  stamp duty
    consanguinity relief, 89–90
    main exemptions, 88
    transfers between associated companies,
      90–92
    young trained farmer relief, 88–9
exploration rights, 26, 27

family companies
  definition, 57
  and retirement relief, 57–8, 69–70
farmers
  activity test, 127–8, 133
  asset test, 127
  cessation of farming, 133
  definition for agricultural relief, 127–8
farming groups *see* trading or farming groups
farmland
  stamp duty relief on transfer between
    relations, 89–90
  stamp duty relief on transfer to young
    trained farmer, 88–9
  see also agricultural property; land and
    buildings
favourite nieces/nephews, 108–9
first in/first out (FIFO) rule, 32–3, 36–7
fixed stamp duty, 82

foreign dividends
  corporation tax, 185
  income tax, 266
  treatment for close companies, 245–6
foreign-domiciled individuals
  capital acquisitions tax, 118–19
  capital gains tax, 25–6
  income tax, 260
foreign earnings deduction, 271–3
foreign investment income: income tax
  overview, 265
  Schedule D, Case III
    deductions available, 267
    foreign rental income, 267
    income sources included under case III,
      265–6
    losses, 267
    non-EU deposit interest, 266
    UK dividends and UK interest, 266
  Schedule D, Case IV
    basis of assessment, 268
    EU deposit interest, 267
    losses, 268
foreign property
  capital acquisitions tax, 117–19
  income tax on rental income, 267
  stamp duty exemption, 88
foreign rental income, 267
free use of property, 123
full-time working directors, definition, 57

gift splitting, 110
gifts
  capital acquisitions tax
    anti-avoidance measures, 110
    basic elements of a gift, 100–103
    date of the disposition, 103–4, 138
    date of the gift, 104, 138
    differences in tax treatment from
      inheritances, 103
    exemption for certain dwelling houses,
      152–4
    exemption for certain receipts, 154–5
    exemption for spouses/civil partners,
      108, 150–51
    gift splitting, 110
    gifts taken free of tax, 155
    overview, 99–100

relief for certain insurance policies,
      156–8
    small gifts exemption, 103, 150
    valuation date, 124, 138
  stamp duty
    deemed conveyance on sale, 86
goods *see* supply of goods
goodwill
  location of assets, 17, 82
  potentially liable to withholding tax, 27
  and retirement relief, 57
  and revised entrepreneur relief, 43–44
  and transfer of a business to a company, 47
government securities
  capital acquisitions tax exemption, 152
  capital gains tax exemption, 23
  stamp duty exemption, 88
group relief
  application of losses
    excess Case V capital allowances,
      206–8
    excess charges paid, 205–6
    excess management expenses, 206
    overview, 204
    trading losses, 204–5
  corresponding accounting periods,
    208–10
  non-resident companies, 203
  overview, 201
  75% relationship, 201–3
group thresholds: capital acquisitions tax
  anti-avoidance measures, 110
  special relationship situations, 107–9
  thresholds for 2020, 106–7
groups of companies
  company capital gains *see* capital gains
    groups
  corporation tax
    disallowance of trading losses following
      change of ownership, 210–11
    loss relief, 201–10
    overview, 199
    payments relief, 199–200
    R&D tax credit, 194
  value-added tax
    group VAT registration, 314–15
    supply of property within a VAT
      group, 315

holding companies
  definition for retirement relief, 58
  double taxation relief, 187–8
  Ireland as attractive location for, 187–8

income tax
  approved retirement funds, 156
  distributions, 73, 229, 236
  employment income
    foreign earnings deduction, 271–3
    lump sum payments on account of death
      or disability, 277
    overview, 269
    retirement lump sum benefits, 276–7
    Special Assignee Relief Programme,
      269–71
    termination payments, 273–6
  exemptions and reliefs
    Employment and Investment Incentive,
      281–4
    foreign earnings deduction, 271–3
    Key Employee Engagement Programme,
      286–7
    Special Assignee Relief Programme,
      269–71
    tax-exempt termination payments, 273–6
  foreign investment income, 265–8
  interest paid to close company directors,
    230–31
  loans to close company participators, 233–5
  loss relief
    Schedule D, Case III losses, 267
    Schedule D, Case IV losses, 268
  returns, 259
  shares
    employee share options, 284–7
    Employment and Investment Incentive,
      281–4
  spouses/civil partners
    joint assessment, 289–90, 292–3
    relief through Employment and
      Investment Incentive, 282
    separate assessment, 290
    single assessment, 290
    subsequent tax treatment of surviving
      spouse/civil partner, 294
    tax treatment in year of death, 291–4
    tax treatment in year of marriage, 290–91

tax treatment on separation, divorce or
    dissolution, 294–6
territoriality rules
  domicile levy, 261–2
  impact of residence, ordinary residence
    and domicile, 259–61
  non-resident individuals' entitlement to
    tax credits, 261
  overview, 259
  rents paid to non-resident landlords,
    263–4
  split-year residence, 262
inheritances: capital acquisitions tax
  basic elements of an inheritance, 100–103
  date of the disposition, 103–4, 138
  date of the inheritance, 104–5, 138
  differences in tax treatment from gifts, 103
  exemption for certain dwelling houses,
    152–4
  exemption for certain inheritances taken by
    parents, 152
  exemption for certain receipts, 154–5
  exemption for spouses/civil partners, 108,
    150–51
  inheritances taken free of tax, 155
  overview, 99–100
  payment through buy-back of shares, 75–6
  payment through insurance policies, 156–7
  relief for certain insurance policies, 156–8
  valuation date, 124–5, 138
innocent errors, 7
instalment payments, 171–2
insurance policies: capital acquisitions tax
  policies to pay inheritance tax only, 156–7
  relief for certain policies, 156–8
intangible assets: capital allowances, 190–91
intellectual property: stamp duty exemption, 88
interest
  arising from Revenue interventions, 6
  income tax
    EU deposit interest, 267
    non-EU deposit interest, 266
    UK deposit interest, 266
  on instalment payments, 171–2
  on late payment, 84, 171
  on overpayments, 172
  paid to directors of close companies,
    230–32

inventories: transfer within capital gains groups, 220
investment companies
    definition, 252
    overview, 252–3
    relief for management expenses, 253–5
Irish incorporated companies, 179

joint assessment, 289–90, 292–3
Joint Investigations Units (Revenue), 4

Key Employee Engagement Programme (KEEP)
    capital gains tax, 38–40
    income tax, 286–7
key employees
    relief on share options, 38–40, 286–7
    rewarded by R&D tax credit, 195

land and buildings
    capital acquisitions tax
        dwelling house exemption, 152–4
    capital gains tax
        acquired 7/12/11–31/12/14: relief on disposal, 24
        potential liability to withholding tax, 27
        and retirement relief, 58
        as specified Irish assets, 26
    corporation tax
        R&D tax credit for expenditure on buildings used for R&D, 193–4
    location of assets, 17, 82
    stamp duty
        mixed-use property, 86
        non-residential property, 86
        residential property, 85–6
    see also agricultural property; development land; farmland; non-residential property; property transactions; residential property
last in/first out (LIFO) rule, 36–7
late filing penalties, 84, 171
limited interests
    cessation of annuities, 145
    deduction as consideration, 145
    definition of a limited interest, 143
    overview, 143
    taxable value, 122, 144–5
    valuation of annuities, 122, 143–4

loans
    to participators in close companies, 233–5
    write-off of participator loans, 235–6
location of assets
    capital gains tax, 25
    general rules, 17
    stamp duty, 82–3
long options, 286
loss relief
    capital gains tax
        interaction with other reliefs, 46
        overview, 23
    corporation tax
        groups of companies, 201–10
    income tax
        Schedule D, Case III losses, 267
        Schedule D, Case IV losses, 268
lump sum payments
    lump sum payments on account of death or disability, 277
    retirement lump sum benefits, 276–7
    termination payments, 273–6

management expenses
    carry forward of unutilised expenses, 254
    definition, 253
    directors' remuneration, 254
    group relief for excess expenses, 206
    relief for investment companies, 253–5
market value
    annuities, 122, 143–4
    free use of property, 123
    general rule, 122
    limited interests, 122, 144–5
    shares in certain private companies, 122
members of the European Parliament (MEPs)
    income payable by the EU, 265
    income payable by the Irish state, 265
micro-entities, 197
mineral rights, 26, 27
minor development, definition for VAT, 310
mixed-use property: stamp duty, 86

no loss of revenue claims, 7–8
non-domiciled individuals *see* foreign-domiciled individuals
non-EU deposit interest, 266

non-resident companies
  in capital gains groups, 218–19
  charge to corporation tax, 178
  company capital gains, 215
  determining non-residence, 178–80
  qualifying for group relief, 203
non-resident individuals
  capital gains tax
    overview, 26
    specified Irish assets, 26–7
    temporary non-residents, 28–9
    withholding tax, 27
  income tax
    entitlement to tax credits, 261
    liability to income tax, 259–61
    rents paid to non-resident landlords,
      263–4
non-residential property: stamp duty, 86
non-wasting chattels, 23, 24

ordinary residence, 15–16, 259–61
overpayments: capital acquisitions tax, 172

participation exemption, 216–17
participators, close companies
  certain expenses treated as distributions,
    229–30
  definition, 227
  loans to, 233–5
  write-off of loans to, 235–6
patents and trademarks: location of assets, 82
payment dates
  capital acquisitions tax, 123, 170–71
  capital gains tax, 21
  corporation tax, 181
  stamp duty, 83
payments relief, 199–200
penalties
  arising from Revenue interventions
    careless behaviour with significant
      consequences, 6
    careless behaviour without significant
      consequences, 6
    deliberate behaviour, 6–7
    full co-operation, 9
    innocent errors, 7
    mitigation, 9–11
    no loss of revenue claims, 7–8

qualifying disclosures, 9–11
    self-corrections, 8–9
    technical adjustments, 7
  late filing penalties
    capital acquisitions tax, 171
    stamp duty, 84
personal insolvency, 155
pre-entry losses, 223
principle private residence relief, 23
professions, definition for service company
    surcharge, 242–3
profile interviews, 4
prompted qualifying disclosures, 9
property transactions: value-added tax
  exempt supplies of property, 310–11
  interaction with stamp duty, 311
  letting of property, 311
  option to tax, 310–11
  overview, 309
  supply of property within a VAT group, 315
  taxable supplies of property, 309–10
PRSI
  exemption with Key Employee Engagement
    Programme, 38, 286–7
  payable on EU deposit interest, 267
  payable on distributions, 73, 229, 236
  payable on employee share options, 285

qualifying disclosures
  amount of penalty reduction, 10–11
  format, 10
  overview, 9
  period to prepare, 9–10
  prompted disclosures, 9
  unprompted disclosures, 9

rates of tax
  capital gains tax, 21
  corporation tax, 180, 185
  deposit interest retention tax, 266
  stamp duty, 85–6
REAP analysis system, 3
relevant business property: capital
    acquisitions tax
  definition for business relief, 134–5
  interest on instalment payments, 172
relevant tax on share options (RTSO), 285
remittance basis of taxation, 23, 25, 260

rental income: income tax
    foreign rental income, 267
    rents paid to non-resident landlords, 263–4
research and development (R&D) tax credit
    buildings used for R&D, 193–4
    clawback of relief, 197
    groups of companies, 194
    micro-entities and small companies, 197
    overview, 192
    qualifying activities, 192
    qualifying companies, 192
    qualifying expenditure, 193
    used to reduce corporation tax, 196
    used to reward key employees, 195
residency *see* territoriality rules
resident companies
    charge to corporation tax, 178
    company capital gains, 214–15
    determining residence, 178–80
resident individuals
    capital gains tax, 25–6
    determining residency, 13–14
    election to be resident, 14–15
    income tax, 259–61
    ordinary residence, 15–16, 259–61
    split-year residence, 262–3
residential property
    capital acquisitions tax exemption,
      152–4
    stamp duty, 85–6
retirement lump sum benefits, 276–7
retirement relief
    disposals of shares, 60–61, 69
    disposals of sole trader business,
      59–60, 69
    disposals to a child, 66–8
    disposals to person other than a child,
      62–6
    and family companies, 57–8, 69–70
    interaction with other reliefs, 45, 56
    marginal relief, 63–4
    overview, 56
    qualifying assets, 56–9
    summary of conditions, 69–70
returns
    acquisition of own shares, 76
    capital acquisitions tax, 123, 169–71
    capital gains tax, 21

corporation tax, 181
    employee share options, 285
    income tax, 259
    late filing penalties, 84, 171
    self-corrections, 8–9
    stamp duty, 84
Revenue audits and interventions
    case selection, 3
    Code of Practice, 3
    interest, 6
    non-audit compliance interventions,
      3–4
    overview, 3
    penalties
      careless behaviour with significant
        consequences, 6
      careless behaviour without significant
        consequences, 6
      deliberate behaviour, 6–7
      full co-operation, 9
      innocent errors, 7
      mitigation, 9–11
      no loss of revenue claims, 7–8
      qualifying disclosures, 9–11
      self-corrections, 8–9
      technical adjustments, 7
    Revenue audits
      audit notification, 4–5
      audits at company's place of business, 4
      conduct of audit, 5
      desk audits, 4
      finalisation of audit, 5
      overview, 4
    Revenue investigations, 5–6
    review procedures, 11–12
    tax due, 6
Revenue Online Service (ROS)
    e-stamping, 83–4
    filing of returns
      capital acquisitions tax, 123, 169–71
      capital gains tax, 21
      corporation tax, 181
      income tax, 259
revised entrepreneur relief
    interaction with other reliefs, 45–6
    overview, 42
    qualifying conditions, 43–4
rights issues, 33–5

sectoral reviews, 4
self-assessment
    capital acquisitions tax, 169–70
    stamp duty, 84
self-corrections, 8–9
separate assessment, 290
separated couples
    capital acquisitions tax, 151
    income tax, 294–6
    see also divorced spouses/dissolved civil
        partnerships
service company surcharge, 242–5
services *see* supply of services
75% subsidiaries
    and capital gains groups, 217–18
    definition for retirement relief, 58
    and group relief, 201–3
share options *see* employee share options
shares
    capital acquisitions tax
        market value of shares in certain private
            companies, 122
    capital gains tax
        acquisition within four weeks of
            disposal, 36
        bonus issues, 35
        buy-backs *see* acquisition of own shares
        disposal within four weeks of acquisition,
            36–7
        employee share options, 37–40
        overview, 32–3
        and retirement relief, 57–8, 60–61, 69
        rights issues, 33–5
        treasury shares, 76
    income tax
        employee share options, 284–7
        Employment and Investment Incentive,
            281–4
    location of assets, 17
    stamp duty, 84–5
short options, 285
single assessment, 290, 293
small and medium enterprises (SMEs)
    definitions, 182–3
    R&D tax credit, 197
    transfer pricing rules, 182–3
sole traders
    retirement relief, 59–60, 69

revised entrepreneur relief, 44, 45
    transfer of business to a company, 47–53
Special Assignee Relief Programme (SARP),
    269–71
special relationships: capital acquisitions tax
    benefit taken by a parent, 108
    benefit taken by a spouse/civil partner, 108
    favourite niece or nephew, 108–9
    minor child of deceased child, 107–8
    surviving spouse/civil partner of deceased
        person, 109
specified Irish assets, 26–7, 215
split-year residence, 262–3
spouses/civil partners
    capital acquisitions tax
        divorced spouses/dissolved civil
            partnerships, 151
        exemption for gifts/inheritances taken by,
            108, 150–51
        separated couples, 151
        surviving spouse/civil partner of
            deceased person, 109
    capital gains tax
        exemption for transfer of assets between,
            23
        sale and re-acquisition of shares, 37
    income tax
        joint assessment, 289–90
        relief through Employment and
            Investment Incentive, 282
        separate assessment, 290
        single assessment, 290, 293
        subsequent tax treatment of surviving
            spouse/civil partner, 294
        tax treatment in year of death, 291–4
        tax treatment in year of marriage, 290–91
        tax treatment on separation, divorce or
            dissolution, 294–6
    stamp duty
        divorce or dissolution, 88
        exemption for transfer of property
            between, 88
stamp duty
    accountable persons, 83
    acquisition of business assets, 94–5
    charge to tax, 81
    conveyance or transfer on sale, 84–6
    definitions, 82–3

stamp duty – *contd.*
  e-stamping, 83–4
  exemptions and reliefs, 88–92
  gifts: deemed conveyance on sale, 86
  interaction with VAT, 86, 311
  interest on late payment, 84
  late filing penalties, 84
  location of assets, 82–3
  overview, 81
  payment dates, 83
  rates of tax, 85–6
  returns, 84
  self-assessment, 84
Standard Capital Superannuation Benefit
  (SCSB), 274
supply of goods: value-added tax
  exports to non-EU countries, 306
  imports from non-EU countries, 305–6
  intra-EU supply
    cross-border VAT reclaims, 305
    distance sales, 303
    purchases by private individuals, 302
    purchases by unregistered persons and
      non-taxable entities, 302
    purchases by VAT-registered persons, 301–2
    sales to unregistered customers, 303
    sales to VAT-registered customers, 302–3
supply of services: value-added tax
  intra-EU supply
    cross-border VAT reclaims, 305
    exceptions to general rules, 304–5
    place of supply, 304
  non-EU supply, 306–7
surcharges
  close company surcharge, 236–47
  for late payment *see* late payment penalties
  service company surcharge, 242–5
  for undervaluation of property, 172

Tax and Duty Manual (Revenue), 76–7
tax rates *see* rates of tax
tax relief *see* exemptions and reliefs
taxable value: capital acquisitions tax
  allowable deductions, 125–6
  calculation where there is agricultural
    relief, 126
  calculation where there is business relief,
    133–4

general principles, 121
market value, 122–3, 143–5
valuation date, 123–5
technical adjustments, 7
temporary non-residents, 28–9
termination payments
  basic exemption, 273
  charge to income tax, 273
  increased exemption, 274
  lifetime tax-free limit, 274
  Standard Capital Superannuation
    Benefit, 274
  tax-exempt termination payments,
    273–6
territoriality rules
  capital acquisitions tax
    foreign property: foreign-domiciled
      individuals, 118–19
    foreign property: general rule, 117–18
    Irish property, 117
    overview, 117
  capital gains tax
    location of assets, 25
    non-resident/ordinarily resident
      individuals, 26–7
    resident/ordinarily resident individuals,
      25–6
    temporary non-residents, 28–9
  corporation tax
    companies managed and controlled in the
      state, 179
    establishing residence of a company,
      178–80
    Irish incorporated companies, 179
    treaty exemption, 179
  general rules
    determining residency, 13–14
    domicile, 16–17
    election to be resident, 14–15
    location of assets, 17
    ordinary residence, 15–16
  income tax
    domicile levy, 261–2
    impact of residence, ordinary residence
      and domicile, 259–61
    non-resident individuals' entitlement to
      tax credits, 261
    overview, 259

territoriality rules – *contd.*
    income tax – *contd.*
        rents paid to non-resident landlords,
           263–4
        split-year residence, 262
trademarks *see* patents and trademarks
trading companies, definition for retirement
    relief, 57
trading losses
    application for group relief, 204–5
    disallowed for group relief following change
        of ownership, 210–11
    see also loss relief
trading or farming groups, definition for
    retirement relief, 58
transfer of a business
    capital gains tax, 47–53
    stamp duty, 94–5
    value-added tax, 315–16
transfer pricing, 181–3, 220–21
treaty exemption, 179

UK deposit interest, 266
UK dividends, 266
Universal Social Charge (USC)
    exemption with Key Employee Engagement
        Programme, 38, 286–7
    payable on distributions, 73, 229, 236
    payable on employee share options, 285
unprompted qualifying disclosures, 9
unquoted shares
    estimation of market value, 122
    potential liability to withholding tax, 27
    as specified Irish assets, 26

valuation
    annuities, 122, 143–4
    business property, 136–7

free use of property, 123
limited interests, 122, 144–5
shares in certain private companies, 122
valuation date, 123–5, 138
see also market value; taxable value
valuation date
    importance of, 123
    taxable gifts, 124, 138
    taxable inheritances, 124–5, 138
value-added tax (VAT)
    group registration, 314–15
    no loss of revenue claims, 7–8
    partially exempt VAT-registered businesses,
        313
    property transactions
        exempt supplies of property, 310–11
        interaction with stamp duty, 86, 311
        letting of property, 311
        option to tax, 310–11
        overview, 309
        supply of property within a VAT group,
           315
        taxable supplies of property,
           309–10
    supply of goods and services
        intra-EU cross-border VAT reclaims, 305
        intra-EU supply of goods, 301–3
        intra-EU supply of services, 304–5
        non-EU supply of goods, 305–6
        non-EU supply of services, 306
    transfer of business relief, 315–16

wasting chattels, 24
wills: stamp duty exemption, 88
winnings, 23, 155
withholding tax, 27

young trained farmer relief, 88–9

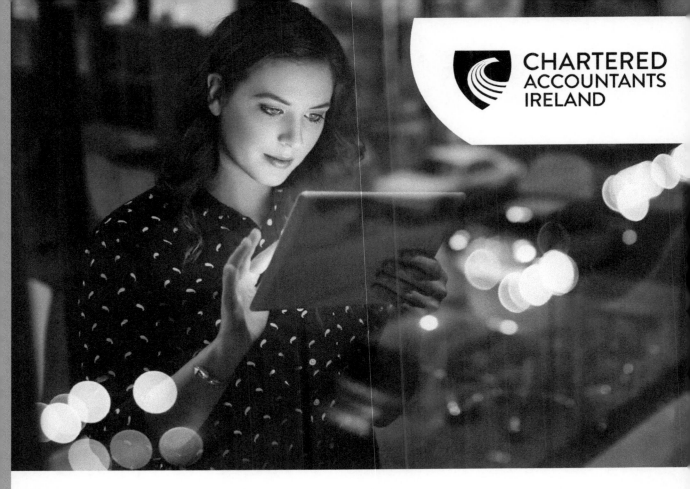

CHARTERED ACCOUNTANTS IRELAND

THANKS FOR JOINING US

We hope that you are finding your course of study with Chartered Accountants Ireland a rewarding experience. We know you've got the will to succeed and are willing to put in the extra effort. You may well know like-minded people in your network who are interested in a career in business, finance or accountancy and are currently assessing their study options. As a current student, your endorsement matters greatly in helping them decide on a career in Chartered Accountancy.

HOW CAN YOU HELP?

If you have an opportunity to explain to a friend or colleague why you chose Chartered Accountancy as your professional qualification, please do so.

Anyone interested in the profession can visit www.charteredaccountants.ie/prospective-students where they'll find lots of information and advice on starting out.

Like us on Facebook, follow us on Twitter.

Email us at info@charteredaccountants.ie

We can all help in promoting Chartered Accountancy, and the next generation to secure their success, and in doing so strengthen our qualification and community. We really appreciate your support.